C000006958

SCHOLARS,
POETS
& RADICALS

'Salute to my generation.'
MAY CANNAN

SCHOLARS, POETS & RADICALS

DISCOVERING FORGOTTEN LIVES IN THE BLACKWELL COLLECTIONS

Rita Ricketts

Bodleian Library
UNIVERSITY OF OXFORD

First published in 2015 by the Bodleian Library
Broad Street
Oxford OX1 3BG

www.bodleianshop.co.uk

ISBN: 978 1 85124 425 6

TEXT extracts from Dorothy L. Sayers' letters and poems (pp. 75–7) reproduced by permission of David Higham; extracts from Nancy Cunard's work (p. 211) reproduced by permission of Robert Bell; extracts from May Wedderburn Cannan's work (pp. 212–14) reproduced by permission of Clara Abrahams; extracts from 'The Last Gallop' from *Façade II* and 'Still Falls the Rain' by Edith Sitwell (p. 215) reproduced by permission of Peters Fraser & Dunlop (www.petersfraserdunlop.com) on behalf of the Estate of Edith Sitwell; extract from Osbert Sitwell's 'Therefore is the name of it called Babel' (p. 216) reproduced by permission of David Higham; extract from H.W. Garrod's *Worms and Epitaphs* (pp. 216–17) reproduced by permission of the Warden and Fellows of Merton College, Oxford; extract from 'A Visit to May Morris' by Margaret Horton (pp. 248–51) first published in the *Journal of William Morris Studies*, vol. V. no. 2, Winter 1982, reproduced by permission of the William Morris Society.

IMAGES items from the Merton Blackwell Collection (pp. 21, 29, 35, 54, 59, 63, 66, 69, 79, 91, 95, 97, 117, 141, 153, 157, 178, 180, 201, 255, 262 and Plates 2, 3, 4, 35, 36, 37, 40, 41, 42, 43) and from the Fletcher–Hanwell–Parker Daybooks (pp. xi, xiii, xv) are reproduced by kind permission of the Warden and Fellows of Merton College, Oxford; p. 37 © Images & Voices, Oxfordshire County Council; image from Edward Bawden's mural (Plate 1) reproduced by kind permission of the Estate of Edward Bawden, photography by Greg Smolonski; images from *Wheels* (Plate 12) © the William Roberts Society.

The jacket shows a detail from William Roberts' design for the endpapers of *Wheels 1919*.

Cover design by Dot Little
Text designed and typeset in 11½ on 14 Monotype Bembo Book by illuminati, Grosmont
Printed and Bound in Great Britain by TJ International Ltd, Padstow, Cornwall
on 90gsm Munken Print Cream

British Library Catalogue in Publishing Data
A CIP record of this publication is available from the British Library

CONTENTS

*This book and research are dedicated to the Warden,
Fellows and Staff of Merton College, Bodley's Librarian
Richard Ovenden and his two predecessors Reg Carr and
Sarah Thomas, who believed in these stories.*

*For grandchildren Nicolas, Guillaume, Senne, Delfi,
Matisse, Victoria, Leon, Frances, Freddy, Noa, Maxime,
BG and my godchildren George and Victoria
– write your stories!*

A DEMOCRATIC SPACE

B Y 1939, many of the houses east of Blackwell's original shop in Oxford's Broad Street had been replaced by Giles Gilbert Scott's New Bodleian. At the same time, the Bodleian's esteemed neighbour expanded and renovated its own old shop. Sir Basil Blackwell, the firm's legendary head, known as 'the gaffer', hailed the result as 'a symbol of our hope for the future'. It was, he said, to books that people would turn to find the 'knowledge and inspiration to build a better world'.

People had been visiting Blackwell's since 1879, when Sir Basil's father, Benjamin Henry, opened his little shop in Broad Street. Bishop William Stubbs, Regius Professor of History, called it the booklovers' 'house of call', and by the time Benjamin Henry died in 1924 the shop had become an institution. 'One does not go there just to buy books,' ran an article in the *London Daily News*, 'one goes there as Londoners go to the Park ... to see and be seen.'

While browsers in Oxford had the run of this 'free library', as the *Manchester Guardian* dubbed it, orders came in by post from those who had set off for, or had gone back to, the 'last loneliest' outposts of the old Empire. But it wasn't only the university-educated who benefitted. When the little-known Benjamin Harris Blackwell, Benjamin Henry's father, came to Oxford in the 1830s, his mission was to educate. In this he was successful. Despite his own lack of formal education, in 1854 he became the indefatigable librarian of Oxford's first public library, which was open on Sundays and after work in the evenings. During the First World War, his son, having been elected as a member of the city council, oversaw its expansion. A book education had now become a *right* – even more so in wartime – not for rich men alone but for all men, as Carlyle had once observed.

Rita Ricketts' latest book, like so many centred on Oxford, is full of eccentric characters and controversies that have coloured its past, and tells a fascinating story of another side of the city. 'Ordinary' people, some of whom were published by Blackwell's, gave themselves an Oxford education at this 'alternative college'. And the Bodleian's newest addition, the Weston Library, is another contribution to this movement to make knowledge accessible to all who need it. Accessed directly from Broad Street via the Blackwell Hall, which has been generously funded by Sir Basil's youngest son, Julian Blackwell, it is yet another sign that the old divide between town and gown is dead and buried. Even better, in the digital age, hundreds of millions of pages of books in the Bodleian as a whole can be viewed wherever there is access to the Internet.

The ideas and the lives that this book documents are also of broader importance than just the Oxford association. They serve as a vehicle for exploring cultural history, especially the history of the book and of reading, during a period when more people were literate than ever before. But the stories within stories told here touch life at many other points: the essential solitude of the human condition; the unquenchable desire for knowledge and the freedom knowledge confers. If there is a major protagonist, it must be 'The Book' itself. Professor H.W. Garrod, classical scholar and former Professor of Poetry, saw books as 'the stronghold of truth'; a truth, Sir Basil later asserted, discovered anew by each generation. Books were also a solace. During the dark days of two world wars, it was through books – 'through the imagination', Sir Basil wrote – that we coped with 'man's inhumanity to man'. But just as important was the 'plain everyday pleasure to be found in reading'. Chaucer's narrator in *The Canterbury Tales* offered a free meal to the pilgrim whose tale was judged the best. There is no free meal on offer here, but there is an invitation to go back and discover forgotten lives in this absorbing and imaginative reconstruction.

Richard Ovenden, Bodley's Librarian

PROLOGUE

THE ARCHIVIST'S VIEW

D IPPING INTO AN ARCHIVE is always exciting: so many varied stories and much myth-making. And the archive of B.H. Blackwell, Booksellers and Publishers – now lodged at Merton College as the Merton Blackwell Collection (MBC) – exceeds expectations. We can only guess at how a tailor's son, Benjamin Harris Blackwell, acquired sufficient book learning to be appointed librarian of Oxford's first free public library in 1854. And at what possessed his son, Benjamin Henry, modest and self-educated, to open a bookshop on a street where Parker's, gentlemen booksellers to the University, ruled the roost. Parker's had outranked all smaller fry – Shrimpton's, Acock's and Thornton's on Broad Street, and Gerring's, Gee's and Richards' in the nearby High Street – since the late eighteenth century. James Boswell paid tribute to Parker's, recalling Dr Johnson's visit in 1784 when the shop was at the corner of Logic Lane; Sackville Parker was then well into his seventies, and Johnson noted, with some surprise, 'I find he has married his maid.' It was a lucky find to discover more of Parker's history in the Blackwell archive.[1] Four shop daybooks record a period of rapid transition from 1794 to c. 1805 as the business passed through a succession of changes, from James Fletcher to Joseph Parker. Their story, and its antecedents, provide the background against which Rita Ricketts has set her finely crafted and meticulously researched stories.

Oxford's book trade, however, began long before Parker's appeared on the scene, and has a pedigree stretching back before even the University was established. Medieval merchants, benefitting from Oxford's geographical, economic and political connections, would have called on scribes to produce books for their schools (guilds of learning).[2] And there may have been other customers. St Frideswyde's, allegedly founded by Princess Frideswyde, the daughter of a minor king who fled to Oxford to escape the clutches of Algar the Mercian King, was a teaching order; if the myth is true, it predated women's colleges by almost a thousand years. And Robert d'Oili's larger religious community at Oseney, to the west of his castle, probably had a school. By the eleventh century, St Mary the Virgin, at the centre of the old walled city, was attracting monks and wandering scholars as well as merchants' sons. A university developed in all but name by the close of the twelfth century, and the appointment of a chancellor in 1214 gave it corporate identity.[3] Serving this nascent university were copyists, parchment makers and other forerunners of a book trade, who congregated alongside St Mary's in the crowded tenements of Catestreet that straddled the line of the old city wall to the east of what is now the Sheldonian.[4] But Dr Johnson's gnomic thrust, 'no man will be a bookseller who has contrivance enough to get himself into a workhouse', summed up their plight.

Students studied a variety of subjects — theology and the seven arts: grammar, rhetoric, logic, arithmetic, geometry, music and astronomy — but they were mostly too poor to buy books.[5] They relied on notes taken down from their tutors and a small supply of chained books at St Mary's. By 1290, monks from Durham Cathedral had erected their *locum Oxonie* on a site north of Broad Street, bringing with them a collection of books, probably on loan from Durham Priory; they would have been either chained or kept in armadios (chests).[6] A century later, newly founded colleges such as Merton operated a similar two-tier 'library' system. This did little to help the struggling book trade, and even when printed books started to be available, by the mid-fifteenth century, only a select few could afford them. Oxford's booksellers suffered other disadvantages. Trade was centred mainly on London, and supply was further restricted in the sixteenth century by 'privilege', a monopolistic patent system operated by the Stationers' Company.[7]

At the end of the sixteenth century Sir Thomas Bodley persuaded the Stationers to give him a copy of every book printed, which could then be borrowed from his library: this was the birth of the Bodleian

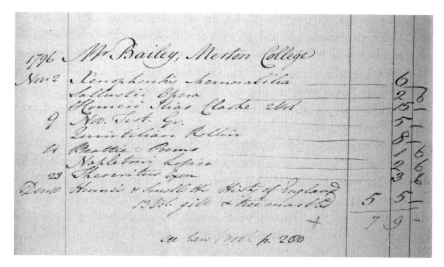

The purchase of standard undergraduate texts from Fletcher & Hanwell
by Merton College student Peter Bailey, November 1796.

Library. But booksellers did not escape the Stationers' tyranny. William
Barley, with a branch of his London bookshop and publishing business in Oxford, was thrown out for breach of their rules. Anthony
Stephens, born c. 1656 in the Oxfordshire village of Appleton (where
Basil Blackwell and his family would settle 300 years later), fared little
better. Bound apprentice to Thomas Gilbert, bookseller and binder of
the University, in 1672, and then to James Good, Stephens matriculated
after seven years as a privileged person, and in December 1681 is said
to have set up as a bookseller and publisher in the Catestreet area; but
he overstretched himself and was bankrupted.[8]

By the mid-sixteenth century, much of the book trade had shifted
from Catestreet and the vicinity of St Mary's to the south side of the
High Street. But one outpost clung on: in 1695 Henry Clements moved
his business to the junction of what had become Catte Street and New
College Lane, now Hertford College's North Quad, and the Clements
family were to be instrumental in shaping Oxford bookselling.

A century before, the medieval Canditch, the broad moat outside
the north wall of the city, had been filled in, making way for new
houses and shops built to a depth of some seventy or eighty feet beyond
the city wall along this new Broad Street.[9] The end of the medieval

religious orders, during the Reformation, also brought Broad Street into the mainstream, as College founders took over the vacant buildings in or around it.[10] The builders had cared little for the convenience of traffic, and the resulting passage between the gate at the northern end of Turl Street proper (just north of Ship Street) and Broad Street narrowed in places to no more than ten feet. It was here that James Fletcher had the prescience to open a bookshop.

It was not only students who milled around Broad Street. Other visitors came, as they still do, to see Sir Christopher Wren's Sheldonian Theatre, the neoclassical amphitheatre for university ceremonies completed in 1669, and the Ashmolean Museum (now occupied by the Museum of the History of Science), which opened a decade or so later. By 1713, the monumental arch of the Clarendon Building completed this trinity, providing a new home for the University Press and a symbolic entry to the University and the world of letters. The removal of the old Turl Gate in 1722, and the Oxford Mileways Act in 1771, which resulted in the demolition of the remaining medieval town gates – the North Gate and the Bocardo (the prison that had held Bishops Cranmer, Latimer and Ridley before their deaths) at the west end of Broad Street included – and the widening of streets, improved communications. Trade in general burgeoned and bookselling became more attractive as the power of the Stationers' Company was eroded; in 1710 an Act for Encouragement of Learning had vested rights in authors and purchasers – the first copyright law.

But booksellers, in Oxford as elsewhere in the provinces, were rarely solvent unless they could pursue a number of trades simultaneously: as printers, general stationers, corsetières, licensed victuallers and boarding-house keepers. By this expedient, a century later, nineteen booksellers-cum-general-tradesmen had established themselves within the city's bounds.[11] Of these, Parker's in the Broad dominated the University market. Their records, the Fletcher–Hanwell–Parker (FHP) daybooks as we may call them, are a rare find, as outside London very few sales records of booksellers survive.[12] They tell us, for example, what the university-educated were reading in the late eighteenth century. There is no record of what is now called 'footfall' in the FHP records, and purchases made by trade and individuals not associated with the University were probably entered in a parallel ledger. But we can presume that the very existence of successful bookshops

The daybook of Messrs
Fletcher & Hanwell, Oxford
booksellers, 1794–5.

like Parker's helped to encourage others on the book ladder: readers, writers, printers, booksellers and libraries.[13]

Undoubtedly, Parker's owed much to their society connections. An ancestor, John Parker, had been a Baron of the Exchequer under Oliver Cromwell, and his second son Samuel was raised to the bench of bishops in 1686 as Bishop of Oxford. It was Bishop Parker's grandson Sackville, apprenticed to his uncle Richard Clements, who began the tradition of bookselling in the Parker family; as the youngest son he was expected to make his own living, and retailing books to clergymen scholars was a more respectable trade than many. In this way the

Parkers became enmeshed in a close-knit web of family and professional ties, in which sons succeeded fathers, nephews succeeded uncles, and apprentices married their masters' daughters and succeeded them in business. His apprenticeship complete, Sackville Parker set up shop at 89 High Street, on the corner of Logic Lane (now part of University College's Durham Building), while his cousin Daniel Price succeeded to their uncle's business on New College Lane, where he would later be patronized by the New College Fellow and diarist James Woodforde.

In 1796 Parker died without issue, and it fell to his great-nephew, Joseph Parker, apprenticed to Daniel Price, to maintain the family bookselling tradition.[14] On completing his apprenticeship and armed with a legacy of £100 from Great-Uncle Sackville, Joseph was drawn by the attractions of London's fashionable West End.[15] But he soon returned to Oxford, in 1797, to become a partner in the Turl Street business of James Fletcher junior and his brother-in-law William Hanwell.[16] On their deaths, Joseph Parker traded as sole proprietor and his commercial acumen ensured the profitability of the business. On the proceeds he rebuilt the Broad Street premises (No. 27) in 1823, incorporating the former Turl Street shop into the family home. Parker's was also appointed as an agent to the University Press and undertook responsibility for the Press's religious publications, which were running at an annual loss. Parker also engaged in publishing in his own right, including John Keble's *The Christian Year* (1827), which proved a great success and ran to many editions.

It was the destiny of the Parker's business, like many others, not to pass by direct descent, and when Joseph retired in 1832 it was his nephew, John Henry, rather than either of his sons, who succeeded to the business. John Henry Parker retained the agency to the University Press while continuing to publish; as well as works by Edward Pusey and others of the Oxford Movement, he produced his own *The Archaeology of Rome* in multiple volumes. In 1866 his son James in turn took over the business. Having lost the agency of the University Press in 1862, the firm thereafter concentrated on bookselling rather than publishing, although it retained the Parker family imprint. James, born over the bookshop in 1833, was well educated (at Winchester), but nonetheless, like Basil Blackwell sixty years later, he was destined for his father's shop. And it was James Parker that Benjamin Henry Blackwell, Basil's father, faced when he first opened on the opposite side of Broad

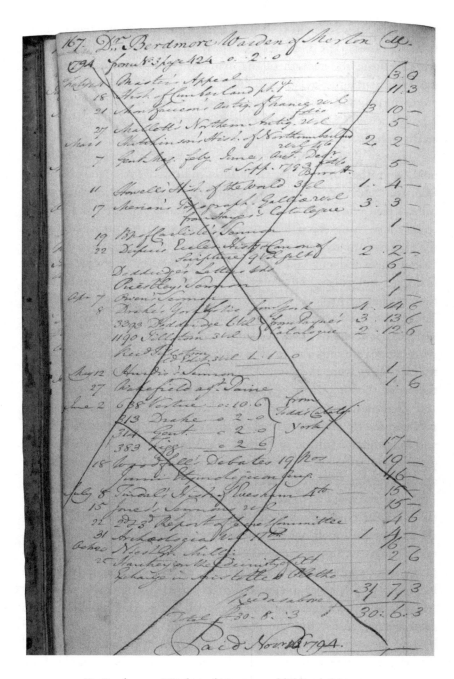

Dr Berdmore, Warden of Merton and bibliophile, was a
regular customer of Fletcher, Hanwell & Parker.

Street. But all was not as well with Parker's as Benjamin Henry might have supposed. The FHP records show that problems with cashflow were limiting the growth of the firm. All tradesmen in those times, even the gentlemanly Parker's, enticed their customers with generous credit terms, and customers were ready to take advantage; it would take Blackwell's until well into the twentieth century to tighten up its credit policies.[17]

The way Parker's customers, and subsequently Benjamin Henry's, paid, or rather didn't pay, their bills indicated the social divide in Oxford. Debts were settled by a gentleman's agreement, meaning customers paid when *they* wanted. Heads of houses (colleges) and Fellows could make things very difficult for a clamorous tradesman. And as for the students, many of the various categories of Noble and Gentlemen Commoners did not take degrees. After spending a couple of years making connections and acquiring a bit of polish, they would escape the clutches of hapless tradesmen by disappearing, often on a Grand Tour.[18] But the poorest students, Batellers, Bible Clerks and Servitors, were easier to nail. They needed a degree to make their way in the world and were required to clear all debts before graduation. Of these, the Servitors were the poorest and the most conspicuous.[19] Working their way through university, they acted as servants to college Fellows and wealthier students. They woke their masters, kindled their fires, polished their boots and waited on them at table, often receiving board and lodging and tuition in return. Distinguishable by the cut of their gowns and seated at a separate table at meal times, they were not allowed to forget their inferior status.

Just as the level of indebtedness was an indicator of social class, so too were the books purchased. Judging by entries in the FHP records, all Oxford freshmen, whether scholar or commoner, bought essential texts: a copy of Simson's *Euclid*, Napleton's *Logic*, some works of Xenophon and possibly a copy of Charles Rollin's edition of *Quintilian*. Napleton might be supplemented or replaced by the *Logic* of Henry Aldrich, and the *Euclid* supplemented with a copy of Charles Hutton's *Mathematical Tables*. But the purchases of the Servitor rarely strayed beyond the curriculum, and their annual expenditure seldom exceeded £3 or £4. Between January and December 1797, for example, John Greenly, Servitor of Christ Church, spent £2 12s on twenty-one purchases, fifteen of which comprised sheet paper, blank notebooks and quill pens, a copy of Simson's *Euclid* and copies of the Oxford almanac.[20] By contrast, wealthier students could afford, literally and metaphorically, to range beyond the set curriculum.

According to the records, the privileged went way beyond classics, mathematics, philosophy and theology to the classic English writers, from Shakespeare, Milton and Herbert to Swift, Defoe and Dr Johnson. The purchase of dictionaries and grammars of modern European languages perhaps presaged a tour of the Continent, or maybe just a desire to become familiar with their literature. Montesquieu, Molière, de La Fontaine and Voltaire all featured on the bookshelves of Fletcher, Hanwell & Parker. In March 1794 William Burrell of Christ Church thought he might tackle Laclos' *Liaisons Dangereuses*, at a cost of 8s 6d, but he must have found that he had misjudged his ability in French, as he returned three months later to buy a copy of an English translation, setting him back a further 12s, plus 4s more for binding. His other purchases that spring and summer included *Robinson Crusoe*, *Tom Jones* and Henry Mackenzie's sentimental novel *Man of Feeling*. (His contemporary at Christ Church, Lord Webb Seymour, younger son of the Duke of Somerset, made book-buying a competitive sport. In the three years January 1794 to December 1796 he racked up a colossal bill of £111 1s 3d.) Burrell's forays into popular literature resembled in many ways those recorded by the self-educated Benjamin Henry in his diaries in the mid-1880s.

Student purchases must have been circumscribed by arcane university rules, requiring all matriculated members of the University to subscribe to the Thirty-nine Articles of the Church and to follow a narrow diet of classics, philosophy, mathematics and theology. Some better-off students were unwise in their choice of reading matter. Thomas Goddard, Gentleman Commoner of Corpus Christi, who started off well in 1795 with the customary copies of Euclid, Pliny and Quintilian, was soon on a slippery slope when he bought the November edition of the *Sporting Magazine*. Subtitled the *Monthly Calendar of the Transactions of the Turf, the Chase and Every Other Diversion Interesting to the Man of Pleasure, Enterprize, and Spirit*, its temptations proved too great and it soon became his most regular purchase; he went down without a degree.

But the FHP records show that the sons of the governing class, who themselves aspired to govern, were reading widely and exposing themselves to new thinking about education and society. Hume,

Rousseau and Adam Smith must have helped to shape a new elite, one committed to the process of social and economic change. Cheaper editions of books and educational reform were also creating a newly literate working class. The passing of the University Reform Acts (1854 and 1877) abolished the extreme social distinctions of Servitor and Gentleman Commoner, and introduced new subjects: history, law and natural science; the range of subjects taught would have created new opportunities for bookseller-publishers. Religious tests of people's beliefs were no longer required, with the exception of theology degrees. And custom in the bookshops must have increased as elections to college scholarships and fellowships were competed for openly.[21] Fellows could now marry and the majority no longer had to be ordained. Colleges expanded, while a class of 'non-collegiate' students, living in approved lodgings, was introduced to provide for students from poorer backgrounds.

Given these changes, it was hardly surprising, then, that Thomas Hardy should have set *Jude the Obscure* in Oxford. Benjamin Harris Blackwell, arriving in the 1830s, must also have divined these shifts. His son and grandson, and so many associated with them, were direct beneficiaries. Oxford was the right place at the right time.

Julian Reid, Archivist, Merton College

INTRODUCTION

WRITE TO BE HEARD

Emily's sister brought the sad news that her youngest brother was killed at the front last Saturday. Both legs shattered, and only regained consciousness long enough to give his home address. Mother sent news that Maggie had given birth to a strong, healthy daughter. Thus we get the whole cycle of birth and death in one day.[1]

Rex King

'WHO'S TO SAY that the ordinary man's life was of no interest?' Rex King remonstrates in his diary. The Merton Blackwell Collection, comprising letters, diaries and fragments of memoirs, is a fund of what may seem like everyday writing.[2] Rex's life, struggling to make ends meet as a booksellers' assistant, was 'ordinary', but his writing was extraordinary. It was prolific, despite a twelve-hour day, six days a week, and, very unusually, much has survived. To read Rex, as Hugo Dyson of Merton College observed, was to discover:

how an important but often inarticulate section of our society lived and felt; its governing ideals, its sources of inspiration, its faith and its strength ... Think of the D. Phil. that could be quarried out of it ... It's part of the Bible of the English people ... an examen of the state of English culture 1910–50 ... and there is a lot he didn't say.

Rescued from bitter poverty when Benjamin Henry Blackwell employed him, Rex proved to be more scholarly than the shop's customers. *The Times* once described Basil Blackwell as 'one of the best read [men] in England', and what he read is apparent in the Collection. His list is almost surpassed by Rex's, however, whose diary entries also incorporate mordant dissections of the texts he studied. Yet the content of his diary was so often full of what Virginia Woolf called 'non-being'. Whereas professional historians had no 'call for [the] personal recollections' of those who lived and died in ill-paid, obscure jobs, she had 'a passion' for them and for 'marginal unvalued literary forms like memoirs, letters and journals'. Much of what she wrote in her diaries would have been dismissed as trivial if she had not been famous: the servant problem, menus, gardening, pressure of work – especially in wartime – fly comments on how people did or didn't behave; the very basic 'yellowing the earth closet'. In similar vein Rex wrote incessantly of 'work, work, work', growing vegetables to supplement a wartime diet, attempts to give up 'villainous red shag', and his petty prejudices: 'a buxom farm lass astride a man's bicycle, carrying her lover upon the step behind! What a blow to Mrs Grundy! An awful sight upon a Sunday!' Rex's story is told in 'A Baker's Son', 'A Moral Witness' and 'The Good Reader'.

Rex's personal recollections as a non-combatant during the First World War, included in 'The Patriots', brought events over there 'over here'. When his pacifist sympathies and Quaker beliefs clashed with his patriotism, he retreated into what Virginia Woolf called 'the life within'. But the prospect of an end to the war brought him only further anguish:

> We have conquered the Germans – now comes the infinitely greater conflict, to conquer all feelings of mere vindictiveness and revenge, to conquer the pride of victory, and to lay the foundations of a new world order. The nation has been rendered malleable by sorrow – God grant that we may be subjected to the moulding influence of the highest and noblest and not wasted and marred by the reactionary forces within the nation.[3]

Yet Rex felt at home in the like-minded company of the Blackwells, who had, as the archives reveal, made a habit of trying to resist 'reactionary forces'. Their story is retold in 'An Oxford Education', because, as biographer Hermione Lee writes, 'there are some stories which have to be retold by each generation': life writing is 'a record of things that few days. The revolutionary movement is spreading in Germany like a flame in dry stubble. We have conquered the Germans — now comes the infinitely greater conflict. To conquer all feelings of mere vindictiveness + revenge, to conquer the pride of victory, and to lay the foundations of a new world order. The nation has been rendered malleable by sorrow — God grant that we may be subjected to the moulding influence of the highest + noblest, + not warped and marred by the reactionary forces within the nation. Oh! for some magian to thrill

'Now comes the infinitely greater conflict',
Rex King's diary, Friday 8 November 1918.

change', so it 'can't be fixed and finalised'. So finding Benjamin Henry's love letters to his future wife, impassioned but very proper at the same time, changed my perception of the man behind the B.H. Blackwell name. The discovery that he had been elected to the city council also showed him in a different light. In 'A Dreadful Radical' he takes on a diehard traditionalist Tory, pushing for policies that seemed radical at the time: better housing, recreational facilities, allotments, half days off and paid holidays for working men. Women, on the other hand, were still 'just' wives and mothers or daughters and unpaid carers. Yet the Blackwell women, in their own ways, were just as ready as the firm's feminist authors, Vera Brittain and Dorothy L. Sayers for example, to become 'Women Warriors'.

Vera Brittain had campaigned for the granting of women's degrees, and her pleas were included in Blackwell's literary series, *Oxford Outlook*. But for many women, the bookshop or public library was their 'university'. This was also where Blackwell's apprentices obtained an education. They were boys from very humble homes, but fascinating, if fragmentary, records of their working lives, their studies and their aspirations have survived in the archive. But not all apprentices were so well placed: the railway hammerman Alf Williams, for example. John Betjeman – who said he 'learnt more at Blackwell's than at

Marlborough or Magdalen' – described Basil Blackwell's account of
Alf Williams as 'one of the most perfect pieces of English prose ... a
touching description of a poor man who wanted to become a writer
... who was a good writer and died in poverty for the sake of being
a writer'. Basil was zealous in preserving all their stories, told here
in 'Scholar Apprentices', believing them to be a 'necessary vehicle of
history'. Or were they fodder for the book he always intended to write?

'Alas,' Basil told his prospective publisher, the 'great book tarries
[because] I only like to write in the sun and there has been none.' Occasionally, 'when time permitted', he would write articles and speeches.
Rex King, enlisted to help, advised Basil to resist the temptation to
strew his work with epigrams and not to embroider facts; Basil parried
that facts were simply things to hang stories on. Basil never did finish
his own book; perhaps there were just too many facts and too many
stories to hang on them. If he had, it would have been very long. Rex
King reported a conversation between 'Fred, a retired college servant
working for us as caretaker, and Jok, understudy to Eleanor [Basil's
secretary]':

> 'Well, Miss, it seems as 'ow Miss Dulcie ain't to be married after all.'
> 'So it appears, Fred.'
> 'So there won't be no presentation, I suppose.'
> 'No, Fred.'
> 'And Mr. Basil won't make no speech.'
> 'No, Fred.'
> 'Tell you what, Miss, if all Mr. Basil's speeches was put together I
> reckon they'd make a book as big as the b ... Bible!'

Although some of Basil's stories came out, he contented himself with
publishing other people's. The early papers relating to their production
were lost, mostly thrown on a skip when the Army commandeered
the premises during the Second World War.[4] But back copies of books,
dating from 1879, escaped the cull and are preserved in the Bodleian
Blackwell Collection (BBC). They alone reveal much of the little-
told story of the early days of Blackwell's publishing. They show, for
example, that publishing for both Benjamin Henry and his son Basil, as
told in 'War on Many Fronts', was a continuation of politics by other
means. The social-minded Benjamin Henry published 'little volumes
of undergraduate verse' and other unknowns who hadn't a hope of

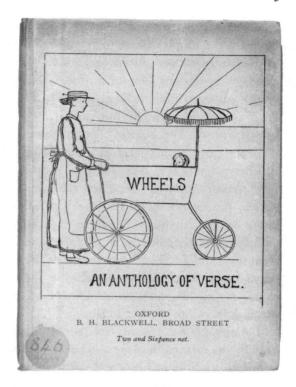

Women on the March,
Edith Sitwell's 'The
Mother', *Wheels*, 1916

gaining an entrée to other London houses. Yet he had a publisher's nose, selecting writing that anticipated the First World War and the sea change in poetic style.

Taking over the publishing side during the First World War, Basil's mission, echoing John Stuart Mill's and his librarian grandfather's, was to publish books that 'might guard against corruption of the intellect and limit the potential for evil'. Basil's 'life writing' is full of grandiose ideas, but he put them to work. Knowledge was power, but 'all power is two-edged', he wrote; 'the knife can kill or cure, gas [can be] a minister of mercy or torture'. Hadn't Aristotle built his theory of ethics on this potentiality of contraries? Basil sought help from 'Paian Apollo, Destroyer and healer', but neither the gods nor warmongering politicians were listening. So he undertook to remind them, publishing poetry that was 'implicitly, if not explicitly, anti-war'. But it also served, as May Cannan wrote, as a 'salute to a lost generation'.

Book covers as much as the contents tell the story of Blackwell's development as a publisher, and much about life in the period (*c.* 1830–

1940). Examples are represented in an extensive series of photographs: there are the simple, inexpensive covers of publications often paid for by Benjamin Henry Blackwell himself, giving way to the youthful Basil's outré designs. He, for a time, was regarded as the *enfant terrible* of the embryonic publishing house, but his gloriously coloured *Joy Street* annuals enticed children and attracted submissions from established writers. The horror of war, especially the First World War, cries out from both covers and titles. And when that war was over, another waged. See, for example, William Roberts' design for the 1919 edition of *Wheels*, depicting machine-like robots.[5] This summed up the Blackwells' view that mechanization 'deskilled workers and killed off craftsmanship'. Eager to halt its 'dead hand', Basil acquired the moribund Shakespeare Head Press, with its fine-printing tradition, great press and genius printer. Stories of his efforts to produce beautiful books in the William Morris tradition and of his life-long dedication to preserving his work alongside May Morris, are told in 'Profligate Printers and a Spellbound Princess'.

Taken together, the Merton and Bodleian Blackwell Collections provide the raw material for this book. Famous or obscure, the characters have a right to be heard and the books merit a re-reading. But more than that, the stories provide a tableau of nineteenth- and twentieth-century history ranging far beyond Oxford. Based on diaries, memoirs and musings, the stories have as much to offer those who study cultural history as those who would like to write their own, and are equally important for those interested in the history of the book and reading. They touch on social, political, economic and literary issues still relevant, contentious even, today. As businessmen and employers the Blackwells had, for example, sought to extract a liberal synthesis from the competing political ideologies of capitalism and socialism, which would enable them to run a business where the individual benefitted from both. Their regard for the individual – access to education and the provision of books – was prescient.

Now everyone who has access to the World Wide Web can have an Oxford education. They can, as Rex King hoped, 'break through the wall of [their] limitations – intellectual and otherwise'. Was it such a vision that prompted Benjamin Harris Blackwell to leave London in the 1830s? We shall never know. But I have hazarded a guess.

ONE

AN OXFORD EDUCATION

Upon my word I think I must take some lessons in love-letter writing … I never was a ladies man, and it's too late to begin now.

Benjamin Henry Blackwell

'TURN AGAIN, Whittington, Lord Mayor of London' goes the refrain. Dick Whittington did return to London to seek his fortune and we can imagine how the sight of St Paul's spire, clearly visible on a fine morning as he came down Highgate Hill, must have enticed him on and stiffened his resolve; as a result he became a 'worthy citizen'. His is a London story. The story of Benjamin Harris Blackwell, the son of a jobbing tailor born in London, is an Oxford story. He *left* London to seek his fortune. As he crossed Magdalen Bridge in the early 1830s, cows still grazed as the countryside met the town; the medieval city nestled beyond, and its spires would have lifted his sights. How relieved he would have been to leave behind the East End's fetid alleys, where beasts on the way to the slaughterhouses fouled the footpaths and victims of gin palaces breathed their last in shadowy doorways.[1] He never looked back.

Like Dick Whittington, Benjamin Blackwell too became a worthy citizen, as the founding librarian of the city's public library.[2] His son was to become North Oxford's first Liberal councillor, and his grandson earned the Freedom of the City and a knighthood. Yet how unlikely this would all have seemed as the young man's charabanc drove up High Street. His reasons for heading for Oxford's 'dreaming spires' are not clear. If he had ideas of becoming a bookseller, he should have thought twice. By the nineteenth century there was a preponderance of booksellers: the University bookseller Parker's, in Broad Street, ruled the roost; Thornton's was in the High, and nineteen others were operating within the city's bounds.

But despite the competition, another London tailor's son, just five years Benjamin's senior, had gone to Oxford and succeeded. Edwin Spiers first ran a circulating library and then a thriving bookselling, stationery and wine business.[3] He was the beneficiary of an upsurge in demand for books from an increasingly literate general public, and a middle-class obsession with acquiring all the accoutrements of gentrification, including a library of fine books.[4] Eventually, Spiers was able to build a house in genteel North Oxford, alongside many other successful tradesmen, and he was to be twice Lord Mayor.

It is not unreasonable to suppose that Benjamin's father, Joshua, knew or knew of Edwin's father, both men being in the same trade. In addition, both families were associated with the church of St Andrew's, Holborn: Thomas Spiers had had his son Edwin baptised there in 1808, the same year that Joshua Blackwell married there. It is not unlikely that Edwin's departure to Oxford would have come to Benjamin's ears. Maybe this was where his future lay? It is well known that émigrés look to follow a path already well trodden, but whatever his reason, it was to Oxford that Benjamin set out with his brother Isaac. He was not to have Spiers' financial success, but he was to give his name to a bookselling and publishing empire that would be to Oxford what Plantin's had been to Louvain 300 years earlier.

How did this come about? There is no evidence that the young Benjamin had any trade, still less any apprenticeship in bookselling. His father was almost certainly interested in books and, as an active teetotaller, Joshua would have benefited from the Temperance Society's library and courses of evening lectures. Perhaps he had treated his son to a book from Lackington's famous bookshop in Finsbury Square? A poor shoemaker's son, Lackington had sold pies to earn the money to start his bookshop, which became so successful that it earned the sobriquet 'temple of the muses'. Observing his mixed clientele, Lackington judged that 'all ranks now read'.[5] How the entrenched gentlemen booksellers in London must have tut-tutted at the idea of rubbing shoulders with the lower orders as they frequented their favourite haunt. And how much louder they would have clucked their tongues at the upstart Lackington's cut-price, 'pay on the nail' policies. When he died in 1815, a third cousin, George, inherited the shop and an apprenticeship there would have been much prized.

If Benjamin had aspired to be a bookseller, Lackington's would have provided the perfect role model. But he had not been apprenticed, probably because he had never had any intention of selling books. His mission in life was to educate. But how would *he* have acquired an education? At the time, Sunday schools of many different denominations provided a basic education, especially in reading, for most children.[6] (Perhaps he had attended Sunday school at St Andrew's – maybe he had met Edwin there?) But the required parental contribution to secondary education, for example to the City of London School, would have been beyond Joshua Blackwell's means. If he had had anything other than an elementary education it would have been at one of the growing number of adult evening schools, run by working-men's associations, social clubs, religious organisations, particularly the nonconformists, and reformist societies such as the Temperance Society. It can only be surmised that it was at this last, where he probably went with his father, that Benjamin furthered his own education.

Among the books in the Society's rooms, the Bible would have been indispensable. Bunyan's *Pilgrim's Progress* was a must for aspirational tradesmen and workers, as was William Blake's new poetry, delivering its stirring exhortations to build a new Jerusalem. The 1820s were also awash with poetry and new novels: Shelley, Keats, Scott. Jane Austen's novels would have provided genteel diversion, and Dumas's (*père*) much-needed excitement. Reading was not the only activity in the Society's rooms. Joshua doubtless participated in lively discussions on the great issues of the day over cups of tea: the right to greater political participation, for example. Perhaps the Society had a copy of Paine's *Rights of Man*, or received leaflets distributed by the early Chartists? Joshua was known to be a maverick. The fact that he was teetotal at all was not out of conviction, but to cock a snook at the government of the day and deprive it of his contributions to the exchequer. But any talk of direct action would have been sheer bravado; hard-working tradesmen like Joshua were too busy providing for themselves and their families.

Chary of Swift and Paine, he and his colleagues would probably have taken Edmund Burke's more pragmatic course: demonstrating their worthiness to vote rather than manning the barricades. Their overriding ambition would have been to see their own sons comfortably settled in a trade. They may have read Rousseau on the benefits of an education, but in the new climate of technical and scientific innovation, education was also a means to an end, a way of capturing some of Adam Smith's 'wealth of nations'. By his late teens, Benjamin was probably working, or volunteering, in the Society's library. But outside, all around, were London's poor, who had no chance of getting a share. Little had changed since Swift had satirized them in *Rhapsody* 150 years before, but they were no matter for mockery. Paupers still starved on the streets, drunks died by the roadside and the unskilled fought each other over half a day's work. Benjamin determined to make it *his* business to rescue them, but in Oxford rather than London.

As soon as he arrived in Oxford, Benjamin opened a branch of the Temperance Society, assisted by his brother Isaac.[7] His next act was to set up a library in its rooms. At the same time, he started a circulating library, which he trundled around on a handcart. This was to provide the funds for his real work: education. In the words of Milton, it was books that 'fit a man to perform justly, skilfully and magnanimously, all the offices both private and public of peace and war'.[8] For Benjamin Blackwell, as for the essayist and philosopher Thomas Carlyle, a book education was a *right*; it was not for rich men alone but for all men. Just as importantly, books were a way of ensuring spiritual survival, or as Shakespeare had it: 'words without thoughts never to heaven go'. Basil Blackwell later wrote that his grandfather had been boldly determined 'to demand a standing among the most important societies for the improvement of man, physically, socially, morally and intellectually'. At barely twenty this was some ambition.

In the Temperance Society's rooms, Benjamin could provide tea and books, but this was not enough if alcoholism was to be conquered. Looking to get support from a wider public, he organized lectures by experts who would carry out dissections, demonstrating the liver damage caused by alcohol. For this dubious entertainment, members of the public would pay an entrance fee. Fighting the temperance cause may have been spiritually rewarding, and may even have yielded a

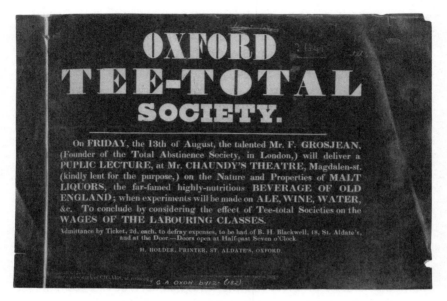

OXFORD TEE-TOTAL SOCIETY.

On FRIDAY, the 13th of August, the talented Mr. F. GROSJEAN, (Founder of the Total Abstinence Society, in London,) will deliver a PUBLIC LECTURE, at Mr. CHAUNDY'S THEATRE, Magdalen-st. (kindly lent for the purpose,) on the Nature and Properties of MALT LIQUORS, the far-famed highly-nutritious BEVERAGE OF OLD ENGLAND; when experiments will be made on ALE, WINE, WATER, &c. To conclude by considering the effect of Tee-total Societies on the WAGES OF THE LABOURING CLASSES.

Admittance by Ticket, 2d. each, to defray expenses, to be had of B. H. Blackwell, 18, St. Aldate's, and at the Door.—Doors open at Half-past Seven o'Clock.

H. HOLDER, PRINTER, ST. ALDATE'S, OXFORD.

Improving 'the standing of Man', Benjamin Blackwell's
temperance work in Oxford, 1830s and 1840s.

small profit, but it was frustrating. In 1839 he wrote an article lamenting that his efforts in Oxford were largely unsupported 'by those who should know better ... We have not one minister of the gospel to assist us, nor one medical practitioner to attempt to dispel the delusions which are generally indulged concerning the qualities of intoxicating liquors.'

His day job, however, proved less frustrating. Circulating libraries were at the zenith of their popularity; most serious books were still too expensive to buy, and borrowing was the means by which many people satisfied their appetite for reading. Somehow, over time, Benjamin must have acquired a nest egg of second-hand books that would cater to members of the University as well as the newly literate. His success encouraged him to put his business on a permanent footing. In 1846, at the age of thirty-three, he took a lease on a small ground-floor property at 46 High Street at £18 per year, and put the name B.H. Blackwell above its door.[9] The little bookshop was sandwiched between the trading establishments of William Loder, pork butcher, and Samuel Prince, baker, and nearby was the family firm of Henry Eagleston, ironmonger and straw-hat-maker, which kept its doors open until 1947.[10] Old photographs show the small parade of shops fronted by an open market, which would have been a further magnet to attract the public across Magdalen Bridge. Adding gravitas was his next-door neighbour living above the shops, J.B. Cardi, professor of French.[11] 'And by lucky chance the road to Headington, Gypsy Lane, Elsfield and Shotover led past his door, bringing scholar gypsies in the course of long afternoon walks.'[12] But did they buy books or just come to browse?

Competition was tough in Oxford and if he was to succeed, Benjamin had to think laterally. Since opening his shop he had traded almost exclusively in second-hand books not available outside Britain. Now he would advertise them overseas. He rightly surmised that the demand for books in America would soon surpass that of the home market. The more progressive Americans had been quicker to embrace scientific and technical education, and this was enabling them progressively to steal a march on Britain's workshop of the world. Added to which, the new steamboats could deliver parcels of books across the Atlantic in two weeks. To advertise his wares in America, he prepared catalogues. A bill survives, dated 11 January 1853, for production by the *Oxford Chronicle*, of 250 catalogues numbering twelve pages. A letter of 30 May 1853 from Mr John Gooch of Pennsylvania presages the development of an export market with which, in later years, the name Blackwell was to become synonymous. Addressed to 'My dear Benj.H.B', the letter thanked the bookseller for his parcel of books 'which almost without exception please', and enclosed a money order for £4 14s 0d in payment, 'much wishing you increase of profitable business'. Benjamin Harris Blackwell had struck a seam of gold.

But not even the chance of making a healthier profit by breaking into the international market could outweigh his passion for books as educators. As luck would have it, Oxford's first city library was to be opened in 1854, a product of the recent Public Libraries Act. Applying for the post of its librarian was a somewhat audacious move on the self-educated Benjamin's part, but his hard-earned reputation as a bookseller and librarian went before him and he won the day. Now he could play an even more direct and active part in workers' education. And his work was soon acknowledged. A letter from the House of Commons dated 14 June 1854 from the MP William Ewart, prime sponsor of the Public Libraries Act, stated that 'the City's first Librarian bore a name which Oxford will always connect with books'.[13]

Although Benjamin Harris Blackwell had joined the esteemed ranks of Oxford librarians, his duties were far removed from those laid down by Sir Thomas Bodley. When the latter had founded the Bodleian Library at the beginning of the seventeenth century, all that was required was 'leisure, learning, friends and means'.[14] 'One wonders,' mused a contemporary, 'how Mr Blackwell and his assistant contemplated the future, in which it was their duty to be in constant attendance on weekdays, from 9.00 am until 11.00 pm (10.00 pm in the winter months) and, after church, from 6.00–10.00 pm on Sundays.'[15] But contemplate it he did. The public library, despite being purged of 'any work of an immoral or infidel tendency', was an immediate success.[16] During its first year, over 13,000 books were issued for reference and its selection of newspapers, metropolitan and local, were widely read. Judging by the daily attendance of over 400, the library's 'handsome room', on the ground floor of the Town Hall, St Aldate's Street, must have provided a welcome respite from the workplace and over-crowded family kitchen.[17]

However, juggling librarianship, bookselling, family duties and teetotal evangelism took its toll. At the age of forty-one Benjamin succumbed to angina pectoris, and his bookshop died with him. Charles Richards, a close friend and fellow bookseller, who had also worked as a librarian for the Temperance Society, valued the stock of printed books on 15 May 1856 as negligible, Richards wrote to the publishers Routledge & Co., hoping they would relinquish their claims for unpaid bills. The response was generous: 'After your letter of this day we will most willingly give up our proportion of the dividend for Mrs Blackwell's use. I only regret that she should have been so badly provided for.'[18] The letter stayed in the Routledge family and, over a century later, a duplicate was sent to Basil Blackwell with the note: 'I am sending you a copy of a letter which bears the signature of your honoured firm and does honour to it, as I do now. *Floreatis semper!*'[19]

The Blackwell name did flourish and Benjamin's grave, beside the Church of St Cross, Holywell, serves as a reminder. The site is ancient and teems with meadow life.[20] Standing clear of the hawthorn, the gravestone is shaded by yew, garlanded with fronds of ivy and heightened in early summer with purple-flowering honesty speckled all around. He lies in the company of many notable book people who in time joined him: Edwin Spiers, who preceded him from London; the writer Kenneth Grahame; the classicist Maurice Bowra, who became Warden of Wadham College; the poet and Inkling Charlie Williams; the drama critic Kenneth Tynan; and John Redcliffe-Maud, who founded UNESCO. And Benjamin's glee can be imagined at discovering himself in the company of the great Victorian church composer John Stainer, hymning himself through eternity.

Benjamin's intention had been to save souls from the demon drink and to improve minds through books. He may well have rescued a few poor souls from the brink, but his true success was that the reading rooms of his public library were crammed full of working people educating themselves, as he had done. It was this increased demand for books, from all social classes and on a wide range of subjects, which formed the backdrop to his firm's eventual success when it was re-established by his son, Benjamin Henry.

A WORKING-CLASS RENAISSANCE MAN

Benjamin's early death left his widow Nancy to provide for their children: Fred, Matilda and Benjamin Henry. Reviving her old dress-making skills, she managed to send them to Price's Dame School, supplemented by Sunday school and church choir. Luckily the Blackwell boys had inherited their father's love of singing. Fred sang in the choir of St John's, part of Merton chapel while still a parish church, and Benjamin Henry was accepted for Queen's College Choir School. This would certainly have furthered his education, but the opportunity was foreclosed when his voice broke early. To make matters worse, family finances made it impossible for him to stay on at school. And so, at the age of thirteen, he began his lifelong career in the book trade, first as an apprentice in Mr Richards' bookshop.

Basil Blackwell, writing of his father, imagined his pangs 'when he was pushed out so early into the world ... just as he had begun to revel in acquiring knowledge and pursuing scholarship'. But Benjamin Henry was not easily deterred. Despite his scant education, he had the demeanour and ambition of a Renaissance man. He considered a working knowledge of Latin and Greek to be essential and, as his diary records, he decided to correct his deficiency in them – a necessity if, as his mother wanted, he had any hope of competing with university-educated booksellers, such as the Parkers. His diary contains the lists of Latin vocabulary he was committing to memory. When trade was slack he turned to Smith's *Principia Latina*, and thus equipped vicariously accompanied Caesar to the Gallic Wars.

His programme of self-education also included literature, classics and music. Studying the Bible and Tennyson was habitual, and he recorded the names of some of the books he read for pleasure, including *Don Quixote* and Pope's *Dunciad*. Always hankering after a life as a writer, he studied the qualities and temperaments of Isaac Disraeli's *Curiosities of Literature* and *The Literary Character*, and George Trevelyan's *Thomas Babington Macaulay*. He admired Macaulay, who had first made a literary name for himself with an essay on Milton. Benjamin Henry committed as much of Milton as possible to memory; on morning runs before breakfast the elegiac 'Lycidas' suited his pastoral mood as he crossed mist-shrouded Iffley Meadow. Like Milton, he had a passionate faith in God and free will, and in the possibility of attaining the 'paradise within'.

Benjamin Henry's diaries, written in a minute hand, also reveal the rhythm of his family life. Sunday was very much Sunday in the Blackwell household.[21] There was no rest, but much music-making, enlivened further at Christmas, Passiontide, Easter, Ascension, Harvest, All Saints and so on, year in, year out. After evensong, musical soirées were held at home. As a zealous Anglican, he took on layman's duties and sang in the choir at SS Philip and James in North Oxford, the heartland of the new bourgeoisie.[22] In these circles charitable work was *de rigueur* and as his wages increased, especially when he became manager at Rose's bookshop, he joined the 'Guild and Burial Society, at 34/8 per annum' and became its treasurer. He served on the committee of the Falcon Rowing Club and the Churchman's Union and was the concert administrator for the Oxford Choral Society (membership '5s per annum'). The Blackwell family all took part in free concerts and carol singing to raise funds.

Ardent about educating others, Benjamin Henry's diary shows him, in his twenties, already on the lecture circuit. He is invited to local boys' clubs, gives a talk on model steam engines to the boys' school, and literary lectures at the Quaker Adult School on George Herbert (second favourite to Milton) and the Wesleyans. He is to take part in many performances of the *Messiah* over the next ten years, and new music with the Orpheus Choir: *Solomon*, which he 'likes very much', and Arthur Sullivan's *Martyr of Antioch* (soon after its debut in 1880), *Elijah* and *Israel in Egypt*, for which, unbelievably, he took time off from the shop and, as the concert administrator noted enthusiastically, 'sold more reserved seats ... than ever before'.[23]

In his diary he mentions writing a paper on teetotalism; he probably maintained contact with the Temperance Society through his uncle Isaac. His own spiritual nourishment came from reading Pusey's Sermons and, chiefly, *Paradise Lost*. Milton had wanted to be judged by his 'inner ripeness' rather than his 'bud or blossom' in his twenty-third year, and if Benjamin Henry had thought to compare himself with this icon, he would have beaten Milton hands down. By twenty-three he had already been working for ten years while furthering his own classical and literary education, collecting quality second-hand books, writing book catalogues for Rose's, networking in the antiquarian and publishing trades, and saving hard so that he could 'go into business on his own account'. He also nurtured an ambition to go into local politics and clearly had socialist tendencies, although he always voted Liberal. So what was he doing 'at a Conservative party dinner'? We can only guess that, in the interests of business and self-betterment, it was expedient to cross the political divide whatever one's personal views.

By the late 1860s, his mother Nancy's reputation as a teacher and skilled embroiderer had taken the family up in the world. They were frequent guests at the houses of well-to-do tradesmen already further up the ladder, and were well off enough to afford a part-time gardener and a live-in servant, who 'had to be taught how to wait at table'. Although Nancy took in lodgers from the University to bolster her income, the drawing room (not parlour) of the house in Holywell Street was lined with books and pictures hung on the walls, and it was large enough to accommodate her embroidery pupils. Here she hosted formal supper parties, and at Christmas the house was full. They were there to see and to be seen at all the concerts (with a marked preference for choral works) and at the theatre. Benjamin Henry mentions *Hamlet* and *The Tempest*, and a reading of *King Lear* by W. Holland in Clarendon Room. They also attended concerts and lectures at the Churchman's Union, originally a young men's club, and used the facilities of its reading room, stocked with newspapers and magazines. Basil Blackwell later construed the Union, housed in a barn-like hall behind 50 Broad Street ('its open pitch roof had a hint of ecclesiastical architecture') as 'an offshoot of the Oxford Movement that had withered away'.

What a dash Benjamin Henry must have cut in his immaculate cricket flannels and tennis whites. An avid follower of the 'Varsity boat race and any other local regatta, and frequenting the Oxford races and St Giles Fair, he sported his new gold chain, straw hat and cane, purchases he noted in his diary. His feet can hardly have touched the ground, with long days in the bookshop and the rounds of teas, dinners and choir-parties – all male affairs at St John's (Merton). Not averse to 'sitting up at cards until the small hours', he noted winning '£1/1½ at speculation', but confessed to his diary that this was rash. He learned to dance the quadrille, and in winter he skated on the iced-over Isis and Cherwell. His big indulgence continued to be the Falcon Boat Club, at 24s per annum. His diaries convey his sense of pleasure as a member of the club. In the height of midsummer, when the light was at its longest, he would go down to the river in the evening and crew for sport:

> In Quelch's four Annis's is said to be the best and Woodward's next (three fours in all) ... Off to Sports, first heat, 7 o'clock, beat Annis's easily, very pleased, got plated cup ... To Iffley to supper (3 shillings) songs and toasts till 11; home by boat 12 – a jolly day altogether ... I am talked of for the Regatta.

In between working, rowing, tennis and cricket, he, like Arnold's Scholar-Gipsy, walked the surrounding countryside: Thame, Shotover ('beautiful view of Oxford'), Port Meadows to Wolvercote, Cumnor Hill, Headington, Godstow, Sandford...

When going further afield, he prepared with home-made maps. These finely drawn sketches guided him on holiday by foot and rail from London to Pontefract, Hampshire to Herefordshire, Sussex to Surrey and Southsea, Leeds to Cardiff, Durham to Suffolk, and Edinburgh to Lincoln. Holidays were always well planned. His itinerary for the Isle of Wight, aged only nineteen, was remorseless:

> 1st day Southampton to the West Coast (on foot) to Thorness Wood through Parkhurst Forest by creek to Shalfleet and then over a bridge to farm – Thorley – Wellow and straight up coast to Yarmouth

– went to George and Bugle Inn. 2nd day Yarmouth round coast
to Cliffsend to Headon Point (397 feet) – Alum Bay, the Needles,
Scratchells, Afton Downs (600 ft), Brook Chine, then regain high
road to Hulverston up to Mottestowe, Longstone and Brixham. 3rd
day Brixham to Chilton much as possible along shore if not on cliff
passing Shipledge to Barnes Chine – Walpen Chine (190 ft), Blackgang
to Chale up to top of S Catherines down to Nilon and Undercliff to
Ventnor to Globe Hotel. 4th day St Boniface and Shanklin Downs to
Cook's Castle, Appuldurcombe, Wroxall – back to Ventnor.

Over the next few years he took in York and Durham, visiting
Barnard Castle, Saltburn and back down to Hull. He didn't stint
himself; dinners were between 1s and 3s and his bed and board often
around 5s, but he spent 11s 6d on books. His holidays and excursions
for one year, he noted, cost £7 10s 0d.

Benjamin Henry indulged in model-engine-building and illumi-
nated missal work, with 'tiny specks of gold and silver paint put on
with a magnifying glass', but book-buying expeditions always came
first. While he was on regular buying trips to London for Mr Rose,
he fostered his own network of publishers. His diary records some of
his purchases from London's publishing houses:

Mrs Beeton's Cookery 7/6
Coleridge 3/6
Shelley 5/–
Keats 3/6
Football Annual 8½d
Smith's *Wealth of Nations* 5/–
Wordsworth 2/6, and Longfellow 2/6 from Ward and Lock
from Macmillan: essays by Arnold, Bacon, Cloughs poems, Herrick,
    Huxley's *Physiology*, Kingsley's novels
Longman: Disraeli, Macaulay's essays and *Lays of Ancient Rome*,
    Mill's *Logic*
Routledge: Carlyle's Essays 18/5, Fielding 3 vols 7/6, 1001 Gems of
    Poetry 2/6, various Dickens at 2/6, Dante 2/6
Simpson and Marshall: Johnston's *World Atlas* 3/6, *Adam Bede* 3/6;
    Mill on the Floss 3/6, *Jane Eyre* 3/6
Bell and Son: Aldines – Chaucer, Spenser, Goldsmith, Milton,
    Herbert, Goethe's poems, Schiller's poems, Horace, Thucydides,
    Virgil, Kant's *Critique*, *The Iliad*, works by Livy, Plato and
    Aristotle.

His taste was eclectic: from books on steam engines, natural history and angling, to Ruskin's strict guidelines for would-be painters and Mountstuart Elphinstone's *History of India* (1841), which anticipated his subsequent commercial dabbling in the markets of Empire. He could seldom resist Latin dictionaries and primers, and works of translation from many eras, including an edition of King Alfred's Anglo-Saxon *Orosius*. Gifts, too, came his way: from the Bishop of Gloucester and Bristol he received an 1860 English Bible. 'Modern' poetry and biography crept in alongside Diodorus Siculus, Diogenes Laertius and Dionysius the Areopagite, Ovid, Carey's *Dante* (1868), Drayton's eclogues and Palgrave's *Golden Treasury* (1875 edition). A life of Chatterton (1837) was a reminder perhaps of the ignominy of poverty, whereas an 1853 life of Francis Bacon was an invitation to 'experience life'. He acquired twenty-two volumes of the fourth edition of the *Encyclopedia Britannica* (1810) and three volumes of Froissart's *Chronycles* (1871 edition). Henry Hallam's *A View of the State of Europe during the Middle Ages*, three volumes (1834) was spiced up by Roscoe's *Memoirs of Benvenuto Cellini* (1822 edition). The *Memoirs of the Life of Colonel Hutchinson*, written by Lucy Hutchinson, his wife, and printed by a descendant in 1806, familiarized him with the struggles of the Puritans; the Hutchinsons would doubtless have looked askance at his copy of Keble's *Christian Year* (1874 edition) bound in calf, which Benjamin Henry had acquired in exchange for 4d and a pack of cards!

Willing sellers to Benjamin Henry were clergymen and schoolteachers, the 'poorer professionals' who, often finding themselves in straitened circumstances in retirement, were glad, his son Basil later wrote, 'of the services of a sort of intellectuals' pawnbroker'. But, as Benjamin wrote on the flyleaf of his 1877 diary, he was also trying to 'keep a check upon my spending, saving, if possible, 100 pounds in the next two years'. He had, since the mid-1860s, taken on private work as a would-be antiquarian, 'some free and some charged'.[24] When his application to become the librarian of the city of Cardiff failed, it only stiffened his resolve to succeed in bookselling. By March 1876 his 'small collection of books', valued at £26 16s 0d, would, he calculated, 'bear a profit, if sold, of 15–20%'. With this collection, some savings and a loan, Benjamin Henry was able to 'open on my own account'. On 1 January 1879 the sign 'B.H. Blackwell, Bookseller' went up over the door at 50 Broad Street and his mother Nancy's ambition to re-establish the family name became a reality.

Nancy's other children had prospered, too. Fred had become a water rates collector and a leading tenor at Christ Church Cathedral 'who from these two sources had a salary of about £160 per annum'. Matilda, who had been a pupil teacher with the nuns of St Thomas, thought to take vows. 'Matilda hinted at being a Sister again. I tell her that she, like me, likes her liberty too well,' her brother recorded in his diary. Instead, she became a missionary in South Africa: 'whither she went [in 1874] for conscience sake' and, after learning Dutch, taught the 'daughters of well-to-do Boer farmers' until she returned to England and married. When Fred married in 1880, Benjamin Henry brought his mother to live with him over his newly established bookshop – a smart move for a bachelor whose ardent search for a wife had been unsuccessful… so far.

A SUITABLE BOY

'Upon my word I think I must take some lessons in love-letter writing… I never was a ladies man, and it's too late to begin now,' the 37-year-old Benjamin Henry wrote in his diary in March 1886. But he was to eat his words, and quickly: within five months of writing them, he was married. At the announcement that he was to wed Miss Lydia Taylor of Norfolk, there must have been some disappointed sighs from Oxford mothers who had entertained hopes that such a suitable boy would settle for one of *their* daughters.

Mrs Ogden, the wife of a successful merchant, had very nearly pulled it off. Benjamin Henry had been friends with her daughter Nellie since 1871. In May 1872 he was invited 'to Mrs Ogden's supper for Nellie's birthday'. By September things were warming up, or so he liked to think: 'Nellie Ogden came and stayed all evening,' he wrote. Further meetings took place and on 1 December he 'took Nellie home at 10.30 to read Macaulay's essays'. On Christmas Day he was invited to 'tea *and* supper at the Ogdens' and did not return home until 3.30 am.

Two years pass, and there is still nothing doing. Benjamin Henry's frustration led him into troubled waters, when he encouraged the interest of a young woman whose intellect he privately disparaged. 'In July 1875 a Miss Mary (Polly) Barwell aged 19½ came to visit Mrs Ogden

A suitable boy:
Benjamin Henry
in the 1870s.

and naturally I came in contact with her a great deal taking her and
Nellie on the water.' Polly, the daughter of a successful seed merchant
from outside Oxford, was, Benjamin Henry confided to his diary:

> very amiable, of a cheerful and yielding disposition but indifferently
> educated and with a slight knowledge of the world ... I could not fail
> to see that I had made an impression on her. Though I was extremely
> careful not to let her see that I knew it. I was charmed by her face
> and manner and felt flattered by her notice. Before leaving Mrs O. she
> said she wondered if I should ever write to her.

Despite his conscience, and his intellectual snobbery, he could not resist
a little dalliance.

> I sent her two photographs with a little off-hand note saying 2/3 High
> Street [Rose's shop] was a bad place to write letters, thus hinting that
> her answer, which I expected, and thought might be rather gushing

had better come there. On the third day it came, beginning 'Dearist Mr Blackwell' and continuing in a similar strain.

Letters are exchanged, even a few kisses snatched. Plainly he is averse to a relationship with an unlettered girl, and attempting to improve Polly's mind he sends her books. He can't help his feelings of 'half-ripened love', but:

> My happiness, my honour, uprightness, everything seemed to vanish in a moment beside a feeling of my foolishness together with a sense of displeasure of God who seemed to hide his face from me leaving me a prey to bitter regrets. I then realised the horror which impels men to drink, but thank god I was not tempted above measure.

Eventually, he summons the courage to write a parting letter. Polly's response came indirectly.

> I received a parcel sent c/o Mrs Ogden [his own mother knew nothing of the affair], containing a few books given by me to her and a very curt letter from her brother, saying that every scrap sent by me had been destroyed and that Polly 'regretted her folly sincerely'.

Within no time, although still recovering 'from the effect of this painful episode in my life', Benjamin Harris takes out Mary Thomas, who sings in the same choir. Yet he still carries a torch for Nellie. His 1881 diary starts with a poem, against which he writes: 'it is enough to love you', but adds she is 'too stiff and formal and not homely enough to marry'. Nothing ventured, nothing gained, he takes Nellie to the Falcon Club dance and out again the next day, not unescorted of course! In the cold winter of 1881 they go skating and walking, but always in company. He confesses that he is rather jealous when Nellie goes out with another friend. Her mother reassures him that there is no one else. Nellie dillies and dallies, sometimes giving him hope. She pays a visit to the shop, and he takes her to his choir performances and is allowed to escort her home. At Christmas, he is again invited to the Ogdens for tea.

In the New Year, Benjamin Henry clings on to his hopes, but sublimates them with 'more tennis and bike riding'. Then comes the blow, Nellie is engaged! But all is not lost: she breaks off the engagement, and he responds to the good news with a gift of a book of Matthew Arnold's poems. At thirty-three and his younger brother married with a baby, 'he is ripe for love', his friends tell him. Some try their hand at matchmaking. He is introduced to Charlotte and her husband George, because Charlotte's unmarried sister, Lydia (Lilla) Taylor, is coming to stay.

Lilla was a teacher, and organist at her village church. Her father, a gentleman farmer in Blo' Norton, near Diss, Norfolk, had lost his livelihood when Canadian wheat flooded the English market. Having worked to provide for her parents until they died, she was now, in her thirties, free to marry. She and Benjamin Henry had much in common. Lilla was caring, hardworking, well-read, enthusiastic about education and had a marked distaste for social division. He found a freshness about her, 'something of the country air'. She was indeed a suitable girl.

Christmas comes and goes and by 1884 Nellie's engagement is off again. Benjamin Henry gives a dance at the Masonic rooms and refers to a new girlfriend, Bessie Swadling. But this is only a diversion; his heart is already engaged elsewhere. In the summer, he meets Miss Taylor in Oxford again and they take a 'stroll in the park'. Before too many days he is taking Lilla punting on the Cherwell in the moonlight – 'with others', he adds coyly.

But old habits die hard and Benjamin Henry still cannot not bring himself to the point; perhaps that was why he indulged his unrequited love for Nellie for so long. Not being financially secure was also a major drawback. Two more years pass, and he and Lilla meet more and more frequently and exchange an increasingly passionate correspondence. During the cold weather in early 1886, Lilla is laid up with bronchitis, and Benjamin Henry writes that he is 'thinking of her lying in bed'! He too is suffering, he has 'a cold and chilblains: nothing to speak of … [but] your smile will cure them … I feel so sure of your excellence as a nurse.' By March 1886 he is teetering on the edge of commitment.

Lilla introduces him to her aunts in London: 'two good, kind, fine specimens of Norfolk woman-hood', and they take in an exhibition at the Royal Academy. On the train back to Oxford he is caught up by a loquacious acquaintance 'that prevented me from dreaming of tempting cherry lips and loving eyes'. He has difficulty sleeping:

perhaps my head is longing for a sweeter resting place … Oh Lilla, don't say again that you love me 'too much'! If God is love his best gift is a heart overflowing with love ... That I do not deserve such love as yours I am truly ready to own, but God loveth a cheerful, generous, unstinted giver and so in any case you shall be blessed, and now goodbye sweetheart.

There are flowers and more letters: 'upon my word I don't know what I wouldn't give now for one kiss – though I shouldn't like to be hurried about it'. He imagines himself in her 'charming arms, the best and warmest of comforters ... I feel I would venture a great deal just now if I could get my head within that noose'. By May the sap is rising and he writes of wanting to make her happy and then corrects himself: 'seeing how happy you have been, it would be more correct to say of *keeping* you happy. I do hope, and pray, my dear Lilla, that I may be able to do this, and may love you more and more...' Days later, he has crossed the Rubicon. 'Your pin scratched my nose,' he writes, meaning that she'd got under his skin. He wants to tell her that he is now able to support a wife, but he can't seem to say it directly. Instead he tells her of the success of his shop, but 'not to brag', which was distasteful to him. He would 'not make a fortune', he explains, but 'if I can live comfortably and quietly, paying my way and bearing in mind the rainy days that must come, I shall be content and in this I am sure you can and will help me'.

Lilla is again staying at her sister's and is again unwell. Benjamin Henry writes of hoping 'that with this change of weather will disappear all traces of cough mixture, pills, glycerine will be put away'. At the end he draws a picture of a warming pan, which can be taken in more ways than one. Two months pass and Benjamin Henry can think of little else but Lilla. Work, choir and walking with men friends provide a degree of solace. He writes of rambling with Mr E. across Marston Fields to Headington and, very out of character, of 'having a smoke on the way in a quiet field'. It was as good a displacement activity as any and he and his friend 'talked on a great variety of subjects without exhausting any of them, [touching on] Darwinism, Mothers-in-law, taste in colours, butter, religion and thought, homes, burials and women-doctors'.

By July it is all settled and Benjamin Henry is buying furniture at auction (Badcock's) for their rooms over the shop. 'You see I have committed myself and you to mahogany in the back, walnut for the front, and pine upstairs.' He is aware that *he* is making the decisions, but 'you never would say if you dislike the things ... I have not kept fashion in view, but I think the things will always be in fashion as long as good honest workmanship is – sometimes I think its day is gone.' Their wedding takes place on 26 August 1886 at 'his own' church, SS Philip and James, and the suitable boy is on his way to becoming a family man.

BROAD STREET

By the time Benjamin Henry married, the bookshop had become the scholars' 'house of call'. Much later, his son Basil compared his father to 'Glorious John', the 'great bookseller' of whom he wrote so admiringly.[25]

John Gideon Wilson was born in Glasgow in 1876 to James Wilson, a journeyman bookbinder and later master ironmonger, and Margaret (née Millar), a sheet-folder in the same workshop. The third of eight children, he was educated at the local Board School and apprenticed at thirteen to bookseller John Smith. Married, in 1908, to Catherine Smart Provan, he had three daughters and one son to provide for. For a while he worked for Constable and then the booksellers Jones & Evans. During the Great War he served in France and Italy, winning a medal for 'Meritorious Service'. His years at Jones & Evans, where he returned after the war, were the happiest. In 1922, at the invitation of Debenhams, proprietors at the time, he managed Bumpus's bookshop. The shop was in the gracious old courthouse at the corner of Marylebone Lane, Oxford Street, and here Wilson emerged as the most famous bookseller of his time. E.M. Forster wrote that the shop 'served as a rendezvous for leading figures in the literary world' and Wilson was a 'friend and inspiration to many of the finest creative minds of the time'. When Bumpus's lease expired in 1935 Debenhams lost interest and Wilson, helped by friends, moved nearer to Marble Arch. Always working late at night and keeping open house, Wilson's devotion obscured his vision of the larger aspects of running a business.

Wilson could not help himself: he found it hard to delegate responsibility and his generosity in granting credit was abused. Changes in the book trade also threatened his enterprise: mass production, mass selling, self-service and mechanization all undermined his personal style of service. He removed to various other premises until he retired

at age of eighty-three, when his eyesight had failed. And in 1963 the
oracle of the book trade died.[26]

Wilson received public recognition, with the award of a CBE in
1948, but remained:

> unassumedly learned ... a loveable man endowed with rare simplicity
> ... He might be found conversing with a poet laureate or wrapping
> up the purchase of a schoolboy. His assessment of authors and their
> books was quick and sure, and his advice, always valid, was freely
> given to authors, publishers and fellow booksellers.[27]

Basil considered stories such as this a 'necessary vehicle of history'.
Wilson's story was certainly a warning to the impecunious, a tendency
of both Benjamin Henry and then Basil on the publishing side. But
despite this, Benjamin Henry's financial success as a bookseller was
assured. His stock, with its array of nineteenth-century texts, grammars
and dictionaries drew in more and more students.[28] Books reflecting his
love of Oxford attracted a wide range of customers. Loggan's *Oxonia Il-
lustrata* (1675) was, at £5, the most expensive single volume in the whole
catalogue. For the antiquarian there was Piranesi's *Le Antichita Romane*
(1756) in four volumes, priced at £5 10s, and a first edition of Hobbes'
Leviathan (1651) at 18s. The catalogue of 1886 reflected changes to the
curriculum and a more extensive selection of scientific and general
volumes. Dr Radcliffe's 'Physic Library' had been re-housed in the
newly built University Museum in Parks Road, and Blackwell's was
the recipient of around 800 volumes of overflow, some containing the
bookplate of James Gibb, architect of the Radcliffe Camera.

New books began to feature alongside second-hand and soon tipped
the balance of sales. New customers diluted the ranks of scholars, and
the Christmas catalogue of 1894 had something for the 'whole family
... for all tastes and all ages'. His sales were a barometer of their choice:
poetry, drama, general theology, history, biography, reference books
– the *Encyclopedia Britannica,* almanacs and annuals, including one on
football. A gift pack for children, 'Our Little Ones' Library', was done
up in a case with silk ribbon at 1s 6d. No less than forty-seven of G.A.
Henry's historical tales were on offer, accompanied by the works of
R.M. Ballantyne, G. Manville Fenn, W.H.G. Kingston, Jules Verne
and Lewis Carroll.[29] As a sign of things to come, L.T. Meade's *A Sweet
Girl Graduate* was included. Meade would have been much to Benjamin

Henry's taste: she had come from Ireland and put herself through the 'university' of the British Museum Reading Room.

Fiction was well represented on the shelves, with over 1,500 volumes, including the major Victorian novelists – with the notable exception of Trollope, 'whose reputation', his son Basil later lamented, 'had sadly collapsed at the time of his death in 1883'. The younger generation of writers were also conspicuous: Hardy, Kipling, Meredith, Bulwer-Lytton, Lever, Harrison Ainsworth, F. Marion Crawford, Marie Corelli and many others long since forgotten. 'Who,' asked Arthur Norrington, revisiting the lists in the 1970s, 'could remember Amelia E. Barr's *Feet of Clay* or *Lover for an Hour is Love for Ever*?'[30]

Changes in reading habits and an increasingly cosmopolitan public led Benjamin Henry to stock foreign texts: the 1895 catalogue included volumes in Spanish, French, German and Italian. He had been appointed by the Oxford Union Society to provide foreign books for its library, so he informed his customers: 'B.H. Blackwell having agents in the leading Continental Cities is enabled to obtain Foreign Works, not in stock, with the utmost promptitude and at the lowest rates.' But he also wanted more two-way traffic. By 1913 foreign trade accounted for 12 per cent of sales, and it continued to grow. American libraries were already sure bets. A selection of promotional leaflets, written in 1902–3, tempted Americans with 542 mid-seventeenth-century tracts, quarto leather-bound, detailing the English Civil War and the Commonwealth, priced at $350.

But the United States was not, as yet, Blackwell's biggest overseas customer. The Indian Institute had opened at the end of Broad Street in 1884, and Benjamin Henry took a special interest in those training for the Indian Civil Service; the bond that developed put Blackwell's ahead of all competitors supplying books to India. Rhodes Scholars, too, started to arrive in Oxford from 1903, and found refuge and familiarity in Mr Blackwell's shop. His hospitality did not go unrewarded. The librarian of Rhodes University in the Eastern Cape, founded in 1904, had known Blackwell's as an undergraduate and knew where to turn to furnish his shelves. Reciprocating, Benjamin Henry had the spines of all the books ordered blocked with the inscription 'Rhodes University'. Similar relationships developed with other South African universities, and with Australia, Canada and New Zealand. These new friends may, at first, have been more a burden than a benefit. Clifford Collins, of

New Zealand's Canterbury College, wrote of his embarrassment at the 'meagre purchases, which for decades could hardly have covered the printing and postage costs incurred'.[31] Yet all this was grist to Benjamin Henry's mill, as he seldom saw things solely in a commercial light. The American writer Orlo Williams lauded 'this Sosius': in his shop 'I may stand from morn to night unchallenged, finding the newest books from all the world, and should I ask for one not there, be it in the language of the hairy Ainu, some all-knowing one can tell me its price and the publisher'.[32]

By the turn of the century Benjamin Henry was shifting his focus to science, medicine, economics, technology. To please his more traditional readers and to attract those wishing to further their general education, he stocked the Loeb parallel translations from Latin and Greek (1906) and two famous series aimed at the general reader: World Classics (from 1901) and Everyman's Library (from 1906). For light relief there was *Mr Polly*, *Zuleika Dobson*, *The Scarlet Pimpernel* and *The Four Just Men*. *Peter Rabbit* and *The Wind in the Willows* could tempt children.[33]

The adolescent George Crutch, apprenticed to Blackwell's in 1921, wrote of his first impressions of the shop:

> On entering one saw shelved rows of books bound in honest calf and morocco, superb buckram and stout cloth. Not a trace of imitation. Folios and quartos underneath counters, Robert's *Holy Land*, a large copy of Ingram's *Memorials of Oxford*, an heraldic item, *Blood Royal*. One walked past new books, sets of Hardy and Kipling and the latest Galsworthy and John Masefield ... One entered a long passage lined with Greek and Latin schoolbooks. Biography and a small Theological section met the eye. Through the swing doors to English literature in the Union Room, were beautifully bound volumes of English poets, sets of Fielding, Richardson, Smollett, and Jane Austen snuggled next to George Eliot. Charles Lamb was near Benjamin Henry's beloved dramatists and one saw the wise Sir Thomas Browne and delectable Sterne. Second-hand theology was to be found nearer to heaven, on the upper shelves of the gallery in the union; appropriately placed since the room was once used for religious meetings. And beyond the Union room, was a treasure house of ancient tomes, vellum bound, the *Biblia Sacra*, St Augustine, St Chrysostom adjacent to the divine Hooker's *Laws of Ecclesiastic Politie*, in full Russian or a cheaper copy in panelled calf. There were mediaeval writers and classical authors, a Spanish ecclesiastic, a Mecca for savants. Here 'They eat, they drink,

Charles Parker and Benjamin Henry in 1906.

and in communion sweet Quaff immortality and joy ...' [Crutch also singled out *Paradise Lost*, book five – he had already caught the Milton bug from his employer.]

A benign atmosphere permeated the shop: a combination of the cloistered calm of the colleges, the Bodleian and a local church ... It may be said that to spend a lifetime working among books is to enjoy a general education in the Humanities kept evergreen by the constant flow of new publications ... to live and work in the intellectual atmosphere conveyed by books must inevitably influence one's intelligence.

But the bookshop was no jumbled Aladdin's cave; it was highly organized and the passport to entry was the catalogue. Inspired by the seminal catalogues of Bernard Quaritch, the legendary antiquarian bookseller of his father's generation, Benjamin Henry made the preparation of catalogues into an art form (he was said to know Quaritch's off by heart). Yet still feeling keenly the deficiency of his education, he included at the end of his first catalogue, in 1879, a disclaimer quoting from Pynson's *Ship of Fools*: 'Styll am I busy bokes assemblynge ... But what they mean do I nat understonde.' He need not have worried. His customers understood perfectly well. Such was the excitement generated, that on receiving a copy of that first catalogue the formidable scholar Ingram Bywater, who 'had not wantonly taken a walk for twenty years', *ran* to Broad Street to secure a rare edition of Pacius' *Organon*.[34]

As Benjamin Henry's confidence grew, so did his tendency to make his own mark. The 1912 catalogue, which included the recently revived Arundel and Medici Prints, had, for example, an annotation drawing attention to Filippo Lippi's *Madonna and Child* that described the artist's 'romantic passion'. Was Benjamin Henry hinting at his own deep-seated feelings? Almost certainly writing catalogues was an outlet for his own creative bent and a substitute for doing his own writing. But the catalogues also gave him a chance to inform and educate: 'to pass on the soul of the past', not only in Oxford but anywhere that the postal network reached. Benjamin Henry continued cataloguing until his death but, mindful of his mortality, he passed on the skill to Will (Rex) King, his hand-trained antiquarian assistant. Will King, indeed all Benjamin Henry's chosen apprentices, were ideal students and, as the 'Scholar Apprentices' tale tells, Benjamin Henry furthered their education in all the ways he could.

Yet when Benjamin Henry died, in 1924, the *London Daily News* reported:

> hardly anyone in Oxford will have noticed the death of Mr B.H. Blackwell ... The average undergraduate has probably never thought of wondering if there was such a person, any more than the average Londoner inquires if there is a real Mr. Marshall or Mr. Snelgrove.

More surprisingly, the University, to which Benjamin Henry had contributed so much, never formally recognized him. But his son, Basil, was to more than make up for the snub. In 1979, Basil was to be seen processing in his doctoral robes in front of B.H. Blackwell's, almost on the arm of a former prime minister, Harold Macmillan. Ironically, it was Frederick Macmillan, Harold's uncle, who had warned Benjamin Henry, exactly a hundred years before, that he was opening his shop on the wrong side of Broad Street; on the north side, the fledgling Blackwell's was right opposite the long-established Parker's. Frederick Macmillan, if he could have watched the proceedings from Elysium's fields, might be wishing he had bitten his tongue. Blackwell's, facing south, proved to be, literally and metaphorically, on the sunny side of the street.

LIFE ABOVE THE SHOP

Basil Blackwell's start in life was inauspicious enough. Born in the bedroom over his father's shop, his first months were spent in the upstairs rooms or parked in an old pram in the small back garden. Once on his feet restrictions were hardly less; the shop was out of bounds, and Basil and his elder sister Dorothy were largely limited to their mother's drawing room, above 'History' on the first floor front. It was a small, cosy room, lined with bookshelves where his father's publishing efforts were displayed. Any adventures here were confined to books and listening to their mother's lively stories. Occasionally, Basil was invited by Dr Theodore Chaundy to play in Trinity's rose garden, and there were excitements too, such as when the circus came to town. He remembered being yanked up bodily by his sister in order to see 'people in Moorish costume, Britannia in her chariot followed by characters from all parts of the British Empire ... in procession down the street'. As a special treat, Fred Hanks from 'the shop' ferried the children around in a basket chair mounted on the firm's quadracycle.

The start of a new university term provided another big diversion. 'Pandemonium broke out as horses' shoes and the iron-shod wheels of carts, coaches and growlers, ground over Broad Street's cobbles. Cabs carried undergraduates, lounging back with all their impedimenta a-top', to their colleges and lodging houses. 'Running behind each vehicle was a young hopeful who followed the equipage with the prospect of earning a few coppers carrying a toff's luggage to his rooms.'[35] But even at quiet times, during the long vacation, the Blackwells seldom took holidays. When Basil was sent to school at seven, his father reckoned he had 'already had seven years of holiday'. His sister, however, was taught at home by their mother until she was of secondary school age, after which she was sent to Oxford High.[36] The curriculum there was as good as that offered at any academic boys' school, and Basil always maintained that Dorothy beat him in the 'grade-grab'. But she was to opt for nursing, rather than attempt to crash through the academic glass ceiling.

Benjamin Henry's choice for Basil was Magdalen College School, which had a reputation for getting its pupils into the University. In preparation he was sent to a local dame school kept by Misses Wilhelmina and Sarah Mardony. Basil remembered that 'learning by heart was very important' and the Bible 'bequeathed me a love for English language'; his teacher, Professor Jenkins, 'had the distinction of declaring prophesies, or what is usually called instruction in Old Testament history'. To his own surprise, and his father's relief, Basil shone among his peers. Living alongside a vast treasure trove of books he came under the same subtle pressure as Samuel Johnson had 200 years before, in his father's bookshop. Basil's father's academic customers also encouraged him; he mentions Leonard Woolley, assistant keeper of the Ashmolean. And Fred Hanks, his father's apprentice, who had enough knowledge of Greek and Latin to satisfy the exacting Mr Blackwell senior, must have drilled the young Basil.

But books were Basil's most reliable teachers; they were open all hours and had no duties to perform in the shop. He immersed himself in the stock.

> I would lie gaping at Fox's *Book of Martyrs*, or at the strange figure on the title page of Hobbes' *Leviathan*, I explored Dante's *Inferno* with Gustav Doré, who led me on to Carey's translation ... I read Sidney's *Astrophil and Stella* and the *Fairie Queen* plus ... random dippings.

On Sundays, far from having the proverbial day of rest, he was expected to continue his education by attending church, which proved to be more than just an education in theology and devotional literature. First came attention to appearance, which marked out social position, or pretension to it. Basil was marched to church 'uncomfortably dressed in an Eton suit, stiff collar and dicky with a brief bumfreezer jacket', regardless of the weather.

The social divide between town and gown was increasingly assailed as newly married dons came to live among the prosperous merchants of North Oxford.[37] The Blackwells had not quite reached these heights, but in 1896 they migrated to the newly developed Linton Road.[38] In their genteel lifestyle at No. 1 they passed muster with both town and gown. Books and music gave Basil and Dorothy a liberal education, and physical fitness was maintained by walking and cycling. In September 1901 Basil progressed to Magdalen College School, which William Wayneflete, the first headmaster of the free school at Eton, had founded in the 1470s; it was here, Basil discovered, that 'Richard Hooker learnt to enjoy the *Odes* of Horace'. Pupils, in the main, were promising sons of aspiring tradesmen, as they had been throughout the school's history – Thomas Wolsey was the son of a butcher,[39] and even a sixteenth-century Master, Thomas Cooper, was the son of a Catte Street tailor.[40] When Basil arrived, MCS had around 100 pupils, some on full scholarships. School photographs show a ragamuffin-like squad scrabbling around in the yard with a football; they would have looked more at home in the back streets than as future members of the professions. How easily life might have been so different for him, Basil thought. His walk to school down the High, seeing rich and poor huggermugger, bare-footed children begging in the street as the fashionable pulled up at the Angel, was another reminder of the social divide.

Bearing this divide in mind, Basil toed the line at school, receiving the first of many prizes at the end of the Christmas term in 1903. His sporting propensities were reported in several issues of *The Lily*, the school's magazine. An account of his contribution to the First IV in 1905 reads: 'Blackwell shows promise and some smartness, and can work without upsetting the rest of the boat.' By the following year, at number eight in the boat, he weighed in at ten stone eight and was a force to be reckoned with.[41] In football, however, 'at right-half Blackwell is willing but wild ... he runs about a good deal, tries hard, and often kicks the ball in the right direction ... as a rule doesn't use his head'.

In the classroom, Basil's bent was for the classics, whose dominance in the curriculum was being challenged by science. MCS had its fair share of university scholarships in sciences and the arts, but, as the Master told the audience at prize-giving with obvious pleasure, the school continued to pride itself on its teaching of Greek: 'out of the forty-one distinctions awarded among well over a thousand candidates from almost all the big public schools, two fell to us, the same number as Eton'.[42] The classics were thought to be essential for the next genera-tion of public servants, army officers and teachers; an unusually large crop of MCS boys became headmasters. At the end of his Magdalen days, Basil, who 'grudged not an hour of the grammar-grind, which opened for me the unforgettable pages of Thucydides and Herodotus', won the classics prize and a scholarship in Greats to Merton College, Oxford. At the time he was perhaps more excited about the appear-ance of his first poem, 'On a Dead Cat', which appeared in the school magazine in March 1906.[43]

No record exists of what Basil thought of his juvenilia, or what Benjamin Henry and his schoolteacher wife thought as their son crossed Merton's threshold. As the first in the family to go to university, surely their cup was full? Education was not only good for a future in the book trade, it counterposed idealism to mere commercial endeavour. The tension between these two strands was to both restrain and liberate Basil throughout his life. His own account catches the flavour of his education at Merton:

> I was some twelve months younger than most of my year; a handicap I found difficult to surmount mentally and physically ... [I was] one of an increasing breed of the students from humble backgrounds who... rather than assuming a divine right of attendance at the University, saw it as an immense privilege.

All around him were reminders of the social divide. Every morning Basil awoke to the sound of his 'scout' clearing out the fire grate. 'That fireplace was my alarum,' Basil recalled. From the warmth of his bed, Basil would watch guiltily as the 'nimble and cheerful Charlie Scarrott' laid the table for breakfast, enquiring of the recumbent Basil 'if he were expecting guests'. Basil had been brought up to respect men like Charlie, 'peace be on the good man, who combined in some measure the functions of valet, butler and chamber-maid, and worked seven days a week without the benefit of a summer holiday'. But the rigours of a scout's life were not to last. Visiting his college almost daily in his eighties, Basil was relieved to discover that 'the hallmarks of the old servant/scout days were gone: the table was not aptly placed for social meals, and the fireplace was no longer in use'.

Yet Basil's student days had been far from hedonistic. He endured a rigorous daily diet of chapel before breakfast, a light lunch (Commons) after physical exercise on the river or rugger on the field, ending with evensong at 10 p.m. Among his closest friends was Austin Longland, son and grandson of country parsons, who was 'early imbued with the untroubled faith and moral discipline which was in the best tradition of devout Victorianism'. 'We studied together, rowed in the eights, walked the Downs and afloat explored the upper reaches of the Thames, opening our minds to each other without reserve.' By Finals, Basil's tutors expected something more than just a creditable performance, but he accepted his Third in Mods (*valde deflendum*) and

Basil Blackwell, an active member of Merton College Boat Club,
in action here in the Summer Eights, 1909.

a Second in Greats as 'fair enough'.[44] He had, after all, put more effort
into making a name for himself in the College Eight. But rowing
wasn't everything and Basil retained 'pleasant and grateful memories'
of his studies and the men who taught him.

Basil had been exposed to the same temptations as Evelyn Waugh's
Sebastian, but he eschewed them; he could hardly have done otherwise
in the Blackwell household. And he accepted that his future was in his
father's shop. But he never saw this as a comedown. Making books
available, selling and publishing them could transform people's lives.
They were just what juvenile delinquents needed, Basil was to preach
in the local juvenile courts. His 'spoil the rod, spare the child' approach
was radical for the times, yet his belief in education, inherited from
his father and grandfather, was, luckily for him, in tune with current
thinking. Politically, however, the Blackwells were often *out* of step.

TWO

A DREADFUL RADICAL

The tendency in both politics and industry is to submerge the individual. Capitalism and socialism, in theory, may be as different as heads from tails: in effect the individual finds them as near as two faces of a coin.

Basil Blackwell

WHILE THE Blackwells could not be easily labelled in the narrow party political sense, they were fierce campaigners on behalf of causes about which they felt strongly. Joshua Blackwell's individualistic attitude to political affairs carried on down the generations. His son, Benjamin Harris, never let a drop of liquor past his lips out of conviction: as a child he had seen too many drunks on London's mean streets – a formative experience. He proselytized against the demon drink among Oxford's inhabitants, but by his own account his campaign fell on deaf ears. His son, Benjamin Henry, was more preoccupied than his father with class prejudice. (His diary entries in the 1880s show a revealing interest in the notorious Tichborne Trial – he doesn't say it, but you can almost hear him thinking: was a mere butcher's son condemned simply because he had the effrontery to impersonate, if he did, someone of patrician birth?[1]) Petty bureaucracy also unleashed his ire: he met a nagging for the non-renewal of a dog licence with the response, '*Vide* Richard III, Act V, Sc. 5, 1.2.' ('The bloody dog is dead!')

Oxford City Council Election, 1911.

To the Electors of the North Ward.

LADIES AND GENTLEMEN,

We venture respectfully to ask for your votes and support at the forthcoming Election of Councillors for the North Ward.

It is doubtless open to question whether the system of party government is best adapted for municipal affairs, but so long as it obtains, it will be generally admitted that something approaching a balance of parties tends to better discussion of public problems, and makes for greater efficiency in government. Among the nine Councillors of the North Ward, the Progressive Party has at present not a single representative; and though matters are not so one-sided in the other wards, this Party, which has had, and will continue to have our support, is so largely overbalanced as to endanger the administrative efficiency of the Council.

Among the many municipal problems of the time we feel that the questions of Town Planning and the due provision of suitable dwellings for workmen are questions with which the Council ought immediately to grapple. Our workers must be decently housed; we should welcome the building of a small number of workmen's houses by way of experiment, and in all future extensions of the City we are of opinion that due regard should be paid to the proper planning of streets and provision of gardens and open spaces, too, the value and benefit of allotments, and should be glad to see their further extension and improvement. Any schemes, therefore, which may be proposed with these objects in view, will have our cordial support.

While we gratefully acknowledge that much has been done to raise the general level of education in the City, we think that the time has come for still greater efforts. The provision of suitable buildings for the Technical School on a suitable site is still an unsolved problem, and unless it be speedily solved, even the present small Government grant of some £450 a year, which under more favourable conditions, we believe, might easily be trebled, will be lost to the City. There seems also to be room for a well considered scheme to bring about a closer co-ordination than has hitherto been devised between the already existing Secondary and Elementary Schools.

particularly the need of a public Recreation Ground and of a ...ut the year has been urgently felt. The erection also at Park ...which a public petition is at present being signed, is obviously ...econd all efforts to meet these needs. We are glad to see that ...nch of the Public Library at Summertown will not immediately ...in the interim means may be found to put it upon a more ...s.

...n us as your representatives in the Council, we should feel it our ...red measures with due regard to efficiency and economy, and ...istration of the City on more Progressive lines.

We are, yours faithfully,

B. H. BLACKWELL,
1 Linton Road.

G. E. UNDERHILL,
10 Northmoor Road.

Published by the Oxonian Press, Park Ena Street, Oxford

A Liberal agenda: B.H. Blackwell takes matters in hand.

Benjamin Henry was in his own quiet way a thorn in the side of many of those with vested interests in the status quo. And despite the demands of the shop, he was prepared to take this further. He had taken an interest in the Liberal party since the early 1880s and attended their constituency meetings. In the general election of 1881 he voted Liberal and continued to do so for the rest of his life, although at the time he wrote, 'I cannot find fault with the Foreign Policy of Lord Beaconsfield [Disraeli].' It was only in 1911, when the Liberals were making waves with their welfare and income redistributive policies, that Benjamin Henry decided to stand as a candidate for the local council. His wife, Lilla, was just as passionate about his causes and he considered her the more radical of the two. Had she urged him to stand? They were both despairing of the one-sided, Tory bias in local politics. Benjamin's manifesto was all for greater political democracy and participation:

We venture respectfully to ask for your votes ... It is doubtless open
to question whether the system of party government is best adapted
to municipal affairs, but so long as it obtains, it will be generally
admitted that something approaching a balance of parties tends to
better discussion of public problems, and makes for greater efficiency
in government. Among the nine Councillors of the North Ward,
the Progressive Party has at present not a single representative; and
though matters are not so one-sided in other Wards, this Party, which
has and will continue to have our support, is so over-balanced as to
endanger the administrative efficiency of the Council.[2]

Benjamin Henry was duly elected, breaking the Tories' stranglehold.
But even so it is difficult to label him as a Liberal; he might just as
easily have stood as a Socialist candidate if the fledgling Labour party
had had a foothold in Oxford. Although he was under the Liberal
umbrella, he would never have submitted to the Whip, had there been
one. He did not think along party lines; in fact, he doubted whether
'party politics was appropriate for the business of running a city'. The
priority in his manifesto was to sort out municipal problems. 'The
question of town planning and the provision of suitable dwellings for
workmen' must be immediately grappled with: 'our workers must be
decently housed with gardens provided, more open spaces for public
recreation in the City and more allotments ... more bathing places
available all year and a cabman's shelter'. He also stressed that efforts
must be made to 'raise the general level of education', always top of
his list of priorities.

How did Benjamin Henry's agenda go down with the hidebound
burghers who dominated the council? No doubt he was as unpopular
with them as he was with the Oxford dons who perpetrated their own
brand of class distinction, gown seemingly looking down on town.
Even though he had come up in the world and was acknowledged as
scholarly by many in the University, his publicly aired loathing of this
ancient divide drew fire from an unnamed don at Corpus Christi who
denounced him as 'a dreadful radical'. Yet by disposition, Benjamin
Henry was never radical. Like Private Willis in *Iolanthe*, he simply
despised those who left 'that brain outside,/ And vote just as their
leaders tell 'em to'. He could, and would, think for himself.

His preoccupations were not constrained by party political boundar-
ies. He shared Disraeli's earlier concern with public health, and his zeal

for moral reform was as palpable as Gladstone's. With more than a touch of William Morris's Utopian Socialism in his makeup, he was influenced by the 'gas and water socialism' espoused by the early Labour party, which urged that municipal utilities and provisions be placed under public control.[3] His track record as an employer, however, with his shared-ownership scheme, time off for education, and promotion within the ranks, should have veered him towards both the Fabianism of the Webbs and Eleanor Marx's brand of democratic socialism. In his diary entry of 9 March 1882, Benjamin Henry wrote: 'Arnold Toynbee died today, a great loss to Oxford and the working classes.' His sympathies with the working classes were manifold: at the start of the year he had written of his concern about the Irish famine, and in spring the economic consequences for ordinary citizens of the collapse of the Oxford Building Society.

In the shop Benjamin Henry was to import allies. A much-esteemed employee Rex King, recruited during the war, had applauded the German Socialists, 'who worked to the eleventh hour to try to prevent war, organising meetings in every town of importance'. Their ideas, he wrote, 'were destined to play a great part in the future of Europe'.[4] But in wartime, voicing such sentiments was, to put it mildly, ill-advised. Benjamin Henry was pragmatic and it was classic liberalism, from Mill to the contemporaneous Hobhouse, with its central concerns for the freedom of the individual, which most nearly mirrored his private philosophy.

Despite his pragmatism, he couldn't help but ruffle the feathers of the die-hard Tories who, although fellow tradesmen, had graduated to the more showy Italianate villas of North Oxford. His chief political rival, and a particular bugbear in Benjamin Henry's career in public life, was Cyril Vincent, the printer. Vincent's grandfather had been headmaster of a church school at the beginning of the nineteenth century, and Vincent was the senior partner in an established printing firm, with branches in High Street, St Giles and Cowley Road. Conservative in politics and a prominent worker for the party, Vincent was 'a fearless debater and one who held strong opinions'. He was also Benjamin Henry's superior in the layman's hierarchy of the church: Vincent was the people's warden and Benjamin Henry a mere sidesman. As a boy, Basil remembered a sight that must have left him spitting: Cyril Vincent strutting to Matins resplendent in 'silk hat and frock coat', when during the week he wore a journeyman's apron and an old cloth cap while working with the compositors in the family's firm. Vincent nevertheless epitomized the division between the established merchant class and their workers, and his presence was to dog Benjamin Henry's time as a city councillor. He bagged all the new initiatives: he was the first chairman of the Old Age Pension Committee and he pipped Benjamin Henry to the post of Library Committee Chairman. Did Benjamin Henry feel that Vincent was flouting him, and the memory of his dead father, when he insisted that the library 'increase the supply of literature that the rate-payers *wished* to read'? Benjamin Harris's preference, of course, had been for access to educational books for everyone, irrespective of their social status.

Education was the preserve of the Library Committee and on this subject Benjamin Henry didn't hold back. Although he acknowledged that 'much has been done to raise the general level of education in the City', he urged its members to make 'still greater efforts'. Long overdue was 'the provision of buildings for a Technical School on a suitable site; a government grant of £450 pa would be lost if the council did not act'. He also pressed for 'closer co-ordination between the already existing Secondary and Elementary Schools'. Fearing for the future of the branch library in Summertown, which eventually closed in 1917, much needed to be done to improve facilities at the ever-popular central library, where his father had once presided. 'The lending department had very poor lighting and ventilation, and, as a matter of urgency, the public had to have direct access to the books on shelves and a selection of good books should be open on the counter.' Benjamin Henry would hardly have been able to believe his ears when the grant for non-fiction books was increased. In 1913 the number of library volumes rose to 23,571, and then to 24,662 the following year. The average rate of borrowing was 340 books per month. Despite the privation of the war years, readership went from strength to strength. At the end of the first year of the war, loans were up on 1914 by 4,780 books, of which 2,000 were children's.

Given the rapid increase in library use, standard reference books were continually updated and the stock replenished. A reference table was provided, but newspapers were to be excluded from the area – an unwelcome diversion perhaps? More periodicals were taken, the *Political Quarterly* for example, but what, Benjamin Henry asked, was to be done to alleviate the crowded conditions, especially in the ladies' room? Suggestions from library users were welcomed and, rather ahead of the times, a visitors' book was installed so that the Committee could take note of them; election results were also to be displayed in the library. An early sense of equality for those with disabilities prompted the suggestion that a Braille department be set up: had this need arisen because of the war-wounded? The Library Committee made gifts of books to the prison and loans were made to the Bodleian. One wonders what the humble public library could offer to its mighty neighbour. However, they must have worked together closely as the Committee recommended that the librarian should join with authorities of the Bodleian Library to attend the Library Association Conference when it was held in Oxford in September 1914, and in 1916 Benjamin Henry was sent to represent the council at the Association's conference, as a member of its executive.

In the Committee's records there are some obscure references to 'discretionary powers for certain books': was this censorship? Benjamin Henry's librarian father would have certainly felt the need. By 1917 all departments of the library were so overcrowded that admittance had frequently to be refused. The ladies' room partition was removed to make space, and open access for non-fiction increased attendance even further. Much encouragement was given to teachers from the technical schools, who were to be allowed to borrow non-fiction while preparing for exams. A catalogue for the junior department of the library was compiled and an extra grant of £50 for educational books, £5 for French books; books were loaned to children's clubs, evening schools, for girls in East Oxford, for example, and to those following university extension courses. The Committee looked after the education of the library staff too: they authorized payment of any examination fees, as well as covering the cost of any books needed. In 1915, the librarian was instructed to attend the Workers Education Association conferences, just in case he was out of step with modern times.

During the war, the library received many gifts of books, paintings and photos. Discarded books were sent to the Children's and Cowley Road hospitals; those not wanted were sold as scrap to provide extra funds for the library. But contingency plans had to be made to use the reference library for the GPO if hostile aircraft appeared. And there was mounting pressure on the Committee to find a solution to staff shortages while men were serving at the Front; as the war drew to an end, the situation was exacerbated by the influenza epidemic. It was left to the Committee to find ways of filling the gaps as more and more male staff members were called up, although their positions were kept open for them until they returned. Opening hours were continually reduced and on one occasion the library was shut for two weeks.

Despite not acceding to the Chair, Benjamin Henry must have found satisfaction with the Library Committee's achievements; it was, nonetheless, a spending committee. Regarded as politically suspect in some quarters, Benjamin Henry was confined to ordinary membership, not chairmanship, of several other spending, rather than funding, committees: Public Improvements, Allotments, Hospital, General Purposes, Playgrounds and Public Bathing Places, Mental Deficiency (administering the Act of 1913), Highways, Sewers and Lighting. Councillors sitting on spending committees always had to haggle for money and had little power to twist the arm of Conservatives, like Cyril Vincent, who served on all the important financial committees. The minutes of council meetings read much as they would have for Alice Holtby, the first alderwoman of East Riding, whose experiences were used in her daughter Winifred's most famous book, *South Riding*. (Indeed, it is reasonable to surmise that Benjamin Henry may eventually have met Winifred if, as seems likely, she had accompanied her friend Vera Brittain when she came to wartime readings in the shop.)

Despite the minutiae and monotony of council meetings, Benjamin Henry must, at first, have been diverted by his time away from his day job. It was right up his street when he was instructed to take photos of the city's collection of silver plate for Mrs Rhoda Murray's history of Oxford, and he was on familiar turf when arguing for further suitable land for 'more allotments in Sunnymeade and Summertown' and land for children's recreation: 'it was lamentable that more was not provided for citizens and children'; the council was 'living in the past'. Benjamin Henry's support for the provision of school meals, implemented in 1913, and the council's job-creation policies was axiomatic. And he would have been heartened that the council was providing work for prisoners, if only to discover that they were employed on mending the drains. The unemployed were also used for public works, in compliance with the Unemployed Workmen Act. Helping the unemployed was essential, but those employed should, Benjamin Henry thought, find a dignity in their work. Like William Morris, he had a horror of the shoddiness and vulgarity of commercial production and the consequent degradation of the workers in the sweated trades. But by the end of 1914, with most of his male staff at the Front, how frustrated he must have been when he had to withstand endless rounds of meetings taken up with sanitation, waterworks and the purity of gas. The tramways debate, persistently occupying the Highways Committee, must have raised his adrenalin – there was always some kind of dispute going on between William Morris, who owned one of the lines, and his rival, the Oxford Electric Tram Co., but Benjamin Henry was all for more money being spent on roads.

As a member of the General Purpose Committee, it was his duty to ensure compliance with both the National Insurance Act (1911) and the Shops and Offices Act (1911). This would have been manna for him. A profusion of demands followed, from hairdressers for instance, who demanded their compulsory half-day in line with the Act. On the Allotment Committee he faced further demands for land, and during wartime there were problems of access and rights of way. It was hard to find extra land, but the need to grow your own food was even greater. Coming to the rescue, the Clerk of the Dean and Chapter of Westminster Abbey granted the Summertown allotments a further twenty-two acres at a rent of £45 with a lease for twenty-one years. In wartime, the pressure on the council to undertake charitable work also intensified. A grant towards searching for those who had been reported missing in the war was made to the Red Cross, and when the Oxon and Bucks Light Infantry Regiment were camped in Oxford, the Committee voted a grant of £105 to cover the cost of hosting and entertainment; what the 'entertainment' consisted of is not minuted!

Benjamin Henry helped achieve much in the six years he sat on the council, but on 22 October 1917 he wrote to resign his seat: 'with very real regret ... A decision which is a great cause of disappointment but cannot be avoided ... the demands of an exacting business carried on under great difficulties make it impossible'. The fine he should have paid for leaving early was waived. Looking at the minute books of the Library Committee, it is clear that virtually everything progressive and educational, everything that Benjamin Henry held dear, went through unopposed. But his work, both there and on various other committees, was mostly unsung and has long since been forgotten. The minutiae of council work suited his temperament and the issues that arose fitted with his personal ideology. It was important work: ushering in and propelling along social changes that would increase access to education, decrease class divisions and improve the living conditions of working people. Non-confrontational as he was, he would brook no opposition from those whose vested interests frustrated his efforts to help others to help themselves. His ideas were typical of the type of reforming politician who moved with the changing times of the early twentieth century. Being a 'little Liberal' in a world where those who wielded the most influence were still 'little Conservatives' was not always a popular or comfortable position to be in. Radical he must certainly have seemed to that don of Corpus and his ilk, and it was a perception that probably cost him a much-coveted honorary degree.

Given his father's experiences in local politics, it was not surprising that Basil was wary of political party activism. His parents had been card-carrying Liberals, but he preferred direct democracy, upholding the freedom to speak his mind 'without reserve and rancour'. Perhaps bolstered up by his élite education, he felt confident enough to extract his own political philosophy from competing ideologies, a distillation of 'capitalist and socialist all at the same time'. In the first Dent Memorial Lecture in 1931, he tried to explain his emerging personal philosophy: 'the tendency in both politics and industry is to submerge the individual. Capitalism and socialism, in theory, may be as different as heads from tails: in effect the individual finds them as near as two faces of a coin.' Running the family firm, he sought to 'extract from these two systems the means to run a business where the individual benefitted from both'. It was an orthodoxy deeply imbedded in the Edwardian zeitgeist: the fight for greater equality, for universal suffrage, for women's social and political rights, for education, for better living and working conditions, a redistributive taxation system and greater literary, artistic and creative freedom. They were ideals his father had fought over in the council chamber and they both upheld in their shop and publishing house.

Yet running a business which depended on the support of a broad range of customers, the Blackwells had to tread carefully. Could they have done otherwise? Basil risked putting his head above the parapet: he published new works that, especially in wartime, could have been contentious, and orchestrated a campaign against mass production, which he believed dehumanized labour. After the First World War, both he and his father acknowledged that 'people would no longer accept the treatment which had been meted out to them' before. They were capitalists, out to make a profit, but this necessary evil was tempered by the concern for the well-being of their workers, chiefly for their education and advancement. Added to this, the very act of selling books in their shop, which came 'from the great traditions of European Literature', provided a common heritage of learning that would impart 'its healing power'. That books, anthropomorphically, could heal, was typical of Basil's brand of idealism.

For the Blackwells there was something almost sacred about books, and a long-running iniquity operating in the world of antiques and antiquarian bookselling went against everything they believed in. The Ring was a semi-secret agreement among certain dealers to bid up prices at auction. This was a practice even the leading Victorian antiquarian bookseller Bernard Quaritch had tried but failed to vanquish. Benjamin Henry had been afraid to face them down, but Basil wasn't, although despite his efforts and government legislation, nothing improved.[5] Then, following a renewed public outcry in the mid-1950s, Basil dashed off a letter to *The Times*. He always maintained that this letter, 'stating my intention to compile and publish a list of booksellers who would state in statutory declarations that they had no part in the Ring', moved the Booksellers' Association 'to add to their rules'. His letter resulted in a flood of correspondence, and the newly knighted Sir Basil led the charge by signing an informal agreement that he had never, and would never, take part in any Ring. But only sixty-seven members out of a total of 300 followed suit. *The Times* insisted that 'debunking the Ring would take more than a gentleman's agreement'.[6] A decade later Basil wrote to *The Times*: 'I am told that the Ring still operates, but cautiously. At any rate ... the harlots are off the streets.'[7] This was an example of idealism that paid off.

Dealing with the Ring was a productive exercise of his idealism, but in general it troubled him. He felt himself, like Heraclitus, beset by contradictions and confounded by paradoxes. He grappled, for example, with the *idea* of democracy. 'Whither representative democracy today,' he wrote in 1936, 'in great matters as in small, it is the precious but imperilled legacy of the nobler past – precious because it allows that every man is master of his soul and that his soul by itself has worth;

imperilled because we have forgotten that the best gifts of life need
ever to be watched over.' As President of the Booksellers' Association,
he worried about the lack of democracy in his own back yard:

> The tale of attendance at our [Booksellers'] Council Meetings gives
> me to believe that either members think that the business of the
> Association can be left safely in the hands of the officers, or that our
> Council Meetings do not afford scope for single members to speak
> their minds. If the first be true, I am sorry, for that way lies mischief.
> Bureaucracy is only less evil than dictatorship. If the second be true,
> then too am I sorry, for the blame is partly mine. I fear that the
> business of the Association may have grown so much that such a big
> body as our Council, meeting so rarely, cannot deal justly with it.

Basil, for example, 'lamented the size of modern bureaucracy', as he did
'modern enterprise and modern finance ... whither the human scale of
the craftsman, of the individual, had gone'; these were arguments used
by Bertrand Russell in his 1948 Reith lectures, and echoed by J.K. Gal-
braith in 1966 when he challenged the New Industrial State. Loathing
of this industrial state had shaped the Blackwells' public consciousness
and, most probably, kept them in Oxford, where vestiges of an earlier
gentler time were still evident, or so Basil hoped.

But even in Oxford, and in the surrounding countryside, 'a different pack of knaves was at work'. Basil could barely contain himself.
His father, an early convert to environmentalism, had followed the
art critic John Ruskin's influential campaign in the mid-nineteenth
century to preserve Oxford, and would have read of William Morris's
exhortation: 'I wish to ask if it is too late to appeal to the mercy of the
dons to spare a few specimens of the ancient town architecture which
they have not as yet had time to destroy, such for example, as the little
plaster houses in front of Trinity College.'[8] While on the city council,
Benjamin Henry had been one of the majority who refused permission
to take away the cobbles in Merton St, although the residents protested
that they were very noisy. (Basil's daughters, in due course, equally
deplored the desecration of Oxford's heritage, lamenting, in the rush
to provide chain stores, the demise of its famous High Street names:
Fuller's, Cadena and Elliston's.)

Basil, Betjeman-like, took up the cudgels. Something had to be
done about traffic, the erosion of Port Meadow and the encroachment

on common land by Medley's Boat Station. He shared with William Morris's daughter May a horror of motorized boats on the river. And, to set an example, he had 'restored the Well in his village of Appleton, to celebrate The Festival of Britain'.[9]

Training his eye on the whole of rural England, he protested against the wider despoliation of the land. Central government had 'imposed the order of the town onto the countryside: mains drainage, new houses uniformly grouped together, the bussing in of village children to the outskirts of towns'. He suggested that they, and their rural counterparts, should read Wordsworth, 'an authentic countryman'. But, Basil added, the rural idyll was a fallacy which had infected:

> town-dwellers ... since the days of Theocritus, the Alexandrian townsman [whose] singing shepherds and goatherds adorned the Sicilian landscape only in the imagination of city folk ... This pastoral fallacy of the poet, so well seen in Virgil's Eclogues, and he as a farmer certainly knew better, infected the literary tradition of the West.

He cited Shakespeare and Housman's *Shropshire Lad*, which had 'dominated the urban view of the countryside'. But, plain to see, the *Rural Rides* of Cobbett's days could no longer tame the restless spirit now that cars jammed the roads. Modern man, Basil argued, 'sees the country as something to run through in a car, somewhere to have a picnic or ... [to] commute [from]'.[10] Basil himself had migrated to the countryside, to escape the restrictions of urban life, but his father, who never owned a car, stayed close to the city. '"See Naples and die" is an ancient proverb,' Benjamin Henry had written in his 1915 city guide.[11] 'But Naples is a far cry ... and Oxford is readily accessible ... all those who ... love beauty, should rest unsatisfied until they have feasted their eyes on ... that city, in whose praise poets innumerable have sung.' He invited 'the unaided stranger to ... see the colleges and other sites and to take full advantage of [Oxford's] art and music ... abundant wild life and geological attractions'.[12]

Benjamin Henry would have been astonished at the extent of his son Basil's commitment to public duty. It was common knowledge that they had not always seen eye to eye, but he was not the lightweight that his father feared he might be. Basil's dress, as a young man, was too flamboyant and dandified for Benjamin Henry's modest taste. Much worse, he mixed with the Garsington set, the group of socially minded writers and artists, many of them part of the Bloomsbury group, who congregated around Lady Ottoline Morrell at her home just outside Oxford. Basil claimed that they helped to 'form his psyche'. He was once accused of being one of Lady Ottoline's 'young men' and of social climbing. 'Lady Ottie,' he recalled, 'was a very kind soul who loved taking care of young men ... helping them in their early years: she came to the conclusion I was a young man to be helped ... Eventually, I had gently to indicate to her that I was getting married and in a fairly substantial position!'[13]

Benjamin Henry's objections to the Garsington set would have been moral and religious, but despite their louche lifestyles, they were proponents of the very reforms he had worked for. Their ideas spread through the intellectual circles of the universities, lending support to the movement for economic and social reform, which gathered momentum during the Depression and after the Second World War. John Maynard Keynes – a prominent member – advocated that putting money in the pockets of workers would boost investment and employment. The Huxleys, Aldous in particular, and possibly T.S. Eliot too (never really an insider), were wanting to rediscover the spiritual in the midst of the material. William Beveridge and Rab Butler, more serious members, were more akin to Benjamin Henry and wanted something concrete: an extensive welfare system, universal free education and a higher school-leaving age.

Benjamin Henry might well have approved of his son's old Garsington friends when they much later embarked on the 'ban the bomb' crusade. Bertrand Russell sailed into the wind and was jailed for his part in the anti-nuclear demonstration of 1961. But while Basil applauded the pacifists' stance – 'war has reached its apogee with the nuclear bomb' – he did so at a safe distance; he would never have risked imprisonment and expulsion from his college as Russell had done. Neither did he become a supporter of the radical left in the Labour party, who were pressing for unilateral disarmament, or of the mainstream Gaitskellites, who were more pragmatic. Basil doesn't say what he thought of the famous 'Fight, fight and fight again' speech of 1960, in which Gaitskell argued that unilateral nuclear disarmament would destroy not only Britain but the Labour party, but he would almost certainly have concurred. Might it be supposed that Basil could have felt differently about Labour? But the Attlee government's decision to give the go-ahead for Britain's atom bomb had been made in camera, which was decidedly undemocratic.

Yet that same Labour government, in power for six years after the Second World War, had embarked on a programme of social welfare and educational reforms of which Basil heartily approved; that is, until a subsequent Labour government put an end to grammar schools. He was never convinced that the Labour party 'could combine the economic necessities of private enterprise with concern for the individual', and now this was proof enough that it was not to be trusted. When Labour came out against the Common Market, portraying it as a capitalist club, Basil was even more critical. Did the memory of two world wars, together with the ensuing escalations during the Cold War, mean nothing to them? He didn't write directly about it, but after the failure of Britain's entry bid in 1963, Basil came out firmly in favour of membership. He was opposed to Labour's idea of a referendum; he didn't have confidence that the average member of the public could think, still less speak, for itself. 'What was the point of holding a referendum on Europe?' he asked. 'We keep upwards of five hundred dogs in Parliament at a comfortable salary, and now are we are expected to bark ourselves? Can more than one in ten people in the street give an intelligent and valid answer to the question – in or out?'

European integration was, for Basil, too important to leave to the general public. 'How else can we prevent what Toynbee called "the new wine of nationality" from making "sour ferment in the bottles of tribalism"?'[14] He saw dangers inherent in the national pride that might prevent integration.

> What does most harm in the world? ... What I am thinking of does harm everywhere every day. Motorcars do, but they can give lots of pleasure and are useful. Is it illness? But illness always makes us kinder, brings out the best in us. What I am thinking of brings out the worst in us. Now we are getting warm ... When we are unkind and unfair, what is it that makes it so hard for us to say we are sorry and ask forgiveness? Now I think we have it, pride! It catches us out, blinds us. We do not know we are being proud until it is too late.

Over Europe and other matters, Basil found himself squarely in the Liberal camp, but it was not until the early 1980s that he participated

directly in party politics. Labour was in disarray, and widely pronounced unelectable; Thatcher, whom he blamed for reinventing the
old divide between 'them' and 'us', seemed unchallengeable. This
threatened the principles of participatory democracy and 'some other
alternative had to be offered up to the electorate'. Basil's thinking was
summed up in a fundraising letter he received from Lord Lloyd of
Kilgerran of the newly formed Social Democratic party:

> The future of our nation and our way of life ... are all under threat
> and the threat comes from within ... There is competition from
> German and Japanese manufactures, a scarcity of oil and other
> resources and a re-emergence of the Cold War ... Most of our
> troubles are of our own creation ... we have put up with a system of
> industrial relations, which divides companies into 'them and us'. The
> result is low productivity, low investment, lost markets and lost jobs.[15]

It was a tale of woe, one that the very elderly Basil fretted over as
he sat at his lectern. The old industries had long gone and British trade
was in the doldrums. He felt impelled to contribute to a reconstruction,
especially as his business did not seem to be unduly beset by these ills.
He had no time for Conservatism as 'the natural party of government',
which had done far too little for private industry; or for the Labour
party, which, he wrote, was divided by the ideology of half-baked and
much misinterpreted Marxism. He could, at least, help to break the
stranglehold of the established parties. Basil duly sent a contribution
to the fledgling SDP, and an accompanying letter:

> I joined the SDP as a life member: life membership doesn't mean very
> much in my case ... I hope that the Liberal Party ... will coalesce
> with the SDP and set about recruiting the vast body of moderate
> opinion which is unable to express itself to-day. It is very difficult
> to get enthusiastic about moderation, but this, I think, is what we
> must achieve, working for the moderate majority. For the moment,
> you must count on me as looking with lively sympathy from the
> touchline; but in my ninety-third year I don't count for much.[16]

There was something of old Joshua Blackwell, their tax-avoiding
great-grandfather, in Basil's sons, Richard and Julian, who formed their
own company to outwit the taxman. (Basil, too, had tried his hand at
this when, in the 1940s, he opposed the government's 'evil form 6D3

designed to keep antiques at home', especially aimed at exports to America, and he despaired at the 'struggles of young publishers' when 'so great a proportion of any profit went to the tax-gatherers'.) His sons' device was rather more self-serving. Richard told *Punch*:

> It started when Roy [Jenkins, Labour's Chancellor of the Exchequer, 1967–70] came up with some silly disclosure thing requiring companies to tell their secrets: the chairman's weight, typists' consumption of Rich Tea biscuits, and a lot of other nonsense besides. I said 'Balls to that' so, when we founded our subsidiary, our lawyers solemnly filed the name 'Up Jenkins' with the Board of Trade. There were ructions though. So, publicly anyway, we were obliged to turn the prefix into the initials: U.P. Jenkins.

Transparency in public life was not yet fashionable, despite the hoo-hah over the conduct of cabinet minister John Profumo, which had propelled the Conservatives out of office (and Richard was fond of expense account lunches at the Playboy Club in London!), but U.P. Jenkins was his way of getting his own back on a left-wing government. When the Labour government devalued the pound in 1967, Richard hoisted his political colours to the mast: a black flag was unfurled and flown high above the shop for all to see; his father made no comment.

Wanting to keep Middle England's end up, Richard 'founded a mainstream book club with an editorial committee of Jo Grimond, John Patten, Leon Brittan and Alan Peacock'. The club aimed to produce books for 'the silent audience who were angry with Britain's continuing economic decline and distressed by deteriorating social conditions, values and quality of life'. The first authors included Mary Warnock, Robert Conquest, Paul Johnson, Timothy Raison, Charles Carter and Lord Windlesham. It could be seen as a rival to the Left Book Club of the 1930s and 1940s run by Victor Gollancz, but Richard argued that it was above 'the insanities and absurdities of Left and Right' which were 'neither relevant nor desirable'. Was the irony lost on him?

Richard and his brother Julian also fought the good fight that Carlyle had put up against protectionism in the book trade in the late nineteenth century. 'Price-cutting was suicidal,' Richard insisted. 'Books were different and the end of [Frederick Macmillan's] net book agreement would mean no *means* to maintain high standards of service and supply.'[17] What Benjamin Henry would have thought of his grandsons' somewhat reactionary forays into public life can only be guessed at. He would, however, have applauded their support for the University, Richard's success as a classicist and Naval officer, Julian's skill as an oarsman, and his political decision in 2010 to put the firm in the hands of his workers, a move which Julian has described as putting on 'the human face of fascism'. But it was Basil's daughters who truly inherited and carried forward the radical torch, especially Penelope and Corinna.

THE MARCH OF THE DAUGHTERS

As a young child, Penelope attended the Dragon School, one of the few girls enrolled at the time. She was a feisty character who usually wore off her aggression playing hockey and cricket, but on one occasion was rusticated because she had been caught fighting. She alone of the Blackwell daughters had an Oxford University education: like her father and mother, she read Greats, graduating from Somerville in 1937. At university she veered to the left, becoming a staunch supporter of 'those free spirits who went to fight in the Spanish Civil War', although she was later to become a prominent Liberal. But things were not so easy with Basil's strong-minded and high-flying daughter.

Just before the Second World War, Penelope taught English to a group of Jewish children brought out from Germany, who were billeted at the house of the Jessels, a Jewish family prominent in the world of law. (George Jessel had been the first Jewish Master of the Rolls at the time Disraeli was very successfully making a mockery of religious discrimination.) There she met Robert Jessel, who was to become a distinguished journalist. Basil is said to have been afraid that the Jewish connection would hold Penelope back. Was this more out of fatherly concern for his daughter's future than out of prejudice?[18] He didn't prevent Penelope from marrying in 1940 at the age of twenty, despite his reservations – it is doubtful he could have, in any case. After marriage she went to work at Oxford House, a settlement in the East End of London doubling as a social centre, air raid shelter, legal aid clinic and nursery, which became 'rooted in the affections of people in Bethnal Green'. Typically, when she served in the ATS, she refused promotion to the rank of lieutenant as she preferred being a corporal 'where she could stay more in touch with the ranks'.

After the war she toyed with the idea of becoming an archaeologist, but in 1954 her husband Robert died from leukaemia, probably as a result of exposure to radiation while reporting on nuclear testing in the Pacific. Like her great-grandmother Nancy, she was left to bring up her children alone. Penelope took up personnel management at the London School of Economics, and it was here that she started to mix with prominent members of the Liberal party. While an undergraduate, Penelope had flirted with Labour, but 'how could she be involved with any group that regarded people as the masses, rather than as individuals?' Like her father and late grandfather, she now found her natural place was with the Liberal party, and she stood as a candidate for the first time at Hall Green, Birmingham, then for North Oxford, Petersfield and Wellingborough (twice). People queued to hear her speak, but she was not elected. Subsequently she vented her spleen on the party, which, she maintained, had 'lost the intellectual excitement of the Grimond years'.

Undeterred, Penelope took on other political roles, both at home and in the international arena. From 1970 to 1972 she served as president of the Women's Liberal Federation and was a member of the Women's National Commission set up by Harold Wilson in preparation for going into the Common Market. She worked on the proposals for the Sex Discrimination Act, sat on a foreign affairs panel and was a member of a group supporting small businesses, thinking in that instance perhaps of her grandfather's difficult pecuniary start. Like him, she had to content herself with local government. In 1980 she was elected to the West Oxford District Council, and her list of causes rivalled her father's and grandfather's: the Civic Trust, Abbeyfield's Housing Association, the National Trust, the Woodland Trust, Greenpeace and the Open Spaces Trust. She, too, was involved in further education, teaching social policy at Plater College, Headington Hill. Branching out, she went on a study tour of India, and led a delegation to the West Bank.[19]

There is no record of what Christine thought of her daughter's public role. But what did Penelope think of her mother's lack of one? Did anyone notice when the Leader of Oxford Council, bestowing on Basil the Freedom of the City, stated publicly that the scroll bearing his name should also have been inscribed with Christine's? Was it compensation enough that 'the City would henceforth regard her as an "honorary, honorary" citizen'?[20] Was this enough for her daughter

Corinna Blackwell in
the Wrens, during the
Second World War. She
caused so much trouble
they made her an officer.

Penelope? And what was her opinion on the glass ceiling that persisted
at the shop? Basil's youngest daughter Corinna certainly protested, and
continues to do so.

Despite her obvious academic gifts, which showed when she worked
in the 1940s, Corinna ended up as nothing more than her father's
minder. But she says this suited her. Like her grandfather, Corinna
was interested not in self-furtherment but in championing the causes
of others. She always regretted that the firm was not unionized, op-
posing her father who thought his benign patronization would suffice.
Her political activities were not confined to Broad Street. During the
Second World War Corinna joined the Wrens, and she set off a protest
at their conditions of work. 'We had to carry pales of effluent from
the latrines across Portsmouth, and we were a laughing stock,' she
recalled. Not knowing quite what to do with such a defiant recruit,
'they made me an officer: I was working in Portsmouth on D-Day'. She
was seconded as a cipher officer to the RAF, subsequently supervising
the dismantling of aircraft.

When she returned from the war, she explained, 'I was not as determined as a woman like Vera Brittain,' and, although qualified, she
did not go to university.[21] Instead, she helped on the publishing side:
like her Ancient Greek namesake, Corinna nurtured writers; she also
preserved the firm's archive. She didn't work after she married in 1948,
but in 1975 she returned to Broad Street to assist her father, who was

by then in his eighties. She was the favourite of Adrian Mott, her father's old business partner, who wrote that Corinna 'radiated the Blackwell charm'. Still caring for the staff in the shop in her nineties, she is no fading flower. She remains a staunch environmentalist, just as her grandfather, father and sister Penelope more publicly, and her artist sister Helen more privately, had been. She is continually riled when she sniffs the faintest injustice: her Blackwell predecessors, particularly her grandmother Lilla, would have been proud of her. Although, like Penelope, Corinna is at times 'radical', she is never 'dreadful'. And, like all the Blackwell women, she has always had a strong sense of duty.

THREE

WOMEN WARRIORS

To us the degree is not a mere titular distinction ... it is the symbol
of that abolition of unreasoning sex prejudice, of traditional fear
and unsubstantiated distrust which we look for from the coming
years.

Vera Brittain

G IRLS PLAYED very little part in Basil Blackwell's life as an adolescent. True, there were girls in the family and carefully vetted
acquaintances at church, but he attended an all-boys' school and undergraduate life was almost exclusively an all-male affair. Everything had
to be left 'to the inner fantasy life'. 'Female undergraduates,' he recalled,
'were remote mysterious creatures and chaperones were de rigueur.'
One of his friends confessed to never having spoken to a girl during
his entire time at Merton.[1] Basil remembered 'a few girls, not accorded
matriculation at the time, coming to lectures in pairs' and, in one case,
he recalled, 'chaperoned by a nun ... Only one of them in the Greats
School took any care of her appearance; we rejoiced in her elegance
and grace and discovered her name from a scrutiny of her bicycle.
Verily, Phoebe W. had her reward; she married her history tutor.'[2] For
Basil, this was 'a proper ending for a clever girl'. In his Victorian way,
he 'didn't on the whole' think of women as intellectual, 'for women
generally are not kindly disposed to books, which lie about and harbour
dust, and cost money that might be better spent. A woman collector of
rare books is *rarissima avis*.'[3]

Yet Basil's life and work were shaped by women, and did he not remember that his mother and grandmother had both been bread-winners? Just what his grandmother, Nancy, would have thought of his chauvinism will never be known. What is clearly apparent is that for her, it was her husband's, and then her sons' careers that came first. And this was a tradition that continued. Although the Blackwell women were all 'clever girls', they spent their lives serving others, especially men. This was a tradition that had started with Nancy when her husband died young.

Born Anne Stirling Lambert in London in 1823, she had followed Benjamin Harris when he migrated to Oxford. It is reasonable to suppose that she was either a dressmaker's daughter, or had been apprenticed in that trade, because Oxford trade directories of the mid-1850s confirm Nancy's occupation as 'dressmaker'.[4] By then a widow, with three children to provide for, she had no alternative. This, Basil later insisted, put her among the 'great Victorian women, who thought more of their duty than of their rights'. Benjamin Henry wrote in his diary of the great debt he owed his mother, and yet Nancy's story would have been lost if it had not been written down by her grand-daughter Dorothy. 'Left with little or no means, she [Nancy] moved from The Turl to cheaper quarters at 1 Jews Mount [now the site of Nuffield College].'[5] Her fine needlework, 'in the best traditions of the Oxford Movement, embellished many a ceremonial ecclesiastical vestment'. And it brought her to the attention of the Conventual Sisters of St Thomas, whose habits she was asked to make. But Nancy also found a niche in a secular and more lucrative market. Her 'elaborately sprigged waistcoats' were all the rage among Victorian undergraduates, who reminded Basil of Thackeray's young Pendennis. Basil explained that Pendennis and his friends 'were rather dressy'. They would dress themselves up in their embroidered waistcoats 'to dine at each other's rooms, just as other folks would when going to enslave a mistress ... but what follies will not youth perpetrate?'[6] It was a folly the Black-wells were to profit from.

In 1874, as the family's fortunes picked up, Nancy moved them, together with a boarder-apprentice and a servant, to 46 Holywell Street. It was a large and spacious house, where lodgers could be taken in during term time.[7] Here she also ran an embroidery school, as an old lady reminded Basil many years later: 'I was talking on Christmas Eve

[1954] to a little old lady of 99 who remembered that her sister came as a pupil to my grandmother's little school of embroidery.'[8] Benjamin Henry's diaries and letters also give some personal details of his mother. 'Her Majesty the Queen Mum ... would wear Buckingham lace on Sundays', and in the evenings she gave 'supper parties with singing around the harmonium', an instrument which Benjamin Henry had 'purchased on June 11 1866 costing 66 shillings, of which £2 was given on account in the first instance'.

Within a year of Benjamin Henry opening in Broad Street, Nancy went to live with him 'over the shop'; she never owned her own house. She had written to her son that she 'rejoiced in the idea of sharing with the couple when they should be married', but she was only briefly to live with Benjamin Henry and Lilla; in June 1887, less than a year after the marriage, she died, and was buried alongside her husband and her elder brother John. (John Thomas Stirling Lambert (1807–68) had been a cabinetmaker, an Army schoolmaster and, later, tended the gardens in Abingdon Road. He and Nancy shared a Lambert steeliness, but he must also have had in common with his brother-in-law a fierce regard for a classical education: he once refused to make a cabinet because the owner knew 'nothing of Latin'.[9])

Nancy had much approved of her schoolteacher daughter-in-law, Lilla. They had much in common – the Blackwell men, it seems, had a penchant for choosing women who could weather adversity. Both women had had to endure relative poverty when the family bread-winner died. Basil described his mother as 'a free spirit, with something of the country air about her', while Dorothy saw her as a latter-day Boadicea 'because she was a fearless fighter against injustice'. Lilla, her four sisters and one brother, Jack, had enjoyed a carefree and happy early childhood in and around their father's farm. Lilla always found it 'difficult to adjust to the stratified society' of Victorian Oxford. She inveighed against the gulf between town and gown, a stance her husband agreed with, even though most people regarded the divide as 'untraversable and fixed'.

Her children – Dorothy, born in 1887, and her brother Basil, who arrived two years later – were largely confined to the living quarters above the shop; holidays were rarely taken and playing in the street or behind the shop was frowned on. They were also taught at home for the first years. While the children would have been introduced to

Anne Nancy Stirling
(Lambert) Blackwell, 1887,

J. GUGGENHEIM   56 HIGH ST, OXFORD

literature via the Bible, sitting on benches just like the pupils in the
schoolroom in Blo' Norton where Lilla had earlier taught, they were
most avid listeners to their mother's high-spirited stories of country
larks on the farm. Lilla's memories from the mid-nineteenth century
enabled her children to imagine times, places, sights and smells virtually unknown to them, but described in terms 'so vivid', Dorothy
wrote, 'that they always remained with me'. Dorothy described her
mother as 'a small village girl always showing off in front of her peers'.
On one memorable occasion, when she had taken the mickey out of
the village zany (idiot), the jest rebounded on *her*. Lilla had dressed up
in old clothes and swaggered about the village, but just then the real
zany turned up and gave her the chase of a lifetime.

Their house, Lilla told her children, had been 'roomy and pleasant ... with French windows opening onto the lawn, and hanging
creepers'.[10] Her story of harvest home parties held at a neighbouring

farm was a favourite. She conjured up for them 'the hay cart as it was brought round filled with clean straw', a picture of herself and her little sisters laid in it and covered with a tarpaulin to keep their muslin party dresses clean. After the journey, the 'horses [were] black with sweat in the stable' and kegs of brandy immediately opened. Her cousins were invited from London, and much sport was had at the townies' expense. The harvest supper was a feast, and the fun a release after months of hard work. Everyone sang, and, as Masefield was to evoke in 'Land Workers' (1942): 'the singing lingers in my ears, from wagon-tops, while bearing back the end of harvest to the stack'.

The Norfolk relations they had never met were also brought alive for Dorothy and Basil through their mother's stories. Their grandfather John Taylor, Lilla told her children, was much respected 'as an honest and upright man ... a strong, thickset man with a golden spade-beard and kind blue eyes'. On market days, 'he put on his square bowler hat and drove his horse and cart spanking through the lanes to Diss'. On rare, unforgettable occasions, Lilla was allowed to accompany her father to market. She loved to wander away from the din of stock auctions, where the farmers were haggling over prices, to tantalize herself with the colourful wares displayed on the general stalls. If she were very lucky, and as her father's favourite she often was, she came away with some new ribbons. But these happy memories were soon to be overlaid by tragedy. The face of rural England was changing forever, Lilla explained. After the repeal of the Corn Laws, the livelihoods of small farmers were increasingly threatened by the influx of cheap wheat, mostly from Canada. It was a paradoxical situation. While cheaper bread was a welcome subsidy for the urban poor living on meagre wages, many small farmers were going bust. And John Taylor was one of them. Dorothy recorded her mother's heartbreaking account of the day their farm went under the hammer. Sitting by the open bedroom window, Lilla watched her father down below in the farmyard. 'In front of his eyes, the whole disastrous spectacle was played out as his horses and farm possessions were all being sold.' As so often happened when a livelihood is removed, John Taylor 'never really recovered and his good strong life passed largely unrewarded'.

Lilla also conjured up her beloved brother, Jack, 'riding high on his horse across the wind-swept fields' of Norfolk. His 'fine horsemanship was legendary', as was his reputation as an amateur vet. But he was also 'one who would put on the gloves and take anyone on'. Jack may have been quick to rise to the bait, but he was also admired for his compassion and fearlessness.

The fields, at that time, had dykes rather than ditches with straight walls, and if a heavy carthorse slipped in, he was boxed and helpless. Then the cry would go up 'Fetch Jack Taylor'. Putting a halter round the animal's neck, and with complete control of a very steady horse, he would drag the animal inch by inch out of the dyke. One jerk would have been fatal!

Jack was especially broken up by his father's death – so much so that he never settled down to life on the farm afterwards. So, strong as an ox and used to the outdoors life, John emigrated to Canada to go 'fur trapping and seek adventure', Benjamin Henry wrote in his diary on 4 April 1883.[11] As Dorothy and her brother sat at the tea table, above the quiet shop where their father worked so late, they were fired up by tales of their uncle's freer life; he became the stuff of family legends. 'He was still spoken well of in his native village,' Dorothy recorded, 'many years after his death.' Jack was always on his sister's mind and she even foretold his death. 'My mother always had a vivid dream of being at a horse fair when someone near was going to die,' Dorothy wrote, and described the tossing manes and red nostrils that were the portents of disaster. 'Lilla woke my father up at 2 am to say, "I have been in the horse fair and Jack is dead". And surely news came that Jack had died at that time, tragically, from an overdose of laudanum.'

Lilla's vivid imagination, if not her telepathy, was certainly a characteristic that her son Basil inherited. But her daughter had her feet on the ground, and considerable talents too. She was, just as much if not more than her brother Basil, the family biographer. She recalled life over the shop as 'rather sober', and 'just as much so at Linton Road in North Oxford'; 'never any parties ... almost no entertaining of any sort ... alcohol was not served, even on special occasions'. Her father may have had 'no time to play with his children', but he did 'broaden the range of their reading'. Dorothy remembered him offering '5/– if she and her brother would read all of Spenser's *Faerie Queen*'. Basil 'went to his father and said he had read it and quoted the bit about the dragon being sick in the woods and went on quoting this at every meal until he got his 5/–'. Dorothy got her 5s too, but only after she had solemnly read through the whole work.

Basil, Dorothy recalled, rubbed his parents up the wrong way. On one occasion she went away with her parents and Basil had a big party. Chastised by his father, Basil insouciantly excused his behaviour on the grounds that he 'was engaged'. Dorothy recalled an earlier occasion when she and her brother were caught scrumping. Basil remembered that

> we were put across my mother's knee, my sister first as she was the elder. I do not know whether she was spanked the harder, but she was in great distress, and I conceived the idea of asking God that some of her pain should pass to me. I thereupon prayed, and then asked her whether the pain had diminished, but she still howled loudly, and said very firmly, 'No!'

Dorothy, small but strong, admitted to being competitive with her brother, giving him the run-around on the tennis courts and busting herself trying to beat him in swimming races. She was a good horse-woman and 'rejoiced in long walks through the Oxfordshire country-side', as her father had done. Her brother would go on bike rides with her, but 'he had a three gear bike on which he would go at great speed'. Dorothy followed him 'on her old boneshaker often in tears, as he would not wait'.

Benjamin Henry and Lilla were determined that their daughter would be as well educated as her brother. In fact, Basil was in danger of being beaten in the classroom. At Oxford High School, according to her brother, Dorothy 'responded to the mark-grubbing discipline of those days by a weekly score of "Red As"'. After her first term she took the Ada Benson Divinity Prize, which she declared 'a bad start'; it added to her worries about being seen to be 'stolid and sullen' when the fashion was for girls to pose as giddy-headed and very feminine. Dorothy was no fading flower. She hated cant, and refused to obey the 'snobbish rule that you could not walk home with any girl unless both your mother and her mother had given prior permission'. Obeying it would have left her outside the group of more 'modern' girls who visited one another, for tea, after school.[12] On top of school and home-work were the obligatory music lessons, as was the fashion. But she had an aptitude for music, which came from both parents. She 'studied the piano under Dr Ernest Walker, the musical genius of Balliol, and later played first fiddle in Dr Allen's orchestra' as well as becoming a member of the University orchestra. Sometimes arranging events for

Dorothy (Blackwell) Austin, an indomitable matron in the Second World War.

The Ladies' Musical Society, she once invited 'Dame Ethel Smyth who was very difficult and terrorised Walker'.

Despite her obvious academic promise, university was not on the agenda for Dorothy, although women's colleges had been founded a generation before.[13] Like her mother, grandmother and aunt Matilda (Benjamin Henry's sister), Dorothy was a carer and chose, or perhaps was helped to choose, an *appropriate* calling. She trained as a nurse, and was, Basil wrote, 'formidably competent'. At the outbreak of war she was one of the first hundred VADs (voluntary aid detachments) accepted for overseas service, and for over three years she worked in tents in northern France. Returning home, Dorothy fell for one of her brother's friends, Sumner Austin, whose ambition to be an opera singer had been thwarted by the war. Austin was training in Germany in 1914, and the prospect of a pianist wife no doubt helped him to contemplate a return to his chosen career.[14] When war came again, being a linguist and German specialist, he acted as an interpreter in Army Intelligence.[15] Dorothy, meanwhile, returned to the wards as a matron. Family folklore has it that during the endless nights of the Second World War, she survived by 'kipping anywhere'; on one occasion 'as she slept on a laundry basket, she was sent flying down the corridor during a bombing raid'.

After the First World War, Dorothy and her husband settled in Kensington. Her nephew Julian remembered his aunt as 'an intelligent and very kindly old battleaxe'. Remaining childless herself, Aunt Dorothy would invite her brother's family to rare treats in London, where they 'would be taken to the theatre and treated to chicken and chips afterwards'. Her husband, an intellectual and much to the Blackwells' taste, became the family Father Christmas during the festive season.[16]

After her father's death, Dorothy was well provided for, but the family business passed to her brother, and her mother stayed with her son in Oxford. Dorothy watched her brother continue with her father's good work, but many years later at Encaenia, when Basil received an honorary degree, she regretted that their father had not been similarly honoured.

While Dorothy continued her nursing career, her brother expected his wife to give up hers. Christine Blackwell, born Soans, was like Dorothy a teacher's daughter.[17] A graduate linguist with 'outstanding honours in Classics', Christine was a part-time assistant to Gilbert Murray when she came to know Basil. As a successful classicist in her own right, and employed by a Greek scholar, she could hardly put a foot wrong. Gilbert Murray's esteem was evident; his book, *Four Stages of the Great Religions* (1912), had a charming inscription: 'Christine Soans, Part Author, her book'. Murray's boyhood had been spent in Australia and, brought up by his widowed schoolteacher mother, he had very modern ideas about women's role in society – views not altogether shared by the Blackwell men. (They did share other ideals, however; like the Blackwells, Murray was a Liberal whose hatred of war never extended to taking a pacifist stance.)

Nothing has been written about Christine's politics, but it seems likely that she too had Liberal leanings. Initially at least, she was less inclined than the women of previous generations to forsake a career for marriage. In old family photographs she always seems to be away from the main group; while the family poses outside the door of her father's schoolhouse, Christine is reading quietly under a tree. Another photograph, less characteristic, reveals her becomingly in a long, white coming-out dress.

When Basil met his wife-to-be 'at country dancing', he already had his eye on her:

> From the windows of my room in 50 Broad Street adjoining my father in 51 there is a view of the fairway between the old Ashmolean Museum and the Sheldonian Theatre and of the westernmost windows of Duke Humphrey's Library over the Divinity School. Before many months regularly at 10.30am there appeared at that window an adorable young woman, one of the talented maidens engaged upon the revision of the Bodleian Catalogue; I stood at my window and we waved hands in mutual support.

Christine made the first move, sending a letter to the shop:

30 St John Street
Oxford

July 2 1913

Dear Mr Blackwell,

I wonder if you would do me a favour. I have a friend who has been offered the right of translating a German book into English if she can find an English publisher for it. It is a book on Germanic Mythology by J.R. Schlender and has been very successful in Germany. My friend does not quite know what publisher to approach, or what kind of terms they offer, or whether there is any opening for a book of this kind in English. Do you think Clarendon Press would be best? They always seem the kindest in espousing lost causes. Any other publisher of course has to consider whether a book is going to pay or not.

The translation isn't done yet, and nobody of course would bind himself to take it until he has seen it. But I wonder if you could tell me whether there are any prospects for a book of this kind and whether it is any use approaching a publisher until the MS can be produced.

It is a shame to trouble you, but I am quite ignorant about the procedure in these cases, and so is my friend it seems.

Please don't answer till you have time – after Henley.

Yours sincerely

Christine Soans

Marion Christine
Soans, *c.*1910, before
her marriage to
Basil Blackwell.

Christine seems already to have a grasp of the problems of publishing. Was it this that recommended her to Basil? He thought of her as 'an entrancing maiden with the brightest of blue eyes and a pastel rose complexion, which never faded'. Christine had her hair cut in a short bob, when it was still not quite the done thing, which met with her father's disapproval. But far from being an early 'flapper', she had more the air of the schoolmistress; certainly she looked very competent.[18] In her bearing she gave an impression of severity and independent-mindedness, similar to Dorothy. In fact, in personality, Christine was very like her sister-in-law-to-be. She was clever, but level-headed, and a counterbalance to Basil's over-imaginative tendencies. While Basil wallowed in the romance, it was Christine, who had had no previous thoughts of marriage, Basil wrote, who 'came to the point'. But when the banns were called at St Andrew's Church, Christine was angry at being described as 'a spinster of Ramsgate'. After her marriage, in 1914, Christine largely set aside her own academic pursuits. Although there were occasions when 'her lively mind and far-ranging abilities' were of 'inestimable help' to Basil in his business, they were little known of outside the family.

While Basil was kept at work, Christine took off to visit her parents in Ramsgate. In her letters she writes teasingly to him 'not to forget' her and pleads with him to come soon, as their eldest son is prone to 'throwing things at the dinner table' and their eldest daughter is getting 'above herself'. Christine swapped Euripides for buckets and spades, but she found time to maintain her enthusiasm for the classics, and she certainly needed bags of Euripidean 'impassioned sympathy' to tame five children and an energetic husband. Thinking of the garden back home, Basil was ordered to 'deal with the spuds' and 'watch the pears'. Yet even when he did come, he would skive off and put his nose in a book. When Christine challenged his behaviour, as she frequently did, he had at the ready a phrase from Ecclesiastes: 'a scholar's wisdom comes of ample leisure and if a man is to be wise he must be relieved of other tasks'. It can easily be imagined what Christine thought of that!

At home there was no shortage of work. The success of the family business meant that Christine was able to help in the house, but there would have been mountains of hand-washing, and wood to be chopped daily to replenish the fires fuelling the hot water system. Christine became known for her stalwart work ethic, which she put to good use during the Second World War.

Christine's country mother-in-law, Lilla, had initiated her into the mysteries of horticulture; a talented gardener, Lilla produced prodigious quantities of fruit and vegetables. When Christine and Basil settled in the village of Appleton, they acquired a huge piece of land which was husbanded to feed a continual stream of evacuees and their relatives, not to mention members of staff recovering from serious illnesses; the entire tribe, staff, family and friends, would be invited home to tea.[19] She also entertained and befriended her husband's book-world customers and a flow of writers. Basil claimed that he had his wife to thank for securing May Morris's cooperation in publishing more of her father's work: 'she could coax May Morris into shy merriment and persuade her to rehearse delightfully a nocturnal argument of cats'.[20] More often than not, Basil would slip away to read or go down the garden, and Christine was left to do the entertaining. Roger Highfield, Merton's Emeritus Library Fellow, remembered Basil 'still scything as guests came up the driveway' and Christine reprimanding him: '"Basil, people will think you are the gardener", to which he lied, "I *am* the gardener".[21]

To entertain her family and close friends, and contain any over-exuberance, Christine would organize rigorous programmes of 'family dramatics'. The library curtains were pulled across and the Blackwell thespians would bring to life the hero King Croton Hoton Thologos and others of Basil's concoction.[22] Christine expected everyone to join in. Adrian Mott derived 'great pleasure and suffered intense agonies' from her famous hospitality. 'There have been frightful occasions when she made me dress up and try to act in plays! ... Once she even went so far as to insist on my playing the flute (fortunately behind the scenes), to the alarm and despondency of all concerned.'

Christine came across as a bit bossy.[23] She had to be, if she were to tame Basil. Her regime kicked off at the break of day when, wanting her rest, she would ignore his early morning rituals. Getting out of bed at five-thirty to swim in the Osse Dyke Brook, even in the snow, Basil would perambulate in the adjacent woods until warmed up, then disport himself naked on the lawn, communing with his muses and out-singing the dawn chorus. His children would hear him as he bounded back up the stairs to the rhythm of some favourite from *Hymns: Ancient and Modern*. He was expected to prepare his own breakfast, for which she funded him £1 a week.

Julian Blackwell remembered Christine as a 'benignly neglectful' mother. After his birth in 1929, with by then five children in tow, the Blackwells had swapped North Oxford for village life in rural Appleton. Designed on William Morris principles, the house was modest and bare. Furnished with heavy unpolished oak tables and chairs, it had the look of a rambling cottage.[24] It must have been a haven of freedom for the young Blackwells, who were often observed romping barefoot down the lanes. Basil referred to them jokingly as 'the Philistines'. But for Christine's headmaster father it was no joke. He heartily disapproved of the children's 'local accents' and thought they were 'in need of a good deal of disciplining'.[25] But Philistines they were not. They all inherited their parents' and grandparents' love of books and received an academic education – as important for the three girls as for the two boys. Julian remembered a ferocious argument when his elder sister Penny was 'roasted' for not working as hard as she might. But a broad education was just as highly valued, and the house boasted a large and

Two of the 'Philistines': Corinna and Penelope,
Osse Field, Appleton, early 1930s.

ever-expanding library, which fed the children's minds. Given that both their parents were classicists, it is no surprise to learn that their daughters were named Helen, Penelope and Corinna (Korinna, the Ancient Greek poet, was alleged to be the teacher of, and rival to, the better-known Theban poet Pindar).

Despite Basil's insistence on a good education for his daughters, and his acknowledgement that he didn't know 'how the women in the family could juggle so many things', he had no intention of letting them run the shop. Unlike his strong-minded women at home, women chosen to work at Blackwell's were to be well educated, but not too much, and biddable. During and after the First World War, women had been needed in the shop to replace absent men, and Basil enlisted his wife's help to find suitable candidates. She suggested that girls from the local grammar school with creditable passes in the school certificate might be useful to the firm. For one or other reason, a considerable number of qualified girls were unable to go to university, as Christine herself had done. Befriending the headmistress of Oxford's Milham Ford School, a customer of Blackwell's, Christine initiated her plan. Basil claimed it as 'one of his educational experiments', but always credited his wife with her active part in choosing among the candidates.

The history of Milham Ford School serves as a record of the ups and downs of educational legislation.[26] The school had started in the 1890s, when there had been scant provision for studious girls, in the private house of Misses Emma and Jane Moody in Iffley Road. When it moved to Cowley Place, it took its name from the nearby ford. The school was sold in 1904 to the Church Education Corporation, and by 1921 it had 245 pupils in the preparatory department alone. Like those at Oxford High and Magdalen College School, teachers of academic subjects were expected to have degrees. The curriculum was even fuller than that of a comparable boys' school, and games were as competitive and places in teams as fought over. In addition to the usual academic subjects, girls also undertook handwriting, map and botanical drawing, nature study, domestic economy, music, elocution, lacrosse, hockey, netball and physical exercise, sometimes cricket but no mention of rowing.[27]

When Eleanor Halliday went to the school in the 1920s, with a county scholarship, it was under the redoubtable leadership of its second headmistress, Miss J.S.H. McCabe (MA), who reigned from 1912 to 1931.[28] The school had a good track record, its pupils often awarded senior city scholarships, which enabled them to take up much-sought-after places in medical schools and in a range of subjects at Oxford University: St Hilda's took three of its girls in 1923, called 'home students'. Others took the Civil Service examinations or trained as teachers, nurses, librarians and secretaries. When Eleanor finished school in 1929, of the fifty-five students who left with her, two went to Oxford University; two to London University; two to teacher training; two to nursing; two to OUP; one to library work; one to Wolsey Hall; one apprenticed in business; one to a bank; seven to secretarial; and the rest to other schools. Eleanor was one of the seven destined to be a secretary. Basil wrote her story, beginning with her interview. His account is a period piece. It reveals as much about *him* as about Eleanor. His first thoughts were of her looks and demeanour: she was 'well-grown, manifestly in vigorous health, grave in her manner. She sat still and answered my questions with the directness and sincerity of a healthy mind.' How could Basil resist? '"Yes, I think we could make good use of you; can you start here on Monday?" She shot to her feet; "Thank you," she said, and sped down the stairs, swift, it seemed, as Homer's Iris. Here, methought, is astonishing energy, and if her mind can match it, here indeed is a pearl of great price.'

Eleanor was to stay for nearly forty years as Basil's 'peerless secretary'. Having 'certificate French', Basil wrote, Eleanor 'worked at first in our Foreign Department' under (of course) 'an exceedingly able and well trained young Dutchman'. She 'responded with enthusiasm, and as I watched her development I was satisfied that my first assessment of her virtues was right. After two years I decided that those virtues must have further scope.' But what he had in mind was not promotion, but a course of shorthand. When she had mastered it:

> I had a grave talk with her. I told her that I wanted her to study my mind and methods in business matters (in bookselling and publishing) and in public affairs, so that she might grow to be, as it were, my spiritual deputy. She assented; it was an act of dedication. For thirty-seven years, unclouded by any misunderstanding, she gave me the whole loyalty of her generous spirit and devoted her boundless energy to the service of the firm in all its aspects. She never betrayed a confidence, and won the confidence of all.

What had Eleanor thought when she accepted the role of 'spiritual deputy', even though 'she knew all the procedure of bookselling and publishing, and could help out any section in difficulties'? She wouldn't have complained; 'she had no moods and she never quarrelled ... Not even the emotional stresses of preparing for marriage impaired the quality of her work,' Basil wrote of her.

But perhaps an inner frustration fed her tobacco addiction? Basil was devastated when Eleanor died of lung cancer at the age of fifty-five. 'She took with her,' he wrote, 'half my competence. I loved her.' In her honour he made a bequest to the library of Magdalen College School. In its tribute to Eleanor *The Bookseller* wrote of her as 'the greatest darling ... her voice delighted: the very breath of goodness and gaiety ... how odd to be brought to the verge of tears by the death of a woman one has never seen'.[29] 'Was there ever such an obituary?' Basil commented. But did he or his bookselling colleagues learn from this painful experience? Probably not. After all, Basil persisted to believe, 'within no time ... a ring would appear on the third finger of the left hand, and then comes the family'.

After Eleanor's death, other women of similar calibre came to work for Basil. One he described as a cross between 'Wordsworth's Lucy and Messina's Reading Madonna'. Like Eleanor, she 'spoke little and to the point'; it was Basil who did the talking. His role he saw as being akin to that of 'a college tutor or senior public-school master ... with only noble thoughts'. He must have been convincing.

As chairman of Blackwell's, Basil would arrive at his desk with a posy of his wife's roses, when in season, offering them to his 'frippets'. He insisted that the term was meant to convey 'a sense of distance, respect and verbal playfulness'. Did he know he was on shaky ground? Had he felt the need to explain himself to his old friend Arthur Norrington when he told him that he 'enjoyed loving friendships'? Norrington agreed with him: 'I do think warmth and feeling is positively good for us, and the lack of it is bad for us.' But where was Basil's 'distance, respect' when the firm still ran a Miss Blackwell competition in the late 1970s? Was it just playfulness? Was it appropriate for the workplace? Was it a failure on his part to take women seriously?

Basil's thinking was typical of his time. Yet as a member of the debating society in his last year at secondary school, he had proposed the motion 'That this House favours the extension of Parliamentary Suffrage to women'.[30] He must have noticed the achievements of women during the First World War, which did much to secure them the vote.[31] And in December 1918 women had taken their newfound political duties seriously, more so than many men who had long had the vote. Rex King, who had not long been working at the shop, wrote in his diary: 'Yesterday was polling day all over the country. The women folk rose to the occasion and apparently outnumbered the men in many districts.'[32] But in the workplace there were no openings for women in management. And at home Basil wanted nothing more than that his women should serve him. Christine, for her part, concurred: her husband was the breadwinner and his career had to come first. But beyond the Blackwell family, things were changing.

In the wake of the First World War, younger women students in Oxford were busy challenging sexual and social mores and fighting for academic equality. Standing out was twenty-five-year-old Vera Brittain, who, having been so 'war-absorbed' was trying to heal the 'scars upon my heart'.[33] 'As no one talks heroics now, and we/ Must just go back, and start again', she threw herself into the feminist fray.[34] In her combative article, 'The Point of View of a Woman Student', published in Blackwell's Oxford Outlook, she urged the University authorities to award women degrees. 'To us the degree is not a mere titular distinction ... it is the symbol of that abolition of unreasoning sex prejudice, of traditional fear and unsubstantiated distrust which we look for from the coming years.'[35] Five female heads of the women's colleges attempted to thwart Vera's revolutionary journalistic efforts when she was invited to write a regular column for the *Oxford Chronicle*. But in 1920 Vera was able to write optimistically to *The Times* that 'our hour has been long delayed, but we are beginning to believe it is near at last'.[36]

On 11 May 1920 Vera's prediction came true. At last, a university statute permitted women to matriculate and graduate. Vera, her friend Winifred Holtby, and Dorothy L. Sayers (who had been awarded first class honours in 1915), were among the earliest women graduates. But academic success did not take top priority with Vera, which probably cost her the First she had been predicted. Even before she finished her degree, her *Verses of a VAD* (1918) were published in London by Erskine Macdonald. Written in an attempt to assuage her grief, the collection gave her the beginnings of a reputation beyond Oxford. But 'death, relentless', Vera wrote, 'left you lonely there', and she had seized upon the invitation of Basil and Dorothy Blackwell (who had also served as a VAD) to attend their Saturday evening reading circle.[37] Although there was a great reluctance to talk about the war, Vera's poems, which she would almost certainly have read in the circle, showed how little she had forgotten, still less recovered, from the loss of her brother, her lover and so many friends. The traumatized Vera welcomed this weekly respite and she wrote to her mother that 'he [Basil] has taken a great fancy to me and is much disposed to help me ... [But] he is married with two little children, so don't get excited.'[38]

Basil did help Vera, inviting her to edit *Oxford Poetry* in the Michaelmas term 1920, together with C.H.B. Kitchin and Alan Porter, and with contributions from Robert Graves, Edmund Blunden, L.P. Hartley, Roy Campbell and Louis Golding. Winifred Holtby contributed 'The Dead Man' and Hilda Reid, also at Somerville, 'The Magnanimity of Beasts'. Vera's poem 'Daphne', inspired by her friend Winifred, had exhorted the 'Youth of the world, just awake to the glory of day'. It was to have been developed into a novel, presenting a feminist exposé of university life in male-chauvinist Oxford.[39] Winifred's dark poem was uncharacteristically gloomy: 'I am hungry for their pain.' Was it, perhaps, an expression of sympathy for her friend?

Both Vera and Winifred were to become ardent pacifists, but they continued to wage their feminist war mercilessly. In 1934 Winifred contributed a story to the third number of *Lysistrata*, another non-profit-making publication from Blackwell's. She lightheartedly admonished the establishment (of men) who chose to employ women teachers who did not wear lipstick over those who did! In the previous issue, Virginia Shull had suggested 'one of the ways to overcome these prejudices was to promote every opportunity for free intellectual intercourse between men and women'.[40] Virginia Woolf, writing in the same issue, took a similar line: 'Why not bring together people of all ages and both sexes of all shades on fame and obscurity so they can talk without mounting platforms, or reading papers? Why not abolish prigs and prophets? Why not invent human intercourse? Why not try?'[41]

Basil did try, but his attitude to women remained paradoxical: while he wanted to help women writers break down barriers in the literary world, he was not yet ready to share power with them. May Wedderburn Cannan had discovered something of this inconsistency at OUP. She had played a pivotal role at the publishing firm during the war, yet afterwards she had to accept secretarial work: how else was she to earn a living? She was also a writer, but acknowledged that 'one cannot keep oneself on verse'.

But one woman who entered the Blackwell ambit wanted to do just that. Dorothy L. Sayers was born and bred in Oxford, where her father had been a canon of Christ Church and headmaster of its choir school until he departed for country parishes in the wild fenlands. After finishing her studies at home (she had hated school), she came back to Oxford as a Gilchrist scholar at Somerville, from 1912 to 1915, briefly overlapping with Vera Brittain and Winifred Holtby in her final year. Dorothy's antics raised more than a few eyebrows in the University. In 1915, when the War Office commandeered Somerville as a military hospital, Dorothy arranged a farewell party where guests had to play at being sleuths, investigating the mystery of the body in the bath.[42] That year she also co-authored the going-down play, *Pied Pipings*, in which she played H.P. Rallentando, based on Hugh Percy Allen, the conductor of the Bach Choir. Her swan song was a pastiche of 'I've Got a Little List' from Gilbert and Sullivan's *Mikado*:

The nymphs who stroll at breakfast time in nightgowns made of silk;
The people who remove your books, your matches and your milk;
The blighters who drop catalogues and whisper in the Bod.,
Or whistle Bach or Verdi as they walk across the quad;
The superficial sceptic and the keen philanthropist;
They'll none of them be missed! They'll none of them be missed!

The song echoes her own little list of misdemeanours. She had stayed out at night, smoked, talked in the library, endured the imposition of fines and conjured up imaginary love affairs. When war broke out her poor eyesight had prevented her going to France, as Cannan, Holtby and Brittain had, so she turned to love and the Bach Choir – Hugh Allen being the main attraction – and writing poetry instead. Cut adrift from Oxford after finishing her degree, she tried to earn her living as a teacher in Hull. But she could not help thinking of her friends in Oxford and those on active service:

Stuck waist deep in a slimy trench
Your nostrils filled with battle stench
The reek of powder and smoke of shell,
And poison fumes blowing straight from hell.[43]

Muriel Jaeger, a Somerville contemporary, wrote to tell Dorothy that Hugh Allen had lain down his baton in the middle of rehearsal and in tones of great emotion adjured the whole choir to listen to the poem.[44]

Stuck in Hull, Dorothy was deeply unhappy. She hated the teaching, her digs were unspeakably cold and Hull was a prime target for the Zeppelins. The only high point was earning three guineas for a prize poem, a pastiche of an allegedly unpublished Robert Browning poem about Don Quixote.[45] Writing may have been a solace, but it would neither earn her a living nor get her back to Oxford, and she mourned the 'Good days that will not come again'.[46]

But if teaching didn't sit well with her writing ambitions, then maybe publishing would? Could she break into this male-dominated world? Virginia Woolf had just set up the Hogarth Press in London, with her husband Leonard. Dorothy had no money, and her father's parish stipend would not have stretched to support any such venture, but he did have Oxford friends. Canon Sayers, then vicar of Wisbech in Lincolnshire, wrote to Benjamin Henry Blackwell to ask if he would take his daughter as an apprentice publisher. By this time, 1916, Basil was keen to expand his embryonic empire, and had enough work to justify employing an editorial assistant. Early in the New Year, Basil interviewed the 24-year-old Dorothy in his father's workroom. She had already been, informally, to his North Oxford house, but this was a serious occasion and Dorothy tried to rise to it. She turned up for the interview 'dressed formally in a blue serge costume, but with informal yellow stockings', Basil noted. Yellow stockings notwithstanding, Dorothy got the job. She was to be employed as Basil's 'pupil editorial assistant, starting at Easter, 1917'. Over the moon, she dashed off a long letter to her friend Muriel:

> Well, now, everything is settled. I shall go to Oxford somewhere about April 25th and establish myself in a bed-sitting room at 4 Manor Road, my landlady being one Mrs Christopher Wren. On April 29th, I enter on a year's pupilage with Basil Henry Blackwell, who undertakes, in the words of our agreement, 'to instruct the pupil fully in the mystery of publishing', 'on consideration of receiving the sum of £100 [paid by her father], to be re-paid at the weekly rate of £2.' … I am to have a dear little room, perched high up in Mr Blackwell's shop, and looking down on the Caesars – bless them! My duties will be the writing of letters, the reading of manuscripts and the learning of the whole business, from discount to the 3 colour process. It is going to be fun – but strenuous. I shan't get any holidays, I suppose, except Bank Holiday and early closing day – but let's hope I shan't want them … It's immoral to take a job solely for the amount of time one can spend away from it, which is what most of us do with teaching.

She continued the letter, giving her impressions of her future employer based on the previous meeting with him and his family at their home. Dorothy's description of Basil is intensely personal. Had she fallen for him or was her writer's eye working overtime?

> Mr B is a darling – he looks about seventeen – but he has a young wife, and a yet younger baby, so I suppose he is more than that. He is not very tall, and very slight, and he has hair of a warm mouse-colour, only rather more reddish than mouse – which forms a lock, or wave, on one side of the parting. His forehead is pleasing, being rather low and broad … and his eyes grey and bright with rimless

pince-nez. His complexion is palish, and I should say that he would probably freckle if exposed to the sun. His mouth is fine, merry and pleasant in expression – his chin pointed, giving an air of great alertness to his countenance. His drawing-room has a sofa full of cushions, on which he has a habit of sitting sideways, his feet drawn up upon the seat, and his hands clasped about his knees. He smokes a pipe with a curly stem – his teeth and ears I neglected to notice, but I suppose they are good, as they did not intrude themselves in a distasteful manner upon my attention. The action of his hands in taking down one of the volumes with which his shelves are so liberally stocked, is caressing and slightly. His voice is quick, nervous and somewhat high, and his conversation lively and full of humour … he wears his hair slightly long, but not sufficiently so to lay him open to aspersions of being silly or Byronic. His dress was a grey suit, with a soft shirt and purple tie. For walking he had a loose coat approaching Khaki in colour, a soft green hat, and a muffler of the Merton college boating colours. He obtained a Second Class (degree) and rowed in his College Eight; his enfeebled eyesight, and an unfortunate liability to sunstroke and malarial fever, relegated him to class C3 under the present military arrangements. He has a dog called John, and a white cat called Michael.[47]

Dorothy had such high hopes, but it was to end in tears. Her difficulties could perhaps be attributed to the misogyny of the older generation; Basil, despite being only in his early thirties, was imbued with the old prejudices. He soon began to fear that his youthful and 'very bright' pupil was 'more interested in being published than in performing the detailed but repetitive and meticulous tasks required of a trainee editor'. Dorothy would not have denied it: by accepting a job at Blackwell's, she hoped to get more of her work published. As to her methods of achieving this, her poem 'Womanliness' is revealing:

The Master of the house came in and sat him down to dine,
And I served him on my bended knee with bread and meat and wine
With a peacock stuffed with peaches, in his pride for all to see,
And the name of that resplendent dish was 'Golden Flattery'.[48]

But Basil was not susceptible. Did he half fear she might turn her considerable affections in his direction? 'I remember that she had kissed me when my son Richard was born. I did not respond'; most unlike him!

When James Brabazon's biography of Dorothy was published, Basil, then over ninety, told *The Times* that 'he thought she was highly sexed'.[49] But when Janet Hitchman's earlier book had revealed that Dorothy had had an illegitimate son in 1924, Basil had flown to her defence.[50] 'I regret the book: a catch-penny, scandal-mongering work.'[51] Ralph Hone was also working on a biography of her at the time, yet Basil was reluctant to cooperate when Hone wrote asking him for information. 'Wait until he writes again', Basil wrote over his unanswered letter in pencil.[52] Subsequently he relented, writing to Hone of Dorothy's literary achievements. He thought of her, and had published her, as a poet, but she had also contributed to his *New Decameron*: 'The Priest's Tale' and 'The Mistress', and the prologue in volume 1; and an essay, 'Eros in Academe', in *Oxford Outlook* (1919). Her first full-length detective story, *Whose Body?* (1923), had been 'written under the desk' while she was working for him. He didn't say any more.

If Basil thought that Dorothy's writing had got in the way of her work, and that her hopeless pursuit of an old Oxford flame, Eric Whelpton, was a further distraction, he kept it to himself. The unattached Whelpton, invalided out of the Army with shattered nerves, was fair game, but a big personality like Dorothy's would have probably been too much for him. And for Basil too: he confessed that 'in some ways I think she brought out the worst in me'. Basil undoubtedly liked obedient, submissive 'serving' women (like Eleanor Halliday); Dorothy was challenging and argumentative. Yet he judged that Dorothy's 'critical faculty was pretty good', and he admired her 'vivid intelligence, courage'. If so, then why hadn't he thought to make Dorothy's job more rewarding? (Vivien Greene, Graham Greene's wife, later described her as his secretary.[53]) But 'she was not a systematic worker' and Basil detected a

> slight strain of coarseness in [her] mind [and] her religious convictions were too obtrusive and caused me to be provocatively sceptical ... She had a crucifix on her desk. I can still see her now hammering one of the nails, which had become loose, while continuing an argument on a subject, which was in no sense religious.

Looking back, Basil remembered her devotion to the *Chanson de Roland*, amidst other heroic literature.[54] And he described her as a mistress of fantasy, which was rich coming from someone whose

Basil Blackwell,
Cornwall, late 1920s.

wife continually tried to curb his. Her fantasies found expression in Lord Peter Wimsey, in the Christ in *The Man Born to be King*, and harked back to Hugh Percy Allen. Basil's whimsy sent him in search of a male replacement; he chose his friend from Merton days, Adrian Mott. 'And so ended an association of some three years' with Dorothy, whose 'witty, lively and gallant mind was a stimulating experience'. He had dispensed with her editorial talents with a mixture of relief and reluctance, describing her employment as 'like harnessing a racehorse to a plough'.

Dorothy soon moved to London, whence most of Basil's writer-protégés flitted.[55] But although, Basil wrote, 'we parted, with somewhat restrained disapproval on both sides', they always kept in touch; he kept a large folder of news cuttings about her progress.[56] They actually had much in common. Both were devoted to good causes: Dorothy participated in an Oxford group dealing with the issues war raised for Christians and, like Basil and her contemporaries writing in *Wheels*, she felt keenly the social and economic consequences; they were all part of a groundswell that was to lead, after the Second World War, to further educational reform and greater equality. Dorothy's passion for the classics coincided with Basil's, and on a more mundane level they shared a love of cats and bell-ringing. Such connections led Vivien Greene to jump to conclusions: she made public her theory that:

> there was something about the light-hearted, high-spirited and what could be called 'debonair' personality which, when combined with a pointed nose, fair flat hair and a tendency to quote from Edward Lear's verses (never the limericks) and particularly from the *Hunting of the Snark*, which convinced me that here was the original of Lord Peter Wimsey.[57]

Although it was with her aristocratic detective that Dorothy L. Sayers made her literary name, Basil had always thought Dorothy would be a serious poet until 'the enervating influence of the novel' claimed her.[58] He knew that she had been penning her first while working for him, but it was no coincidence that during the three years Dorothy was 'in harness', Blackwell's lists were almost bursting with women poets, and together they had succeeded in making women's voices audible above the din of war. In 1917 he had published Agnes Edith Metcalfe's *Women's Effort, A Chronicle of British Women's Fifty Year Struggle for Citizenship* and, in 1919, *At Last: Conclusion of Women's Effort*. And in publishing *Lysistrata* in the 1930s, Basil would surely have won a 'blue' for supporting women's writing. If the University was hidebound, then Blackwell publishing was not. But did he regret not making better use of women employed in his firm? Probably not.

However, when it came to male employees, his attitude was markedly different. He promoted them every bit as much as his father had done, and many of his apprentices became scholars in their own right. *Lysistrata*, apart from promoting women's rights, had been a mouthpiece criticizing the 'deadening effect' of an Oxford (University) education: 'The percentage of inquiring minds in Oxford must be incredibly small ... Let the schools of dialectic and rhetoric be immediately re-opened with a flourish.' Blackwell's apprentices, despite their humble origins and lack of formal education, were chosen for their inquiring minds and did flourish.

FOUR

SCHOLAR APPRENTICES

> Have you considered a habitat among books, to live and work
> among the great minds of the ages? Not in the confines of a library
> but in the distinct activity of an academic bookshop?
>
> George Crutch, apprenticed to Blackwell's

S ONGS AND STORIES about apprentices are as old as the hills. Accounts written by them, and subsequently preserved, are much
less common. There are, of course, exceptions. One such was Alf
Williams, the railway-hammerman-cum-Greek-scholar who started
his apprenticeship in the railway sheds of Swindon. He remains an
extraordinary example of someone who, despite grinding poverty, put
scholarly endeavour above any material ease or reward.

THE HAMMERMAN POET

'Here is the tragic story of Alfred Williams: a genius whom we refused
to recognize – until too late,' ran a belated story in the *North Wilts
Herald*, fifteen years after his death.[1] Rectifying their omission was
probably due to Basil Blackwell. Basil had immediately recognized
Alf's genius, but only just in time to make a deathbed promise to
Alf's wife, that he would save her husband's Sanskrit scholarship.[2] On
a personal level, it is easy to guess why Basil was so attracted to men
like Alfred Williams. His poverty would have reminded Basil of his

own father's childhood privations. Lacking a formal education, Alf had been unsuccessful in his application for the librarianship of the Swindon Mechanics' Institute, just as Basil's father had been unsuccessful in his application to the city of Cardiff. Alf and Benjamin Henry were both puritanical to a fault and, brought up without a father, they had both been sent out to work at an early age.

Alfred Owen Williams, born in South Marston, Wiltshire, in 1877, was the son of a Welsh carpenter and a farmer's daughter, and the fifth of eight children. When his father deserted them, his mother sold home-made sweets and delivered newspapers in order to feed her brood. Alf's education was rudimentary, and at the age of eight he became a 'half-timer' at school so that he could get paid work with a local farmer. The outdoor life suited his temperament and love of the countryside, but the prospect of better wages, much needed by his mother, lured him inside to join two of his brothers at the Great Western Railway works in Swindon. He worked first as a rivet hotter, then as a furnace boy in the stamping shop; eight years later he was promoted to a drop-stamper. Operating powerful machinery exhilarated him – just as well as he was to remain in this hot and physically demanding environment for twenty-three years. He prided himself on being the best hammerman in Swindon, but he had other ambitions too. Writing what must have been his first poem when he had been in the stamping shop for only a few months earned him the sobriquet 'hammerman poet'. Landscape painting was another of his pastimes, fitted in before and after a twelve-hour shift. He also tried his hand at oil painting: 'a portrait of Mr Gladstone, undertaken when he was only 18, found a following and others sold locally'.[3]

During the day shift, Alf 'used to chalk, on the frame of the steam hammer which he tended, the characters of the Greek alphabet, that he might learn them while he worked', Basil wrote. 'So he began to teach himself enough Greek to read the Tragedians in their own words and to lecture on their plays to popular audiences.' Unbeknown to him, Alf was supporting Basil's crusade to save the teaching of Greek and anticipating 'Warde Fowler's prophecy before the Classical Association' in 1920:

> The seeds of Greek will be for ever in this land – hidden beneath the soil, they will reappear and blossom whenever the chance is given them, like the sweet violets that invariably show themselves in my

woodland country whenever a bit of old cover has been laid open to the fresh air and the sun.

Aspiring to escape the sheds, Alf make his own programme of study. He always read in his dinner hour and then, to the astonishment of his workmates, in 1900 he embarked on a four-year English literature course at Ruskin College. In the meantime, the tall, gentle, blue-eyed Alf had caught the eye of Mary Peck, a moulder's daughter; she was to dedicate her life to him, and at great personal cost. They were married in 1903, and Basil was told how 'they set up their house literally, by taking bricks out of a lock in the derelict Berks and Wilts Canal, and using them to build with their own hands the house', appropriately named Dryden Cottage. They lived 'almost unknown to their neighbours, but sufficient unto themselves, he for Letters only, she for Letters in him'.[4] Alf worked late into the night, only to rise at four each morning to study modern, as well as ancient languages, before cycling four miles to Swindon to be on time when the hooter sounded at six. Unbelievably, he also found time to wander the countryside, collecting songs and folklore. These did, however, bring him tangible results. In 1909 his *Songs in Wiltshire* were published, followed by *Poems in Wiltshire* (1911), *Cor Cordium* and *A Wiltshire Village* (1912) and *Villages of the White Horse* (1913). They evoked the land he knew and loved:

> The friendship of a hill I know
> Above the rising down
> Where the balmy southern breezes blow
> But a mile or two from town;
> The budded broom and heather
> Are wedded on its breast,
> And I love to wander thither
> When the sun is in the West.[5]

Resembling a latter-day medieval peddler, he subsidized his meagre pay selling his poetry and translations door to door. His books were highly regarded and sold well locally at the time, and he was invited to lecture at the very Mechanics' Institute that had previously rebuffed him. His fame even prompted an invitation to talk and dine from a group of London poets.[6] But his extra-curricular activities rattled his employer, the GWR:

> In the huge army of workers employed by the Great Western
> Railway Company there must naturally be men of exceptional and
> diverse talent, men whom a modest competence would have enabled
> to delight their fellows with artistic beauty, but whom the harsh
> realities of life compel to bury their talents, to the permanent loss of
> their day and generation. Happy the man with enough strength of
> soul and body to rise superior to circumstance, to cherish his ideals
> amidst the harsh realities of a life of toil and to bring fruition to his
> precious gift. The man with scientific or mechanical talent finds the
> way open before him; his power can be valued in pounds sterling and
> are readily marketable; but what shall a great commercial company do
> with a musician, a poet or an artist? It is non-plussed![7]

It need hardly be said that Alf's not 'readily marketable' talents went
unrecognized by the GWR. What he thought of this became clear in
his classic account, *Life in a Railway Factory*, written 'at night in twelve
weeks'. If it had been published while he was in the GWR's employ,
he would almost certainly have got the sack.[8] But his workload was
taking its toll. Violent heart pains, similar to the ones that killed Basil's
grandfather, and a troubled digestive system forced Alf to give up the
taxing work. Finishing his last day in the forge he gleefully chalked
a single word *Vici* ('I have won') above his furnace. Now his *Life in a
Railway Factory* could be published without recrimination. The *Daily
Chronicle* called it 'a book of revelation', while *The Times* considered it
both a work of 'pure literature' and a serious 'social study': 'his subject
is real life, the result is admirable'. As was to be expected, the GWR
was less than pleased. The *GWR Magazine* accused Alf of sour grapes.
'He detested the factory ... its buildings, simply because it shut out
views of hills and fields, were like fortresses or prisons.' His fellow
workmen, fearing contamination, stood clear of the book. Very few
copies were sold and Alf was bitterly disappointed.[9]

It was 1916. Alf thought of emigrating to Canada, but war was
raging and, in spite of his poor health and being near to the age limit
for active service, he enlisted. Before joining, his *Folk Songs of the Upper
Thames*, collected by cycling nearly 7,000 miles in the process, was
published and it established him as an authority.[10] His *War Sonnets and
Songs* were also published during this time. Posted to the Royal Field
Artillery in India, he taught himself Sanskrit and explored the great
literatures of the East, and even contemplated staying there. Instead,

in 1919, he returned to a life of poverty in South Marston. With a grant from the Royal Literary Fund he sustained himself and Mary while he continued his study of Sanskrit and finished *Round about the Upper Thames* (1922); *Selected Poems* followed in 1926. But what was to become of his Sanskrit scholarship? Could he find a publisher? Hearsay suggested that Basil Blackwell's publishing house was more open to the outsider than others. Sensing that his days were numbered, and with no money to go in person to Oxford, Alf parcelled up his work and posted it off.

John Betjeman singled out Basil's version of Alf's story as:

one of the most perfect pieces of English prose ... a touching description of a poor man who wanted to become a writer, and who starved in order to do so, and who was a good writer and died in poverty for the sake of being a writer. That is a true publisher for you – a man who can appreciate the sacrifice of a man like Alfred Williams.

Basil takes up the story of his first (and only) meeting with Alf Williams.[11]

Some years ago there reached me through the post a typescript on thin green paper, bearing the impress of a hard-worn typewriter. The accompanying letter stated that the work was a translation from the Sanskrit, that the Professor of Sanskrit at Oxford had written an introduction, and that if we should decide to publish the book and thought that pictures might be able to add to its attractions, a certain young artist might be able to make them for us.

Basil was immediately in thrall to this chance manuscript by an unknown author. The translator's Preface showed that Alfred Williams could write English; the professor's introduction testified to his scholarship. The address typed on the letter gave the name of a village near Swindon, and the best course seemed to be to invite him to come over to Oxford and discuss the matter.

He replied that he would be happy to come, and on the appointed day he arrived punctually, a man seemingly in his fifties and with a charming smile. As soon as he entered my room I was aware that I was in the presence of a rare spirit, but being slow, and often wrong, in my estimate of men, I could not tell what lay behind the serenity, the cheerfulness and the gentleness which both his face and his manner revealed. Our discussion raised no difficulties. He would

revise his typescript according to my suggestions, and bring it to
Oxford again in a week or two to meet the artist and to complete
the preliminary plans for publication. When was his train? He had
bicycled.

He courteously excused himself from lunching with me, for he was
anxious to be getting home. I thought that a meal between two rides
of twenty-seven miles could hardly be amiss, but let it go at that.
When I proposed a day for the next meeting, a look of pain came into
his eye as he asked me, very gently, if the day after would be equally
convenient, for his wife had just undergone a very serious operation
of doubtful value, and the day I had offered was that on which he was
to bring her home from Swindon hospital. So 'the day after,' and the
hour of 2.30 was agreed, and Alfred Williams went his way. At noon
of the day appointed came a telegram: 'Alfred Williams died in his
sleep yesterday.' It was signed by a name unknown to me, and there
was no address. Two or three days I was asked if I would see someone
who 'wanted to tell me about Alfred Williams'; and there entered my
room the man (as I soon learned) who had sent the telegram.[12] He was
stone-blind. He told me that he had been Alfred Williams' closest
friend, and that he felt I ought to be told the whole story. He felt it
was due to his friend and due to me, and as he sat before me with the
strange stillness and slow speech of the blind, this honest man spoke
words that made my ears tingle. 'Heart failure?' I supposed. 'Well,
that's what the doctor said, but I'm afraid it was starvation ... that
and bicycling into Swindon every day, and then up that hill up to the
hospital to see his wife. You see, we found his bank book, and since
Christmas he has spent only twenty-six pounds (it was then late June),
and there was little left.

'Even so Alfred Williams had saved a bit, for we found in a drawer
a pound note pinned to a bit of paper on which he had written "for
port-wine for Mary"; and I fancy he was starving himself to give
her comforts in hospital.' 'And she? Was her operation successful?'
'It was a forlorn hope. It's a cancer, you see, and she can't last long.
She had been looking forward to coming home, and her husband
had promised to come for her early on Friday. She was sitting at the
window looking out for him when the news came to the hospital that
he had been found dead in his bed. They did not know how to tell
her, and she sat there waiting and waiting ... Now she's home, and so
near gone that, when I sit by her bed, sometimes I strain my ears to
hear if she is still breathing, and can't hear a sound; and I'll say gently,
"Are you there, Mary?" and she'll whisper, "Yes, Harry."' (It was
Lou Robins she referred to as Harry.) And so, bit by bit, came out

the story of Alfred Williams and his wife Mary; how a country boy, like Jude the Obscure, he was set to work in the fields, but his thirst for learning drove him to devote himself to Literature, helped and encouraged by the village girl he married ...

But the sales of poetry even before The Great War were small, and even with the help of articles and lectures, can have provided but a stepmotherly portion to this devoted couple. On his return to England (after the War) he pursued his studies, and out of them had come the Translations which he had offered me. 'They thought a lot of him in London,' said the blind man, 'and only last week (the last time he was with me) he told me that the Prime Minister had written to tell him that it had been decided to grant him a Civil List Pension and sent him a cheque for £50 to carry him on for the present. But I fancy he knew what was coming for him, for he came over to me and gripped the arms of my chair so hard that I felt them tremble, and said, "Harry, it's too late."' He had learnt by then that his wife's case was hopeless. And now his wife's one care was that his Sanskrit books, the great Lexicon, Grammars, etc., should be given to the University Library. Could I help her there? I asked if it would be a comfort if I went to see her ('It would indeed'), and arranged to meet the blind man at the house in South Marston a day or two later.

I found the little house they had built with their own hands, and entered the sitting-room. Small, clean, furnished with the bare needs for sitting at table for food or work, austere as a cell, it contained Alfred Williams' books. They stood on a small desk by the window, eight or ten books, the nucleus of a Sanskrit scholar's working library. There were no other books to be seen; and it was manifest that to equip himself with these costly volumes he had sacrificed all his Greek and Latin and English books. I went upstairs. The bedroom was as bare as the room below. In the bed, the clothes pulled up to her chin, lay the dying woman. The ivory skin was drawn tight on her face, and her neck was wasted almost to the bone. Only her eyes moved. Beside the bed sat the blind man, and between them on the floor was a case containing all Mary Williams' earthly treasure. I was asked to open it, and there was the revised typescript, which Alfred Williams had promised to bring to Oxford. There was nothing else in the case save discarded sheets of the same work. It was all of a piece with the sense of finality that possessed that house.

Mary Williams' first care was for the Sanskrit books, and I promised to see that they were well bestowed. We then spoke about the typescript, briefly, for it was clear that words were costly in that room, and I said I would lose no time in producing the book. We had

spoken simply and with a kind of unearthly serenity about the books
and the typescript, but as I took my leave I felt that I must tell Mary
Williams that I should always remember gratefully my meeting with
her husband, for he was one of those who left you a better man than
he found you.

Like summer tempest came her tears. 'One of the best,' she
whispered.

I left the house and drove home on that summer afternoon with
that sense of awe which once or twice in a lifetime takes a man,
when, for a moment, and without desert, he is caught up in the high
triumph of one of the rare spirits of mankind.

'His translation of the *Panchatantra* brought these ancient moral fables
to a contemporary audience,' Basil wrote.[13] *Tales from the East* followed
in 1931. In 1950 an Indian librarian wrote of his joy at reading Alf
Williams' *Tales*, the Blackwell editions duly accorded 'a place in our
fine Goethals Indian Library'.[14]

In what stark contrast stands Lord Nuffield of Morris Motors fame,
an Oxford boy who started as an apprentice bicycle maker and ended
up a millionaire, yet eschewed books completely. He once told Basil:
'I am a craftsman; I get nothing from books; show me or let me find
out for myself; machinery is metal logic.'

Within the bookselling trade, however, apprentices were typically
eager to improve their minds and dedicate their lives to books and
learning. Some, like Dorothy L. Sayers, even had themselves apprenticed specifically with the intention of learning about how to write and
get published. In the 1940s and 1950s, to escape relative poverty and
not being able to afford university, Brian Aldiss continued his education
as an apprentice with Sanders Bookshop at 104 High Street, Oxford.
There he found his footing as a writer, and his first book was a lively
diary-cum-novel called *The Brightfount Diaries*; the title, of course, was
a take-off of Blackwell.[15] More than 100 years before, Bernard Quaritch
had, after serving his apprenticeship, set up his own bookshop with
scarcely more assets than Benjamin Harris had had when he first came
to Oxford.[16] At one time Quaritch owned the finest stock in Victorian
England, but as his stock rose in volume, book prices fell. He died in
1899 virtually penniless. In contrast, Benjamin Henry combined the
'art of scholarship with the science of making both ends meet'.[17] And,
it must be added, a talent for educating his apprentices and his son.

'ONE OF THE BETTER COLLEGES'

An article in the *Oxford Morning Post* in 1906 averred that 'the greatest educative influence of Oxford resides neither in Bodleian, nor schools, nor tutors, nor lectures, nor college societies, but in the excellent management and most liberal facilities of one of the best bookshops in the world – Mr Blackwell's'.

Mr Blackwell himself – Benjamin Henry – had not been directly exposed to the system of tutors and lectures and college societies as a boy; he was self-taught, and he was determined to pass this habit on.[18] Apprentices were encouraged in their studies, and everyone had access to Blackwell's 'free library', where the staff acted as research assistants. In a letter to Basil Blackwell, John Betjeman once declared that he had 'learnt more at Blackwell's than at Marlborough or Magdalen'.[19]

Admissions policy at the Blackwell 'alternative seat of learning' was to take the most promising 'natural scholars' straight from school. Typically, apprentices came from impoverished backgrounds and had no hope of affording further education. It was not unlike the medieval tradition, when the colleges would take poor boys singled out by their parish priest. At Blackwell's, wrote Hugo Dyson, Fellow of Merton, they became 'scholars of one of the better colleges, Blackwell's'. Blackwell's freshers did indeed count themselves lucky. George Crutch, apprenticed in 1921, wrote that 'working among books is to enjoy a general education kept evergreen by the constant flow of new publications'. In one's peregrination round the shop carrying a large pile of books, Crutch recorded:

> you would meet Mr Blackwell, who would ask if you knew who Aristophanes was, and if you did not know would suggest politely that you become acquainted ... the fully fledged apprentice would be expected to know where to look for *The Frogs*, a Ruy Blas (Victor Hugo) or a Gray (*Elegy* or *Anatomy*?). And you had to know if the book was in folio or duo decimo.

Books conveyed an intellectual atmosphere, but other aspects of college life also characterized Blackwell's. Early apprentices were steeped in the Anglican choral tradition; several sung in the same choir as Mr Blackwell. On weekdays their chapel was the shop floor, where their master would join them as they sung lustily to let off steam.

Harnessing youthful proclivities was a continual challenge. While apprenticed, alcohol and marriage were forbidden. The White Horse next door and two more watering holes just down the street were a temptation some apprentices could not resist. Women were less in evidence. Precious few were seen in the colleges, and Blackwell's first apprentices suffered the same deprivation as students. Basil recalled that the first young woman employed to undertake secretarial duties for his father 'proved too upsetting for the male staff'. The second, 'a discreet red-haired maiden who lived in the odour of sanctity', was all too soon 'claimed by the holier estate of matrimony'. A favourite haunt for young ladies was the Cadena café in Cornmarket, where *Tales from Vienna Woods* was played by a string quartet. It is doubtful if any of Blackwell's male staff ever penetrated this haven.

Like their peers in the nearby colleges, apprentices took to sport. Cycling was an easy option, necessary too as a means of delivering customers' books, running errands and taking notes when the telephone was still little used. Geoffrey Barfoot, who was apprenticed in 1913, recalled being sent out on reconnaissance on Mr Basil's bike.

> when the airship Delta came down in University Park ... It nearly ended in disaster for in my excitement I brought back the wrong bike. Mr Basil said it was a better bicycle than his own but I had better nip back and change it for the right one. My luck was in, for I was able to make the exchange without being spotted. The bicycle was rather high with two cross bars so that it was not easy to reach the pedals from the saddle. In sliding both ways on the saddle it was rather a strain on the seat of my rather worn trousers and repairs to the same had to be effected by my long-suffering mother.

Rowing, cricket, soccer, hiking, drama and choir were all part of the Blackwell 'curriculum'. Productions were put on for the local prison and Blackwell's teams, especially in cricket, did well against the University's. There is nothing on record to suggest that the players versus men divide caused any upset. But whether imagined or not, Geoffrey Barfoot felt keenly the social difference: 'Mr Basil was still rowing for his college and during Summer Eights I was given time off to run with the students along the river bank to shout for Merton.' He felt he was 'looked upon as a "Towny"' in the Oxford of gown *above* town: the University elite versus the proletariat.

Cycling enthusiasts: B.H. Blackwell with Fred Hanks,
William Hunt and his team of apprentices, 1892.

Barfoot's reaction wasn't surprising. Aged only four, he had witnessed his father's pauper's funeral, 'one of the last walking funerals recorded' in Oxford City. 'All the family resources had been used up burying my grandmother a few weeks before. My father's coffin was loaded onto an open handcart and pushed through the streets with the mourners following on foot.' There was no welfare state, and to make ends meet Barfoot's mother worked as a charwoman in the daytime and a school cleaner in the evening.

Cooking, mending and cleaning at home had to be supplemented by my sister and eldest brother. We got ourselves off to school – cleaned our faces and necks and ears, brushed our hair and put on patched clothes. At seven I helped my mother with the school cleaning and in term delivered newspapers to the colleges.

On Saturdays, when only ten, Barfoot became a butcher's boy; working for twelve hours with two full meals provided, he had 'one shilling to take home and a good joint of meat'. Yet he did well at school.

My very good teacher, at St John's Cowley [a higher grade school],
invited me to tea and encouraged me to finish the 'top standard'. On
the strength of a very flattering letter from him, good fortune came
my way at the age of fourteen. I secured employment in the service of
that revered gentleman Mr Benjamin Henry Blackwell, who decided
that here was a case whereby he might make a 'silk purse out of a
sow's ear', at best he had a good try.

Wages were

2/6 to 5/– per week for boys; women's approximately 5/– to 10/– and
men 20/– to 25/– and seniors (men) rarely more than 30/–. Overtime
was expected, unpaid, but our generous boss gave us two weeks with
pay during the University vacation, in addition to the five national
day holidays. Due to his generosity, because of family poverty, I
received the highest boys pay of 5/– per week.[20]

Barfoot rose through the ranks to become a director, one of a
number to do so. Master Fred W. Chaundy, Benjamin Henry's very
first apprentice, predating Barfoot by thirty-five years, went on to run
his own shop.[21] Master Fred Hanks, the second apprentice, joined in
1883 and stayed until he dropped.

Fred Hanks was only five when his father died, and, he wrote:

the only education my mother could afford was provided by an
elementary school at 2d per week. A year or two later St. Philip and
St. James Boys' School was opened. Under the extramural tuition
of my dear old teacher Mr Dermer, I learnt a little more French and
some Latin up to the first book of Caesar. At the age of nine I became
a choirboy at the church of SS Philip and James … Mr Blackwell, a
senior chorister, sat in the pew immediately behind me. Like most
boys, I tried to bolster my appearance by using hair lotion. This
particular lotion (bless it!) must have had a rather offensive odour.

One Sunday morning Mr Blackwell spoke to Hanks for the first
time.

He asked me, nicely and kindly, if I would mind *not* using this
particular hair lotion. The next Sunday I obediently turned up with
my hair in its natural and inoffensive state … You can imagine my
surprise when after the service Mr Blackwell, thanking me nicely,
placed a shilling in my hand.

Hearing that Mr Blackwell required an apprentice, Hanks boldly applied. 'Whether the hair-oil did the trick or not I don't know.' He recalled the signing of his indentures:

The scene is a room in a house, No. 36 Woodstock Rd., the date is July 1st 1883; present B.H. Blackwell, his brother Mr F.J. Blackwell, my mother and a little boy – myself. I promised on the Bible: to serve faithfully for five years, not to waste the Goods of the said Master ... not contract Matrimony within the said term nor play Cards or Dice Tables ... haunt Taverns or Playhouses.

In return, Hanks was to be rewarded with 3s 6d a week, rising to 10s in his fifth year. His working hours were as arcane as the dictates of apprenticeship law. Officially from 8.30 a.m. to 8 p.m., they were much extended at the start of term. But it posed no hardship. 'I hardly knew what it was to have a father, and Mr Blackwell tried to some extent to fill that gap ... In a fatherly way, he invited me to share his hobbies.' When the shop was quiet, Hanks assisted with the cleaning and reassembling of two model railway engines, 'and then we shared the pleasure of seeing them working'. If Mr Blackwell was out of Oxford, Hanks came to act as 'a bodyguard to Mrs Blackwell and the children ... When they took holidays I watered the window boxes, fed the much prized cat and took charge of the shop.' On 29 May 1889, Hanks played midwife's attendant when Basil Blackwell was born.

His first duties in the shop were more mundane, however, especially in the summer vacation when trade was slow. The entire stock had to be given

a thorough dusting ... There were no such mechanical implements as Hoovers to assist us, so we had to devise our own methods. We would take two packing cases outside the shop, on which we placed a long board. The books were carried out, an armful at a time. The proverbial duster saw action, and in addition we took two books at a time and banged them well together. As rivals on the other side of the road followed suit, the noise and reverberation that resulted can well be imagined.

Hanks was next initiated into

the most useful and economical method of opening the parcels ... Economy was strictly observed and I was taught that the string should be cut in such a way as to preserve as much as possible. The packing paper, too, had to be salvaged and reused. Mr. Blackwell himself taught me how to pack a parcel.

Mastering the basics, Hanks' duster was replaced with a pen, and he was taught to 'prepare the educational catalogue, commonly known as the potboiler'.

Hanks' schoolboy knowledge of French and Latin enabled him 'to cope fairly successfully with books in these languages'. But when faced with German, he was at a loss.

> Before long Mr L.A. Selby-Bigge, a fellow of University College, came to my aid [Blackwell's paid the fees]. I visited him once a week, after business sometimes as late as 10 o'clock. He used to say, very kindly, that while he taught me to read, I taught him a little grammar. That may have been so, for at that time I was ploughing through Otto.[22] I had a wish to go to Germany when I had finished my apprenticeship, but *res augusta domi* [poverty] prevented this, and as the French proverb says, *où la chèvre est attachée il faut qu'elle broute...*

So Fred, tethered to Oxford, grazed there – and was amply compensated.

> My dear old chief, anxious as ever to encourage, rewarded me with a bonus due to the high turnover of foreign books. A rival, Williams and Norgate, on the other side of the street, had for a while threatened Blackwell's supremacy in the foreign field. But not for long, they ceased trading in September 1901.

Alongside running 'Foreign' and acquiring 'a little learning', Hanks was expected to write letters and keep the books.

> Every letter had to be written by hand, a state of affairs we cannot imagine today ... Before the Lamson-Paragon system of bookkeeping, all credit sales were entered into a daybook, and later transferred to a ledger. To prevent misposting, I called out the items from the daybook, while Chaundy checked the entry in the ledger; many of the entries in Ledger No. 1 contained a good deal of Mr. Blackwell's neat hand writing.

At the start of a new term, daily routine went to the wall and overtime was obligatory. After a thirteen-hour day, Hanks would hoist

'Honours for ordinary folk': *Fête champêtre*, 1933, held in Appleton,
where Basil Blackwell lived, to celebrate Fred Hanks' jubilee and the
conferment on him of an honorary MA by Oxford University.

a sack of parcels on his back 'in order that they could be delivered at
the porter's lodge before the gates were closed at 9 p.m'. Local deliveries
were made on Mr Blackwell's quadracycle; the contents of scholarly
libraries bought out of town were sent on by rail.

As the purchasing of libraries increased, so space in the shop
decreased.

> After some years Mr Blackwell purchased the adjoining premises of
> Lockwood's the tailor. You can imagine our delight when we drew
> up the blinds of No. 51 and exposed *two* windows to the public gaze.
> Before long the buildings behind: a caretaker's cottage, a dispensary,
> and the Churchmen's Union, were amalgamated.

Knocking away the dispensary removed the sorry sight of

> wretched specimens of humanity crowded into our back yard waiting
> for the doctors who attended three of four mornings a week to
> dispense medicine. The Union continued to be used for readings and
> meetings ... On some occasions it was let to a professional boxer, who

gave lessons to undergraduates, and in the morning was the evidence, on the floor, that much blood had been spilt.

Hanks associated fire, as well as blood, with the room.

One day, by good luck, I happened to be at that end of the shop when I was amazed to hear a terrible screaming by a female and at the same time a vivid flash of light passed by the window. Running as quickly as I could, I found the daughter of the keeper of the Union on fire and about to enter the house. I seized her, rolled her up in the mat just inside the Union passage and tore away the burning pieces of her dress. She had been dusting a table in the reading room and while she was standing with her back to the stove her dress had caught fire.

Less dramatic, but equally memorable, was the time Hanks spied through the keyhole on Paul Verlaine. 'The room was bare, lit only by two candles, and the only other person present was the Regius Professor of Modern History, Yorke Powell, successor of J.A. Froude.' Noted for having befriended refugees after the Paris Commune, Powell was keen to foster French poetry; Verlaine, Mallarmé and Verhaeren all lectured at Oxford under his auspices.

Hanks dined out on his memories of the notables who came to the shop, and the story of his recruitment must have reached the ears of other choristers, including William Hunt. Hunt, another apprentice who rose to become a director, also kept a diary, but sadly it has not survived. We do, however, get a picture of him through his colleague, Rex King:

Hunt did so much to place Blackwell's upon the map ... many scholars the world over are his debtors for his advice and help in finding the books they needed ... I should describe him as a slightly belated product of the Samuel Smiles self-help school of thought ... he was of the old school: for all he was magnanimous and warm-hearted, in his position as director, he was hierarchic. While he was studiously differential to those above him, he used to sit in judgment at the Charles Reade desk, putting the fear of god into idle apprentices. 'If the customer knows the book so must we. Find it,' he would bark at them. But he gave them presents of Dickens each Christmas. Hunt let it be known that mere assistants should be honoured to sit round the table with him.

William Hunt playing cricket:
Oxford v. Cambridge Booksellers, 1912.

IN AND OUT THE COUNTING HOUSE

Charles Field, who was to become one of the founding directors when Blackwell's became a company, arrived in the counting house back in the memorable days when it was in the charge of Uncle Fred Lambert, Nancy Blackwell's brother and uncle to Benjamin Henry. Tommy Templeton, apprenticed in 1926, remembered him well and fondly.

> Uncle Fred was a colourful character, with the neatest handwriting imaginable. After a lifetime as a pest control officer in local government, he retired to his nephew's shop to help assemble catalogues and keep the ledgers. When Uncle Fred died of appendicitis, the only means of transporting him to the hospital was by handcart.

Field soon assumed control of accounts in the 'flea room', once a bedroom in one of the cottages immediately behind No. 51, overlooking Bliss Court where the New Bodleian is now. He worked at a long sloping bench with two assistants and an office boy, equipped with steel pens lodged behind the ear when not in use. Tommy Templeton remembered:

> I was now his *office* boy. Not just a job but a *position*; the biggest snobs are in the working class! My chief duties were to put into alphabetical order the day's invoices and answer the company telephone. The office measured 20ft by 10 and along one wall was a very high desk at which I stood to work (I had to stand on a box).

All day long they copied entries from the long, parchment-bound daybooks into the ledgers, under the name of the customer concerned, which were transcribed onto account forms and sent out for the end of term. It was legendary that Blackwell's encouraged long credit. 'A certain Lord Chancellor's [the Earl of Birkenhead] three-figure account had not been closed since his undergraduate days. [He] bought books by the yard and had them sumptuously rebound; a practice that must have depressed rather than enhanced the value of many first editions … Yet Charles Field had invincible faith in his debtors,' Templeton recalled:

> it was part of his sweet nature. 'Oh, he'll come up,' he would say when the time was overripe to pass an account into the hands of professional extortionists. And how often he was right. [Tommy remembered with shock news of a debtor 'found kneeling at his bed with a written sheet before him on which he prayed God's mercy for taking his life by a shot. The money-lenders had extorted his last asset …'] … Kind-hearted as ever, Field took me as a youth in his little three-wheeled Morgan on numerous little outings, which were a great joy to a still poor youth. When I was newly wed he learnt that I could not afford even a crystal set wireless, so he gave me a two-valve set with loudspeaker. His favourite saying was, 'If it's not in one place it must be in another' and time and time again he would find an account in the ledger when I had said it wasn't there … I suspect that he did not always agree with his fellow directors for I have seen him return from Board meetings red of face and scowling … [But] little has gone right in the Accounts since his death.

Field suffered from malaria caught in Gallipoli during the First World War, Templeton recorded. 'He came to work when he should have been in bed and died sooner than he should have.'

Templeton, very much alive and adventurous, was often sent to do valuations. Arriving to price some books in a large Victorian house, he was informed that they were:

> in a chest in the cellar and the key to the cellar could not be found. The only means of access was via the coal shute. Not wishing to return empty handed, I precipitated myself into the cellar. Arriving with a thump, I discovered the chest in a corner and prized the lid open. Imagine my horror when I discovered not a treasure trove of books, but a soggy mass ... I turned away in disgust and, feeling like the Count of Monte Cristo planning his escape from the Chateau, I contemplated my return to the world outside. The only way out was back up the coal shute!

Just as undignified was his brush with a local Mother Superior. Called to value some books at an open order, he mistakenly turned up at a closed convent.

> I was subjected to a severe scrutiny by a beady eye, and asked my business. I explained. The grille closed. The keeper of the gate withdrew to convey my message. After some considerable delay I heard within the sound of bells ringing, the hurried scurry of footsteps and the slamming of doors. All the inmates had to withdraw from any possible contact. When eventually I was admitted and led through long bare corridors to the Mother Superior's sanctum, I met with a very frosty reception. Duly escorted from the premises by the keeper of the gate, her beady eye expressed even greater disapproval than before. Fortunately my proper destination was close at hand, and I was relieved to discover that it belonged to a much milder order.

The moral of the story, Templeton wrote, was 'always read your instructions carefully'.

It was Templeton's job, training for the counting house, to buy stamps for the parcels.

> I was given a piece of cardboard on which was written '£3 for stamps please'. This token was inserted into one of the mechanical miracles of the age. I can only describe it as a wooden tube that went vertically from the shop through the floor of the room above. In the square tube was a miniature 'lift' measuring about 5 ft by 2. Placing the cardboard on the lift, I administered a sharp kick aimed at the bottom of the

tube whereupon an unknown deity whisked it away to the office (the counting house). By and by, the little box would thud to the bottom and lo! There were three one pound notes; the equivalent of two months wages.

Templeton remembered many good times:

> on sunny afternoons we apprentices were urged, 'to take a frisk' ... being sent on shopping errands and not accounting for any delay in returning ... When the doors closed to the public on Thursday afternoons, we played indoor cricket on a pitch that had the benefit of a good run-up in the English department on the ground floor. Screwed up balls of paper sufficed as balls, with similar, larger, ones for footy. It was good practice for the annual matches against the Cambridge Booksellers, and there was always great anxiety among the younger members of the staff until the teams were announced... Another more singular source of competition involved seeing how high up the rungs of the bookshelf ladders anyone could spring at a single jump. One of my particular accomplishments was to hang headfirst down the spiral staircase suspending my feet from the top rail; one ill-timed performance scared the wits out of an unfortunate customer on the way up!

A 'less dangerous sport was to lean out of the front windows and spot the passing toffs: royalty, politicians, poet laureates, and other notables, on their way to University ceremonies'. But close proximity could be alarming. Hanks recalled such an occasion: 'Fred Chaundy had been sent to collect some books from the rooms of Charles Dodgson in Christ Church; he had called early only to find the author still in bed. Hearing the door, Dodgson emerged to open up clad only in his shirt. Turning his back, he stooped down to recover a pile of books from the floor. But his shirt was only a "cutty-sark" – it had no tail!'

Searching for something more enticing, Templeton had his eye on the young ladies recently admitted to clerical and secretarial posts. He would attempt to lure them down to the safe, where the company's ledgers were deposited at the close of each day. There were no doubt adventures, but we had best draw a veil on these, as Fielding did over the doings of his hero Tom Jones.

The apprentices risked 'being caught smoking behind the pub's lavatories, known as Hell's Kitchen' and, like their customer students, were 'prone to the fruits of Ceres, quickly obtainable at the White Horse next door'. Several of the apprentices were at first 'under the sway of the chief packer John Brayne: a rather Dickensian character who chewed and spat tobacco'. Barfoot remembered that while the White Horse was strictly out of bounds, 'old John Brayne liked his pint. On many occasions I "kept pike" while he nipped off there for a very quick one. Beer in those days was 2d. per pint: the value in salary of 20 to 30 minutes work for a man.'

Working conditions may have been Dickensian by today's standards, but Templeton counted himself lucky. 'Paradoxically, the Great War served Blackwell's well, bringing an increased demand for books … and wages were increased accordingly.' By 1926, Templeton had worked '6 days for fifteen shillings a week', and in 1936 he was earning £4 7s 6d. 'No consumer durables tempted us, there was no TV, and cars were only for the rich; the cinema cost ninepence. I managed to put down a deposit on a house and buy second-hand furniture; even a walking holiday in the Ardennes.'

Another to benefit from the good times at Blackwell's was Frank Timbs, who began in March 1925 as Charles Field's 'boy'. A good cricketer, with a talent for colouring prints, he stayed in the counting house for forty-seven years. Timbs also left behind a fragment of memoir:

> I had been interviewed by Basil Blackwell and William Hunt. Mr. Blackwell had asked if I read much and I replied four books a week. He replied that I liked books too much. Mr Hunt had been shocked when I confessed to not liking G.A. Henty, nor have I since. At all events the place was mine at 7/6d a week. My mother took 7/– to pay for my board, clothes and haircuts. The sixpence left didn't stretch far, even in those days. My duties were to enter in a small black book the names and addresses and postage on all the parcels, stick stamps on and struggle with them to the post office: it was a struggle for I was a small boy.

Edgar Hine, too, started as an office boy. After military service in the First World War he joined the firm as a '35/– a week improver'. In his memoir he wrote that 'my meteoric rise from office boy to director was beyond my wildest dreams'. Originally apprenticed to H.G. Gadney at 2–3 The Turl, Hine came to Blackwell's when Basil took over his business in the late 1920s. Hine 'was so grateful for a job:

there was mass unemployment and I was [to have] a salary increase of 5/– per week, with three weeks paid leave and Bank holidays'. By the 1930s, Hine was Hanks' deputy, and one of his jobs was book-buying. 'The publishers' reps were resplendent in morning dress, and a limitless source of gossip.'

Reggie Nash also came from Gadney's, where he had been a packer:

> My packing department was a 13th-century crypt where I was also responsible for keeping the books clean, not an easy task if one recalls that semi-circular construction of stones and dust ... My only joy in the seclusion of the crypt was the discovery of several Stevensons, Kiplings and Hardys, which I had not read at school. There was also J.H. Patterson's *Man-Eaters of Tsavo*, I read this twice in quick succession. Some twenty years later I relived the book as I walked up and down Tsavo Station Platform and crossed the Athi Plains – the 'man-eaters' were seldom seen but often heard! At Gadney's, I was instructed that all books must be daily lined up with the front of the shelves – a ritual which I then imagined to be some off-shoot of parade ground smartness ... But my promised apprenticeship was never forthcoming. I visited my old Headmaster with a view to reverting to my first love – the Army. I well remember his advice, 'wait for another year or so'. One day, while tidying the books on the shelves I attempted to speed up the operation by running the palms of my hands along the shelves. A quiet voice behind me warned me that I was running a risk of picking up splinters with possible after-effects and absence from work. I was given an expert demonstration of the correct way of carrying out the task; it was sound advice and has remained with me to this day. I remember wondering how that particular gentleman had known of this bookseller's ritual.'

Nash later discovered he:

> had been speaking to Mr. Blackwell, who on subsequent occasions watched with interest the result of his good advice. One morning, a year before his death, he offered me indentures. I still recall the joy of seeing each room, passage and staircase of the shop bursting with books. The Union Room was no longer the *ultima thule*; it should have been obvious to anyone that Blackwell's could never have a last extremity. Just as it was obvious to the apprentices that the indoor cricket pitch had to go. But the games went on. Mr Herbert Steele, late of the Gunners and another apprentice turned director, was always prepared to blow us off the face of the earth. Was this why he

kept a brace of 45s beneath his desk? We deserved his threats, we were always missing when 'Suttons up' was announced; Suttons meant that they were bringing the books on Wednesday that we had ordered two days previously.

If still up to no good, the apprentices had Mr Hanks to contend with. John Alden, apprenticed in 1929, remembered Hanks' 'fine singing voice and stirring strains from Gilbert and Sullivan would echo up the stairs, sounding a warning of his approach'. At his interview, Alden, destined for forty-two years of service, found himself discussing the pleasures of cycling with Basil, then five years into his chairmanship since the death of his father. Alden boasted of his cycling prowess: 'I fancied myself as a lesser H.V. Morton.' Instead, Alden was shown how to convey books on 'a strangely contrived wooden stretcher prone to accidents round corners'. Sent to widen his experience among Blackwell's remaindered books, which were housed in the Davenant bookshop then opposite the Examination Schools, he had been much alarmed by the politics of its chargehand, Bert Piper. Piper was the resident Marxist and not popular, but a 'whiff of communism and left wing sympathies was accepted' as long as they did not obtrude.[23] But the workers knew where their bread was buttered and their education taken care of. These benefits advanced them socially, added to which they rubbed shoulders with customers more or less as equals.

The acceptance of the booksellers by the University and other bibliophiles was just one indication of social changes afoot, especially after the First World War. Gone were the days of fictional characters like Emma's protégée Harriet, who was thought to have got above herself. Like Don Calogero in *The Leopard*, Lampedusa's famous tale of social change, booksellers were too useful. They were also more accessible than cloistered academic librarians. Blackwell's staff were ever-willing researchers and their knowledge came from the most up-to-date sources: newly published books.

While priding themselves on the service they provided, Blackwell's staff nonetheless minded their Ps and Qs. Nash recalled that if any customer asked for a book shelved elsewhere, 'we moved at speed around the building: front shop, up the famous spiral to Foreign on the first floor, to Periodicals and the Catalogue rooms on the second floor, returning through the Union Room with its fascinating balcony'. The left-wing Piper was unlikely to have been so obliging, but he attracted a following: Alden remembers him introducing socialists such as G.D.H. Cole, Patrick Gordon-Walker, John Redcliffe-Maud and perhaps J.B. Priestley, who was to be a founding member of the Campaign for Nuclear Disarmament in 1958. Alden also recalled visits from Hilaire Belloc and Sir Charles Oman, the famous military historian of the Peninsular War period, and 'the thrill of serving Colonel John Buchan, Harold Acton, Sir Henry Marten [of Marten and Carter's Histories], Sir Robert Birley and Lord David Cecil'. Reggie Nash remembered 'the crush outside the shop when the King George VI opened the New Bodleian ... A.P. Herbert was in the procession and gave saucy winks to the Blackwell girls'.

Nash recalled:

> A very great favourite at Blackwell's was Professor Sir Charles Firth, the foremost historian of the Civil War. On a rainy day he would invariably return to the shop for his umbrella, only to be informed that it was hanging on his arm beneath his gown. Best of all was Lady Ottoline Morrell, who would arrive in her carriage and four, bringing in with her an aroma of a beauty parlour.

Edgar Hine remembered Mr Asquith, Robert Bridges, the former poet laureate, the first Lord Birkenhead, John Masefield and W.B. Yeats. Dull moments could have been relieved by fantasy, prompted by the sight of J.R.R. Tolkien on the lookout for goblins. Saving civilization, and taking his daily exercise at the shelves, would have been Basil's old Mods tutor, Professor H. Garrod of Merton. Hard on his heels came Robert Graves, the future poet laureate John Betjeman, T.S. Eliot, Stephen Spender, Cecil Day-Lewis and W.H. Auden, accompanied by Christopher Isherwood, Louis MacNeice, William Empson, George Fraser and Angus Wilson. Politicians came too: Herbert Asquith was a regular, and later, in the 1950s, the *New Statesman* reported a rare sighting:

> Tired of politics after an extended cabinet crisis, [the Israeli Prime Minister Mr David Ben Gurion] flew here for the sole purpose of spending four days at Blackwell's bookshop in Oxford. His cabinet and diplomatic advisers tried to dissuade him on the grounds that no one would believe such a ridiculous story.

But Ben Gurion had learned Ancient Greek in order to read *The Republic*, 'and Blackwell's has a fine collection of Platonic Scholiasts. In an age of barbarism it is a pleasant thought that anyone who penetrated to the back rooms of Blackwell's last week and spied a little white-haired man on top of the step ladder would have seen a prime minister indulging his secret vice.'[24]

SCHOLARLY TRIBUTES

Even out of hours, Blackwell's shop assistants were expected to study. The firm paid for staff attendance at night school, but books, studied at home, were their mainstay. Reggie Nash wrote that 'the hundreds of volumes that made up the Everyman Library, alone provided an almost complete experience'; they represented 'the re-birth of literature with a thousand doors to open'. He had 'spent a whole week's wages to purchase three of the volumes, priced at two shillings and one and sixpence'. They were just as popular with customers 'and the records kept for a period show that we sold a volume every twenty minutes'.

Basil's regard for the scholar manqué matched his father's. Indeed some recruits went on to make a name for themselves with their own works: Reginald Gibson with his *Sir Francis Bacon* and Christopher Francis's *Catalogue of Theology and Church History*. Rex King and George Crutch provided huge support for Basil Blackwell and were the source of many of his draft speeches and articles.[25] Crutch was Basil's unofficial research assistant and wrote a long essay for him on the influence of books, while a close comparison between Basil's and Rex's writings shows the extent to which Basil came to rely on him for his speeches and articles.

In the wake of the Second World War, education reforms brought a new wave of apprentices with university entry-level qualifications but whose parents needed them to work rather than continue their studies. But did they ever achieve the bibliographic mastery of the first apprentices, George Crutch asked? Crutch was as much a teacher as a bookseller; he couldn't resist trying to impress academic customers, not in a common room but leaning over the counter: 'Dryden used very few, if any, images from nature. Did you know that much early poetry was written without any knowledge of metre?' This would have delighted the early modernists who frequented Blackwell's. In turn, Crutch and John Alden acknowledged the debt they owed *their* teachers, Bob Rowles and particularly Rex King. 'I began to grasp something of the classification of subjects, till some time later I could recite the books of Cicero and could tell which were available in Kelly's Keys or Bohn's, or the Loeb Library, the latter was considered rather expensive at ten shillings per volume.' In his spare time, Rowles was a beekeeper and a church and social worker, but he still found the time to prepare the classics catalogue: 'Macmillan's Elementary classics,' he asserted, was the series on which the business had been built. Nash regarded Rex King 'as Chief among the educators'; he taught the skill of cataloguing, passed on to him by Benjamin Henry, and his knowledge was just as prodigious: 'he was blessed with a marvellous memory for books, and even knew if they were on the shelves of Parker's or Thornton's'.

One of Rex King's most successful pupils was Edward East, who was to succeed him as resident antiquarian. East, the last scholar apprentice to be engaged by Benjamin Henry, in 1923, was given the University's seal of approval with the conferment of an MA, *honoris causa*, in 1973. He came on the recommendation of the Bodleian librarian, Sir Arthur Cowley. His speciality was cataloguing libraries: R.G. Collingwood's, Sir Arthur Evans's, Sir George Grierson's, Hugo Dyson's, F.P. Wilson's, A.T.P. Williams's (Bishop of Winchester), the Williamscote Library of the Loveday family, and John Masefield's all passed through his hands. Tommy Templeton, too, for all his high jinks, was scholarly. His more lasting contribution to French literature consisted of writing and producing a widely read bulletin, which had very detailed descriptive notes, extracts and reviews. He also became something of a foreign trade specialist: 'India was our biggest customer in the days of the British Raj. This was a time of great expansion in higher education here and in the Empire. Civil servants going out from Oxford carried the flag.' One of his contemporaries, George Bunting, destined to be a director, pioneered sales in South Africa. He tasted the academic high life when he was sent to Paris, to purchase the library of Professor Gustave Cohen of the Sorbonne.

The reach of Blackwell's scholarly staff thus spread beyond the confines of Oxford, as a letter received in 1947 from one West African hopeful suggests:

You may please help me because I do not want to disgrace myself in
the 'Cambridge Examination'. You know a lot of money my parents
are wasting on me in the College, and if it comes to the time to sit
for the Cambridge Examination and I fail to get grade One with
exemption then it means I have not impressed them well. So for all
these reasons, I think I will get a help from you. If I receive the list, I
will send the money to you in order to get the books in time. Include
also the following:– (1) Greek Book. from Form 2 to 6. (2) Science
Book. from Form 2 to 6. (3) English Books. As for this send different
kinds because this is the only subject that I like well. (4) History
Books, Story Books, Essay Books, Latin Books, Letter writing Books,
and many others.

    I remain,
        Your dutiful boy,
          Owusu Albert.

N.B. Send Grammar Books also. This is also important.[26]

It was now expected that former apprentices, who had been trained
along generalist lines, 'should display all the qualities of a bookseller
specialist: be able to catalogue and write and layout for printing, know
all the standard works, understand the techniques of scholarship and
to know the real purposes of a university: to discover truth'. This
was a tall order, and Basil was anxious to attract 'raw talent' from the
grammar schools, such as Merlin Bulborough, apprenticed in 1938, who
came from Basil's old school, MCS. The 1944 Education Act provided
yet more qualified applicants who came as 'school-leavers with a string
of creditable exam passes to their names'. They too calculated that a
good job with prospects was 'preferable to the expense of going to
university only to face an uncertain job market afterwards'. But their
studies continued.

    It was obligatory to digest Aldis's *The Printed Book*, Campbell's
Higher English and Hudson's *Outline of English Literature*, and those who
showed an aptitude for research were given a Bodleian reader's ticket.
There were educational days out too, with visits to other bookshops
and libraries in a hired charabanc. Lectures and readings were put
on for them, including readings given by Dorothy L. Sayers and the
poet laureate John Masefield. John Alden suggested that just 'watching
the progress of the books themselves' would be sufficient education.
'Which would become bestsellers; Priestley's *The Good Companions* and

Massingham's *World Without End* had this honour at the time.' Was the poetry of Eliot, Auden and Isherwood to be the hallmark of modernism? Science, too, came in from the cold. Finding this to his taste, John Alden retrieved the stock of science books, which 'hitherto had been housed so high off the floor they could only be reached by extending ladders'.

Some of Blackwell's 'dons' arrived ready-made. In 1936 Tony Pullen (whom Christopher Francis classed as a scholar bookseller whose classics catalogues 'were the life-blood of our trade') came as Head of Classics. Frederick Dymond, previously a consultant for the world-famous Hirsch Library in Cambridge, joined in 1955. For a time, he made Blackwell's music department the largest and busiest in the United Kingdom. Christopher Francis, who joined in 1952, 'went straight upstairs to Theology'. Having failed to find a religious vocation, and constantly grieving at the loss of the Latin liturgy, Francis had been an assistant in a country bookshop in Petersfield, but there was no call for his theology, which he counted his only asset. Seeing an advertisement placed by Blackwell's for 'in-charge theology', Francis jumped at the chance.

Francis drew scholars from around the world. His crowning glory was his own work of scholarship: *Catalogue of Theology and Church History* (1978).[27] He too was rewarded with an MA, *honoris causa*, from the University. The eminent theologian Henry Chadwick lauded Francis as integral for two decades not only to one of the greatest academic bookshops, but also to the serious study of religion and theology in the English-speaking world:

> As successive conferences of biblical and patristic scholars assemble or meet in Oxford, it is easy to see that the learned papers they read to one another are really secondary. The primary purpose of their presence in Oxford is to see their deeply respected friend, and, with his help, to fill gaps in their working libraries so that the proceedings of the conferences themselves have a role comparable to that of a chorus in a Greek play. The real action is in Blackwell's ... for Christopher Francis knows us all. His mind has a retrieval system for both books and individual scholars. Above all, he cares for the now threatened enterprise, the learned book.

Rex King had described the book trade as midway between a trade and a learned profession: 'whereas other retailers work by weights and measures, a bookseller is concerned with an individual book'. Triggered by the retirement of Bob Rowles in 1947, Rex penned a tribute to Blackwell's scholarly booksellers.

> Let us not grow fat like Jeshurun's ass and bray at our accomplishments without recalling with gratitude the hard patient spade-work put in by those who laid down the foundations of a business which now enjoys a world-wide reputation. They set the wheels of the chariot moving, which has now gained a terrifying momentum, and it ill becomes us to imitate the fly in the fable who, sitting pretty on the axle of the swiftly moving chariot, exclaimed, 'What a dust I am making!' These early pioneers worked for hours in less pleasant conditions and for a remuneration that would unnerve the present generation ... It is not meet that these unsung heroes should pass into oblivion ungarlanded and unsung.

Basil always regretted that his 'scholars, given their knowledge and years of learning' were not remunerated as they would have been in other professions. 'It may be taken for granted,' he argued, 'that the brains, energy, and long hours required of the bookseller would yield far richer results if applied in most other forms of business.' Nonetheless, he concluded, the rewards for those who stayed the course were 'greater than those in the more commercial world and much more than just wages'. This was a sentiment with which Rex King was in accord.

> The scholar-bookseller is an anachronism in this giddy age, distracted with its cinema, radio, television and speedy means of travel. He is almost as extinct as the Dodo – the few tottering old specimens I know are more or less museum pieces, maintained and inhibited by wealthy firms who can afford their upkeep. Left to himself, he would be quickly exterminated. It was only in Victorian days that a bookseller could live on a few pence a day like the one depicted in Beatrice Harraden's novel *Ships That Pass in the Night*. So long as he had a shelf full of Gibbon and a box of snuff, he was quite content.

Rex could have been describing himself.

FIVE

A BAKER'S SON

To read him [Rex King] is a little like seeing an athlete at Parson's
Pleasure. It's part of the Bible of the English people – writ in lives
rather than ink. It is canonical and there is such a lot he didn't say.
What would people to-day make of his struggle to find himself in
finding books, people and ideas? *I* have no idea.

Hugo Dyson, Fellow, Merton College, 1945–63

M OST PEOPLE familiar with Oxford will know of Thomas
Hardy's *Jude the Obscure*. Hardy's protagonist was fictional,
but there were many such characters in real life; Oxford seemed to
attract them. At one of the meetings of Oxford's city council, where
Benjamin Henry Blackwell sat on the committee of the library, 'there
was read a letter offering for the acceptance of the Library a considerable collection of standard works in the field of English Literature'. The
writer offered the books 'in case frequenters of the Library should still
have an itch to read something after exhausting the popular papers
on which apparently the Library grant was mainly expended'. It was
signed W. King. 'My father,' wrote Basil, 'scrutinised the books and
found them to be a poor man's library judiciously chosen, well used,
and well kept – the result of many previous sixpences hardly come by.'
Then a penny dropped. Benjamin Henry had already heard of him.
This W. King had been in the audience when he (Benjamin Henry)
had given a lecture on George Herbert at the Quaker Adult School.
Afterwards King had written to him commenting on the text 'in such

a knowledgeable fashion that Benjamin Henry sought him out'. In conversation, he discovered that King, a baker's boy, had lost his job with the GPO because of long illnesses and had endured a period of almost desperate poverty. But he also 'revealed a mind stored with reading and acute in literary judgment: manifestly the mind of a born bookman'. Remembering this, and being short-handed because of the war, 'my Father invited Rex, as he was commonly known, to come and work in the Secondhand and Antiquarian Department of his shop'. (At the time it was a function – rather than a department – run mostly by Benjamin Henry himself.)

Basil described Rex as being 'of middle height and slender build; he had a fine head with a profile reminiscent of Henry Fielding's save that Rex showed signs of suffering and meditation'. Rex King was born in 1886 in Chesterton, near Cirencester, some thirty-five miles from Oxford. Basil described him as coming from 'plain peasant stock'. Had the university-educated Basil forgotten that his pedigree was rather similar? Basil's maternal grandfather had lost his farm (in Norfolk), and so it seemed had Rex's father, who had ended up peddling buns and cakes at county fairs. Like Jude, in his early years Rex had studied his books while working in the bakery. He and his brother were paid one penny per hundred for trimming currants off their stalks. Assisting his father while he sold his wares had its dangers. 'I wish Rex had recorded, as he told it to me, a hideous experience in his boyhood.' Luckily, Basil, who relished his story, wrote it down.

> Returning home by train after a fair at Chedworth perhaps, or Fosse Cross, little Rex sat alone in a compartment until a horrible fellow blind drunk and raving tumbled in. He saw the boy Rex and with threats to rip him open and tear out his guts made a lurch at him. Rex contrived to wriggle under the seat, where he listened to ogre-like threats and curses, and watched the brute's hand and foot as he fumbled about in dazed search for his victim. He managed to escape at the next station, but the fearful memory was still vivid as he spoke of it some fifty years later.

Rex's was a boyhood full of childish fears. He'd shrink from going with his cousins to gather wood in the fields, causing his aunt, who wanted the firewood, to fly 'into terrible paroxysms of passion and threaten to thrash me'. At harvest time, he was as nervous of gleaning (or 'leasing') corn 'in case the field had not been given a final raking, and we should be hustled off by an irate farmer, accompanied by a fearsome dog'. But each Christmas, in compensation, 'I used to receive a Christmas cake made from the leased corn'.

It might be thought that Rex would have felt on safer ground when he won a scholarship to Cirencester Grammar School, but he remembered his schooldays as 'a nightmare of unimaginable horror'. Despite, or perhaps because of, his academic prowess, Rex was seen as fussy and was commonly called 'Mother King'. He liked to think of himself as a sportsman, but his only ever boast was of winning a race one sports day. One of his fellow pupils sped into the tea tent to tell Rex's father – 'Mother King has won a fountain pen' – confusing 'Mother's' father utterly. Any further sporting triumphs eluded him.

And it went on. As there was no possibility of going to university, he accepted a position as a monitor, then pupil teacher, at Powell's Church of England Primary School in Cirencester.

There was I, a prodigy of learning, but nevertheless a small nervous weakling, put in charge of a small gang of hooligans led by a budding pugilist rejoicing in the sobriquet of Banger Jackson. Being fully aware of my fear, these sons of Britain made my existence a continual hell. I bought off the ringleaders with gifts of cakes, and sometimes the odd halfpence, both pilfered from my father's shop, and this blackmail once enacted was never allowed to drop. They waylaid me on my journeys to and from school and menaced me with fearsome oaths and emphatic fists, and I was allowed to proceed only after the promise of some, more, placating gift.

Only once did Rex 'flare up in a despairing attack' on one of his tormentors, 'a boy called Draper with an extraordinarily narrow head'. Rex managed to 'blacken Draper's eye'. He did not appear at school the next day and Rex was left 'a bewildered victor'.

Rex's recompense was £5 a year, 'paid quarterly by cheque'. Rex remembered the thrill 'with which I presented it for payment at the bank: and my subsequent disappointment when my mother deducted 20% towards my keep'. While at school Rex became addicted to a local second-hand bookshop, spending 'many hours reading and choosing for his collection such volumes as his few pence of pocket money could stretch to'. Such was his life until his second encounter with Benjamin

Henry and the assessment of his gift to the library. Rex King joined Blackwell's in 1916 and he was to spend the rest of his life there among the second-hand books, a fortuitous outcome after such an unhappy start to his adult career.

Rex had so much in common with Benjamin Henry and his apprentices. All had suffered from the ignominy of poverty, and this had made Benjamin Henry all the more determined to help others: to publish writers 'unknown to fame' and to educate his workers to such a level that they would not be looked down on by the University. Without Benjamin Henry's offer of employment, Rex would have endured a life of abject poverty. Forever mouldering away in one of George Eliot's 'unvisited tombs', his writing would have died with him.[1]

An inkling of the way his own writing may have shaped up can best be judged by the diaries that have survived him. His entries reveal different facets of his life: antiquarian, Quaker, adult education teacher, poet, philosopher, book reviewer, husband, father and son, and so much more. They bring his words and ideas on books, life, love and war out into the light. I think Dyson, who died in 1975, would be surprised by the extent to which they still resonate today.

George Crutch, looking back on his apprentice days, recalled his impression of Rex. 'He distilled within himself a golden blend of Quaker, Scholar and Antiquarian. Deeply read in literature and philosophy, his early acquaintance with the Stoic philosopher Marcus Aurelius caused the spirit and temper of his mind to be a little on the austere side,' reminding Crutch of the 'redoubtable Samuel Johnson ... Sincerity and integrity shone through him and he was guide and friend to all who approached him unpretentiously.' Crutch thought him 'a man born out of his time ... Had he experienced the advantages of a university education, he would have occupied a chair of English literature.' But Rex's lot was 'to live out his life amongst Blackwell's store of books; indeed, aside from Fred Hanks, he was the only one to know the extent of the stock'.

'Rex was as happy as a difficult home life with a Xanthippe and two discordant children would permit,' Basil recorded.

> His marriage had been a case of 'the nymph pursuing the faun pursued', and the nymph, under the stress of hard times and a

jealousy of Rex's intellectual and spiritual prestige among the Quaker community, became a scold. At the close of the day, he returned to something like a penitentiary, which, as the years passed and his wife's health declined, became increasingly exacting ... His loyalty nevertheless was undeviating.

But at work he was appreciated. 'University tutors often consulted him, to be presented diffidently with a nugget from his "golden treasury" of learning. When touched he could reveal considerable erudition,' recalled George Crutch. His scholarly knowledge of Coleridge particularly marked him out; Rex left behind a hardbacked exercise book full of marginalia concerning Coleridge, gleaned from the libraries of dead scholars which he frequently had to price and classify.[2] Working long hours in the shop, and burning the midnight oil compiling catalogues, it is astonishing that Rex found time to write anything. As far as we know, he wrote two diaries, a series of articles, poems, book reviews and memoir fragments. He gave all his written material to Basil Blackwell for safekeeping at Christmas 1938. Some of his poems and reviews were published, and his two diaries/commonplace books, written between 1918 and 1927, and in 1939, have only recently been rediscovered.[3]

THE RICHES OF THE COMMONPLACE

That Rex's diaries – his life writing – have been preserved at all makes them uncommon: the annals of the poor were seldom considered important enough to keep. And writing, and indeed reading, was often deemed to be a time waster. Historians, wanting to penetrate their world, 'keep running into the vast silence that swallowed up most of mankind's thinking', as Robert Darnton has perceived. 'Later the emerging discipline of book history, which tapped archival resources, allowed a way into this mystery – mass observation surveys, memories, diaries, memoirs, school records, library records, letters to newspapers, fan mail even.'[4] Margaret Lane, in her introduction to Flora Thompson's *Country Calendar*, wrote that she found it hard to classify the work of a 'cottage child', whose writing blossomed 'without education or encouragement'. It was perhaps 'social history', but more 'alive'. Flora Thompson 'dwells on the humble details which social historians either do not know or leave out'.[5]

Academic fashion has changed. Historians have tapped into the rich seam of previously hidden lives. David Kynaston, for example, in his *Tales of New Jerusalem,* gives weight to the stories of ordinary citizens, to the 'everyday as well as the seismic'.[6] Thomas Hardy, whose family circumstances put higher education out of reach, championed the self-taught and the underclass, 'humbly recording diverse readings' in his novels.[7] Richard Altick, scholar and historian, brought them under academic scrutiny. An unusual pursuit in the 1950s, he searched for and collected autodidacts' writing from the nineteenth century. One study yielded over 2,000 documents.[8] Jonathan Rose's exhaustive study in 2001 of working-class reading provided further fodder for historians.[9] Stefan Collini, in a review of Rose's book, sees it as a vital part of our history. 'If we could recover the reading practices of past generations, we would be in touch with an experience that was at once intimate and formative.'[10] Rex King's diaries would have been a prime example of what Altick and Rose had looked for, if they had been able to find them. Luckily Basil kept them and gave them to Hugo Dyson, bibliophile and Emeritus tutor in English Literature in Merton College, to read.

Dyson wrote to Basil of the journals that they reflected 'both how an important but often inarticulate section of our society lived and felt: its governing ideals, its sources of inspiration, its faith and its strength'.[11] He later wrote that it was 'indispensable material ... worthy of an academic study' and should be fed into any history of Blackwell's.[12] Dyson applauded Rex's:

> sceptical intelligence, impatient of sham and show, and a faithful
> spirit. He touches life at so many points: the essential solitude of
> the human condition; the unquenchable desire for knowledge and
> the freedom knowledge confers; some of the traditional kindly
> earnestness of the way of The Friends; the labour and fascination
> of the trade in old books; the spirit that governed the relations of
> its hierarchy of members and associates; the day to day traffic of
> catalogue and parcel; an examen of the state of English culture circa
> 1910–60.

His journal shows his 'immense respect for individuals combined with an astringent and critical outlook – tremendous humility and self-criticism is mingled with independence and self-respect'.[13] It was well known in Oxford that Rex did not tolerate fools gladly. Awareness of this trait, and first-hand experience of the sort of Oxford characters Waugh had portrayed in *Brideshead Revisited*, provoked a gnomic thrust from Dyson. 'Rex did not live in a world where the young are paid and begged to read and think and talk and study, but in a world in which you had to pay for and earn all your privileges. If some paid in false coin, Rex was not one.'

To read Rex, Dyson continued:

> is a little like seeing an athlete at Parson's Pleasure.[14] His writing is part of the Bible of the English people – writ in lives rather than ink. It is canonical and there is such a lot he didn't say. What would people today make of his struggle to find himself in finding books, people and ideas? *I* have no idea.

Despite his praise for Rex, Dyson criticized his immature prose style and considered some of the material 'trite'. Was he judging King as a self-taught man rather than as an educated equal? Perhaps he did not give the diaries the close reading they deserved. Had he failed to notice, for example, how often Rex studied Greek and Latin texts ('sufficient to cope with classifying books'), that he learnt Spanish, Danish and French, and tried out other languages? '14 July 1918: commenced learning the Danish Norse language ... It is a very fascinating tongue, and promises many hours of pleasure in its acquisition.'

If by 'trite' Dyson meant the everyday or 'commonplace', then Rex was in good contemporary company. Flora Thompson, born ten years before King in a similar locality and humble village cottage, was the exemplar of 'rigorous plainness'.[15] The diary of the solidly middle-class E.M. Delafield was famed for its 'ordinariness',[16] and Virginia Woolf's diaries are studded with what some would regard as minutiae. Compare, for example, Rex's entry for Whit Sunday 19 May 1918: 'After tea, we all went for a short saunter through the meadows – one dazzling cloth of buttercup-gold, shimmering in the declining sun. The hawthorn hedges one mass of blossom, as though burdened with a sudden fall of snow. God never loses his ecstasy in the renewal of spring'; with Flora Thompson's, written around May 1921: 'Along every lane and hedgerow ... nature's embroidery ... blue eyes of speedwell, silvery stitchwort stars, cowslips, coltsfoot and violet ... and dead nettle with honeyed coronets of rich cream'; and Virginia Woolf's Tuesday 28 May

His steps are God-haunted — but, maybe,
He is but the ghost of his fears!! He fears
God, but within his fear there is also a
dutch of affection, the pushing out of
his heart's tendrils lest haply he may lay
hold upon God....

O! ye early Victorians!
I saw this night that which would have
shocked your respectable decorum! A
buxom farm lass astride a man's
bicycle, and carrying her lover upon
the step behind! What a blow to
Mrs Grundy! an awful sight upon a
Sunday!

' O! Ye early Victorians! I saw this night that which would have
shocked your respectable decorum!', Rex King, diary, 9 June 1918.

1918: 'The important thing was the weather. We had the best display
of flower yet seen – wall flowers in profusion, columbines, phlox, huge
scarlet poppies ... peonies about to burst.'

Quentin Bell, writing of his aunt Virginia Woolf's diary, declared
it to be 'plain-sailing', unlike her critical writings, which were difficult
and 'sometimes formidable'.[17] Rex wrote:

On the whole, the rich are far less interesting than the poor. Their
money can, if they choose, bring them laziness, which they share
with the tramp and to about as good a purpose. It can secure the
indulgence of animal sensations with all manner of luxurious
accessories. It is doubtful whether they relish their seven-course
dinner any more than the farm labourer relishes his crust of bread
under a flowering hedge. Some fatal laws block the way to felicity
along this line: the law of familiarity, which robs sensation of its

first flavour. Every indulgence brings in a diminishing return. We
read of Roman Emperors who offered rich rewards to anyone who
could invent new pleasures. One has only to read Petronius to see
how the world was ransacked to find such pleasures. But they are at
the last unable, from the whole complicated apparatus, to extract one
satisfying drop.[18]

Rex was equally dismissive about the benefits of travel and change
of scene, frequently the subject of the diaries of the better-off. 'It
is enough to rub shoulders with the average globe-trotter to be dis-
illusioned ... John Brierley calls to mind how, at a Swiss hotel, when
an expedition was being planned, a British tourist exclaimed, wearily,
"I suppose it is just the same there as here, a lot of mountains and that
kind of thing".'

On closer acquaintance, the diaries of Woolf, Thompson and King
have more in common than might be supposed. They all used them in
a practical way, as exercises in writing; what Virginia Woolf described
as 'limbering-up'.[19] They are full of jottings about books and ideas
that sprang from their study.[20] All three confided to their diaries their
'life within'; for each of them, the diary was a solace and a therapy. It
provided a tool for recovering possession of the self and for survival.
Men, as well as officers, in the trenches kept diaries for these purposes.[21]
Away from the Front, King, Woolf and Thompson were preoccupied
with the horror of war and its aftermath, but we read of them recovering in their gardens, or the countryside. Rex's holidays were always
spent on the old stomping grounds of his childhood, where his family
still lived; paying holidays, at the seaside or anywhere else, are never
mentioned 'due to the famine stricken leanness' of his purse.

SATURDAY 10 AUGUST 1918
Handed over reins of office to B.H.B. at 5 o'clock: and made my way
to the G.W.R. Station where I found Emily and the children awaiting
my arrival. Fairly comfortable journey – except from Didcot to
Swindon, when we were all tightly packed in the corridor. Caught a
glimpse of Father's old 'farm' at Chesterton. In one corner of the field
was a well-defined circle of healthy stinging nettles – an eloquent
epitaph on his unfortunate well-sinking venture, in which he dropped
so much money to no purpose. Of the sties and other buildings there
remains no trace. Sic transit Gloria mundi. Joe met us at Cirencester
Station, and we found the old town improved considerably. Bishop's

premises at the corner of Crickdale St have been demolished, and
replaced by quite an imposing structure – incidentally permitting
a marked widening of the street. Above all, and dominating all,
stands the noble tower of the fine old parish church. The old home
in Crickdale St has had its improvements: the Yard levelled-up, the
pump renovated, the plum-tree sawn off, and other minor alterations.
Alice gave us a hearty reception and a sumptuous repast.

MONDAY 12 AUGUST 1918
We saw Flo, her husband, and Harry at Chedworth station [part of
the King family had moved from Cirencester to Chedworth]. Putting
children and luggage into the donkey cart, the procession started
towards Gilgal. Granny met us at the top of Blakesmoor; but I had
great difficulty in getting to her owing to the excitement of Trix,
the dog, who nearly ruined my suit of clothes in his mad endeavour
to show his pleasure in seeing me again. Granny looking a trifle
'summerish' like me. We were all charmed with the house, which is
very delightfully situated on the upper slopes of the hill. One end
of the house, together with a nice patch of grass – euphemistically
called 'the lawn' – is pleasantly shaded by a walnut tree. There is
a nice garden, well stocked with flowers, old fashioned herbs, and
vegetables, and also, a paddock of considerable size, chiefly devoted to
plum-trees, poultry and potatoes!

SATURDAY 24 AUGUST 1918
Went for a walk round Mr Dunstan's farm to get my last glimpse
of Chedworth, before returning to Oxford. Another very hot day.
Mother and Trix accompanied us to the station, and Trix tried
hard to get in the railway carriages with us. We had three hours
in Cirencester, and whilst Emily explored the old church, Jimmy
and I went for a short walk through the beautiful park – along the
Windsor Walk to the Octagon, and thence through the Dark Walk
to the Cicely Hill Gates and home. Met cousins Eileen and Maggie
in Crickdale St, and stopped to pay our respects to the latter's brown
faced little baby … The trains were very crowded all the way from
Cirencester to Oxford, but we were very favoured all through the
journey, and dropped into seats almost as if they had been reserved
for us. We were glad to get home, however, as it was swelteringly hot
in the stuffy, crowded carriages.

Every year follows a similar pattern: Rex is happy on holiday, and
depressed on his return. His diary entry for Thursday 26 August 1920

describes his fortnight's holiday as 'twelve days of Paradise, with a touch of Purgatory at each end of travelling' and returning to work he is 'feeling very depressed and irritable'. He loves to work on the 'sweet disorder' of piles of old books, which he quietly classifies, but is too often taken from this refuge to work painstakingly on catalogues or sent out to auctions or to value collections. However, he is also beginning to make a name for himself in the bookselling world.

SUNDAY 6 OCTOBER 1918
Had an offer yesterday to take over managership of Horton's shop at Cheltenham. Were it not that I owe a debt of gratitude to Mr B.H.B. for taking me up two years ago as 'an unknown quantity', I should have seriously considered the offer.

SUNDAY 15 DECEMBER 1918
On Friday – being the fateful thirteenth of the month – I had an offer from a local bookshop, which from the monetary point of view – and in the number of hours – was a great improvement upon my present condition. On the other hand, I have always experienced friendliness and consideration from Mr Blackwell and I know that to leave them at this particular juncture of affairs would cause him considerable inconvenience. At the same time, it is no use blunting the fact that my present wage is not sufficient 'to carry on' in these iron times ... and a rise of £60 was not to be winked at! Then too, when the fellows return from the army, they may regard me as having climbed into power and position over their backs. These and a hundred and one other considerations kept my mind in a perpetual ferment. At last, through the good offices of Mr Hanks, I obtained a talk with Mr Blackwell, who with characteristic tact and kindness brushed away the baseless fabric of my fears – and I decided to remain, at least, for the time being ... Mr Hunt has been home for twelve days leave and I have had his invaluable aid for several hours each day. Notwithstanding, the hours have been long and the work very wearisome.

Rex, like Thompson and Woolf, was frequently fretting about not finding enough time and energy to write. Thompson put aside writing to cope with small children; Virginia Woolf was under pressure trying to run a small press, and Rex had no free time because of his day job. Here, particularly, is the universality of their diaries. But Rex's diary is uncommon in that it tells us about the books he is reading in order to educate himself. He makes no overt mention of any intention to write books, but considerable play of the poems and review articles he has published. Before he came to Blackwell's, according to fragments of notes, he had reviewed *The New Parent's Assistant* and (the American) Winston Churchill's *A Far Country*:

> the title's allusion is to the Prodigal Son: the novel has been described as a biography of the inner life of an American romanticist – it follows his childhood and into manhood – it is alive with real people (the sort he mixed with) – feminism interest is strong – a tour de force of ideas of modern life.

He continued in earnest once ensconced in the shop, despite long hours of work: perhaps his confidence had had a much-needed boost?

THURSDAY 28 AUGUST 1919
A month has elapsed since my last entry – the pen having been displaced by the typewriter. Have written a resume of humorous experiences at shop (during the war) and sent off to 'Book monthly'. Have also written a 2,000 word article on 'the Churches Conception of God – Is it adequate for today?' I have sent this to the Ideal Literary Agency.

Rex called his own collection of poems:

> Sparks From a Dull Flint ... They are shallow. Shallowness may endure for a night but disclosure cometh in the morning. The words of the true man are of pure gold, weighted with sincerity, but the witticisms of the shallow are of base metal beaten out in the smithy of the brain. The latter are but sparks from the anvil, whilst the former glow with living fire from the altar of the man's inner self. One is dust and chaff; the other, the golden grain.

His world was a far cry from that of Virginia Woolf, who had the encouragement of a confident literary milieu. In life and time Rex was so nearly Hardy's Jude.[22] In his writing he is more Flora Thompson, in her earlier years before her work was published. 'To be born in poverty,' wrote Flora Thompson, 'is a terrible handicap to a writer.'[23] The fictional Jude, his creator Hardy, King and Thompson had no prospects other than to further their education while in paid apprenticeships. At the end of her life, Flora Thompson succeeded as a writer, despite her humble origins. Hardy's Jude still stands as a reminder of the frustrations a lack of formal education inflicted on those aspiring to find acceptance in the literary world.

Flora Thompson wished she could 'make the earth and the stones speak and tell her about all the dead people who had trodden on them'.[24] Virginia Woolf maintained that she had 'a passion for "the lives of the obscure", and for marginal, undervalued literary forms like memoirs, letters and journals'.[25] She is thinking mainly of women, 'always urging them to write their life-stories'; why hadn't she read Flora Thompson's? Maybe she wasn't in touch with working-class writing, men's or women's? Their lives were certainly obscure, but not their stories. Rex, like Thompson, was able to write authentic accounts of peasant life because he came from those roots. In his writing we discover something of how he lived, cameos that provide an insight into the everyday in a time and place that was not usually recorded.

FRIDAY 16 AUGUST 1918
Walked to Cirencester with Emily to get weekly meat ration, a very enjoyable walk, taking just under two hours. Returned by 10.33 am train, well laden with toys and foodstuffs. Jimmy met us at the station, although very lame by reason of a bad cut on his knee … Evie was much tormented by harvest bugs in bed, and after ten minutes fighting and scratching, she burst out with the quaint piece of consolation that 'They are all laid down but one now, Mum!' She also comforted Jimmy by telling him that his knee was worse than all her chilblains put together – the various localities where the said chilblains were then gravely enumerated.

But, as often as not, his entries were primarily concerned with ideas and conjecture. He wanted to know how to live, rather than to tell how he lived. In his own subdued way, he raged against the puerile every bit as much as Jude. It was a way of cementing his identity, which was often lost in the run-of-the mill days of work. It was a work in progress, a hint of the serious books he would have liked to write. Like the avid diarist Virginia Woolf, he 'copied out fine passages from the classics … written down the names of great writers … lists the names of books that have actually been read'.[26]

So was Rex's diary a furtive attempt to write his own life story, or his autobiography? The dialectical nature of the text supports the idea that perhaps he wanted to engage with some as yet unknown reader. Diaries, commonplace books, memoirs, letters and other materials are often the mainspring of autobiography and biography. Did Rex give his material to Basil for safekeeping because he knew that he, Basil, intended to write his own autobiography or history of the firm? The Norrington history of Blackwell's (1983) made no identifiable use of Rex's writing, and by the time the research was undertaken for *Adventurers All* (2002), the diaries had been lost; luckily they were recently rediscovered.

Hugo Dyson called Rex's diary 'the nearest in spiritual quality to Edwin Muir's *Autobiography*'. In reproducing his writing, are we playing the role of his biographer? Michael Holroyd warns us that the biographer is a 'grub street merchant'.[27] Almost certainly Rex wanted his work to be read, published even. And even if he didn't, Basil did. 'I asked him to let me have again an intimate journal, which he had been writing for some months in 1935–9, and had shown to me at the time. I had returned it, urging him to go on with it, but the War put an end to that.' Long hours in the shop, two children to provide for, an ailing wife and his own ill-health 'robbed him of the time to write books he should have written'. Poverty too played its part. At lighter times of the year, and to supplement his wages, he grew vegetables in the garden and he relied on fruit from his family still living in the Cotswolds. But, as his diary reveals, he still found it hard to pay the rent and to feed his family. The pathos is gently felt.

SUNDAY 8 AUGUST 1920
A gloriously fine day, and taking advantage of it, we took our tea to 'the Sandhills' – a bracken sprinkled, hilly spot on the edge of Stow Wood. After tea, we indulged in cricket and rounders, and the boys [Jim and Harry] climbed trees and entered into other noisy and boyish diversions. It was a very enjoyable evening, with a dash of vinegar in it, for on arriving home we found notice to quit.

In September 1924, after a wet and dismal summer, his daughter started at the Central School in Oxford. He did not write of any scholarly hopes for his children; he was too busy: Benjamin Henry was sick and so Rex had to do the work of two.

Benjamin Henry died a few weeks later and Basil immediately asked Rex, who had then been at Blackwell's for eight years, to be head of the 'so-called' Antiquarian department. 'There,' Rex explained, talking of himself in the third person, 'thanks to the continued progress and initiative shown by the other departments, he has been allowed to remain ever since – an ornament to the trade.'[28] Basil described him differently.

> His self-acquired book knowledge had scope and his personality impressed itself on all who dealt with him. It seemed that he could assess the value of a book by holding it in his hands. Touch his mind at any point and he responded instantly with literary allusion, shrewd criticism, apt folk saying or aphorism. His speech was vividly phrased, spiced with aphorisms, and presented with the wry humour of his native Gloucestershire.[29]

Rex had had at least two offers of better-paid managerial positions elsewhere, but he stuck where he 'could be hourly among books and repay the kindness shown to him by both the Blackwells'. Rex battled with depression until the end of his life, but his remedy was the inner world of books. They provided, he said, 'holiday adventures of the soul … refreshment for the spirit'.

Recovering from another bout of depression while 'vegetating in the Cotswolds', he considered the immutability of life – the 'building up, disintegration and decay' – hardly guaranteed to cheer him up. But Rex was not afraid of death. 'Fear is the greatest thief in the world, directing the attention of many to imaginary ills and misfortunes on the far-distant horizon, whilst he is busy picking their pockets of all present happiness.' He took his own ill-health in his stride, and lived thirty years after he had penned these 'unfinished fragments of a meditative half hour in the dusk of twilight'.

When Rex died in October 1950, Basil, as his friend and confidant, wrote:

> Early in the year it was manifest that Will King's health, always frail, was failing fast. We did all we could to lighten his duties at Broad Street, leaving him free to come and go as he pleased … As his strength waned, his wife's illness made increasing claims upon it; nevertheless, he spared himself no part of his duty (for loyalty was of the essence of his nature), and sustained by some power that he could only ascribe to 'a miracle of the Grace of God', ran his straight race to its merciless end.[30]

Rex would have been greatly surprised to know that his death would bring accolades, not just from Basil, but also from London's literary press and the University.

Arnold Muirhead (bookseller and one-time classics teacher) wrote to the *TLS* asking that King's death should not go unrecorded: 'for many book collectors Blackwell's has long meant first and foremost "Rex" (as he was known) ... He undoubtedly influenced the formation and extension of many private and public collections by the libraries he bought and the fascinating catalogues he compiled of their contents.' The man himself is so memorable, he writes:

> On first acquaintance shy and retiring to the point of diffidence, he would in congenial company unbend ... and let his knowledge of books, his love of anecdote, a rather sardonic sense of humour, and an unexpected power of mimicry have full play. His own predilections were for Coleridge and Lamb, and to their works he bought a scholar's devotion and insight (his wife's illnesses robbed him of the time to write books he should have written) ... Some of us regretted that the University never recognised with an honorary degree his undoubted services to learning, but all the collectors here and in America ... will hold him in affectionate and grateful remembrance ... Blackwell's will never be quite the same without his presiding genius.[31]

Rex had graduated from what Dyson termed the 'university of life'; there is no record of his wanting any other kind of qualification. We do not know if Rex was disappointed at himself when the University awarded his long-standing and more sociable colleague Fred Hanks with an honorary degree. He is there in the photograph of the party that followed, yet his face gives nothing away. Rex was very different from the larger-than-life Hanks. He was introspective and averse to small talk. But after his death, the University did acknowledge Rex's contribution. John Sparrow of All Souls, for example, expressed much the same sentiments as Muirhead.[32] And the Bodleian Library put it on their *Record*:

> it seems fitting that we should pay tribute to a man who served so well the interests of book-lovers in Oxford. A member of staff in Blackwell's for thirty-four years, and for many years manager of the Antiquarian Book Department, King was completely master of his

subject; his pungent comments and still more his silent appraisals of books were often more informative than another's disquisition, and the Library benefitted from his knowledge and judgement on innumerable occasions.[33]

Writing in the autumn of 1923, Rex attempted to sum up his own private philosophy. Montaigne had taught him that 'external occasions take both flavour and colour from the inward constitution'; Marcus Aurelius and St Paul that the 'only way forward is the inward way'.[34] This, rather than any narrow religious canon, informed his philosophy of life. His pursuit of knowledge continued, keeping pace with his doubts. Like Dante, he loved 'to doubt as well as know'. One of Rex's chief doubts concerned the role of the church. This led him on a pilgrimage to Quakerism.

SIX

A MORAL WITNESS

Men and women are asking for the bread of human comradeship.
But the Churches offer them the stone of sectarian wrangling
and bitterness ... The history of man presents no more poignant
tragedy than this appalling wastage of moral force.

Rex King

BENJAMIN HARRIS BLACKWELL's philosophy of life, and his evangelism, must have commended him to the Quakers, but as a bookseller he had experienced a brush with one of Oxford's Friends in the 1840s. Called to the house of a devout Friend to value some books, part and parcel of an antiquarian bookseller's life, he was courteously enough received. The grave Quaker showed him the books and asked, 'Wilt thou take tea?' Not wanting to trouble his host, Benjamin Harris politely declined. But as so often must have happened, the valuation took longer than expected. And presently the Quaker's wife came in bearing a tray with teapot and pleasant nourishment. He graciously thanked her. But his pleasure at the sight of the sustenance was short-lived. Almost before she had left the room, the door flew open; the Quaker entered, seized the tray and carried it off, saying, 'Thee hasn't to tell a lie in my house.' How diminished the sober, and usually much respected, Benjamin Harris must have felt. Yet he had much in common with the Quakers. He had set out to save souls in the teetotal rooms and the public library. His son's intention too, when he set up in his father's trade, using Milton's words, to 'perform justly, skilfully and magnanimously, all the offices both private and public of peace and war', reads almost like a Quaker text.[1] In common with the Quakers – indeed with all the dissenting offshoots – the Blackwells shared a commitment to social reform, greater educational opportunity and repugnance for anything that curbed liberty.

One of the beneficiaries of both Blackwell and Quaker evangelism was Rex King. While settling in at the shop, and relatively new to Oxford, he was trying to decide which branch of the Christian church to attend.[2] There were many to choose from: since the infamous conflicts between Jewish merchants and Catholic scholars in early medieval times, the 'Vineyard of the Lord', as John Wycliffe once dubbed Oxford, had been a hotbed of religious contention.[3] Ridley, Latimer and Cranmer, whom Mary I, 'Bloody Mary', had burnt at the stake for heresy, were prominent Oxford Protestants; Jesuit priest Edmund Campion, hung, drawn and quartered at Tyburn on the orders of Elizabeth I, was a junior fellow of St John's College.[4] During the English Civil War, Cromwell persecuted fellow Protestants as well as the Rome-inclined; in retaliation, Royalists twice put Milton's books on the stake.[5] There was a plague on both their houses when George Fox's Society of Friends (Quakers) emerged, only to be persecuted in turn.[6]

In the nineteenth century Quakers were still debarred from public office and university fellowships, along with other dissenters from the established Church, Roman Catholics and non-Christians.[7] The Oxford Movement of High Church Anglo-Catholics, notably John Keble, Edward Pusey and John Newman, seemed in danger of holding Oxford in what Geoffrey Faber described as the Church's 'death-like grip', where faith took precedence over reason and science. Despite being on the outside, Quakers and Wesleyan Methodists were influencing members of the University, and the wider community of Oxford Anglicans. Men such as John Ruskin, Thomas Huxley and Charles Darwin were in the vanguard. Huxley had taken off the gloves to 'Soapy Sam' Wilberforce, in a famous exchange over Darwin's idea of evolution.[8] And he won the bout.

Quakerism, with its open and questioning ministry that had no time for doctrines, theories and beliefs that were taken as irrefutably true, appealed to a new generation of scientists and entrepreneurs. This was especially true in university cities. But with its seemingly classless membership and opportunities for education – provision of Sunday schools for children and adult schools after working hours – Quakerism attracted autodidacts to its fold. It is no surprise, then, that Rex, like Hardy's fictional Jude, chose to settle in Oxford, and he was spoilt for choice when considering a Nonconformist place of worship. The University boasted its own Congregationalist stronghold, Mansfield College, founded the year of Rex's birth. But Oxford's townies had their own flourishing establishment, the New Road Meeting House, which brought together all Nonconformists except Quakers. Dating from 1721 and re-founded in 1788, the chapel thrived under the 35-year ministry of James Hinton.[9] Studying Hinton's work over a century later, which he placed on a par with Carlyle's *Sartor Resartus* and George Fox's *Journals*,[10] Rex was drawn to New Road. Yet despite his admiration for Hinton, Rex for some years described himself as a spiritual vagrant, dilly-dallying between the Congregationalists and the Quakers.

Rex's quandary invaded his dreams:

> I had the misfortune to arrive on this planet at the tail end of the Judgment-Day-Hell-Fire-School of theology … I often lay awake for hours after I had been put to bed imagining the tragic horrors of the Last Trump and the dire torments of everlasting fire. The prophecy that the sun was to be turned into darkness and the moon into blood before the terrible day of the Lord, was taken very literally by me. I often crept out at night to take fearful glimpses at the moon, and experience relief when no vestiges of blood appeared on it. I imagined myself as scourged by an Egyptian taskmaster, and often swooned off to sleep under the pain of the imagined lashes.

Happier dreams were of angelic choirs, when Rex dared 'not to stir lest the music cease'. Attending the morning service in the parish church in Cirencester one summer Sunday in 1918, Rex writes longingly:

> How the music of the old hymn tunes intertwines itself into the fibres of one's being. Were I trembling upon the point of indecision between Baptist and Quaker – the memory of stirring notes of an organ would push me decisively into the fold of the former. Not that I should remain long: for I love not the hurdles of any sect.[11]

Rex's questing is reflected in the numerous articles he wrote for a local newspaper, reviewing books on a wide range of religious matters, from the vexed question of the authorship of the Gospels (Percy Gardner's *The Ephesian Gospel*)[12] to the peaceful co-existence among different Eastern faiths (Herbert A. Giles's *Confucianism and its Rivals*). The Quakers, Rex believed, were 'the least prone to [this] sectarianism: God has no favourites ... The cry of the wastrel is as readily heard as the pious petition of the Plymouth Brothers.'[13] And it was the Quakers, Rex was coming to believe, who 'most nearly speak to our condition ... Men and women are asking for the bread of human comradeship. But the Churches offer them the stone of sectarian wrangling and bitterness.'[14]

Teaching and writing gave Rex a chance to try to get his ideas straight.[15] He wrote many other reviews, but the most regular recipient of Rex's theological thoughts was his diary. Here he was free to roam, his internal debate informed by copious reading. Ploughing through a minefield of dogma and prejudice, he declared not only his hate for both the tyranny of a sect or an accepted body of beliefs, but for the confining of God to the churches. Turned off by Anglican doctrine, even more so by the 'lush mansions' of Roman Catholicism, Rex was beginning to wonder if God could be found in *any* of the churches.[16]

THURSDAY 9 SEPTEMBER 1920
If a man has wrong suppositions in his mind concerning God, he will be wrong through all the parts of his religion ... The God of the churches is apparently an Old Testament survival – an Eastern monarch, who is approached by gifts and flattering, by adulation and fulsome praise; who is pleased by the recitation of liturgies, the swinging of censers, the meticulous performance of so-called acts of worship and devotion. The churches in thus setting up a God that desires these specific acts of devotion, and in substituting an arbitrary, artificial service of God in place of a true service to meet real needs, have fostered a false religiosity, which allows mere adulation of the Deity to make amends for a lack of proper behaviour towards man. No one has stated this fact with more insistence and passionate conviction than James Hinton. 'Put up,' says he, 'a loving of God that is not a loving man, and man's strength is squandered on idle things and mischief; he has no power left to love his neighbour, and he avenges himself for his waste – makes an equilibrium – by not loving his neighbour.'

At work, although not usually very sociable, Rex engaged in heated religious discussion with Mr Cooper over the tea table.

He, it would appear, handed over his soul to the Roman Catholic Church, to escape pessimism and gain comfort and ease of mind. If one can once accept the central act of the R. Catholic worship, and the presence of the Christ in the water or bread, the other anomalies of their system should prove easy to swallow. Personally, I could find no reverence for a God who was influenced by such mumbo-jumbo. Mr C. retorted that I was entirely arrogant on such matters, and had no 'historical sense'. Incense had been associated with religion from the very beginning, etc etc. I retorted that other very objectionable practices also went hand in hand with religion in its early days, and that the mere antiquity of a practice was no logical argument in its favour. We spilt many words and came to no conclusion, except of the impassable gulf between our religious views. We finished with a pinch of snuff, as an offering on the altar of good fellowship. Alas! To how many is religion an extra spice, a condiment in life, and not a spur and urgency to that true worship of God, in the service of one's fellow man.

If Rex's anticlerical stance made no converts at work, he had more luck outside.

THURSDAY 13 JUNE 1918
Got into conversation with a Mr Brazil coming home in the bus – apparently of a deeply inquiring mood, and an acquaintanceship to be fostered. Gave him Theodore Parker's 'Discourse' to read: hope it will prove effective. He is an inveterate enemy of clericalism under any garb.

Rex may have reached people through chance encounters and regular reviews of new theological works, but more reliably receptive were those who attended his lectures at the Quaker Adult School. Rex, like Benjamin Henry, anticipated Charles Williams (the poet and colleague of Basil's from OUP days) in concluding that teaching in such venues was more rewarding: audiences were more open-minded compared with those in the University. Rex was as good a teacher as anyone formally trained, if not better. His preparation to lecture on 'The Historic Christ' was impressive: H.J. Bridges' *Religion of Experience*,[17] D.W. Forrest's *Christ of History and of Experience*,[18] Matthew Arnold's *Literature and Dogma*, T.R. Glover's *The Jesus of History*[19] and N. Schmidt's *The Prophet of Nazareth*.[20] Lecturing at Cowley Road Adult

School he takes on Browning's poem, 'Paracelsus'. It is a moral tale, food for himself as well as his audience. Is Paracelsus so involved in his quest for knowledge that the rest of his life has become atrophied? 'I have become wise, and discovered that I am a fool,' he admits. Yet silence 'may be golden, as Carlyle so vociferously and noisily declares, but, oftentimes, there is a good deal of lead in it'.[21]

Six weeks later he was flooring them with the *Religio Medici* of Sir Thomas Browne, which Basil admitted never having mastered.

SUNDAY 19 SEPTEMBER 1920
Very small gathering, but appreciative. Mr B.H.B. honoured me with his presence. True holiness is true healthiness ... the secret of Christ can only be learnt by living the Christ-like life: no poring over the Gospels will disclose it.

For Rex, the war compounded his attempt to unravel the mysteries of life, and also his search for a home among the churches. Protest at the prolonging of the bloodshed was widespread. Opposition was not restricted to the Quakers. In *The Great Silence*, Juliet Nicolson writes: 'Disillusionment was commonplace in conversation among fighting men, and poets at the Front began to reflect the shift in feeling. Although they remained a thorn in the side of arch Jingoists, many Quakers were patriotic, volunteering for active service and non-combatant duties.'[22] The Nobel Peace Prize would be awarded to Quakers worldwide in 1947, for their relief work in the field. In the summer of 1918, as the war draws to an end, Rex writes of his own confusion.

SUNDAY 2 JUNE 1918
I regret that I do not take altogether kindly to the type of young men who frequent the Friends – although of course, I am included in that indictment. Despite the toughness of their consciences, they are in the bulk a pasty, effeminate, crotchety set. I must confess that those who in defiance of their religious traditions have donned the soldier's uniform, are of a much superior type to their queasy-conscienced brethren.
At the same time, one would not belittle the courage of the genuine objector – whose ordeal of contumely and scorn is not one easily to be borne. I have never, however, been able to accept unreservedly the Quaker attitude towards war – much as I hate and condemn it.

Despite his reclusive personality, for which he continually admonishes himself, Rex sees the advantages of adhesion to some religious body, which may 'multiply one's opportunities of doing good and as a vehicle for expressing opinions, even if they are extravagant and ill-digested'.

WHIT SUNDAY 19 MAY 1918
The open ministry of the Friends ... creates a charitable atmosphere in which views may be dispassionately judged. One is able in this way to discern oftentimes a vein of truth in the crudest utterance. For instance, at this morning's gathering one speaker endeavoured to prove that the great European catastrophe was not the result of hatred, but of love. Love, that is, of the different peoples for their own native land. Stated in this bald way it appears an absurdity: quite a Chestertonian paradox. It is one of those partial truths. More difficult to scotch than pure error. The fallacy arises in the comprehensive meaning of the word 'love' – which may be used with a dozen different significations. It is evident that a 'love' which leads to a long nightmare of mutual murder and unparalleled slaughter is not the 'love' of which Paul gives a minute spectrum analysis. Another speaker gave a spirited exposition of the blessings of those that make the most High their habitation. A man who is conscious of the encompassing presence of God will live in a mountain top atmosphere of calm. Exterior circumstances and conditions will have even less and less power to influence and unsettle his mind. One might even imagine that a vivid, persisting awareness of this encompassing presence – this divine aura in which we live, move, and have our being – would act as a shield against the germs of contagious disease?

Rex had found God on a short saunter the same afternoon, where the meadows were 'one dazzling cloth of buttercup-gold, shimmering in the declining sun. The hawthorn hedges one mass of blossom, as though burdened with a sudden fall of snow. God never loses his ecstasy in the renewal of spring.' The next day, Monday, provides a perfect (bank) holiday, and he takes his children on an energetic climb up Shotover, east of Oxford. 'The joyous earth [is] bathed in brilliant sunshine, and cooled by caressing breezes. The children gathered two armfuls of blue bells [and] amused themselves in making daisy chains. What a wealth of innocent and costless pleasure is open to the child-like heart.' Rex sees three small mushrooms, which had pushed their delicate white crowns through the hard gravelled path at the top of Headington. 'What a tiny parable to the understanding heart.' When the spell of fine weather broke in early June, Rex has more earthly thoughts: the rain 'is very badly needed, and hundreds of allotmenteers will rejoice'. Back at New Road Chapel that same evening, he listens to the Rev. Hobling preach 'with great truth that it is a disaster when the Godfearers are driven from the churches — not for them, but for the church'. The church has its problems, Rex agreed, but secularism was worse: 'it causes artificial barriers between men, equally good and equally sincere'. He was all for staying in the fold — but which one?

Still contemplating joining the Quakers, Rex read Fox's *Journal*.[23] It helped him to transcend everyday difficulties.

> It is a book full of energy and rugged sincerity. How bracing and purgative is the salt of his utterance. 'And I went to Chesterfield, where one Britland was priest. He saw beyond the common sort of priests, for he had been partly convinced, and had spoken much on behalf of truth, before he was priest there; but when the priest of that town died, he got the parsonage, and choked himself with it.' This gift of rural, picturesque speech belongs to all those who pierce the veil of convention and reach the bedrock of reality. How often does it flash from the pages of Thoreau: 'How many a poor immortal soul have I met well nigh crushed and smothered under its load, creeping down the road of life, pushing before it a barn seventy five feet by forty, its Augean stables never cleansed, and one hundred acres of land, hillage, mowing, pasture, and woodlot!'[24]

Rex, thinking of Fox walking shoeless through the streets of Lichfield in the depths of winter, 'crying out "Woe to the bloody city of Lichfield"' jumps to Ezekiel the prophet:

> who on so many occasions performed apparently foolish and grotesque actions at the behest of God. A striking parallel might be drawn between the experiences of these two God-intoxicated men ... After his mission was accomplished, Fox continues, 'the fire of the Lord was so in my feet, and all over me, that I did not matter to put on my shoes any more, and was at a stand whether I should or not, till I felt freedom from the Lord so to do'.

Pondering Fox's simplicity and 'indifference to physical conditions', Rex explored his own moral code and the nature of faith. Yet again he sought the help of Thomas Browne's 'magnanimous, generous-hearted first book' of Marcus Aurelius. According to Rex, Thomas Browne's work put other religious works, especially English religious poetry, in the shade. Rex read a lecture delivered before the Royal Society of Literature by the 'Gloomy Dean' (William Inge), who attributed the lack of 'a supreme poet' in the Roman Catholic religion to the rigidity of its theological system. Rex saw the poetry in Browne's work as stemming from his emotional nature, which 'frequently flushes and colours the hard outlines of his ethical code'. Browne, he wrote, saw himself as having 'protection from above', and he cited others:

> who have striven to follow the gleam: Epictetus is assured of it; St Paul holds fast to this conviction of overruling benevolence, even when in prison. 'All things work together for good to them that love God' [Browne wrote] ... To the living oak, deeply enrooted in the soil, rain, sunshine, wind and storm, all contribute to its strength and rugged beauty; but once cut off from the soil, the same elemental forces work for its destruction and decay.[25]

In other words, Rex believed, Man cannot live without God. Yet he still admitted to gnawing doubts.

THURSDAY 30 MAY 1918
Rested for a while on the bracken, and read Robert Buchanan's powerful 'Ballad of Mary the Mother'. The Ballad is daringly conceived, and skilfully contrived, but it has not the haunting melodic beauty of 'The Ancient Mariner' – traces of which poem, however, are discernible, here and there ... The viewpoint of the ballad is that Christ was of illegitimate birth, charitably concealed by the kindly Joseph and that he was a deluded fanatic 'who aspired to break, and who misinterpreted the laws of God, and who perished of necessity, like a fly on the wheel'.

Rex concluded that having faith surmounts all.

SUNDAY 2 JUNE 1918
At the [Friends] Meeting this morning my mind was exercised as to the nature of faith. Faith is not a mere intellectual assent to a creedal statement, or belief in any formulated scheme of salvation, or the adoption of a ceremonial cult. Men of a creed are all too plentiful, but men of faith are difficult to find. To have faith is to have such a deep-rooted assurance of the reality of God and the eternal realities that it affects one's whole outlook and activities. One's faith consists only in those things that determine one's conduct and one's valuations

of life. To say that we have faith in the unseen, and then act as though our vision was limited by the worldly and material, is to give a lie to our affirmation. The man of faith launches out adventurously on the current of his deepest intuitions – not hugging the shores of personal comfort, nor veering with the wind to compromise with the conventions and usages of his time...

WEDNESDAY 5 JUNE 1918
'Jesus Christ. Thou amiablest of characters. I trust that thou art no impostor, and that thy revelation of blissful scenes of existence beyond death and the grave, is not one of the many impositions which, time after time, have been blamed on credulous mankind.' What a sceptical confession of 'trust'! And what an apt footnote to Buchanan's 'Ballad of Mary the Mother'. How doubt gnaws at the vital roots of the strongest characters!

But – and Rex continued to use the views of the Rev. Hobling as his touchstone –

an unquestioning faith is born of insecurity and fear: your dogmatic Christian is often a dull, phlegmatic Christian – there is a cold, rocklike stolidity about the unquestioning certainty of his faith. Your God-fearer hopeth all things. But there is a tremor and a timidity lest his hope is a mirage. He fears to believe, lest his beliefs prove him a dupe. His steps are God haunted. But, maybe, He is but the ghost of his fears!! He fears God, but within his fear there is also a clutch of affection, the pushing out of his heart's tendrils lest haply he may lay hold upon God.[26]

Despite his respect for Hobling's views, Rex was finally on the point of resigning from New Road, although he was afraid of being isolated.

FRIDAY 21 JUNE 1918
The problem of the sincere searcher after truth is a very difficult one. Whilst he cannot avow allegiance to any sect – by reason of the very catholicity of his mind – he yet feels the barrenness of spiritual and intellectual isolation. If urged by his gregarious instincts into a church, he feels that he is thwarting his message by adopting the garb of a party. Such is the dilemma.

Back at his family home in the Cotswolds, Rex attended an open-air service of Congregationalists where the Rev. Hobling is preaching. A 'bounteous tea' gave him a taste of what life might be like after the war.

THURSDAY 4 JULY 1918
... Farmers very busy with their hay crops. The country was clothed in its summer beauty ... The services were held in a large orchard attached to the manse. The chief speaker was the Rev. F.G. Spurr, who, in the afternoon, spoke on prayer; and in the evening spoke of the necessity of reconstruction after the war. The honours of the day went to Rev. Hobling who in a quiet address took us to the uplands of the spirit...

Rex derived hope from Hobling's words – and a few chapters of *A Wayfarer's Faith* by Edmund Harvey reaffirmed his belief in prayer.

WEDNESDAY 10 JULY 1918
These are particularly stimulating religious essays, full of strong, wholesome meat. 'Every evil desire overcome is a victory to our brothers, and not merely for ourselves. Our lives are intertwined one with another, and constantly, unseen and unknown to ourselves and each other, we influence one another for evil or for good ... Truth is beautiful in the mouth of a friend, but most divine when it is seen in the heart of an opponent. The devil had delight to seek for faults in Job; let us seek rather to see, with Christ, the good in the heart of the publican.' Those who would aspire to the mount of vision, must humble themselves in prayer. Prophecy is born of prayer.

It was difficult for him to climb to any summit when gripped by indigestion: 'what a thing is man when a little underbaked flour and water disturbs his moral and spiritual equilibrium!' Rex had perhaps had too much rich country food, or was he in a lather about going back to work?

After a rare easy day at business, Rex studied the text of a lecture given by the Rev. David Smith on 'The Divinity of Christ' and made a note of Smith's 'strongest points': 'Had the evangelists been setting forth their own conception of a holy man, they would have depicted Jesus after the likeness of Pharisee'; 'Bronson Alcott once said to Carlyle that he would honestly use the words of Jesus, "I and the Father are one". "Yes," was the crushing retort, "but Jesus got the world to believe Him."'[27]

This did as little to help Rex's spiritual progress as the Quaker meeting of the previous day (Sunday 21 July), where 'he did not feel the uplift of previous occasions. The dead-hand of reserve and formality was on the gathering.' By contrast:

> After tea, we all went to New Rd. Mr Hobling gave an inspiriting and arresting address on Ezekiel's vision of 'the chambers of imagery'; which carried me back to one of my earliest attempts at preaching when I had the youthful audacity to speak from the same text. Mine was a much more gloomy and morbid exegesis than Mr Hobling's. I still shudder at the very recollection of it...

A couple of Sundays later (4 August) marked the fourth anniversary of the war, and again Mr Hobling impressed, speaking 'with the eloquence of a righteous passion. His out and out sincerity blazes through all shams and counterfeits; and he has much of the rugged, uncompromising austerity of the old Hebrew prophets.'

On holiday the following Sunday (11 August), Rex and his family attended the old chapel in Coxwell Street (Cirencester), where the preacher does not measure up to Hobling. 'His matter was passable, but his manner and delivery were very irritating. He shouted most strenuously: but even so, his words went no deeper than our ears. Personality and power of character were quite lacking.' That evening, Rex indulges his old passion at a hymn festival in the parish church:

> The hearty congregational singing by over a thousand voices of some of the old hymns, set to massive and majestic tunes, was extraordinarily impressive, and will remain an exhilarating memory for many days. The children exhausted by the change and excitement of the last 24 hours, dropped off to sleep and were not even awakened by the trumpet tones of the new setting of 'For All Thy Saints'.

Back in Oxford, Rex returned to the Congregational Chapel, where on Sunday 18 August he enjoyed a homely address on 'The Lord is Thy Keeper': 'Nothing can thwart a single and unshakeable will. 'Tis in ourselves, and not in our stars, that we are underlings. The difficulty is to choose amidst a multiplicity of ideals – all legitimate, maybe – but waging an internecine strife against one another.'

The following Wednesday, in a state of agitation, Rex takes a closer walk with God – you can almost hear him humming Cowper's beautiful hymn. 'I made a review of my life: its thwarted purposes, its cruel disillusionments, my struggle with darkness, my weakness of will, the crumbling away of my early aspirations under the necessity of gaining money. I spread the whole matter out in prayer, and asked for strength to do the tasks ahead' – one of which is to overcome his indecisiveness.

SUNDAY 25 AUGUST 1918
Awoke full of melancholy and sour humour ... went to New Rd, but I was in no frame of mind to benefit by the service. Mr Hobling spoke on the words 'I am the vine' and he thought that in these teetotal, total abstinence days we did not grasp the full significance of these words of Christ. We needed to regain something of the joy and intoxication of the early Christians. I went to the little chapel at Headington at night. The preacher, a young local, was quite unknown to me; but he was considerably above the average local. He gave a message rich in consolation on the words 'He seethe every precious thing'.

When, a few weeks later, Rex received a visit from Mr New, 'asking if he might register me as an "attendant" at the Friends' Meeting ... I refused to be classified and docketed'. On Sunday 15 September, he noted among the Friends the frank wonder and insouciant manner of a child, in contrast to:

the bent heads and furrowed brows, heavy with care and perplexity, all round him. How much happier should we be if we could make life less of a problem and more of a ground for happy, beneficent activity. The pain and suffering around us should not be allowed to lose themselves in the sandy wastes of thought, but should be diverted into channels of activity ... Arthur Gillett spoke very suggestively on the difficulty of knowing which is Caesar's, and which is God's.

Unsated, Rex went back to New Road in the evening, to welcome Rev. Hobling after his holidays.

SUNDAY 22 SEPTEMBER 1918
Another quiet resting place on life's pilgrimage! Went to the Friends meeting in the morning, but everyone seemed filled with a superfluity of talkativeness. Both schools of thought – the ultra-orthodox and the progressive – were well represented. An old gentleman made

a weighty and impressive utterance on 'Sin and Forgiveness' – but
continually lapsed into anachronistic allusions to David as a
'Christian'! A young man stole a shaft from the armory of Voltaire,
but blunted its edge in the talking. He spoke learnedly, but tediously,
on 'making God in the image of man'; and his speech was aptly and
concisely driven home by a few words from Dr Gillett. Had a short
conversation with Miss Quick, who is blossoming out as an ardent
Liberal – and discourses most eloquently on tariffs, protective and
otherwise...

The jury was still out for the Quakers. Rex attended a midweek study
circle, where both Quakers and Congregationalists were contending:

Dr Jackson made rich use of Marcus Aurelius, and even quarried from
Pharisaic material – an unexpected source – as collected in Abraham's
book on *Pharisaism and the Gospels*. The discussion was seconded by
Mr New, who was succeeded by Mr Cadoux who rode rough-shod
over some of the tentative conclusions of Dr Jackson. Mr Cadoux is
a 'whole hogger' in the matter of forgiveness. Other speakers were
Miss Quick, Cowley Rd Congregational Church (a poor, halting
speaker); Miss Wells; and the secretary of the electric company (a
strict evangelical, with an apt illustration garnered at Jerry McAuley's
Mission down in Water St).

That Sunday (29 September) he is more comfortable at the Quaker
meeting: 'What a blessing if we would walk softly in regard to religious
dogmas and opinions. Surely our ignorance does not justify our blatant
and noisy dogmatism. There are none so sure as the empty headed.'
    Rex, still unsure, attended a study circle at Hammington Hall, the
Quakers' meeting place.

WEDNESDAY 2 OCTOBER 1918
Dr Gillett was in the chair and stretched out the field for discussion
on 'the Religion and the future'. He was not altogether happy in
his subject and did not define his talk within the necessary limits.
His chief points were that religion in the future would place more
emphasis on 'service' and on the power of the resurrection, as opposed
to the crucifixion. This last point was evidently reinforced by the
arguments of Silvanus Thompson's 'A Not Impossible Religion'. The
discussion opened with a guerrilla attack by Mr Brazil, who is still
obsessed with 'the laws of god' and 'the laws of nature'. The debate

was blistering away into a running fire of questions, and it was only with difficulty that we got back to the main point at issue. A soldier made a good point when he said that the Mosaic law of 'equal justice' – 'an eye for an eye, and a tooth for a tooth' – was an advance on the unbridled revenge and scorn of vendetta, which perhaps wiped out a whole family for the murder of one; and that Christ lifted the whole matter to a higher level by insisting on 'love and forgiveness' rather than the exaction of equal justice. I made a few remarks in a ragged fashion – which caused some merriment and some surprise. I was not altogether happy in my performance and made at least two slips against good taste ... my abstention from public speaking for such a long time has had its effects...

'We have conquered the Germans'. Rex King's diary, 8 November 1918.

By November, the war, at last, was at an end. But Rex battled on, continuing his spiritual education.

SUNDAY 24 NOVEMBER 1918
My reading has been of a desultory and varied nature from the diaries of Abraham de la Prynne (Camden Society), the essays of Sidney Smith and J.H. Leckie's 'Authority in Religion'. The last book is a very exhaustive and convincing examination of the nature and source of authority in religion. It is a mine of rich suggestions. What he says of supernaturalism; is worthy of note. 'What does supernatural mean? Does it mean "miraculous"? If so, how can it apply to spiritual relations? "Miracle" is a term that belongs to the realm of physical things. It means an apparent break in the action of the laws which govern the material universe, and has no oppositeness at all as applied to the things of the soul ... when we are dealing with spiritual facts we are in a region where all is supernatural, but nothing is miraculous.'

Miracles apart, Rex found the world in political disarray at the turn of the year, compounded by the seizing of Hammington Hall by the Army demobilization board. Rex sought comfort at a Quaker meeting 'where Dr Gillett spoke with much forcefulness and truth on the relationship between the individualistic and socialist conceptions of religion'. After the Easter break, Rex was in a better frame of mind:

TUESDAY 22 APRIL 1919
It has been a glorious Easter – Good Friday being like a day in midsummer ... I had intended walking from Wantage to Shiverham over the Downs, but the famine stricken leanness of my purse prevented this happy expedition. Still, I had a very restful time, pottering about the garden, indulging in short walks, reading Leonard Merrick and reviewing books for 'Oxford Chronicle'.

THURSDAY 1 MAY 1919
May Day came in shrouded in cold mist and rain and May garlands were conspicuously scarce. Dr Gillett's suggestion – made at the study circle – that inspiration in the biblical sense was really 'spiritual perception' was a most fruitful one. At the same time, it does not appear adequate to cover the element of enthusiasm – using the word in its primary signification, as 'god-filled' – which is present in some of the impetuous prophetic utterances. Even in the realms of poetry,

1. In this detail from panel 1 of Edward Bawden's History of Oxford mural, books are slipping from the hands of Sir Thomas Bodley to fall into those of boys from St Paul's School. This panel depicts other Oxford characters: Walter de Merton, John Wycliffe, Chaucer, the Wife of Bath with the coffins of her four husbands, and Duke Humfrey.

London 2 Farringdon Street
June 28. 1853

Dear Sir,

After your letter of this
day. we will most willingly
give up our proportion of the
dividend for Mrs Blackwell's use
& only regret — that she should
have been so badly provided
for — We remain

Dear Sir Yours Very Truly

Geo Routledge & Co

2. George Routledge's letter, releasing Benjamin Harris Blackwell's widow Nancy from outstanding debts, demonstrates generosity and fraternity within the book trade.

Isle of Wight
Thursday July 9
From Southampton to West Cowes
to Thorness Wood by beach through
Parkhurst Forest by creek to Newtown
to Shalfleet a mile or so past Shal
fleet and close to a little bridge turn
to left down lane to Ningwood Farm
turn to right & pass Wellow follow
the Yar to Thorley (abt 12 miles)
pass Ch across Thorley rivulet to
right & straight up to coast (views of
Lymington near Hurst C & N. Forest)
to Yarmouth (Inns George &
Bugle (nine electors in 1832) George
Inn anct mansion of Sir R. Holmes
ent^d Ch 2° in 1671

3. Fit to go up in the world: Benjamin Henry's walking holiday
in the Isle of Wight, at the age of only nineteen. His itinerary
was demanding. In his diaries, he characteristically sketched
and annotated the routes he planned for his holidays.

50 Broad St
Oxford
July 22/86

My dearest Lil.

I am afraid you will
be disappointed at not receiving
this this morning, but when yours
arrived yesterday I was just going
to that Sale of Badcock's where I had
to stay shewing till about half
past two so I hope you will see
that there was no time.

I am glad you found your friends
all well and that Jackie was
better. I can fancy how excited
he was at seeing his dear old
Auntie who must have loved
him like a mother, sister and

4. Benjamin Henry's courtship of Lilla Taylor,
a girl with 'something of the country air about her'.

5. Benjamin Henry Blackwell spared no effort in book production,
despite limited resources. He demanded as much from the physical
book as from the text. The cover of this slim poetry volume
of 1880, with A.E. Housman of St John's to be found among
the contributors, hints at his interest in William Morris.

HYMNS

THE YATTENDON HYMNAL
EDITED BY ROBERT BRIDGES
AND H. ELLIS WOOLDRIDGE

Ed: Stereotyp:
Music & Words
only

Oxford: B. H. Blackwell, Broad Street
London Agents: Simpkin & Co., Limited
1 9 0 5

6. Benjamin Henry, an enthusiastic church chorister, added the
Yattendon Hymnal to his list in 1905. Edited by Robert Bridges, with
Harry Ellis Wooldridge and H.C. Beeching, it was arguably the most
important book to bear the B.H. Blackwell imprint. In its field, it had an
influence way beyond the rural parish for which it had been prepared;
Vaughan Williams' *English Hymnal* owed much to it.

THE
BROODING
EARTH~

a Story of
Mashonaland

BY

ARTHUR
SHEARLY
CRIPPS

OXFORD
B·H·BLACKWELL.
LONDON
SIMPKIN & Cº Lᵀᴰ

7. *The Brooding Earth*, published by B.H. Blackwell in 1911. Arthur S. Cripps,
educated at Trinity College next to Blackwell's, became a parish priest
in Essex and then a missionary in the 'brooding' plains of Mashonaland,
Africa, where he was honoured for many years after his death.

8. B.H. Blackwell's own contribution to the defence of Belgium,
1914, with a cover design by Elsie Lunn. Inside, the frontispiece
features the famous *Punch* cartoon depicting the King of the
Belgians declaring his soul unconquerable by the Kaiser.

9. The art of suggestion: is this soldier going 'over the top' –
or coming down to meet his woman and dog? Blackwell's book covers
were designed to show what the text described. Grace Mary Golden's
poems, 1917, give a women's perspective on war: the nurse, the sister, the
widow, the mother and the 'old maid' whose lover 'sleeps in France'.

10. Bernard Gilbert, from the fenlands of Lincolnshire, was a lucky discovery.
B.H. Blackwell published his *Rebel Verses* in 1918. Gilbert's poems advocated
rebelliousness in the face of death. A.P. Herbert's *Half-Hours at Helles*, 1916, is
dedicated to Lieutenant Colonel Leslie Wilson, DSO and MP, and the officers
and men of the Hawke Battalion. Both authors spoke for the Blackwells.

11. The Blackwell series *Initiates* included Captain Geoffrey Faber's *In the Valley of Vision*, Eleanor Farjeon's *Sonnets and Poems*, Aldous Huxley's *The Defeat of Youth* and Edith Sitwell's *The Mother and Other Poems*. *Songs for Sale* is an important anthology, illustrative of the work of many Blackwell 'war' poets: male and female, combatant and non-combatant.

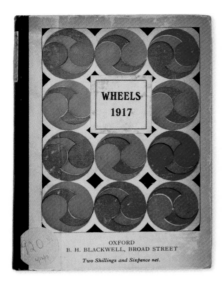

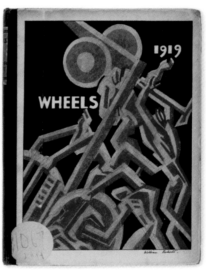

12. *Wheels 1917: A Second Cycle*, edited by Edith Sitwell, includes contributions from all three Sitwells, Iris Tree, Aldous Huxley, Sherard Vines and E.W. Tennant. The cover design, suggesting wheels in motion, is by C.W. Beaumont. The cover for *Wheels 1918*, depicting a sky pilot by Lawrence Atkinson, conveys edginess and a radicalism that suggests the influence of Wyndham Lewis and the Vorticists. *Wheels 1919* was dedicated to the memory of Wilfred Owen. The cover and endpapers are by renowned war artist William Roberts; gun drill is a metaphor for war but also for the dehumanization of labour. Roberts took evening classes while an apprentice; a scholarship to the Slade put him in the company of Paul Nash, Dora Carrington and Stanley Spencer.

13. Bernard Gilbert's 1919 volume of verse takes men home from the war 'back to the land' – to the farms of the Fenlands. They are shell-shocked, 'shuddering'. Will they find solace in their homelands? The cover, artist not known, is a graphic portrayal of the displacement and confusion felt by returned servicemen.

14. Leslie Stephen, Virginia Woolf's father, celebrated his first ascent of the Alps with the first edition of this book in 1871. It became a mountaineering classic long before Blackwell's published it. Did Basil Blackwell hope that European conflict could be resolved by such endeavour? Aldous Huxley's *Selected Poems* was the poetry of a new world – but was it 'brave'?

"AT LAST"

CONCLUSION OF "WOMAN'S EFFORT"

From " Punch," 23 Jan., 1918.
Reproduced by special permission of the proprietors.

By A. E. METCALFE

OXFORD : B. H. BLACKWELL, BROAD STREET

One Shilling and Sixpence net

15. This volume complements A.E. Metcalfe's previous work, *Women's Effort* (1917). But, he concedes, it was hardly a conclusion. Under the terms of the Representation of the People Act, 1918, 'women were far from having won complete freedom'; a quarter of adult women were excluded until 1928, although the war had shown them all to be 'worthy'. This small book conveys simply and concisely the vicissitudes of women's fight, and the ambivalence of many men.

THE COMPLEAT

THAT MOTLEY DRAMA, OH! BE SURE
· WITH ITS PHANTOM CHASED FOR EVERMORE
· THROUGH A CIRCLE THAT EVER RETURNETH IT
IT · BY A CROWD THAT SHALL SEIZE IT NOT ·
SPOT · IN TO THE SELFSAME · AND MORE OF SIN
· WITH MUCH OF MADNESS · THE SOUL OF THE
· AND HORROR ·
P.·O
L

SHALL NOT BE FORGOT,

SCHOOLMARM

HELEN HAMILTON

PRICE TWO SHILLINGS NET

16. Helen Hamilton's verse story, 1917, of 'promise and
fulfilment', was dedicated to women teachers who, unstinting
of effort, strove to make education more human.

FOR THIS ALONE
R.P.L.MOGG.

17. In 1943 Blackwell's published *For This Alone*, written by Sergeant
R.P.L. Mogg, who, having left journalism to join the RAF, was shot down
over Germany and taken prisoner. In the preface Basil Blackwell wrote:
'the world of letters is the gainer for in captivity he [Mogg] has discovered
in himself a poetic gift of very high quality ... A fellow prisoner, Sgt J W
Lambert, has transcribed and beautifully illustrated these poems.' By publishing
it, Basil Blackwell hoped yet again to 'extend the healing power' of poetry.

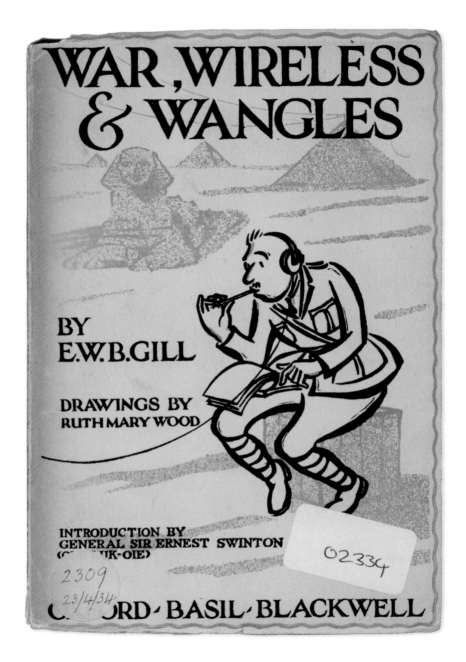

WAR, WIRELESS & WANGLES

BY
E.W.B.GILL

DRAWINGS BY
RUTH MARY WOOD

INTRODUCTION BY
GENERAL SIR ERNEST SWINTON
(————UK-OIE)

OXFORD·BASIL·BLACKWELL

18. Published by Basil Blackwell in 1914, Major E.W.B. Gill's book takes
a light-hearted swipe at military leaders devising strategies 'that any child
could unravel' and desk-bound experts deciphering codes with paper
and pencil. Gill divulges the gaffes, stupidities and petty jealousies of
'a huge disjointed machine'. But they were, after all, only the 'ordinary
failings of mankind'. The illustrations were by Ruth Mary Wood.

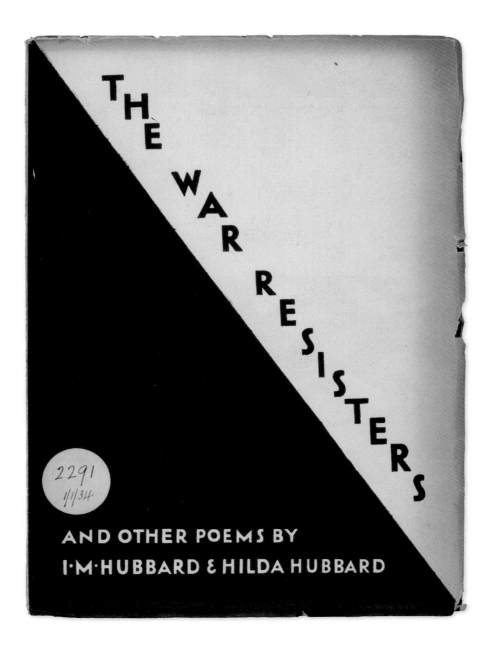

THE WAR RESISTERS

AND OTHER POEMS BY
I·M·HUBBARD & HILDA HUBBARD

2291
1/1/34

19. I.M. and Hilda Hubbard's poems were published by
Shakespeare Head Press in 1934. Incensed by war, they write
of the 'desolate mother' whose sons had been taken and of
ever-pervasive fear. There is no doubt about impending war.

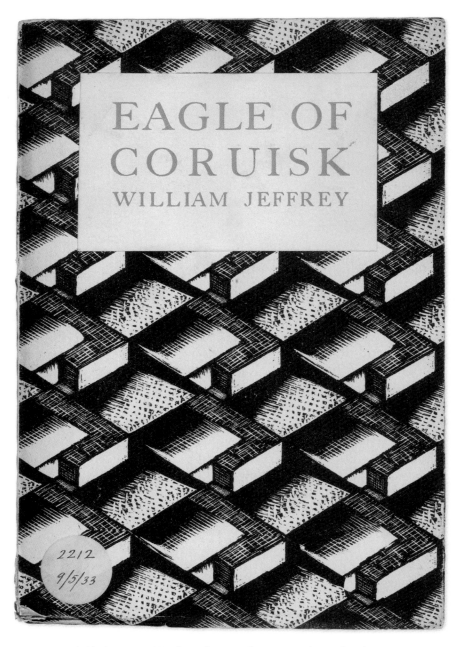

EAGLE OF
CORUISK
WILLIAM JEFFREY

20. A Shakespeare Head production from 1933, this jacket (artist unknown) has an Escher-like graphic look, consistent with the symbolist thrust of the text. The Scottish poet William Jeffrey, the son of a colliery manager educated at Glasgow and Edinburgh universities, was gassed in World War I. His love of the sea and sky, where the sea eagles fly, must have earned him a sympathetic reception at Blackwell's.

NOUGHT RIVALS WATER: GOLD, A FIRE
THAT FLAMES
ILLUMINING THE NIGHT, ALL WEALTH
OUTVIES;
   And wouldst thou chant, my soul, of contests won
  Look not for day-beams in the lonely skies
    From any star more radiant than the sun,
        And for no greater Games
  Than great Olympia's, whence the welcome strains
    Of bards flow forth, acclaiming Cronus' Son
    In this fair home of God-blest HIERON,
Who wields the right o'er rich Sicilian plains.

He gathers every virtue's flower and prime;
    And music spheres him in enchanted air,
      Such joyous music as we minstrels make,
   When oft the table of a friend we share.
      Take down the Dorian lyre! Let VICTOR wake
      The sweetly-mused rhyme,

3

21. Pindar's *Odes*: a publisher in defence of the classics.

The Woman Doctor.   The Professor.   The Psychic Researcher.

The Schoolmarm.   The Poet.   The Priest.

The Courier.   The Lady of Fashion.   Her Maid.

The Master-Printer.   The Detective's Friend.   The Bureaucrat.

22. Boccaccio and Chaucer both painted word-pictures of fourteenth-century life. Basil Blackwell decided to make his own *New Decameron*, in seven volumes, from 1919: 'The truth which we find in the Parables and in Aesop's Fables, the truth which, to generation after generation, unfailingly makes its appeal.' Aided and abetted by his old friend Michael Sadleir, he gathered together storytellers such as John D. Beresford, L.A.G. Strong, Compton Mackenzie, L.P. Hartley, D.H. Lawrence, Sherard Vines, William F. Harvey, Evelyn Waugh, Horace Horsnell, Norman Davey and Wilfred Blair. He included stories from tailor's son Alfred E. Coppard, who was among those who met to read Elizabethan drama in an Oxford pub, and Robert Keable, who left the priesthood after the First World War. Female contributors included Vita Sackville-West, Naomi Royde Smith, Storm Jameson, E.M. Delafield and Dorothy L. Sayers.

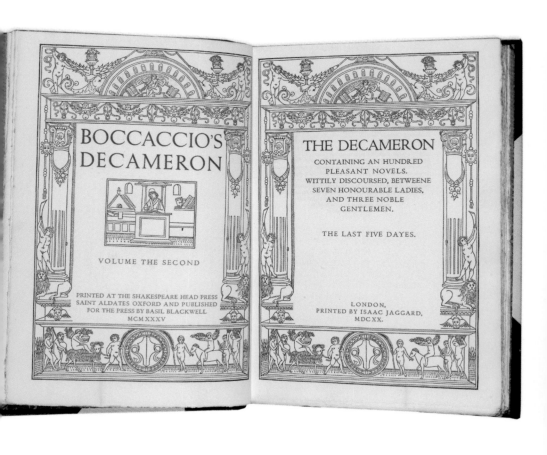

23. Title spread of the Shakespeare Head Press *Decameron*, vol. 2, 1935.
The series was designed to have the Venetian flavour of the scholar printer
Aldus Manutius; three copies were printed on vellum. Printed in black and
blue with ornate capitals, it also featured blue-gold marbled end papers.

❡ A CLERK ther was of Oxenford also
That unto logyk hadde longe y-go.
As leene was his hors as is a rake,
And he nas nat right fat, I undertake,
But looked holwe, and ther-to sobrely;
Ful thredbare was his overeste courtepy;
For he hadde geten hym yet no benefice,
Ne was so worldly for to have office;
For hym was levere have at his beddes heed
Twenty bookes clad in blak or reed
Of Aristotle and his philosophie,
Than robes riche, or fithele, or gay sautrie:
But al be that he was a philosophre,
Yet hadde he but litel gold in cofre;
But al that he myghte of his freendes hente
On bookes and his lernynge he it spente,
And bisily gan for the soules preye
Of hem that yaf hym wher-with to scoleye.
Of studie took he moost cure and moost heede,
Noght o word spak he moore than was neede,
And that was seyd in forme and reverence,
And short and quyk and ful of hy sentence.
Sownynge in moral vertu was his speche
And gladly wolde he lerne and gladly teche.

❡ A SERGEANT OF THE LAWE, war and wys,
That often hadde been at the Parvys,
Ther was also, ful riche of excellence.
Discreet he was, and of greet reverence;
He semed swich, hise wordes weren so wise.
Justice he was ful often in Assise,

11

24. Benjamin Harris Blackwell could be seen as a nineteenth-century
reincarnation of Chaucer's Clerk of Oxonford, depicted here. The idea for a
Shakespeare Head edition of *The Canterbury Tales* came from Basil Blackwell,
but credit for the end product must go to master designer and typographer
Bernard Newdigate. According to the publisher's advertisement, it was
issued in 'eight large octavo volumes', starting in the autumn of 1928. The
text is from the Globe edition, and it is printed on Batchelor's Kelmscott
handmade paper, using Caslon Old Face type. The headings and initials were
drawn by Joscelyne Gaskin, and the illustrations are hand-coloured.

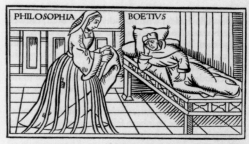

INCIPIT LIBER BOECII DE CONSOLA-
CIONE PHILOSOPHIE

Carmina qui quondam studio florente peregi.   Metrum 1

ALLAS! I, wepynge, am constreyned to bygynnen vers of sorwful matere, that whilom in floryss-chyng studie made delitable ditees. For lo! ren-dynge Muses of poetes enditen to me thynges to ben writen, and drery vers of wrecchidnesse weten my face with verray teres.

⁋ At the leeste, no drede ne myghte overcomen tho Mu-ses, that thei ne were felawes, and folwyden my wey (that is to seyn, whan I was exiled). They that weren glorie of my youthe, whilom weleful and grene, conforten nowe the sorwful wyerdes of me, olde man. For eelde is comyn unwarly uppon me, hasted by the harmes that y have, and sorwe hath comandid his age to ben in me. Heer is hore arn schad over-tymeliche up-on myn heved, & the slakke skyn trembleth of myn emptid body.

⁋ Thilke deth of men is weleful that ne comyth noght in

VOL. V   b   I

25. The text of the fifth volume of Chaucer, 1924, is that prepared by Mark Liddell for the Globe edition of the *Works of Chaucer*, edited by A.W. Pollard. The headpieces were drawn by Lynton Lamb from woodcuts in a copy of Boethius printed at Lyon by Simon Vincent, *c.* 1508–25.

FROISSARTS CRONYCLES

TRANSLATED OUT OF FRENCH BY SIR JOHN
BOURCHIER LORD BERNERS · VOL · II PART IV

PRINTED AT THE SHAKESPEARE HEAD PRESS
STRATFORD-UPON-AVON AND PUBLISHED FOR
THE PRESS BY BASIL BLACKWELL OXFORD
MCMXXVIII

26. Printed on hand-made paper and adorned with hand-coloured armorial shields, as befitted the chivalric revival of fourteenth-century England and France and an author whose work did much to inform understanding of that century.

THE · X · BOKE

HERE BEGYN
OF SYRE TRY
OF THIS PRES

⟨ HOW SYR TRUS
KYNGE ARTHUR
TELLE THEYM H
THENNE sayd A
be ye can dyscry
beere, ye are wor
the armes. As for that say
tram I woll answere you
de was yeven me not desy
Morgan le fay. And as
II B

THE NOBLE & JOYOUS BOKE ENTYTLED LE

MORTE DARTHUR

NOTWYTHSTONDYNG IT TREATETH OF
THE BYRTH LYF AND ACTES OF THE SAYD
KYNGE ARTHUR: OF HIS NOBLE KNYGHTES
OF THE ROUNDE TABLE · THEYR MERVEYL-
LOUS ENQUESTES AND ADVENTURES
THACHYEVYNGE OF THE SANC·GREALL
AND IN THE ENDE THE DOLOUROUS
DETH: AND DEPARTYNGE OUT OF
THIS WORLDE OF THEM AL.
Whyche boke was reduced in to Englysshe
by the well dysposyd knyghte
SYR THOMAS MALORY

⟨ The Second Volume

⟨ Oxford: Printed at the Shakespeare Head Press
Saint Aldates and published for the Press
by Basil Blackwell Broad Street
MCM XXXIII

27. The Shakespeare Head Press 1933 edition of the 'unique' *Morte Darthur*
printed by Wynkyn de Worde at Westminster in 1498, with woodcuts
copied from that edition and the Press's characteristic marbled endpapers.

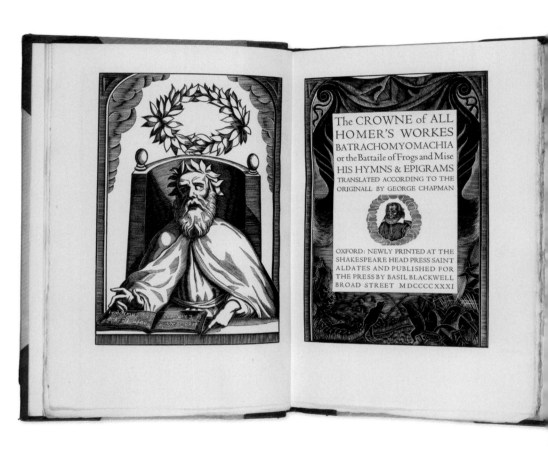

28. A monument to the work of Bernard Newdigate.

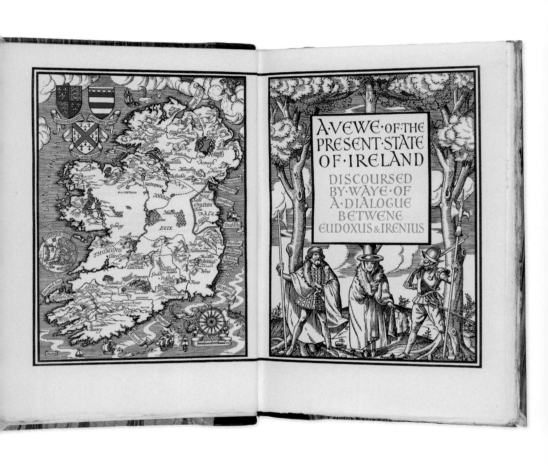

29. The Shakespeare Head Press edition of Edmund Spenser's *A Vewe of the Present State of Ireland* is based on MS. Rawlinson B 475 in the Bodleian Library, a manuscript which Matthew Lownes entered in the Stationers' Register, 14 April 1598. The glosses in the margin are written as in a Dublin edition of 1633. MacDonald Gill drew the map of Ireland forming the frontispiece and title page. The letters follow the first edition, printed by Henry Bynneman in 1580.

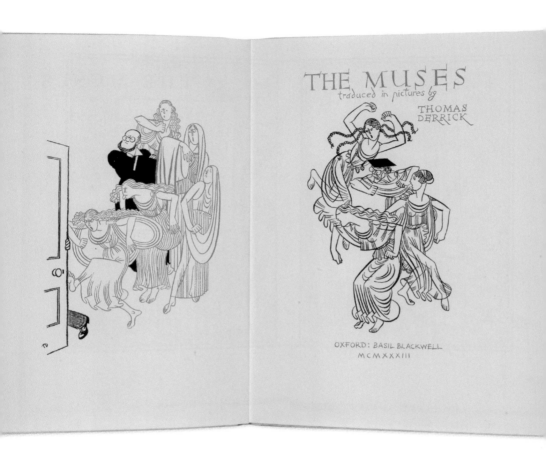

30. Thomas Derrick conjures up *The Muses Traduced in
Pictures*, in memory of Sir William Smith, author of the
classical dictionary. Shakespeare Head Press, 1933.

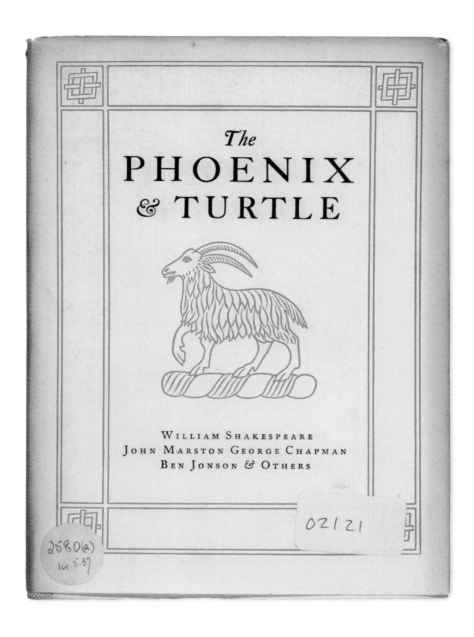

31. *The Phoenix and the Turtle.* 'In an age', Basil Blackwell wrote, 'which regarded the pre-Raphaelite as a Victorian episode, William Morris's faith was to be preached entire, his crusade to be carried on.' And to carry on the practices and ideas of Morris was just what he intended to do. He took as his model Morris's Kelmscott Chaucer, published in 1896. For Basil Blackwell this was the epitome of everything the fine craft of printing should be.

CHAPTER XI
Paper-Making in England

THE first English paper-maker was John Tate, who established a paper-mill near Hertford about 1490. Some authorities state that the mill was at Stevenage, but it is more probable that the mill was on the Stevenage side of Hertford, as there are several names still in use

Fig. 33. Sorting and cutting rags. The woman is drawing the rags across the knife to cut them into pieces small enough for the beating engine to deal with. The box on the right is divided into compartments for the various qualities of rags.

there which indicate the existence of a paper-mill.

John Tate, the younger, who started the paper-mill, was a citizen and Mercer of London, and he was the son of Sir John Tate, who was Lord Mayor of London in 1496. We have indisputable evidence that Tate was making paper about this time, in Wynkyn de Worde's famous English edition of Bartholomaeus, 'De proprietatibus rerum.' The paper on which this book is printed contains Tate's watermark, an eight-pointed star en-

106

32. A historic account, illustrating the origin of early paper-making in China, and its progress over a millennium, *Paper-making by Hand* venerates all those invisible characters that travailed in the early paper mills. Fittingly printed on handmade paper, it is a demonstration of the Blackwell's respect for the whole book.

S. $4^1/2 \times 4^1/2$ inches   T. $5^1/2 \times 5^1/2$ inches U. $4^1/2 \times 4^1/2$ inches
V. $7/_{10}$ inches thick   W. 6×6 inches   X.

S is a printed tile in Merton College library. T is a printed bit in Blewbury Church, also drawn by Manning from the Post Office site. U is a printed Thame Park tile. V is an inlaid and keyed Osney tile in the Ashmolean. W is a printed tile in Merton Church. X is an inlaid bit in Dorchester Abbey.

33. Loyd Haberly's *Mediaeval English Paving Tiles*, which he illustrated, was produced by Shakespeare Head Press in 1937. It is a stunning record, in which Haberly urges us to look down at our feet, as well as up at the stars.

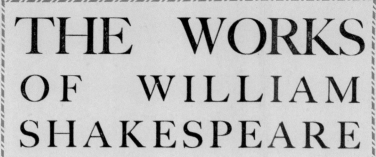

THE WORKS
OF WILLIAM
SHAKESPEARE
Gathered into One Volume

1280
pages

$5.00

NEW YORK
Newly Printed for the Shakespeare Head Press
and Published by
OXFORD UNIVERSITY PRESS

34. Basil Blackwell's one-volume Shakespeare, produced at a
widely affordable price, was a tour de force. Its success may have
convinced him that the way forward for his publishing firm was not
to produce finely printed belles-lettres, but rather to make the classics
accessible on the one hand – and to make a profit on the other.

SHAKESPEARE HEAD PRESS

33 St Aldates
Oxford

Founded at
Stratford-upon-Avon
1904

ENQUIRIES & ORDERS *for*

PRINTING

received HERE

35. Bernard Newdigate's book of samples.

PUBLISHED FOR THE GIRL GUIDES ASSOCIATION

Tales
for
Brownies

BASIL BLACKWELL · OXFORD

36. Newdigate 'outreaches' to the Girl Guides.

37. *Bed-time Fun for Boys and Girls.* Some of these
activities might not be conducive to sleep...

38. These verses for young children are as captivating as any, and the exquisite intricate woodcuts, first published by Benjamin Henry Blackwell, then Basil Blackwell from 1919, have made these volumes into collectors' items.

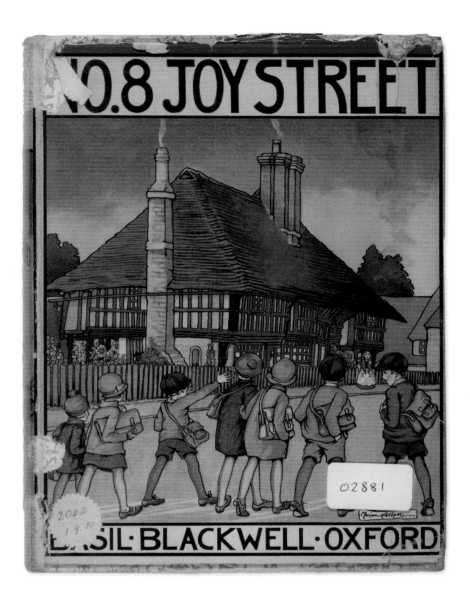

NO.8 JOY STREET

02881

2044
1.9.30

BASIL·BLACKWELL·OXFORD

39. The cover of the eighth edition of *Joy Street*, 'A Medley of
Prose and Verse for Boys and Girls' published annually by Basil
Blackwell from 1923. Contributors over the years included Walter
de la Mare, Hilaire Belloc, Compton Mackenzie, Eleanor Farjeon,
G.K. Chesterton, Edith Sitwell and A.A. Milne.

Basil Blackwell's
Books for Boys & Girls
1936-37

BROAD STREET · OXFORD

40. Despite the liberal Blackwell's commitment to women's education, there
is more differentiation in this 1930s list than would be acceptable today.

41. The vital role of the book in history: the advertisments on the following pages are a symbol of Blackwell's support for literary emancipation.

42. 'Good Books Build Character.'

43. 'More Books in the Home!'

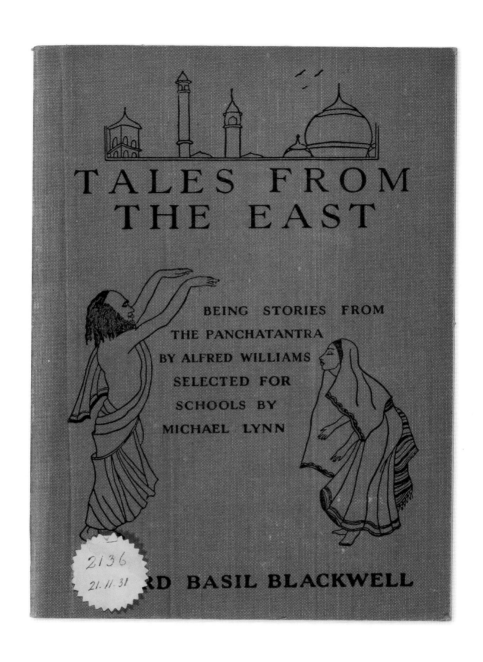

TALES FROM
THE EAST

BEING STORIES FROM
THE PANCHATANTRA
BY ALFRED WILLIAMS
SELECTED FOR
SCHOOLS BY
MICHAEL LYNN

RD BASIL BLACKWELL

44. Alfred Williams's version of these ancient fables was published for children by Basil Blackwell in 1931, but was intended as much for adults to read. The simple but beautiful illustrations are by Peggy Whistler.

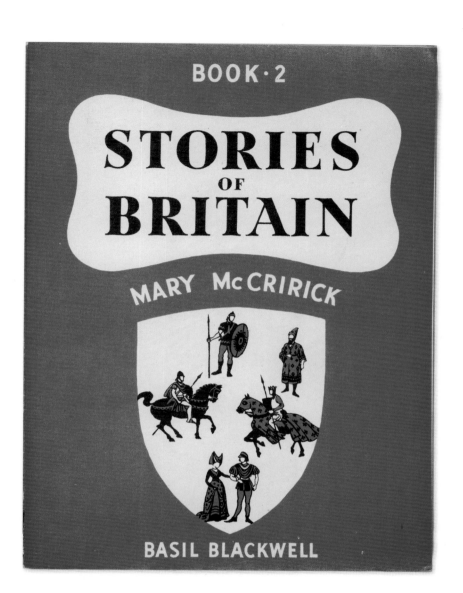

BOOK·2

STORIES
OF
BRITAIN

MARY McCRIRICK

BASIL BLACKWELL

45. Mary McCririck's *Stories of Britain*, Book 2.

46. Expanding children's horizons –
and securing a future in educational publishing.

47. For Julian Huxley, who was passionate about education, science is poetry is imagination. He came to the attention of Benjamin Henry Blackwell when he won the Newdigate Poetry Prize in 1909; he was also a contemporary of Basil Blackwell at Oxford.

Ludwig Wittgenstein

The Blue And Brown Books

Preliminary Studies for the 'Philosophical Investigations'

A Blackwell Paperback

48. A 1972 paperback version of a Basil Blackwell 1958 production, which reputedly was chosen in preference to *Asterix*.

we have instances of the same yeasty mental ferment forcibly seeking an outlet – very noticeably in the case of Shelley; it is 'a fire in the bones'. Yet even here, 'perception' may be a potent factor ... It was Jeremiah's perception of the true nature of religion that made him burn with scathing indignation against the rottenness and falsity in the worship around him.

MONDAY 2 JUNE 1919
Went to the Adult School in the evening, and listened with enjoyment to an animated – and sometimes, trenchant – discussion upon the question 'Can democracy exist without Christianity'? There was a large number present and we did not arrive at any solution. The honour of the evening went to Mathew Webb – 'the poor devil of an artist', who in a few quiet words showed that service of others was the real essence of Christianity and Socialism. The opening speaker favoured an ascetic type of Christianity. This was ridiculed. The representative of the evangelical school was also 'roughly handled' by a soldier from Lancashire, who was on fire with righteous indignation. An Indian made an interesting speech and thought that as 'suffering' was an essential factor in the Christian scheme it was wrong to attempt to alleviate it. Judging from the twinkle in his roguish eyes, I think he was indulging in a little 'leg-pulling'.

Through June Rex spent time with the Friends, listening, learning and thinking: 'a long windy discourse about the futility of politics and the divisions in the ranks of the Quakers ... Dr Gillett sensibly reminded that differences of opinion could co-exist with a real unity of spirit'; 'A restorative hour at the Friends ... Mr New spoke long on the need of solidarity and the breaking down of class-distinctions'; 'Went to Dr Gillett's in the afternoon to meet a few undergraduates who are anxious to revive Adult School work in Oxford – Quite a large gathering, full of glad, youthful enthusiasm.'

SUNDAY 20 JULY 1919
Still wet, but Jimmy and I trudged down to the Friends meeting. Miss Paske, being on holiday, the children's preparatory class was not held – much to Jimmy's disappointment. He relieved the tedium of an exceptionally dead morning with a rapid succession of distinctly audible yawns and sighs! Mr New opened with a dull wooden homily on Bishop Ken's morning hymn 'Awake, my soul, and with the sun, etc.' As he, with a naïve irony, pointed out it is not only on arising

from our beds that we need to prod our souls into wakefulness. His
remarks, however, elicited a charming interpretation of 'the Sleeping
Beauty' from a lady Friend. There is a 'Sleeping beauty' in every
soul; however set round with prickly breans and thorns, if we can
only awaken it with a touch of love ... Read a very lucid 'Outline
of Theosophy' by G.W. Leadbetter – sang a few 'hymns and spiritual
songs' – and then to bed.

MONDAY 29 SEPTEMBER 1919
The last day of official 'summer-time' – tonight we are commanded
to turn our clocks back an hour. So as to get back to 'God's time'
again. It has been pelting with rain unceasingly all day since eleven
o'clock and one is loathe to put back the clock to lengthen such a
dreamy day! Perhaps it was the thought of putting back the clock
that dragged into the dome of consciousness the memory of King
Hezekiah for whose consolation the shadow on the sundial went ten
degree backward. This morning, at the Friends meeting, the words of
[that] old king who had recently gone down to the gates of death – 'I
will go shortly all my days' recurred again to my mind. The strong
and robust are all to exult fiercely in their Health – little knowing by
what tiny advances death may creep in. But those who have looked
into the eyes of death, come back with quieter step and lowlier mien.

At the end of 1919 Rex read G.M. Gaillard's *A Living Christianity*,
'the work of a progressive scientific mind'. But his mind was on politics: was the rise of Labour compatible with the Kingdom of Heaven
and where did Quakerism stand?

SUNDAY 29 FEBRUARY 1920
Last night I attended a very inspiriting meeting at 115 High Street,
when Richard Westrope – familiarly known as 'Brother Richard'
– opened a lively discussion on Labour and the Churches. He
identified Social Democracy with the Messiah of the second Isaiah.
He gave an illuminating survey of the rise of Labour ... alluding
to the significant fact that the year 1906, which witnessed the
rebirth of democracy, was the commencement of a steady decline in
membership in all the churches.

THURSDAY 1 APRIL 1920
Went to a lecture on Sunday evening, at 115 High St on what
Quakerism stands for by Mr Braithwaite – The President of the Adult
School Union. The remark that the Kingdom of Heaven was already
breaking into the present order was a very helpful one...

SUNDAY 2 MAY 1920

Opened the discussion at the evening meeting of the Friends on The
Revolt of the early Quakers against the Authority of the Church and
the Bible, Dr Hind was in the chair. The question was awkwardly
framed – as the centre of authority had already been moved from the
Church to the Bible before the emergence of the Friends.

WHIT SUNDAY 23 MAY 1920

Going to Adult School, I overtook Mr Williams, who told me he
had been studying the new Rent Bill instead of the Bible. Dr Gillett's
interesting address on Truth and Tradition, dwelt very largely on the
question of Punishment and Coercion. Mr Gray Jones, of St John's
College, opened the discussion and I was thrust into the Chair. I was
not quite unprepared, for Mr Williams had hinted in the afternoon
that I ought to be able to make a useful contribution to the discussion,
so I had carefully thought over my position. Nevertheless, it was a
Chestertonian situation – a Presbyterian and a lapsed Baptist in charge
of a Quaker meeting.

Rex pondered, as he continued his denominational pilgrimage.

SUNDAY 20 JUNE 1920

... to the Congregational Church in the morning, and the gloom
born of dripping skies was intensified by the chilling coldness and
barrenness of the service. The congregation consisted of nine persons
– including the minister's wife. The inner tragedy of the mistrust that
exists between minister and people is a very sad one. Immured within
his manse all the week – except when he wanders into the road and
lanes away from the village – he has lost touch with the people.

SUNDAY 11 JULY 1920

At the Meeting some very helpful words were spoken on 'By
their fruits ye shall know them' – the speaker remarking upon the
pragmatic temper of the age. He emphasised the action and re-action
of 'what we are' upon 'what we do' ... Dr Gillett spoke suggestively
upon 'man cannot live by bread alone, but by every word that
proceedeth from the mouth of God'.

The next Quaker meeting was swamped by an inrush of American
delegates to the All Friend's Conference, but Rex found glory in the
commonplace.

SUNDAY 22 AUGUST 1920

Elbert Russell gave a powerful address on the inadequacy of 'Justice' as a Way of Life. He spoke again in the evening on the Meaning of the Cross ... The breadth of a man's culture is marked by his ever-deepening sense of the interconnectedness of things – both in the realm of behaviour and in the realm of knowledge. The commonest object and the slightest act have ramifications which branch out into the infinite. He sees the glory in the commonplace.

The world was begotten in mystery: and whatever theory we adopt of the origin of the universe, we are involved in the 'miraculous' or 'supernatural' – either as a violation of the order of nature, or a transcendence of the order of nature.

Rex was still busy sorting out his own ideas. His criticism of organized religion and its institutions, the unsatisfying spiritual fare dished up by the different sects, is similar to that in *Jude the Obscure*. But, unlike Hardy, Rex had no doubts about his faith. What people sought was *love*.

SUNDAY 5 SEPTEMBER 1920

An oppressively hot, steamy morning. The meeting was well attended. A lady visitor spoke helpfully upon punishment, alluding to the anomaly that whilst we accepted the dictum of 'returning good for evil' as a divine rule of life, yet we often thought of mishap or misfortune as punishment sent from God? ... Despite nearly two thousand years of organised Christianity, man is still incurably religious; and the steady, continual trend away from the Churches, is not so much a proof that men and women are becoming indifferent to the higher concerns and finer issues of life, as that they are growing more dissatisfied with the conception of religion offered to them by the churches – whether those churches are High, Low, or Broad; whether established, or disestablished; whether Baptist, Congregationalist, or Methodist. I believe that man's religious appetite was never more sane and wholesome than it is today; and it is the very sanity and healthiness of his craving that excites his strong moral taste against the unsatisfying spiritual fare provided by the various churches. The roots of the misconception of religion, which is driving thoughtful God-fearing men into the wilderness, strike far deeper than the oftentimes-superficial differences that split up organised Christianity into a multitude of sects. Man does not want a religion that is a mere spice and condiment to life; nor yet a religion that is a reshuffle of wilted dogmas and opinions...

There is within man a large reservoir of moral energy – capable, if rightly directed, of cleansing the Augean stable of our own social, industrial, national, and international life, and of lifting men to a higher level of mutual service. But, alas, this unlimited reservoir of moral force has been allowed to filter into thin, meandering channels of useless activities: the meticulous performance of ritual and ceremony; the singing of hymns, and a hundred and one other so-called acts of devotion. Worse than all of these has been the foolish expenditure of mental and moral energy in the cockpit of theological and ecclesiastical controversy, on the fierce embittered warfare of creeds and opinions. The history of man presents no more poignant tragedy than this appalling wastage of moral force.

Rex was slowly coming to a decision. Almost a Quaker, he was appointed to the Library and Evening Meeting Committees, but still, for him, worship was not confined to any religious gathering.

THURSDAY 9 SEPTEMBER 1920
A man's religion should be the basic centre of his whole being, from which all the line of his activity should radiate ... His working hypothesis of life should unify all his ideals and correlate all his activities, so that his life should resemble a cluster of branches from one stem. But once admitting that certain times and seasons, or certain acts, have a specifically religious character, an ever-widening fissure is made in the moral life that is fatal to wholeness, holiness and sincerity of character. The seamless robe of life is torn into 'secular' and 'religious'. The kingdom of a man's inner life, instead of being whole and indivisible, and ruled from one central source, is split into two or more petty states, each having its own code of laws and sets of moral sanctions. Much of the discrepancy of character, which is stigmatised by the world's coarse thumb as hypocrisy, is simply the results of setting apart particular times and observances as definitely religious. The professing Christian, who in business life is guilty of sharp practices, is not necessarily hypocritical, but, for the time being, his motives spring from that cluster of practical considerations, prudential maxims, and rules of conduct, which have gathered round his commercial life. His religion is a thing apart, whose authority does not extend over this portion of his life.

After much soul-searching, Rex finally took the plunge.

Worcester Place
Oxford
11 October 1920

Dear William King,

I am very happy to tell you that at the Witney Monthly Meeting, held here last Thursday, you and your wife were accepted as members of the Society of Friends. Please excuse me for not writing at once. I had hoped to see you, and in the rush of things, forgot to call.
I am glad to assure you that your application and our Report were received by the Meeting with universal sympathy. We all look forward to your membership with a deep sense of satisfaction. We are conscious that you are already a friend and that you are already in a position to help us to a truer understanding of our inheritance and a truer application of our faith.

I hope you will forgive the shortcomings you will surely find, but that you will not regard them as inevitable or hopeless; that you will fearlessly point them out and help us to correct them.

Believe me truly thy friend
Edmund New

Rex the Quaker, though, continued to wrestle with good and evil.

THURSDAY 14 OCTOBER 1920
... The problem of evil is too frequently allowed to ruin into mere speculative channels. Instead, this passionate feeling of intolerance and disgust in the face of world evil and world suffering should be regarded as the voice of God urging us along useful paths of service to alleviate the suffering and remedy the evil.

EASTER SUNDAY 27 MARCH 1921
Five months have passed since my last entry, and I am brought round to another method of approach towards the problems of evil suggested in my final paragraph of 14 October last year. This evening, I opened a discussion of 'Signs and Wonders in Divine Guidance', which led to the conclusion that there were signs all about us that the world needs mending; signs of the needs of our fellow men whose craving after the so called supernatural and miraculous, was a sign of spiritual morbidity and lack of tone.

We all have our times of spiritual depression – hours in which physical derangement darkens the windows of the world; days in which shattered nerves make life simply endurance. We become crushed with overwhelming thoughts of the uselessness of it all. The gigantic forces of evil, organised and entrenched, make us feel so helpless. We feel that we should like to slip out of the conflict and create a little monastery or retreat for ourselves, somewhat apart from the mad vortex of life and its problems. There is a craving for some opiate that will stifle the cries of this world, and give us rest. We feel that God sits afar off, and does nothing. Probably, like the exhausted prophet under the juniper tree, all we need is sleep and food.

We often think of matter as of something wholly outside of and apart from God ... We cannot with our corporeal senses discern the reality of anything, only its phenomenal and conditioned aspect. God's messages to us are no less messages because they are the natural efflorescence of subconscious processes, or because they fall from the lips of friends, or because they come from the pages of a book, than if they were blazoned across the sky in letters of fire. God's intimations come along the pathways of law and everyday experience.

WEDNESDAY 22 FEBRUARY 1922
J.N. [Mr New] spoke well at Meeting this morning on Man Friday's pertinent question to Robinson Crusoe 'and why did not God kill the Devil?' ... However we may disguise the ugly facts of evil – as 'atavistic tendencies' or 'the ape and the tiger within us' – the essential problem is still with us.

The devil is within us, and Rex's remedy was prayer and fasting and the adoption of reverent wonder.

SUNDAY 23 JULY 1922
They say miracles are past; and we have our philosophical persons, to make modern and familiar, things supernatural and causeless. Hence is it that we make trifles of terrors, ensconcing ourselves into seeming knowledge when we should submit ourselves to an unknown fear ... In 'All's Well that Ends Well' these words, put into the mouth of Lafeu, have a strange tone of modernity. They might have been written, anytime. Men have always been fond of 'ensconcing themselves into seeming knowledge', never more so than in the later half of the 19th century. The proud intellect, intoxicated by its unquestioned triumphs in many realms, thought itself equal to solving the riddle of the universe, seeping away mystery. Hackel and Buchner, with a dogmatism unequalled in theological spheres, announced with a flourish to trumpets that the idea of God was an unnecessary hypothesis. By the simple conjuring trick of putting into the hat all that they wished to get out of it they succeeded, for a time, in deceiving a superficial and over-credulous public. People were hypnotised by glib phraseology; by the light coinage of

superficial knowledge and constant talk about scientific laws, into accepting mere generalisations of observed phenomena as adequate and satisfying explanations.

We now know that science has solved none of the great and ultimate problems of life. It has only wrapped them up a little differently. They cannot tell us how such strange beings as ourselves came to inhabit this strange world. They can only echo the words of Sir Thomas Browne 'that we are men, but know not how'. The inherent improbabilities of another life are nothing to the inherent improbability of our being here at all, and perplexing ourselves with such questions. Whatever our attitude towards life may be, certainly it should include 'a sense of reverent wonder'.

The fresh arrangement of the child in the face of bird, flower, star, and tree should be transmuted into the humiliation of the wise before the ever-deepening mysteries of the universe. Many of us become case-hardened by use and wont, and in a world teeming with the marvellous remain unmoved and almost immoveable. Thus the demand for the extraordinary and sensational in fiction, the horrific and terrible! A true culture brings the faculty of surprise into the so-called simple and commonplace, and enables one to see the heart of mystery in flowers, stone, and tree. One sees the wonderful network of relationships that enmeshes the whole of creation. Dust, grass, insect, beast and man form a wondrous circle of being in endless flux. There is no need to race hither and thither in feverish haste to see the marvelous and sublime, it blossoms at our feet and overarches our heads.

Wonder is the dower of the child, but the hardly won acquisition of the man. Thrust out, for a time, by the proud pretensions of the meddling, pragmatic intellect, it returns at last enriched and sublimated. The 'gross rusticity of vulgar heads' is displaced by a 'devout and learned admiration'. Religion, too, has lost its sense of wonder. All mystery has been squeezed out of it; it has become almost synonymous with universal good will and social service. We have lost the poetry and beauty of the forest by cultivating merely economical trees. We must recapture something of that first fine careless rapture of the first Christians if we are to strike at the imagination of the world. The mysteries of faith and 'the marginalities of religion' are shouldered into the background, and all things reduced to the measure of man's mind.

With all this on his mind, Rex had little more to confide to his diary. The conclusions he came to in July 1922 were summed up in the first stanza of a poem, part of a collection he subsequently dedicated to Basil Blackwell.

Wistful Wonder! Thou that art
Priceless gift of childlike heart!
Pure religion's seed *and* fruit,
And of *poesy*, the root!
Mellow wisdom's fairest flower!
Manhood's crown! But childhood's *dower*!
Cleanse our eyes, that life may be
Ever touched with mystery

At the end of Rex's life, Basil wrote:

> From time to time he honoured me with his confidence, and during
> his last weeks at home I had several talks with him on terms of simple
> friendship, though most, I think, was said, as formerly, in the clasping
> of hands … his last talks with me, reveal the constancy of an austere
> spirit loyal to the Quaker discipline and to that of Marcus Aurelius –
> the spirit of one stretched upon the 'rack of this tough world', but in
> whom there was 'no shadow of turning'.
>
> Anyone who knew of or worked with him must be aware that
> we have lost something irreplaceable in his mastery of his calling,
> and the knowledge and judgment which he drew from the store of
> his vast reading. But this is not all. As I reflect upon the witness of
> his life and conversation, and upon the meditations recorded in his
> journals, a question insistently presents itself to me (I write with no
> sense of exaggeration): have we at Blackwell's these thirty-four years
> entertained unawares one who may deserve the tremendous title of
> Saint? [28]

Basil tended to hyperbole, and Rex would have been deeply embar-
rassed by such effusion. He wouldn't perhaps have minded being called
a *sage*, but even if he were, it was only because of his reading. Books
had provided him with a livelihood, an Oxford education as near as
it was possible to get without actually attending the University, and
they were his solace. While he read pagan and Christian texts and
'the works of the great Greeks and Romans – Plato, Aristotle, Cicero,
Seneca … the simple parables and sayings of the Galilean Peasant were
the bank and steel to the souls of countless multitudes, a light to their
path a foothold in the uncertainties of existence, and have opened up
unending vistas of thought and speculation'. Rex confided his inner
thoughts and ideas to his diary, while the books he was reading and
learning from refuelled his mind.

SEVEN

THE GOOD READER

To acquire the habit of reading is to construct for yourself a refuge
from almost all the miseries of life.

Rex King

B Y TWO OR THREE GENERATIONS before Rex's time, reading was
no longer an elite preoccupation, and children, as well as adults,
derived excitement from it.[1] Supplementing the traditional solid fare
of hymns and Bible readings were stories from the classics, poetry
and encyclopedia. If 'penny dreadfuls' were forbidden territory, more
ambitious readers could have a go at the weekly or monthly serials;
Pickwick Papers, first serialized in 1836, was a wild success.[2] But despite
the fact that literacy had substantially increased by the second half of
the nineteenth century, that books cost less because printing and paper
were cheaper, and lighting in the home was brighter, reading for pleasure among the toiling classes was limited to the few hours outside the
working day.[3] In addition, there is scant record of what they read.[4] For
researchers into working-class intellectual life, such as Jonathan Rose,[5]
Rex King's diaries would have been manna. They provide not just an
account of his life at work and at home but, with the copious lists of
the books he read, they are his *florilegium*. Books were his university,
just as others, who became famous writers – H.G. Wells and George
Bernard Shaw, for example – studied in libraries open to the public.[6]

In this world of books Rex was able to connect with the whole of
human thought and experience. Books were his 'boon companions'. He

Oxford 1930s, never alone with a book: 'To acquire the habit
of reading is to construct for yourself a refuge from almost
all the miseries of life', William Rex King, 1886–1950.

walked with them and talked about them in his diary. Reading made
his world go around; it was his solace, even when he was served with
notice to quit his rented house or had to have all his teeth extracted
because he could not afford to have his 'rotten battalion overhauled'.
As literary historian Stefan Collini suggests, books furnish the mind
in a form the bailiffs cannot repossess.[7]

Rex's choice of reading material was not always educational, in the
narrow sense, and some he described as illicit. Even as young as eight,
he used to walk long distances in the country around Cirencester to read

> surreptitiously halfpenny romances and boys' papers of the baser sort
> ... not allowed at home. By a kindly dispensation of providence, my
> boyhood was coincident with the days when Britannia was fervently
> and vociferously believed to rule the waves, and it was the fashion
> to put small boys into sailor suits. My sailor blouse, with its loose
> bulging cut and encircling elastic band, was admirably contrived for

my nefarious purposes, and I never walked abroad without a supply of contraband literature concealed about my person.[8]

Escaping after church, Rex would spend his pittance of pocket money at the newsagents kept by Mrs Dike in Cricklade Street, Cirencester. He wrote of buying 'Union Jack, a halfpenny periodical of exciting fiction, that was to become famous in its second number with the introduction of Sexton Blake for lovers of detective stories'. This he 'devoured secretly with great relish. This was the start of my interest in literature.'[9] But there was nothing secret about his habit.

> I became known as 'Penny Dreadful', which ... was uttered with such venomous scorn that I never failed to wince under the taunt. My chief tormentor was a very superior boy who lived at the Lodge Gates of Cirencester Park ... but I have the wicked satisfaction of knowing that retribution befell him – as on the rude children who shouted 'Go up, thou bald-head' to Elisha the prophet. My tormentor has been penned ever since behind the counter of a small provincial stationer's and bookshop not a hundred miles from his enormities.[10]

In finding his niche at Blackwell's, Rex fared better. 'Happy are the souls,' he wrote, 'who find congenial space for their labours ... life for them is prolonged holiday ... I am able, at will, to absent myself from the ledger and play truant with Phoebus, in his flaming chariot, or sport with Boreas in the idle fields of air.'[11] But he would have liked to have the freedom to become a writer, as his account of Hugh Walpole's literary beginning suggests. 'By a strange coincidence upon looking in the Sunday Dispatch [Rex is probably writing this at the time of Walpole's death in 1941] a first paragraph riveted my attention. "When eight years old, the son of a former Bishop of Edinburgh, managing to slip away from his governess, went into a bookshop, and bought a pile of penny classics, including The Talisman. (Later in a statement on the wireless he admitted to buying a Penny Blood, Marigold the Pirate). These books he smuggled home under his sailor blouse, and read secretly at night by candlelight in his bedroom." That was the start of his interest in literature.' But here the parallel ends. Walpole's childhood reading would have been like that described in 'that well-known passage in the fifth book of The Prelude where the poet congratulates Coleridge and himself that in early childhood their reading was unrestricted'. Less fortunate children were 'hourly watched, and noosed ... This unhappy lot was mine, for in my young boyhood I was tethered to a patch of scant pasturage – and had I not strayed into forbidden pastures – those "dumb yearnings" and "hidden appetites" of childhood of which the poet speaks would have starved of their food.'[12]

But the pasturage of Rex's childhood was not so very scant. Even as an adolescent he acquired considerable knowledge of the great English poets, partly due to the cheap editions increasingly available at the time, but also to his teachers. In his 1939 diary he mentions, with affection and admiration, two teachers at Cirencester Grammar School. Rex, like Basil and Basil's contemporary at OUP, Charles Williams (who, arguably, is at least as famous as Walpole), had the chance to go to a local grammar school, although Rex and Williams were scholarship boys. The school library would also have made up the deficit of books at home. 'The family library – forgive the word – was a heterogeneous collection of odds and ends ... a goodly number of hymn books and prayer books, with which ingenious devices were made to serve as the basis for our Sunday amusements; secular literature being strictly forbidden on that day.' The six volumes of Cassell's *Our Own Country* Rex deemed 'most excellent', but 'a surfeit of which gave me for ever after an unconquerable distaste for topographical works'. 'Watt's *World to Come*, Richard Baxter's *The Saints' Everlasting Rest*, Bunyan's *Pilgrim's Progress*, an imperfect copy of *Latham's Falconry*, three odd volumes of *Buffon's Natural History*, with some extraordinary wood engravings, a few books on confectionery, a birthday book, and a small tattered dictionary with many leaves missing' completed the King family's collection. 'Apart from *The Pilgrim's Progress*, which was enlivened with some spirited engravings, this was miserable fodder for a growing and explorative mind. And did I bleat piteously for more books? I was silenced at once with the undisputable fact that "I had not read all the books in the house".'

As an adult Rex accumulated:

pocketable volumes of viarian sustenance for fugitive and solitary walks. Time would fail me to enumerate all the volumes of this growing and ever-changing collection, but one is almost certain to find copies of *Emerson's Essays*, *The Meditations of Marcus Aurelius*, Coleridge's *Aids to Reflection*, Carlyle's *Sartor Resartus*, and above all many editions and translations of what in later years I am becoming to treasure as one of the world's greatest books, *The Imitation of Christ*.[13]

Sir Thomas Browne's *Religio Medici* was also a constant companion. 'This book is like an old-world garden full of charm and delicious freshness with flowers of rich thought and beautiful expression in wonderful profusion – well stocked with fruits.'[14] But as Rex sets off for church, he slips into his pocket, 'as viaticum for my homeward walk through Stanton St John, the Temple Classics edition of Wordsworth's *Prelude*'.[15]

Rex's own prelude was an article, 'The Day's Illusion', written and published in 1906 when he was only twenty. He conjured up a 'utopian State, a New Jerusalem', although not in the manner of William Morris or William Blake. His finger posts were the Platonist Sir Thomas Browne, Calvinist Carlyle and James Hinton. Of these he singled out Hinton, who had breathed life into Congregationalism in Oxford in the late eighteenth century but was now little known. Rex read *The Longer Life, Studies in Hinton's Ethics* by Caroline Haddon. 'In the chapter on Hinton the Seer, a contrast is drawn between him and Carlyle. Theology is not a sacred cow, but "the allegorical presentation of philosophy", "truth in the form of fiction".'[16] References to Hinton's work occur repeatedly in Rex's first, more extensive, diary. He was, for example, 'working the rough ground of Hinton's thoughts in *The Law-Breaker*' but feared the book too obscure, 'like some of the poems of Browning [and assumes] knowledge, which, unfortunately, the reader does not always possess'. He included himself in this indictment; he made little headway, for example, in his endeavour 'to pierce through the crust of Spinoza's ethical and political philosophy even with the help of James Allanson Picton' (another Congregationalist minister).

THEOLOGICAL TEXTS AND QUESTS

Judging by Rex's diary entries, and his reputation, it is religious works that come out top. As Fred Hanks once remarked at the Blackwell's staff tea table, Rex 'ought to have been an old Hebrew prophet'. 'This may be somewhat prophetic in itself,' Rex wrote in his diary, 'although his apostrophe to me as Jeroboam did not reveal a very strong grasp of Old Testament History.'[17] Away from the Old Testament, Rex continued his search for the truth with the less orthodox Hinton, more especially in his life and letters where Hinton's 'repeated injunction was "do not shut up the question"'.

sitting down to a sumptuous repast — with cream sandwiches of several layers, + almost as large as the table. There were several saucy damsels there — one especially in pink tights with a tiny tip of leather on the end of her foot. Upon the men + horses returning from the field, we got up to allow them to pass through a large wooden partition behind us. My little puss, exuding a very powerful + enervating perfume, began to clip me in her arms + shower passionate kisses upon me. Upon struggling to free myself from her intoxicating embraces, I awoke + soon tumbled out of bed ———— .

But now, to come to the sober realities of the day! I had a letter from Robert, who is anticipating a visit to Oxford this summer ... At present, he is having a new floor put down, so he is somewhat muddled and perplexed ———— .

I am continuing my study of Hinton — more especially in his "Life + Letters". His strongest mental characteristic is 'adhesiveness' or 'stick-at-itiveness'. This is illustrated in his oft-repeated injunction to his correspondents — "Do not shut up the question". He never allowed a thought to escape until he had got to the bottom of it. He had a great, unshakeable conviction that man's moral and spiritual emotions are in as true relations with the visible creation as his intellect; that "man's religious aspirations, his love, his worship, his loyal trust in the Unseen, all that lifts him above himself, are not a winding stair of a ruined tower leading nowhere, but are correlated to answering realities".

In which of the ancient Hebrew prophets shall we find a nobler and more heart-stirring vision than his passionate utterance: "I have seen Righteousness taking Pity to her bosom, and going forth, repentant that she has been cruel, to meet those who cannot restrain their passion, and saying to them: you also are my children. I have seen

'Do not shut up the question', Rex King, diary, 24 April 1919.

Hinton never allowed a thought to escape until he had got to the bottom of it. He had a great unshakeable conviction that man's moral and spiritual emotions are in as blue relations with the visible creation as his intellect; that 'man's religious aspirations, his love, his worship, his loyal trust in the unseen, all that lifts him above himself, are not a winding stair of a ruined tower leading nowhere, but are correlated to answering realities'. In which of the ancient Hebrew prophets shall we find a noble and more heart stirring vision than his passionate utterances. [Hinton insists] on the need of rediscovering the truth of the old commonplace maxims.[18]

Rex found in Hinton again and again Schopenhauer's premise from *Religion: A Dialogue*, 'that duties towards God and duties towards humanity are in inverse relation is a truth'. But, Rex commented, there is a great difference between 'knowing it' and 'finding it out'. As he says, 'We know too much, it is our irreverent familiarity with things that blinds us, so that we cannot see that we walk in the midst of miracles ... and trample beneath our feet the sublimest principles of philosophy.' Rex finds a parallel with this in the 'aphorisms of Coleridge in his "Aids to Reflection", a book that influenced Hinton very appreciably'.[19]

Rex consulted more and more theological texts during his quest.

The Christian Idea of God by Rev. W.R. Thomson, is for those whose sturdy minds like clambering amongst the Alps of theoretical metaphysics. Is the Christian idea of God merely the result of theological opinions ... much as the contending poetical claims of Sophocles and Euripides were decided on the Christophanic seals? After hammering my brain with the piece-meal opinions of Theodor Haring and Emil Schaden, Horace Kallen and Ernst Troeltsch and a multitude of others, I felt like Walt Whitman, who having listened to the proofs and figures of the learned astronomer wandered off 'In the mystical moist night air, and from time to time, looked up in perfect silence at the stars'. Outside a work of reference, I have never encountered such a host of high brows as are crowded together in the early chapters of this book. It resembles a brilliant salon, in which the remarks of the host are almost drowned in the general hubbub of conversation.[20]

In contrast, Henry W. Clark's *Philosophy of Christian Experience* and *Christian Method of Ethics* provided Rex with a 'rare insight, the distinction between the things we *do*, and the thing we *are*: while the things we do are often right, the thing we are is always imperfect ... there is little place for mere resolve to do what is right and to avoid what is wrong ... most of us drop into goodness occasionally'.[21]

Lowes Dickinson's book, *The Meaning of Good*, provided some lighter relief. 'Part of the peculiar charm of works of art consists in the fact that they arrest a fleeting moment of delight, lift it from our sphere of corruption and change, and fix it like a star in the eighth heaven.'[22] Laughter too, for Rex, dissipates 'the mists of ennui and life weariness ... But it has its counterpart. The derisive scorn of the intellect, regarding mankind with the amused detachment of the Olympian Gods, much as a child regards the feverish activities of a swarm of ants. Such is the laughter of Leopardi, whose dialogues I have been reading.'[23] Driven indoors by a bitter wind, 'after picking the plums in the paddock with the vociferous aid of the children', Rex indulges himself in 'sensational garbage' (probably a detective story). Feeling guilty, he turns to the Acts of the Apostles:

> By what seemingly crooked ways was Paul's earnest desire to go to Rome – expressed again and again in his epistle to the Romans – at last fulfilled. Many mighty conquerors, with their captives and spoils, had entered Rome along the Appian Way, scattering largesse amongst the turbulent rabble; but now here comes a solitary prisoner, bound in chains, hailed by a few of the brethren from Rome. The triumphal marches of the Caesars and Pompeys are now but a sounding tale, signifying nothing: but the world-wide effects of the entrance of that despicable-looking tentmaker into the Imperial City have been growing into the present day.[24]

Rex may also have been thinking of Quaker George Fox's experiences, which he had read of in his *Journals*. Fox's emphasis on a 'practical, fruit-bearing religion as opposed to a merely "rational" experience' led Rex to explore books dealing with secularism and science, but he always fell back on the intangible. Reading James Martineau, whom he considered to have 'one of the greatest minds of the nineteenth century ... with what delightful ease and freedom does he deal with (in his "Seal of Authority in Religion"), the profound problems of life! Again and again the unerring aptitude of a phrase on an epithet slants an involuntary exclamation of glad wonderment.'[25]

For Rex, the intangible concept of wonder took precedence over rational explanation:

> The scientific temper of the age is averse to mystery ... it will tolerate no half-lights, it does not, like Sir Thomas Browne, 'love to lose itself in a mystery'. It regards many religious conceptions as the riot of an empty and meaningless mysticism – the marsh lights of a disordered imagination. Yet all the ultimate realities of life and the universe are involved in mystery. If the man of faith cannot reduce God to an algebraic formula, no more can science the idea of matter.[26] We now know that science has solved none of the great and ultimate problems of life. It has only wrapped them up a little differently. They [scientists] cannot tell us how such strange beings as ourselves came to inhabit this strange world. They can only echo the words of Sir Thomas Browne 'that we are men, but know not how'.[27]

Rex had struck a seam of thought that Karl Popper and his moderators Thomas Kuhn and Peter Winch were to excavate; one that Freud and Jung were already exploring in the world of psychology. He must have read some Freud since he uses his analysis to probe the character of Firk in Thomas Dekker's *The Shoemaker's Holiday*: 'Firk, has a lovely wit [that] works on Freudian levels.'[28] Present-day psychology, Rex wrote in his commentary:

> has much to say about the important functions performed by the unconscious mind, both in the realm of physical ... and in the mental sphere, in determining mental bias, shaping character, etc. This is also true in the moral and spiritual realm – it is the unconscious that forms the true background and essential reality of our moral and spiritual life.

To substantiate his anti-materialism, Rex read the Rev. H.R. Haweis' *The Key of Doctrine and Practice*, written in 1884, which 'rejects the materialists who puts into their conception of matter all they wants to get out of it'. Rex decries the reductionist, 'the proud, intoxicated, intellect, thought itself equal to solving the riddle of the universe'.[29] He cites the attempt of G.T. Wrench, in his quasi-scientific work *The Grammar of Life,* 'to reduce the multiform activities of human life to three dominant instincts – the self-preservative instinct, the reproductive instinct, and the gregarious instinct'.[30] Rex finds Wrench's book 'excellently provocative of thought', but he comments, 'a man with an hypothesis to prove is a dangerous creature. His strongest weapon is often "his blind eye" to facts that would disturb his theory.' A reading of Haeckel and Büchner draws fire from Rex. They exhibit a 'dogmatism unequalled in theological spheres – announced with a flourish of trumpets that the idea of God was an unnecessary hypothesis. Stainton Moses' book "Spirit Teachings", goes the other way [when he writes of] the dictation of spirits from the other side of the veil.' What would people today think of this? Rex asked, but this 'does not destroy the possibility that these hopes and beliefs *are* the inspiration of higher beings'.[31]

A VARIED DIET, FROM SEXTON BLAKE TO COLERIDGE

Rex's diet of serious reading was often spiced by a 'cheap sensational story of crime and intrigue', which he found 're-creative and invigorating, like a hard drubbing with a bath towel'.[32] He is upbraided for this by a friend, but 'unrepentant, like a dog, I returned to my vomit ... *The Mystery of the Green Car* from the Austrian of Weissl – an enchanting concoction of murder, theft, and high intrigue – à la William le Queux!'[33] In his general choice of books and way of reading them, Rex followed Bacon's dictum. Some were to be read from cover to cover 'with diligence and attention', some 'tasted', some dipped into and 'some few to be chewed and digested'.[34] His choice was uncensored and he tried to keep an open mind. He read and reviewed a controversial new work, *Despised and Rejected*, 'a novel by a new writer treating of Uranianism and Pacifism. It is a very blurred piece of work – very similar in atmosphere to Tremaine's *The Feet of the Young Men*. Its chief interest is in the portrayal of abnormal sex relations and instincts, and its interpretation of the pacifist mentality.' The book, written by Rose Allatini under the pseudonym A.T. Fitzroy, had been banned and copies seized; did Rex get his copy through the Quakers?[35]

Rex's favourite authors, according to his colleague George Crutch, were Lamb, Emerson, Sir Thomas Browne, Wordsworth and Coleridge. But he also had a high regard for Milton, whom he parodied in his own poems, writing of 'Come pensive brute', and 'quips and cranks', for example. Rex much preferred Milton to Tennyson. Paul Elmer More, a contemporary American critic:

found two outstanding weaknesses of Tennyson: 'prettiness' and the spirit of compromise that mars some of his most-quoted work. This latter blemish he [More] illustrates from the stanza of the poet's dead friend into the heavenly host:

> The great intelligence fair
> That range above our mortal state,
> In circle round the blessed gate,
> Received and gave him welcome there.

Now turn to Milton's 'Lycidas':

> There entertain him all the saints above
>   In solemn troops, and sweet societies,
> That sing, and singing, in their glory move,
>   And wipe the tears for ever from his eyes.

Why is it that Tennyson [More asks] leaves us so cold, whereas at the sound of Milton's words the heart still leaps as at a bugle call? To these 'flies in the ointment', I would add the sense of conscious artistry and word-craftsmanship that one feels in many of his best lines ... does not always achieve the level of the art that conceals art.[36]

Rex found further evidence for his scholarly conclusion in a copy of *Mrs Leicester's School* by Mary Lamb; the volume may have been in Henry Beeching's library, which he had classified. He found there some marginalia of Coleridge's, in which Coleridge (STC) is having an imaginary conversation with 'Mr Terry, dramatizer of The Northern Enchanter's History':

STC: But you, I am sure, will rank him (Byron) on a par with Milton.

Mr T: Don't you think Lord Byron nearer to Dante, sir?

STC: Sir! I was talking nonsense, not blasphemy.

A SELF-EDUCATED CLASSICIST

Being able to move effortlessly through the centuries, from Dante through Milton to Coleridge to Gilbert Murray gave Rex a scholarly aura. From Murray's *Religio Grammatica*, 'a defence of the classical tradition', Rex pulled out the idea that 'all great forward movements are based on the study or idealisation of the past'.[37] Understanding the past was essential, and this required a knowledge of ancient languages.

This was a theme Basil Blackwell and the Blackwell old guard, such as Fred Hanks and Benjamin Henry, repeatedly rehearsed. Like many in the University, they feared that scientific subjects would oust classics. At Blackwell's, and from his reading, Rex acquired a level of proficiency necessary for his work.

Rex's knowledge of books loosely classified as classics set him apart. Basil granted that 'such was the extent of his book knowledge that only once I had him at a loss, when I quoted *Give him Long Melford*. But I had to yield to him the palm for reading with enjoyment of *Sartor Resartus*, which after several attempts remains for me but musty fodder.'[38] This was a brave admission coming from someone who had had the run of a bookshop from birth. Rex replied that he simply liked a bone to chew on; an aphorism borrowed from Meredith. His first copy of *Sartor Resartus* had come from 'the wonderful series of cheap books in Cassell's National Library'. Some years later, on a buying expedition, he went to the house of the late Henry Morley, one of the first professors of English Literature (UCL), who had edited the series. His daughter showed Rex the 'originals in red and yellow and blue covers with their advertisements for French Coffee, Borwick's Baking Powder, Mellin's food for infants and Woodward's Gripe Water. She told him that her father had received £5 for editing of each volume.' Such affordable editions not only educated Rex, but enabled him to enjoy 'holiday adventures of the soul'; away from 'the crowd at winter sports or seaside hotels who return sans money, sans energy and sans good humour'.[39]

Rex's days off were mostly spent at home. Customarily he took himself 'up Shotover' with his nose in a book. A favourite companion was 'old Montaigne's *Of the Inconstancy of our Actions*. In his puritanical way Rex felt it was just what he needed 'unless one is to be content to dream and drift, blown hither and thither by the shifting winds of circumstances or by the ever-changing currents of mood and desire'.[40] Rex, who did not want to dream and drift, often chose books for their corrective effect. In his second diary he wrote, in 1939, of the influence exerted by Fielding-Hall's *The World Soul*. 'Cold reserve ... smoothers [the] soul ... Separateness and aloofness are sins.' On the other hand, Rex thought, 'whilst the eye may be a window into the soul, the voice is an open door'. For reinforcement he turned to the work of William Tiptaft:

as eloquent on the blessedness of silence as the sage of Chelsea ...
There are those who mistake a vehemence of speech and a blistering
outspokenness for strength of character – who mistake noise for
power ... the devastating power of fire and flood... but it is a Pyrrhic
victory in which the victor loses more than the vanquished.

This could be, and probably was, a metaphor for life in Oxford, where
he would have been confronted, and intimidated, by those who made
a noise in an attempt to exercise social power.

Like Basil when he first started at Merton, Rex's book knowledge
was a hedge against such superiority, although hard to ignore in
Oxford. As he watched his children playing hit and run, he cast his
eye sideways to the students playing cricket on the adjoining Christ
Church cricket ground and was reminded of a saying of 'Froebel the
great educationalist', that 'a tree had been his great teacher'. Trees, he
saw, provided wood, which provided the bats used by all classes, and
were therefore a great leveller.

Rex did not often waste time worrying about social inequality. He
was too busy serving in the 'Outer Courts of the Temple of Literature,
as an itinerant and peripatetic reader'. In his first diary entry, Whit
Sunday 1918, Rex's release from toil enabled him to 'enjoy a standard
book', which is not possible unless he had 'plenty of leisure, vitality and
mental vigour – a combination rarely enjoyed in these stressful days'.
He selected *The Journals and Letters of Caroline Fox,* 'two delightful and
entrancing volumes, disclosing a most catholic and charming character
[giving] unforgettable glimpses of Wordsworth, Tennyson, Hartley and
Derwent Coleridge, John Welsh and Thomas Carlyle, John Stuart Mill
and J. Sterling, and many other notable characters'. On bank holiday
Monday he read Delolme's *On the Constitution,* 'full of legal phraseology
[but] a readable résumé of England's constitutional development'.[41] Yet
even on work days he would go home to face Asensi's *El Aeronauta* or
Shelburne Essays, which he found 'especially provocative of thought'.

[More] examines Matthew Arnold's famous definition of culture, and
draws a parallel between him and the Earl of Shaftesbury. In the essay
on 'Wordsworth' he supports Jeffery's dictum on 'The Excursion'
– This will not do. Mr More appears ultra-critical, and too austere
in his application of strictly logical rules to some of Wordsworth's
finest passages. The syllogisms of logical reasoning are not the best

instruments for the appreciation of poetry – which [are] rooted in the emotions ... [in] the heart as well as a reason of the intellect. One does not always desiderate a strict consistency in the poet. Still one is glad to find a critic in the tradition of Matthew Arnold and Sainte Beuve.[42]

The next day Rex limbered up, before breakfast, with Whittier's 'Mogg Megone'. Despite some reservations, he was enthralled: 'How skilfully does the poet anticipate the revelation in a later stanza of Ruth's criminal amour by a single adjective, which sets the reader wondering as to its suitability – until the whole story is ultimately disclosed? What thoughts of horror and madness whirl through the burning brain of that *fallen* girl?'[43] He likens Ruth's fierce cry of 'Give me the knife' to the 'dread scorn and resolution of Lady Macbeth'. It is hardly surprising that by the end of the week, with a heavy load of reading material and long days at the shop, Rex was in bed with a bad cold. For light relief, he seized on *Sketches by Boz*, only to strike:

a dark streak, in his [Dickens'] descriptions of Gin Shops, Pawnbrokers, and Newgate. Even here, we may see the germ of those qualities, which were to make Dickens so popular in later years. [His] keen observation, kindly sympathy, hatred of shams, touches of genial humour, are apparent on every page. Here, too, we find his characteristic playing upon two senses of a word in the tradition of Tom Hood ... 'There are some of the most beautiful-looking Pembroke tables that were ever beheld: the wood as green as the trees in the park, and the leaves almost as certain to fall off in the course of a year.'[44]

Still in bed, Rex finished over the weekend Blackmore's 'Creation' in Cooke's Little Series of English Classics. He saw the poem as 'an attack on the philosophical schemes of Lucretius and Aristotle, and difficult to read with any degree of pleasure. Blackmore was widely ridiculed in his day: and with other victims, was pilloried in the "Dunciad" of Pope ... judging from the "Creation" his fate was not undeserved.' Back at work, he re-read:

for the *n*th time that magnanimous, generous-hearted first book of Marcus Aurelius. What a gallery of portraits, with no hard lines of envy or disparagement, but full of rich, warm tones of gratitude and love. What an insight it gives into the nobility and charity of

Marcus himself! What different portraiture should we have had from a Thersites, a Nero, or a Tiberius? Yet I must confess that I feel a grudge against those who dissuaded Marcus from poetry and rhetoric. That he had the rod of poetry in him is evident from the second paragraph of the third book; and had this been watered and nourished, it would have added grace and warmth to his morality.[45]

It is extraordinary what Rex read in one week, laid up in bed and then, on some days, working a twelve-hour shift. Compare this with his holiday reading in August 1918, when he could tick off Robertson on Elizabethan Literature and the autobiography of Benvenuto Cellini. Robertson's book, Rex commented, 'is full of sane, well-balanced literary judgments, and proved a pleasant companion for the afternoon and evening. He is not gulled by conscientious carpentry in verse and his selection of prose extracts reveals an ear delicately attuned to the rich cadences and stately balance of the best Elizabethan prose.'[46] He added a note to read Hooker's *Ecclesiastical Polity*, and also some of the prose works of Nashe, as opportunity arose. Over the next few days, sitting in the shade of the walnut tree, he consumed Parson's *Source of England's Greatness* and a series of lectures by a Gloucestershire minister, then turned to Thomas Dekker, 'not quite such as incongruous a mixture as might be imagined', devouring *The Honest Whore, The Shoemaker's Holiday* and *Old Fortunatus*. He 'found a vein of kindly humour in honest Dekker, and one can imagine him as a boon companion of Charles Lamb in the Elysian Fields'.[47] But Dekker's *Witch of Edmonton* he judged to be 'poor, tasteless, stuff' noteworthy only 'as a partially sympathetic study of a witch. The plot is full of absurdities: and whilst the parting between Frank and Susan is not without a certain sweetness – the latter's oyster-like acquiescence in her own murder is stupid in the extreme. The whole murder scene is an artistic outrage.'

Shaking off his distemper, he gorged on the Jacobean playwright, Thomas Middleton. First, *A Trick to Catch the Old One*: 'a comedy which has affinities with Massinger's *A New Way to Pay Old Debt*s: a well-written robust piece of work', then *The Changeling* and *A Chaste Maid in Cheapside*: 'an uproarious comedy, chiefly notable for its lack of chastity. It is a feast of bawdiness and indelicate situations – but Allwit, the contented cuckold, is a character of some merit.' The following day he read *Women Beware Women* and *The Spanish Gypsy*:

the former tragedy is one of the solution-by-massacre type, but contains one scene which is unsurpassed as a direct transcript from life. I allude to the scene between the scheming Livia and Leantio's old mother. It is unforgettable in its almost surprising naturalness – the dialogue throbs with life. The opening of *The Spanish Gypsy* is also notable for its beauty and high finish.[48]

By the end of his holiday Rex had finished Cellini's *Memoirs*, whose 'antipathies are etched with an acid humour that bites into one's memory'. To cap Cellini, and ward off the 'dread of next week's work', he indulged in Montaigne's *On Pedantisme, Education, Solitarinesse* and, again, *On the Inequalities that there is between us*. He concluded his holiday reading with 'various chapters of the Acts of the Apostles', which reveal a theme much dwelt on by Rex: 'that of the ordinary man become extraordinary; the divine and eternal to be found in the common-place and in the inner-world'.[49]

Back at work, it was some days before he could pause to read. All he could manage, on Sunday evening, 1 September 1918, were two 'shilling shockers' ('now alas! Two shillings each') by John Buchan: *The Power-House* and *The Thirty-Nine Steps*. 'The latter is the richer in incident and sensation; but both are well written and good specimens of their type.' On Monday work was hard, but in the evening Rex managed Felkin's *Introduction to Herbart*. He read the chapter on Herbart's psychology, and found to his surprise that Glover's *Know Your Own Mind* was nothing more than an expanded paraphrase of Felkin. 'He did have the grace to slightly alter one or two of the psychological terms – otherwise, it appears a piece of flagrant plagiarism. Glover, however, has a rare gift of humorous exposition.'

As summer, and hopefully the war, ended, Rex read Hugo's *Notre Dame* – 'a terrible book ... pure, unadulterated horror ... gargoylishly grotesque ... The book is not so fine as "Les Misérables".' Changing tack, he reached for Lange's *Theory of Appreciation and its Application to Pedagogy*: 'An intensely interesting work, and full of raw material for profitable reflection. The Herbartian psychology is certainly a good working method, and its theory of appreciation is exceedingly illuminating upon many mental processes.'[50] In October he read Elizabeth Gaskell, who he thought had influenced *Nicholas Nickleby*. This was high praise from Rex, whose reading was rather short on women writers.

As the people of Lille rejoiced at the sight of the relieving troops, on Friday 18 October 1918, Rex plunged into an exciting story, *The Vulture's Prey* by the contemporary Irish writer de Vere Stacpoole. Days later, tucked up in bed on Basil Blackwell's orders, he read the plays of General John Burgoyne, best known for his role in the American War of Independence: *The Lord of the Manor, The Heiress* and *The Maid of the Oaks*. He had also acquired the works of Solis, including *Conquista de México*. Hearing the bad news of a family war fatality, he turned to *Lorna Doone*:

> What a gift of striking and picturesque phrase the author has! Every page is a delight, 'and we knew that we could not go astray, so long as we breasted the hill before us ... But in truth I used the right word there for the manner of our ascent, for the ground came forth so steep against us, and withal so woody, that to make any way we must throw ourselves forward, and labour, as at a breast plough'.[51]

On 10 November 1918 the Kaiser abdicated. Along with the news, Rex digested some reviews by Edwin P. Whipple, an American critic of the mid-Victorian era. 'His essays on Macaulay have much of the rigor and effectiveness of Macaulay himself. But he hails G.P.R James in an unmerciful fashion.' By the next day the armistice terms have been accepted by Germany. It was raining hard in Oxford, and Rex was too wet and cold to read much. For comfort, he spends a quiet afternoon with Lorna (Doone) and honest John Ridd.

The gloom of the December weather ('its gusts, its storm, and its depression') mirrored Rex's inner feelings. His mood persisted into the New Year, his reading mostly confined to religious texts and commentaries.

By May Day (1919) he was up for a little Shelley. Later in the week he consumed a life of Dickens in the Great Writers series, but the following Sunday (11 May) was, surprisingly:

> a day of literary turpitude – immersed in Sexton Blake and Peter Hunt!!! This latter called 'The Serpent Dog' is the most amazing riot of sheer idiocy that I have encountered. Futurism is a child to it. It is as though Chesterton and Lola had collaborated to write a detective tale under the influence of some baleful, judgement-destroying drug. William! William! Chosen to be an apostle! Poisoning your mind on the Lord's Day in such putrid streams of criminal extravagance.

Three glorious, summer-like days lightened his spirits. When he wasn't planting potatoes and kidney beans, he was holed up with Turgenev's *Virgin Soil* and Bacon's *Essays*. Finishing this sustenance, he reverted to Sexton Blake, 'quite a well-written romance, notwithstanding its horrible cover'.[52]

June called for something more heightening. Rex tackled Penty's *Guilds and the Social Crisis* and Carpenter's *Civilisation: its Cause and Cure*, the poetry of Samuel Daniel, and Beaumont and Fletcher. During two weeks in Chedworth with his family, Rex read Goethe's *Conversations with Eckermann* and Dostoyevsky's *Crime and Punishment* ('a great book'), Taylor's *Philip van Artevelde* and Matthew Lewis's *Bravo of Venice*. Back at work, O. Henry's 'capital yarns' were a digestive, as was 'Goethe's delightful poem *Herman and Dorothea*, full of a noble charm even in its English dress'. A day's respite, in celebration of peace (19 July) was spent with a pipe, Bosanquet's *Social and International Ideals*, and in the South Seas with Joseph Conrad.

> What a connoisseur in the vague, shadowy, instable emotions of the human heart! 'Man', as he says is 'A Smile of Fortune ... a capricious animal, the creature and the victim of lost opportunities ... In the instability of his emotions man resembles deplorably a monkey'. With what a cunning hand does he portray the sombre [and] half-evil.

What Rex admired in the Conrad atmosphere 'is the way worn truths strike home with unwonted forcefulness. His remark in "Freya of the Seven Seas" that "nothing gives away more a man's secret disposition than the unguarded ring of his laugh" is incontestably true – here you catch a man in "emotional undress" so to speak.'

Rex, although always chary of exposing himself, of 'emotional undress', made renewed efforts to get more reviews published. He had hopes of *John O'London's Weekly*, 'a new paper of an anecdotal, literary type'. He sent off two review articles, 'one to John O'London and one to The Daily Express. One of the former was promptly returned – so I retaliated with another on Thursday.'[53] The following month he submitted two more reviews via the Ideal Literary Agency. Waiting for a response, Rex immersed himself in Herman Melville and H.G. Wells and in books needed to prepare for his teaching at the Quaker Adult School. At the year's end, his idle scanning of 'a recrudescence of "Varsity Journalism"', left him out of sorts. 'Following the bad example

of "the Infant" and "the Topay of Ethiopia" we have had in quick succession "The Aunt", "The Spout", "The Goat", "The Cardinal's Hat";
also the official organs of the Labour and Tory Parties, the names of
which I am quite unable to recall.'[54]

Rex started 1920 in better spirits, elated on discovering 'an essay
by Chas Lamb, "Peter's net", in a copy of The Mirror, 1831'. Later,
he 'discovered that it appeared in his collected works under the title
of 'Reminiscences of a late Royal Academician'.[55] Venturing out in
spring 'despite the cold', he attended a performance of Twelfth Night at
Headington's Orthopaedic Hospital and read Grant Allen's monograph
on Charles Darwin: 'a fascinating book, but marred by mannerisms of
style. Allen has a peculiar penchant for double epithets – leashed like
hounds.'[56] But he finds Frances Power Cobbe's work 'full of her usual
good sense'; more high praise for a woman writer.

Over a rain-soaked Easter he read Mór Jókai's Eyes like the Sea and
takes up with another woman author, Elizabeth Braddon: 'Subcon-
sciously influenced no doubt, by hearing E. Morison on one occasion
lift us his voice in defence of that authoress. She certainly has the pen
of a ready writer,' he noted, on reading her Ishmael.[57] Progressing well
away from any tendency to misogyny, Rex looked at Edith Wharton's
The Custom of the Country. He found Beaumont and Fletcher's Scornful
Lady 'an amusing comedy, affording full scope for a magnificent display
of invective – of which Abigail gets more than her share. Loveless the
Younger does not get his deserts.'[58] As if this fodder weren't enough, he
took in Alaric A. Watts' marginal strictures on Wordsworth.

The onset of summer brought Rex a spot of good luck: a postal order
for 10s 6d, for a letter published in the Daily News. Aptly, he was reading
Eugene Field's Love Affairs of a Bibliomaniac, 'a delightful confection, full
of amusing anecdotes',[59] and then took up the following week Boswell's
Hebrides and Crofton Croker's Fairy Legends and Traditions of the South
of Ireland. In June, 'treacherously cold', Rex reverted to spiritual and
philosophical works to ward off a bad cold; 'in bed all the morning' he
devoured 'Sexton Blakes!' From The Palzer Experiment he extracts the
following, "'I can assure you that a man mentally troubled is a diseased
man, and his blood arteries and even his digestive organs show symptoms
of that fact".'[60] This offered no crumb of comfort, so Rex tried Tudor
Jones's The Spiritual Ascent of Man. Back at work in the rain, he fell on
George Henry Lewes's melodramatic romance Ranthorpe: 'crude in the

characterisation with a plot of the Family Herald type, but his comments on life and literature are worth the gleaning'.[61]

His summer holiday arrived at last. Rex walked the Fosse Way and wrote a review of Lofthouse's *Prophet of Reconstruction*. Lending a hand at hay-making, he still found time for Headlam's Bampton Lecture, 'Reunion'. But his frustration with the rain-sodden Cotswolds drove him to buy 'some Red Rag – a villainous black shag' which he smoked while consorting with Massinger's *Roman Actor* and *The Maid of Honour*. 'In Camiola [the Maid of Honour], Massinger reaches the topmost height of his female characterisation.'[62]

Back again in harness, Rex commenced Rolland's *John Christopher in Paris*, with which he was delighted: 'a great book, rich in thought and characterisation'. He also found Metcalfe's *Lowly Estate* 'a very companionable book of essays, in which I encountered many old friends'.[63] By the end of the summer, Rex was 'taking his mind out of cold storage' with Wordsworth, Milton and Crabbe. But for once the 'majestic diction' of *Paradise Lost* failed to grip him:

> I am afraid my aesthetic conscience has been deadened by too much obsession with moral, religious, and philosophical questions. The quotations 'who overcomes, by force hath overcome but half his foe', which occurs in Satan's speech, came with fresh impact, after the terrible experience [of war] which we have gone through.[64]

In Crabbe's 'versified tales' Rex found:

> rough-hewn characterisation but very little insight into the finer shades – the half lights and shadows – of temperament and disposition. His descriptive powers are more at home amongst 'the nettles, charlock and poppies' of impoverished land – in scenes of meagre poverty and meanness than in the beautiful and luxuriant.[65]

In peevish mood at the onset of autumn, Rex read Browning's 'La Saisiaz', 'with its obstinate questionings about the soul and immortality'. But he felt cut off:

> It is a humiliating thing that we are never able to convey to another a true or adequate expression of our thought. As the bird snatched from its leafy hermitage, and the shell taken from the beach, leave behind half their beauty, so the thought or idea torn from its mental background loses the larger part of its significance. Language, too, is a

very imperfect and inadequate vehicle of thought. Some words – such as man, spirit, religion, socialism – seeming single as they are, are really many sided and many-sensed, changing and shifting with the speaker. They are really 'parcels of ideas' and contain just so much as each speaker, or each listener, puts into them. As well hunt a rabbit in a wood with a stick, as try to kill a lie in a hostile mind by force of words.[66]

A sudden burst of Indian summer lightened Rex's mood, drawing him to Shelley's 'Ode to a Skylark', and helping him to face the evening lecture he will give on the *Religio Medici* of Sir Thomas Browne. As winter takes over, religious reading and reflection came to dominate his inner life. Convalescing from another bout of ill health, he was brightened by Ferrier's *Institutes of Metaphysics* and Buchanan's *The City of Dream*:

> The former is the most fascinating philosophical treatise that I have read for many years, and I shall return to it with pleasure when I am in better fettle. Buchanan's long poem might be called 'an epic of revolt'. Many sections are verbose and tedious, but the 'amphitheatre' is a poetical tour de force, being an attempt to portray the spirit of Ancient Greece. Many of the lyrics have a haunting pathos.[67]

Feeling better, he walked up Shotover with Weld-Blundell's version of Massinger's *Virgin Martyr*, which he 're-read with great satisfaction'.

Five months pass without Rex making any further diary entries, explained by 'a bout of spiritual depression'. In the spring of 1921, comforted by 'a botanising ramble to Stow Wood, returning through Elsfield', where he found, 'besides the usual early flowers, wild pansy, hop-trefoil and bulge. Cowslips, Stitchworts, Jack-in-the-Heads, and Cuckoo Spit.'[68] He faced Comte's *A General View of Positivism*, having finished Spencer's *Social Statics*, which he classified as 'Quakerism philosophically stated, at least, as regards his doctrine of force'.

Bogged down at work, Rex makes no more diary entries for the rest of 1921.

RESOLUTIONS AND REFLECTIONS

MONDAY 24 JULY 1922
Having decided to break the tobacco habit, I am purposing each week to replace the ounce of rotting vegetation, by some living leaves from the great tree of literature – thus building up a

permanent source of pleasure and inspiration, instead of dissipating good money in smoke! The first book purchased on the 'anti-nicotine' foundation was Kingsley's 'Water Babies' – a book which I had not read until Thursday last. 'Mon! It is a grand buik!' Written against all pride, vainglorious blindness and hardness of heart. What a wonderfully intimate picture it gives us of the author himself: his sympathy with the poor and downtrodden; his love of outdoor games and sports; his keen interest in nature; his antipathies against Irishmen, Americans, Roman Catholics, and feather-beds. With what gentle irony and genial pleasantry does he allude to individual and social shortcomings. His whip has a hundred lashes with which he tingles the ears of your Aunt Agitates, your Cousin Grannchilds, your dogmatic professors, your fallacious reasoners, your Baxterites, and End of the World Terrorists, your sentimentalists and shut-door and window folks, your puppies and tyrants of fashion, your quacks, pedants, fanatics, bigots, theorists, and bores. He has not the fire, smoke, and sulphur of Carlyle, nor the righteous indignation of Ruskin, but of the effectiveness of gentler methods of attack there can be little doubt.

Chance tossed into Rex's lap a copy of a short work by a contemporary of his, Gerald Gould: *The Helping Hand: An Essay in Philosophy and Religion for the Unhappy.*

Amidst a weedy tangle of irrelevant verbiage, it has flashes of genuine insight. 'One may remain untouched by the greatest and strongest powers, yet respond to the most trivial' is a matter of common experience. There is nothing intrinsically mean in trivial – only relatively so. A brick-wall may be an eye-sore for twenty years, but in some strange vivifying moment of the 21st year, it may be a gateway into wondrous realms of imagination ... In the kingdom of spiritual, even aesthetic, influences – in that ever shifting interplay of thought and circumstance, matter and mind, deed and emotion, which constitutes the raw-material of character – a sigh, a smile, a violet by a mossy stone, may outweigh, in influence, things and events apparently of more importance and weight ... 'One may be blind to the sunrise and the sunset, and find illumination in a candle.' What a forcible illustration of this we have in Coleridge's story of the awakening of his poetical powers. How true, too, as Gould says later, that 'everybody, probably, has moments of sheer physical exaltation, when they feel capable of conquering all difficulties'.[69]

Feeling a spot of indigestion coming on, Rex's remedy was Anthony Trollope's *Ralph the Heir*. He found it restful to get away from 'today's subtle-analytic and psychological novels' into the 'broad highways of Trollope's straightforward narrative and boldly outlined characterisation':

> Mr Neefit, vulgar, illiterate, and indelicate ... is drawn with Hogarthian zest. His wife, too, is drawn with a sure pencil. Wealth, and a dwelling in the fair suburb of Hendon, did not bring unalloyed happiness, for here 'she was debarred by a sense of propriety from making those beef-steak puddings for which within her own small household, she had once been so famous'. What an illuminating glimpse we get of the Rev. Gregory Newton, when we are told 'he thought that Dissenters were – a great mistake'.[70]

Come autumn, he dipped again into Birrell's *Essays*, Cowper's *Letters* and Amiel's *Journal*. 'This last book is full of illuminative and beautiful thoughts fascinatingly expressed. It is a mine that invites further investigation.'[71] As 1922 drew to a close, Rex was attracted by 'two striking novels' by a popular Norwegian, Johan Bojer: *The Face of the World* and *God and Woman*. In both there is 'that stern facing of "pain and suffering" which we expect from Scandinavian writers. He does not truckle to the convention of the happy ending.'[72] For variety Rex tackled *The Prisoners of Hartling* by Beresford, *The Chaste Wife* by Swinnerton, *Blinkers* by Vachell and *This Freedom* by Hutchinson.[73]

Back with his family in the Cotswolds the following autumn, Rex wrote philosophically of pain, love and faith, but said little of his reading. He relied on Mary Slessor of Calabar for contemplations and reflected on George MacDonald's advice in *The Seaboard Parish*. "'It was rather hard for poor Milton, though, wasn't it father." "Wait till he says so dear. We are sometimes too ready with our sympathy, and think things a great deal worse than those who undergo them. Who would not be glad to be struck with such blindness as Milton's?"' But re-reading *Cranford* delighted him.

> A delightful piece of work, as dainty and fresh as a piece of old china, and with all the lavender-sweetness of the little world it charmingly portrays. The amusing foibles and piquant peculiarities of the feminine population of Cranford are done in soft-etching as it were – with no trace of bitterness, or it is a book to place cheek by jowl with 'The Vicar of Wakefield' and the 'Essays of Elia'.[74]

Although Rex continued his reflections, he was less inclined to commit them to paper – life had become too hectic.

In October 1924, Rex was knocked back by the death of his kindly employer, Benjamin Henry. Basil, who admired and respected Rex's deep and wide-ranging appreciation of literature past and present, invited Rex to formally take on his father's mantle, as antiquarian specialist. Rex was so burdened that he wrote little more in his diary, although he mentioned Thackeray's *Esmond* and the letters of Jane Welsh Carlyle. But towards the end of his first diary he reflected, on 4 January 1925, on the nature of books:

> Milton's high estimate 'of the preciousness and potency of good books' is in no wise an exaggeration. The worth of a true book cannot be expressed in the currency of commerce, but in the coinage of thought, inspiration and permanent soul-enrichment. Furthermore, the books we read exert a powerful influence upon our life. We cannot obliterate the ideas received from books: they become interwoven into our mental texture and go so far to make or mar our character: the quality of our thought is the quality of our living. Our outward life is but the expression of our inward thought. The picture gallery of the mind should be enriched with that which is beautiful, pure, wholesome; it should be hung with lofty ideals and noble aspirations, flooded with light of purity and moral excellence.

Since books had such an influence on both the inner and outer life, Rex warned that they must be chosen with care. 'They may either "bless or curse" – they may open up to us a heavenly realm of pure joys and "unreproved pleasures" or drag us down to hell.' But how do we know a good book? Rex asked himself.

> I can offer no better standard of judgement than that of Apostle Paul in his letter to the Philippians: 'What so ever things are true. What so ever things are honest, what so ever things are pure, what so ever things are lovely, what so ever things are of good report' … If we but substitute the word 'books' for the word 'things' we have here a splendid standard of choice.[75]

Thinking of the reader, Rex turns to Charles Lamb:

> In one of his essays Lamb writes of 'a class of sheer readers whom I can never contemplate without affection – the poor gentry, who, not

having the wherewithal to buy or hire a book, filch a little learning
at the open stalls, the owner with his hard eye casting envious
looks at them all the while, and thinking when they will be done.
Venturing tenderly, page after page, expecting every moment when
he shall interpose his interdict, and yet unable to deny themselves the
gratification, they snatch a tearful joy'.[76]

Rex would gladly ally himself with Lamb's 'poor gentry', but his
conscience got the better of him:

I cannot steal so much pleasure without the occasional expenditure
of a few coppers ... Upon one such occasion, I alighted upon a good
clean copy of the meditations of Marcus Aurelius for which – after
a short inward debate between thrift and book-hunger, in which the
latter carried his motion – I deposited a large sum of 3d and trudged
home contentedly. Notwithstanding that I had battened my mind
upon its pages for several years; its nectaries still contain inexhaustible
supplies of mental nourishment.[77]

Rex's admiration for Marcus Aurelius Antoninus, the adopted son and
heir of Emperor Antoninus Pius, knew no bounds.

His reign was troubled. He was called upon to defend the Roman
Empire against the hardy German tribes on the Danube and Upper
Rhine, and against the 'insolent Parthian' of the East. His dominions
were ravaged by plague and famine. His throne was assailed by
Avidius Cassius, one of his generals in whom he placed the utmost
confidence. In the midst of all the dread warfare against savage
hordes, the primal forces of nature, and those of his own blood, he
possessed his own soul in serenity and purity, ever generous and full
of compassion. When he heard of the assassination of the revolted
Cassius, against whom he was marching: 'he was sorry', he said, 'to
be deprived of the pleasure of pardoning him'. Such was the spirit of
this heathen emperor. Tis the debt of our reason we owe for not being
beasts.[78]

Rex would have liked to be as brave as Marcus Aurelius. But he contented himself by reading about him. Reading made Rex a fulfilled
man, in the sense Bacon intended. Books provided the tools for his
writing, and a solace during the long arduous days of two world wars.

EIGHT

THE PATRIOTS

We have conquered the Germans – now comes the infinitely
greater conflict, to conquer all feelings of mere vindictiveness and
revenge, to conquer the pride of victory, and to lay the foundations
of a new world order. The nation has been rendered malleable by
sorrow – God grant that we may be subjected to the moulding
influence of the highest and noblest and not wasted and marred by
the reactionary forces within the nation.

Rex King

IN 1853, at the start of the Crimean War, Benjamin Harris had been
revolted by the 'insatiable appetite of his Library readers for the diet
of blood and gore dished up by the popular press'. It overshadowed his
children's lives, just as the atrocities in South Africa in due course shaped
their children's attitude to war. And war continued to haunt Basil, the
First World War more than any: 'I seldom enter my beloved College
without a pang, for the names of so many of my contemporaries are
engraved on the memorial to those killed in the Great War.' Lest he
should forget, he kept to hand Barbara Tuchman's *The Guns of August*.

As a student, before the war, when Matthew Arnold's Oxford was
still 'whispering from her towers the last enchantments of the Middle
Ages', Basil had sensed impending doom. Studying classics 'would
leave no intelligent boy in any doubt that war was a brutal business'.[1]
Basil's favourite was Thucydides, who had 'provided a rational basis
for war'. But what was rational about the arms race and 'Germany's

Officer Cadet Basil Blackwell, OUOTC, signal section camp, Salisbury
Plain 1908, with T.E. Lawrence cross-legged, front row left.

envious challenge to British sea power'? Basil's contemporaries 'seemed
unconcerned about the Kaiser's posturings', but he felt compelled to
join the Oxford University Officers Training Corps. A photograph of
the signal section camp on Salisbury Plain in 1908 depicts Basil with a
slight, crossed-legged youth sitting at his feet.[2] Even then, recalled Basil,
'we felt there was something extraordinary though indefinable in this
quiet, shy little man, later known to history as Lawrence of Arabia'.[3]
At the time, however, Basil was more mystified by his inability to hit
the target during rifle practice. He attributed his failure to a lack of
skill. When war finally came, Basil emphasized his willingness to serve,
but his bad eyesight, coupled with his susceptibility to bouts of fever,
which had first beset him travelling around Greece as a student, earned
him a 'courteous rejection'.

Instead of going to war, Basil joined up as a special constable, and
during the Second World War he commanded the local branch of the
Home Guard and acted as a fire watcher. (Wanting to play an active
role in preventing a second world war, Basil thought of writing to

ask 'the Pope or some other Christian leader to sequester broadcasting stations throughout the world and recite the Lord's Prayer to a worldwide audience. But before I could put this idea to the Vatican or to Canterbury, Germany had invaded Poland.'⁴)

The Blackwells, men and women alike, were patriotic. Basil's wife Christine gave every support to the war effort: in the First World War she contributed to food distribution (helped by her mother-in-law Lilla, who was a great fruit grower in the large garden in Linton Road); in the Second she ran the food bank in Appleton practically single-handed, and took in refugees. Many of the girls of Basil's youth were the sisters of First World War soldiers, and his own sister, who didn't have children, served as a nurse at the Front; in the Second World War she served as a hospital matron. Their cousin, also called Dorothy, was married to Sir Melville Arnott, who was one of the first medics to enter the Bergen-Belsen concentration camp in 1945, and Basil kept a file of cuttings about the horrors endured by inmates; it added to his indictments of war.

As 'A Dreadful Radical' has told, before the First World War Basil had associated with the renowned pacifists Lady Ottoline Morrell and Bertrand Russell, inwardly digesting their gloomy prognostications. When, fifty years later, an aged Russell entered the fray to 'ban the bomb', Basil was to write dismally of the 'potentiality of contraries' in the physical world that had 'reached its apogee in the atomic bomb'. Basil dealt with the troubling reality of war by making up parables:

Once upon a time there was a man who had a lovely garden but a bad neighbour. His bad neighbour used to break through his hedge and steal his flowers and fruit. The man with the lovely garden did not know what to do to get his own back on his troublesome neighbour. So he went to two advisers and asked them what he had better do. The first one said, 'Here is a packet of gun-powder. Load a gun with this, lie in wait for your neighbour, and the next time he comes through your hedge, shoot him in the leg. Then you will get a bit of your own back.' The other adviser said, 'You can do better than that. Let's make a rocket with gunpowder; then ask your neighbour to come in through your front gate and help you to let it off.' Well, as good fortune would have it, the man took this advice. He invited his neighbour, who came in fearing what he was to be asked to see, and together they lit the rocket. It shot up heavenwards on a path of

Demanding officer: Basil Blackwell in the Home Guard.

gold, made a most joyful bang, and scattered stars of all colours across the sky. The two men watched with delight, standing side by side steadfastly gazing up into heaven.

But he was doubtful of the efficacy of this one. Could individuals be so easily reconciled? They were all too often caught up in the machine; even in the shop, 'young recruits seen to burst with health were fattened up before being sent to fight'. Basil's old school and college friends 'had become cannon-fodder that way, dragged into war by the authorities'.

Apart from Basil, his father, elderly members of staff and a few newly recruited ladies, all the men at Blackwell's were called up. The apprentice Geoffrey Barfoot, called up when still in his teens, kept his tone light-hearted, though, typically, he never divulged what he truly felt:

Len Jarvis, Mr B's male shorthand typist, was the first to go to war. He was a bandsman of the 1st/4th O.B.L.I. and at camp when war was declared. Gradually many of us disappeared. We were lucky for most of us came back, except my old pal Cyril Pinkney; Cyril's first name was in fact Albert; he fell in pas-de-Calais on 23 April 1917 and is named on the Arras Memorial. During my own period as a POW in Germany and Belgium, the Blackwells and their staff contributed to the cost of food parcels sent by the British Red Cross, including bread from Copenhagen. Unfortunately, very few parcels reached me. The first, to my very great disappointment, was a pair of Army boots. They were, however, very welcome for I had been without boots and shuffling along some nine months in a pair of Dutch wooden clogs.[5]

'THE GOD THOR ROSE UP'

On 21 March 1939, Rex King wrote in his diary:

> many times during the last few days of feverish excitement over the rape of Czecho-Slovakia, my mind reverted to the closing months of the Great War. It had concentrated the minds of those working in the shop. Went back to business after tea to sweep the desk of some accumulations of work. Little time or energy for original thought, the inroads of business are becoming day by day more insistent.

Business had gone on, however, and Rex, left behind in the shadows, recorded in his diaries life on the home front in the last months of the First World War. 'The god Thor rose up in 1914,' he wrote, 'and the church could not resist the fierce hatreds that prevailed.' His writing opens a window on to the swirling mix of the mundane and earth-shattering that encapsulate daily life in a country at war.

On Whit Sunday 19 May 1918, he imagined church services in the war zones, 'in the field, on troop ships and in hospitals. There is an uneasy calm in Oxford, as local people went their own way to church, or not.' While he enjoyed 'quiet refreshment' on bank holiday Monday, south-east London was bombed. Writing a diary helped him to survive these outrages, 'to take possession of himself', a benefit written about by Jean-Paul Sartre in his Second World War diary, and by Virginia Woolf, from the safety of her home in the country.[6] Rex attempted to entertain his colleagues with regular correspondence. A letter to Will Hunt 'was full of whimsicalities and exaggerations ... how many untruths does my imagination and love of mystification lead me! I hope the Lord loves a cheerful liar.'[7] Hunt was sick of Army routine, and Rex attempted to divert him on another occasion with his account of a brush with a horseshoe.

Found a horseshoe in Broad St: dismounted from cycle and camouflaged it under my overcoat. Soon after nine, Mr Hanks comes in with the stunning announcement that his son is home on leave unexpectedly. I could do no other than give over my holidays. Walked up and down the shop with an imaginary halo encircling my head: but, immediately afterwards, cut my head severely against the corner of a cupboard. I learned that halos are not so efficacious as steel helmets in warding off injuries. Today's misfortunes, once and for all, have exploded the myth that horseshoes are omens of good luck.[8]

To console himself Rex goes blackberrying with his two young children, in a 'heavy thunderstorm'. Drying out, he reads Montaigne's *On Pedantisme*. 'How long must men philosophise?' Montaigne answers, 'Until such time as they who conduct armies be no longer blockish asses.' That spring, Rex had written of 'a regular singing morning – full of sweetness and light, the singing of birds and the smiling of flowers', only to be dragged down by thoughts of 'that bloody struggle in France, the loss of Soissons, the peril of Rheims and the healthy young lives spilled on the horrible atlas of Mars!'[9]

Rex was fearful as his workmates departed for the Front. But, disallowed military service, he filled a gap: 'The new harness rubs a little for the time being,' he wrote on 4 June 1918, as sales, rather than declining, were booming, with books for the troops and for colonial universities. What was Rex thinking of, sitting in his socks waiting for his only pair of boots to be mended? Had he been talking to the editorial assistant at work, Dorothy L. Sayers, who cannot see socks without conjuring up the mud of Flanders Field: 'the shoes and socks buried underneath it'?[10] Flanders triggered one of Rex's sonnets, written for a dead friend, and another, 'for many youths', prompted by a saunter in his garden.

> I. Lo L.A. Klemantaski (*8th Royal Berks ... B.E.F. 1916*)
> O'erspent by toil, I climb the hillside bare,
> So muse awhile, in Nature's starlet shrine;
> And, as I halt, upon the last incline,
> I see resplendent, in the cloudless air,
> Proud Jupiter and Venus – that same pair
> Of burnished stars, which in the Serpentine
> Were glassed so sweetly on that night divine
> We stole from earth by friendship's golden stain.

But thou, my dearest friend, art far from me,
In noisome trench, on Flander's dreary plain;
Yet thou, perhaps, those flaming orbs wilt see,
And soul with soul will meet in thought again.
May He, whom stars obey, encompass thee,
And crown with joy these months and months of pain.

Death's Caprice
I saunter round my tiny garden plot,
With daffodil and narcissus displayed:
And there! all shattered by a childish spade –
I see with grief, my budding bergamot
That I had nurtured in this favoured spot,
Dreaming of days to come when fruits of jade
Would glow, dependent, in the leafy shade –
But now, my tree and treasured hopes are not!

Thus many youths, with golden gifts endured,
And gracious virtues swelling in the bud,
Are beaten down, e'en in the spring-time flood
Of heart & brain; and War, in captious mood
Despoils both gifted mind and noble blood,
And robs the earth of their beatitude.

Rex's diary continued to chart the course of the war and its effect
on those 'over here'. He noted anniversaries of the fallen that he knew,
and more lives lost, and an accidental death added to the pathos.

SATURDAY 11 MAY 1918
Called at Oxford Chronicle Office for two books for review …
Heard the sad news that Mr Kenneth Graham's only son 'Alastair', a
student at Christchurch, killed on the railway near Post Meadow a
few days ago.

SATURDAY 25 MAY 1918
News received that Richard, my wife's brother, was in hospital,
suffering from the effects of poison gas.

TUESDAY 28 MAY 1918
This is the second anniversary of dear Louis' death. My thoughts have
been hovering around that spot near Béthune, which enshrines his
mortal remains. Wrote a short letter to his mother.

SATURDAY 1 JUNE 1918

June opened with royal splendour this morning. A swarm of bees settled on Broad St a few yards from the shop, and were successfully taken by some enterprising individual, who calmly flicked them into a cardboard box with a feather. The news this morning was of a serious character, and many wonder if Foch's 'army of manoeuvre' is not more or less a myth. It is certain that the French are almost at the end of their resources – after four years of unparalleled fighting, and with a population that has been dwindling for many years. Mr Presley was passed into grade III at his medical examination this afternoon; and is thus liable to be called up for service in fifteen days.

The news began to be more reassuring, thought Rex: 'defence appears to have settled down into some degree of stability'. But still more men were being called up and sent for duty: 'Mr Hanks passed into grade II' and (Friday 7 June 1918) 'Mr Hunt safely landed in the R.F.A.'

TUESDAY 25 JUNE 1918

The news that the Italians had captured 45,000 prisoners dwindled down to between 4,000 and 5,000 in the evening.

WEDNESDAY 26 JUNE 1918

Another harassing day at business (home after 9.40). Mr Hunt paid a visit, he on leave for a few days after being vaccinated and inoculated. He is expecting to go abroad next week.

THURSDAY 27 JUNE 1918

A gloriously fine morning, but filled with the buzzing of aeroplanes. Had a visit from Mr Rowles in full uniform, looking quite robust after a special feeding-up period at Blackpool prior to going abroad.

MONDAY 1–WEDNESDAY 3 JULY 1918

Strenuous toil from morning until night. Mr Rowles came in (Tuesday) to say goodbye before going to an unknown destination ... Mr Cooper collapsed on Wednesday afternoon – probably Spanish influenza which is raging throughout the country, overthrowing tens of thousands ... There are even queues at the chemists for quinine and 'other tonics'. Lord Rhondda died today (Wednesday): his death probably accelerated by overstrains in his office of food controller.

MONDAY 8 JULY 1918

News of the assassination of the German ambassador in Moscow. Mr Hanks to go for medical examination on Friday.

But Rex had the loss of German lives on his mind: 'How terrible to think of the Kaiser's life-long crusade for large families – now that the fiendish end of this gospel of procreation is made clear on the grim battlefields of Europe!'[11] But domestic reality obtruded, in particular food shortages: 'Emily's sister Elizabeth paid us a short visit, bringing a few pounds of blackcurrants for jam. Fruit is very scarce indeed.'[12] (Just after the war Rex was told by a friend at church, 'who had just returned from Austria, having been interned for over four years, that the food in the prison was often better than that of the villages around here. His own condition does not betray any signs of starvation!'[13])

And work is harder: by July 1918, 'the shop is closed at one o'clock each day, consequent upon the continual diminution of staff'. But as the battle on the Marne continues, tragedy strikes close to home.

SATURDAY 13 JULY 1918
Emily's sister brought the sad news that her youngest brother was killed at the front last Saturday. Both legs shattered, and only regained consciousness long enough to give his home address. Mother sent news that Maggie had given birth to a strong, healthy daughter. Thus we get the whole cycle of birth and death in one day.

THURSDAY 18 JULY 1918
More torrential rains in the morning and early afternoon, but delightfully bright and fresh after tea. Went back to business, and broke the back of a large Canadian order. The new big German offensive on either side of Rheims apparently brought to a standstill. French open a counter attack today on a 28 mile front.

SATURDAY 20 JULY 1918
News that my cousin Cecil has been gassed and dangerously wounded, apparently very little hope of his recovery ... In the face of such tragedies – experienced daily in thousands of homes – it is a sin to talk of *good news* from the front. There can be no good news in such a devilish thing as war. Foch's bag of prisoners amount to over 20,000, and about 360 guns ... Mr B.H.B. gave me a nice calf copy of 'Guesses at Truth'.

Rex, like many people, is very sensitive to the weather, and 'reassuring news' that 'the German resistance has broken down between the Ourcq and the Marne, and that the Allies are in full pursuit' coincides with a distinct improvement in conditions. 'It has been, altogether, a bad three weeks for the Crown Prince [Wilhelm, the Kaiser's eldest son], whose popularity should be waning considerably.'

MONDAY 29 JULY 1918
Mr Hanks commences his holiday in an outburst of sunshine. Oxford terribly hot. Mr Hunt removed to a machine-gun school at Uxbridge: a 'better 'ole'. Did two pages of the Rhodes University order ...

WEDNESDAY JULY 31 AND THURSDAY 1 AUGUST 1918
News of the assassination of Von Eichhorn, the German dictator in the Ukraine. Lord Lansdowne launches another lengthy letter advocating an immediate offer of terms.

SATURDAY 3 AUGUST 1918
The sight of a poor Australian youth – once, no doubt, sane and strong – gibbering and moping like a brainless ape in the High St has brought home to me the horrors of war and of its eternal devilishness more powerfully than the hundreds of crippled men about the streets.

The fourth anniversary of the war, Sunday 4 August 1918, 'opens more auspiciously for the Allied cause: the news that the Germans are retiring beyond the Veste towards the Aisne. Over fifty villages were retaken yesterday – that is to say fifty groups of blackened, smoking ruins.' Rex was happier, though, on holiday with his family near Cirencester.

SUNDAY 11 AUGUST 1918
Everyone elated at Haig's success on the Somme: and throughout the day there was a constant stream of people to read the latest telegrams, displayed at Mr Matthew's shop in Crickdale St.

MONDAY 12 AUGUST 1918
Visited the local Food Office to get permission to deal with Cirencester tradesmen; and after bagging a week's supplies, we walked to the M.S.J.R. to entrain for Chedworth. Sat out under the walnut tree reading Parson's Sources of England's Greatness, published about 1850. This author, minister of Ebley, Glos, a liberally-minded man, has something of Cobbett's fire and gift of strong satire – especially in dealing with the bench of Bishops. Played 'hey pass and repass, pindy pandy, which hand will you have'. A happy day.

MONDAY 19 AUGUST 1918
Received a long letter from Mr Hunt, who is now undergoing a nine
weeks course of instruction in the machine gun.

THURSDAY 22 AUGUST 1918
Went to borrow newspaper from Aunt Rhoda: and sat down on a
grassy slope in the orchard to read it, but was frequently disturbed
by the affectionate regard of a little black pigling. Stretched our
skins with deliciously greasy fatty cakes. This has been the only day,
during our holidays, that has been free from the continual droning of
aeroplanes overhead.

Back at the shop, war on a different front was imminent: 'Mr Cooper
fell foul of Miss Whitford, by telling a customer that twenty one of the
fellows had gone, leaving only three to carry on – thus ignoring the
female element! Whereupon the fullness of her wrath descended upon
him!'[14] Rex met some friends 'going to a meeting of working bakers
to formulate a demand for £3 per week minimum wage'.[15] In the real
war, he has an inkling that peace is in the offing, but the problem of
conscience versus duty still troubled him.

SUNDAY 15 SEPTEMBER 1918
Received the news that Austria was inviting the belligerent powers
to a secret, non-binding conference to find a basis for peace. Went to
Friends' Meeting in the morning. Quite a full attendance. A husky
young fellow, wearing a silver cross in his buttonhole, gave us his
experience. He joined the army in the early days of the war, and soon
gained a commission. At a Church of England service, however, light
came into his soul through hearing the 30th chapter of Isaiah read as
the lesson. He felt that as a Christian, his place was not in the army.
He therefore resigned the commission, and became an agricultural
labourer at 25/– a week. He also spoke of the difficulty of praying
in a tent, where no one was in sympathy ... After he had finished,
a uniformed officer spoke of the insidious danger of a religious
ostentation, and thought it better that the tenor of one's whole life
should bear testimony to one's religion rather than set attitudes of
devotion etc ... He also put in a plea for the nobility, selflessness, and
sincerity of the soldiers who were unable to see 'eye to eye' with his
conscientious brother ... He was a poor halting speaker, but his words
were better flavoured than his unctuous comrade.
    I could not help reflecting upon the experience of Chris Laslett
about whose sincere search after the truth there cannot be the faintest

doubt. He has been led by a sense of duty from the Red Cross into shouldering arms with his brother in the muddy trenches. His conscience, delicate though it is, has led him *into* the army and not out of it. The workings of conscience are conditioned by the mental content of the individual, and one cannot usurp the conscience of another ... The fundamental basis of any religious rapprochement must be the willingness to accede to the sincerity of those whose views differ from ours as much as they should give to ours.

'News arrived,' Rex wrote on Monday 30 September 1918, that 'Bulgaria has surrendered unconditionally to the Allied Powers. This will isolate Turkey from the Central Powers and her defection from Germany and Austria should only be a matter of a few weeks.' At the same time, he attended a meeting of the Fellowship of Reconciliation 'on Forgiveness and the Social Order'. A few days later it gave Rex pause for thought.

SUNDAY 13 OCTOBER 1918
Everyone cheered by the news that Germany has virtually surrendered to the Allies and has accepted President Wilson's Fifteen Points. I trust that the new world order that will arise from the blood and chaos of this terrible war will be worthy of its great cost. As Mrs Gillett pointed out at the meeting this morning, it behoves us all to do our part in influencing aright the thought of the nation at this time. There are still many nations that openly flout the idea of a League of Nations and one thundering for a meaningful tariff and a boycott of enemy countries. God grant that the noise they make is in no wise commensurate with their insolence.

MONDAY 14 OCTOBER 1918
Public opinion in England and America is hardening against Germany, owing to the victorious onrush of our armies. The glamour of a great military victory is without doubt a factor in this hardening process, although it has more excusable elements, such as disbelief in Germany's word: the recent sabotages of passenger vessels and the many abominable outrages she is inflicting on the stricken peoples of France in their retreat. Never was the shaping influence of Christian thought more necessary in the council of the nations.

In her diary for 15 October 1918, Virginia Woolf wrote of a meeting with Herbert Fisher: 'we've won the war today ... The Germans have made up their minds that they cannot fight a retreat.' Fisher assured her that he would try to help educate people: 'they'll be trouble when [the soldiers] come back' and reassured her that 'Lloyd George has told me time and time again that he means to be generous to the Germans'. Rex was not, of course, privy to any such inside information, but he, just like her, was concerned about the peace – and about the influenza epidemic.

FRIDAY 18 OCTOBER 1918
News of the evacuation of Lille by the Germans was received today; also of the occupation of Ostend by the British Naval Forces, who subsequently withdrew to prevent the bombardment of the town by the retreating enemy. The people of Lille were filled with delirious joy and could not show sufficient gratitude to the relieving troops.

MONDAY 21 OCTOBER 1918
Began to tackle Rhodes University order after tea. Arrived home about nine o'clock and after reading Germany's reply to Pres. Wilson.

THURSDAY 31 OCTOBER 1918
Mr Hanks came in soon after six o'clock with the news of the surrender of Turkey and the opening of the Dardanelles to the Allied Fleet.

SATURDAY 2 NOVEMBER 1918
News to hand of the apparent break up of Austria-Hungary into its component nationalities ... King Boris of Bulgaria abdicates after a reign of nineteen days.

MONDAY 4 NOVEMBER 1918
A perfect deluge of rain all the morning ... Austria has capitulated, after losing 100,000 men and 2,200 guns.

THURSDAY 7 NOVEMBER 1918
Have received no parcels at shop for a week. Whole railway organisation undermined with the influenza epidemic. Over 13,000 deaths during three weeks in 96 large towns of the British Isles ... German armistice delegates reported to be on their way to meet Marshal Foch.

The same day, Rex went back to the office after tea, because of the pressure of work, and heard news to cause rejoicing:

Mr Basil came in about 7:30 with the news that the armistice had been signed at 2:30 that afternoon. Just as they were leaving

Paddington a reporter from the House of Commons had thrust his head into their compartment and told them the glad news. News also to hand of revolutionary movements at Kiel and other places in Germany.

The good news is momentarily set back, but as the war is obviously coming to a close, Rex's diary carries a stark warning.

FRIDAY 8 NOVEMBER 1918

A wet, cold morning, but all buoyed up with the news of the evening before – which alas! Resolved itself into a rumour! Still we all feel that it can only be a matter of a few days. The revolutionary movement is spreading in Germany like a flame in dry stubble ... Oh! For some magazine to thrill the people of the world with a lofty, grand idea, that should woo them from the lowlands of petty jealousies and narrow-mindedness up to the sunlit heights of mutual trust, comradeship and togetherness. We pray that President Wilson may be unworldly strengthened and upheld to hold aloft the torch of righteousness and magnanimity.

We have conquered the Germans – now comes the infinitely greater conflict, to conquer all feelings of mere vindictiveness and revenge, to conquer the pride of victory, and to lay the foundations of a new world order. The nation has been rendered malleable by sorrow – God grant that we may be subjected to the moulding influence of the highest and noblest and not wasted and marred by the reactionary forces within the nation.

MONDAY 11 NOVEMBER 1918

The armistice terms have been accepted by Germany, and the historic document was signed this morning at 5 a.m. Firing on all fronts ceased at 11 o'clock – being the 11th hour of the 11th day of the 11th month. Within a few minutes of the arrival of the glorious news, Oxford was in a wild ferment of excitement. Flags and noisy bands of youths and soldiers paraded the streets making a dreadful din with rattles, hooters, sticks and pans etc ... The children walked down to Oxford to see the revelry and rejoicing, and arrived back about six o'clock tired, wet through to the skin. Poor Weasel [James] had a sound smacking 'to set up his circulation', and was sent ignominiously to bed – surely a sorry ending to so memorable a day! A small band of Serbian students marched through the town about 8 o'clock singing with wonderfully impressive effect their national songs.

The persistent 'drizzling rain dampened down any tendency towards mafficking' – a portent perhaps of what was to turn out to be, as Rex feared, a pyrrhic victory? On the same day, in London, Virginia Woolf wrote: 'So far neither bells nor flags, but the wailing of sirens and intermittent guns.'

TUESDAY 12 NOVEMBER 1918
News came to hand of the Kaiser's flight into Holland, and also of the shooting of the Crown Prince by revolutionary soldiers. This latter piece of news, although confirmed from two sources, afterwards proved to be incorrect.

SUNDAY 24 NOVEMBER 1918
Mr Hunt gave us a call at business last night: but does not appear over anxious to return to the toil and worry and lone hours of Broad St.

HEALING THE SCARS?

With the armistice signed, the atmosphere was buoyant in some quarters and business was picking up. Rex received an offer from a local bookshop and considered moving on, but his loyalty to Benjamin Henry kept him at Blackwell's, although he worried that 'when the fellows return from the army, they may regard me as having climbed into power and position over their backs'.[16] But Rex felt weighed down by more than work.

SUNDAY 1 DECEMBER 1918
Another week of laborious days. The orders began to fall as thick as leaves in Vallombrosa. This week Nagpur, Anantapur, Cape Town and Calcutta swell the collection in my bottom drawer. Having been seized by the army demobilisation board, the Society of Friends have had to move their abode still once again. A strong wave of resentment is arising in the country against the dictatorial methods of Lloyd George in forcing 'specially selected' Coalition candidates upon the various constituencies. Personally, I can conceive nothing of the 'joint blessing' of Bonar Law and Lloyd George as candidates, who had sacrificed his freedom to gain a mess of pottage.

SUNDAY 15 DECEMBER 1918
Yesterday President Wilson arrived in France and had a tremendous reception. I pray that his ideals may be held steadily aloft, dispensing the ugly vapours that are rising in the sphere of international politics.

And these 'ugly vapours' confirmed Rex's worst fears. With what vain hope in mind had he penned his poem 'Christmas 1915'?[17]

> We pilgrims come to Bethlehem's fair shrine
> In all the dread accoutrements of war:
> And, as we kneel, there soundeth from afar,
> The 'echoing roar of loud-exploding mine'.
> We come, sweet Child, from that entrench'd line
> Which girdles Europe like a fearful scar,
> Because, amid the murk, there gleamed the star
> That lures men's feet to purposes divine.

> Undimmed in splendour by the fires of Hate,
> This God-conceived Ideal shines full clean,
> And woos us to the manger – this dark year –
> To re-affirm, with heart and soul elate,
> Our staunch conviction in that gladsome state
> When Love shall reign and overthrow all fear.

Could his fine words of Love's reign offer any recompense for the 'dread accoutrements of war', for the deaths of twenty million combatants and civilians? No wonder he battled with depression until the end of his life. Through his writing Rex struggled to find peace, or rather love, as he later described in his 1930 poem, 'Sunshine after Shadow'.

> A darkest hour is thrust a seed of light,
> And blustering tempests burgeon into peace;
> Life's dust and heat give place to cool respite,
> And after turmoil cometh sweet release.

> Let not my love decline in Love's increase,
> Nor radiant sunshine hide thee from my eyes;
> When fears subside, let not my love decrease
> But let thanksgiving like a fountain rise
> Flooding my heart & eyes, with thine exceeding peace.

The New Year did little to allay Rex's fears.

WEDNESDAY 1 JANUARY 1919
This fateful year in the history of the world was ushered in with storm and wind: and I fear that these are but portents of storms and insurrections in the political world. Although a strong wind of an

enlightened conscience is blowing slightly through the civilised world
– and men everywhere are straining their eyes towards the dawn of a
better and brighter Europe; yet the powers of reaction are becoming
stridently articulate and the voice of the softer is seldom heard in the
land ... On the continent, Bolsheviks and extremists are undermining
the whole social structure: and it will be a long time before any
stability in government is assured. Paderewski has left his piano to
strike deeper and farther resounding chords in the responsive hearts
of the Polish people. Poland, like a giant awakened, is gathering
together its people from Austria, Russia, Germany and it is rumoured
is sending a large army of occupation to Berlin!'

THURSDAY 2 JANUARY 1919
H.M.S. Iolaire sunk in Stornoway harbour. The failed vessel was
conveying soldiers home for their first leave during the war. About
250 drowned ... Spinoza's teaching regarding the non-morality of
nature is very modern in tone.

SUNDAY 5 JANUARY 1919
Remained in blanket-town until noon, coddling my cold. Wrote
a long humorous epistle to Mr Hunt – probably the last before his
demobilisation. Also wrote to Mr Sydney Cooper, thanking him
for a delicious fruitcake, which he sent us for the New Year. What
ebullient exclamations of delight when the fruit slice disclosed an
amazing weight of currants! Such a stomach stirring sight had not
been seen for two years!

Spring comes and snow lingers, and Rex includes another poem in his
diary on 1 April 1919, but will hope rule over 'blistering hate'?

The wind runs cracking through the frosted sedge;
    And wantons with the snow –
        With loath to go
Clings to the sheltered wall, and thornset hedge;
    On like a silver gleam
Outlines the windings of the tortuous stream ...

The budding willows glint with silken sheen;
    And merry catkins bold,
        All green and gold,
Shake out their tresses, spite of April spleen:
    And in the moss warm ditch,
The [?] flowers their tents begin to pitch.

The heart of man shakes off the winter snows:
    The blackened seams of hair,
      Drink in the rain
Of gentle hope; and, over all there blows
    The soft, fresh wind of god
Mossing the scenes where blistering hate has trod.

It provides a stark contrast to the healing poem 'Snow' that the solid, socially conservative Fred Hanks wrote after the Second World War.

Snow falling, sadly palling
The coffin earth.
Snow creeping, lying, sleeping;
Retarding birth.
See how it whirls
It twists, it curls;
Healing balm;
Pure, calm.
While all above falls on, in love.
Dressing with bandage clean,
The scars where men have been,
As city street and field
To still caresses yield.

Snow falling –
Still falling.
Where'er I go,
Snow – snow!

Rex could never have been as upbeat as Hanks. Could the scars be healed? By May the weather is warmer, but Rex is still depressed. His

inner harmony … has been shaken by the terrible war in Europe: it has 'tilted us out of doors', tilted us out of the armchairs of our snug beliefs, indifference and self-complacency – 'homeless' and ill at ease. It is the world of Longfellow: 'The air is full of farewells to the dying/And mournings for the dead'.

Peace, Rex later wrote in a review of a book by Bishop Robert Scott, could only be found by 'being at home in the universe, in harmony between self and not self'. In a review of F.R. Barry's essays, a tribute to members of Oriel College killed in the First World War, he found common cause with the author who has:

a burning conviction that if the unparalleled sacrifices of all our noblest is to usher in the dawn of a better civilisation ... those of us who remain should do our utmost to mould public opinion. The future of humanity is in our hands, if through indifference we let slip the opportunity our brothers' sacrifice will have been in vain.

Rex was not optimistic, and wrote of his suspicions as the Treaty of Versailles was being signed.[18]

THURSDAY 8 MAY 1919
A gloriously warm spring day, spent the afternoon in gardening. Yesterday the Peace terms were presented to the German Plenipotentiaries at Versailles. They are exceptionally stringent, and how Germany is expected to pay the huge indemnity of 5,000 millions when the bulk of her resources in coal and iron is taken from her, and a tariff universally operating against her, I cannot understand. The fear is that the severity of the terms will drive people into Bolshevik excesses and subvert all responsible Government.

SUNDAY 22 JUNE 1919
The Germans have sunk over forty of their battleships interned at Scapa Flow. This will – at least – prevent any further squabbling amongst the allies.

SUNDAY 13 JULY 1919
The first intimation we had of the signing of the Peace Treaty of Versailles was the mad clanging of the Church bells at Charlton Kings as the train was passing through ...

SATURDAY 19 JULY 1919
This being an official holiday for the due celebration of peace! The children and I walked to St Giles to watch the soldiers march to Christ Church Quad – there to suffer the infliction of a mayoral speech. The weather, however, was not sympathetic and the rain soon damped our ardour, so we caught a bus and came home.

SUNDAY 20 JULY 1919
Mr New, at the Friends', with all precise solemnity, announced that the usual ramble of the study circle and Society of Reconciliation would start from that place on Thursday.

WEDNESDAY 23 JULY 1919
Emily's sister brought us a fine basket of raspberries and wishes us all to go to Eaton for the Bank Holiday. Harvey and Jim are thrown

out of work for the time being owing to the 'peace mafficking' at Coventry. Surely the harvest of peace has been purchased at too tremendous a cost to be treated with such mad hilarity! England is indeed in a very parlous, feverish condition.

Pacifism continued to worry Rex, and no peace could be found in the 'mad clanging of Church bells'. His hopes, in the years following the war, became vested in the United Nations – in 1924 he wrote of Lady Mary Murray (Gilbert Murray's wife), 'who spoke winningly and earnestly, to the Friends, about the League of Nations and of what was being accomplished'.[19] In the years that followed, even before the reality of a second war hit home, Rex continued to be despondent. He wrote of being 'crushed with the overwhelming thought of the uselessness of it all ... We feel we should like to slip out of the conflict, create a little monastery or retreat apart from the mad vortex of life.'[20]

He contemplated the problem of evil, but said little more directly about the end of the war, or its effects, save for a poem, 'His Words were Half-Battles', written in 1928.

Not smooth and facile words, that lightly slip,
A gleam with fancy, from the fluent lip;
But words of power, that falteringly start,
Forged in the furnace of the patient heart,
Tempted by months of sorrow sternly borne,
Of nights and days, and days and nights, forlorn;
When hope itself died down in murky air
Of thwarted dreams, and secret, festering care:
Words born of passion, but cool'd of passions' heat
Held in the clews of silent thought 'till sweet
And clean as daffodils 'mid orchard trees –
These are the words that are half-victories.

For others in the shop, there was less angst and more optimism. In his short memoir, the newly demobbed Geoffrey Barfoot wrote:

Members of the staff began to return, I am not sure who was first – possibly Charley Field, 'Bert' Steele or Piper. My return was delayed as many adjustments had to be made to give fair play for the wartime helpers. Gaffer [Basil] suggested I sit tight – I might make a better soldier than bookseller – for it needed a little time to find a gap for me in the confusion caused by the return of so many prodigals to the fold. However, I returned as soon as the call came. Having left 'Blackwell's' when earning 14/– per week to take on as a solider at 1/– per day – I returned to receive the salary [rather than wages] of £2/10/– per week.

George Crutch, too, shied away from any soul-searching. 'The front shop was very lively during Eights Week – the sisters and lady friends all in splendid hats and elegant apparel ... to these young people things were "frightfully good". The Great War was over and it had been a war to end war. So the future was bright and secure.'

It wasn't long before Crutch's optimism was put to the test. But Basil, even in 1935, was full of bravado. 'If our civilisation must go down in the havoc of war, it will be to the bookshops, or the ruins of bookshops, that the men of the future must turn to find knowledge and inspiration to build a better world.'[21] And while Giles Gilbert Scott's New Bodleian was under construction in 1939, Basil decided to shore up the east wall of the shop: 'it was a symbol of our hope for the future'.

DOCTOR DOKTOR

With so many staff called up and those remaining hard-stretched during the war that followed, surviving memories of Blackwell's in the years of the Second World War are scant. Reggie Nash remembered that the house magazine, *Broad Street*, 'gave us news of Broad Street and of each other until the war was over'. Fred Hanks, by then very elderly, but a regular contributor, wrote jovially about the firm's raffles:

> It is hoped to Raffle a pair of Pure Silk Stockings (no kiddin!) sometime after Easter, which I am sure will go down well with the ladies; and, sometime in May there will be another big Raffle containing, amongst other objects, a Bottle of Gin ... Nothing is too big or too small – very much appreciated if anyone could rustle up a pot of jam, sugar, tinned fruit, treacle, a bottle of some liquid refreshment!

Nash wrote in *Broad Street* of the relief he and other servicemen felt when they returned to the 'blessed shores of England ... to the same peaceful atmosphere of our World of Books', which had been retained for us.

However, by chance there arrived on Blackwell's doorstep a bona fide scholar who, writing in her nineties for her grand-daughter, provides a precious vignette of the bookshop in wartime and also the unusual romance it sparked.[22]

Herta Doktor arrived in England in 1936 as a German-Jewish refugee, having escaped the Reich via Italy and Switzerland. Although granted British citizenship, it turned out to be impossible for her to find a position commensurate with the doctoral degree in linguistics she had attained in Germany. Initially she found work as a nanny and a nurse, but visiting her cousin in Oxford, she took an immediate liking to the town and decided to live and work there.

> So I went to Blackwell's. A very surprised Miss showed me the way to the *souterrain* to meet a really old man in his seventies, Mister Hank. I said: 'I am looking for a job!' Coming back the next day to meet Mr Blackwell, I introduced myself and continued: 'I like this place and do you think I can find a job with you?' I recounted my CV; this seemed to impress him, so he mumbled, 'Yes, yes … I'll give you two pounds a week and you can start on September first.'
>
> In the beginning I worked in Periodicals, all girls were addressed by their Christian names, the men with their Surnames; I wasn't addressed with my title: titles don't play that role in England. After several weeks, I was installed in the department for the supply of books to British and Allied Prisoners of War. The books, supplied by the Red Cross, were channelled through Blackwell's, which paid less postage than the Red Cross. Donated books were also collected and processed by Blackwell's.

Finding a huge backlog, which was preventing POWs getting the books they wanted, Herta worked her way through the pile and wrote to the recipients.

> They were thrilled. Especially those who had ordered books on crafts and trades, they were anxious about losing too much time in their professional training. Some of them came to see me later, when on leave. But after the European railways were bombed, it was harder to deliver. We were also put in charge of contacting military personnel. And so I met my future husband Willy Haas. As a captain in Bombay he wrote movie-scripts, and had just written his third in 1940, when his producer went bankrupt. He himself actually never saw this film, but I did; subsequently a young man from Berlin, Christoph von Ungern-Sternberg, wrote a brilliant thesis on my husband's work in India, and he arranged for me to see this movie. Willy Haas was in

India with the British Army, he held no British passport, he was a Czech of German Jewish origin. He was moved to a small town in southwest India. He held the position of a censor, his assignment was censorship of all German mail, no matter whether it had been written by God-fearing Jews or Nazis, the Brits didn't really care from whom it came ... As there was no bookseller in the town, somebody recommended Blackwell's: so he became my customer. And I always complained: 'Oh, goodness, those high-browed books, no one else orders such books, such sophisticated stuff.'

In my department there was another German refugee, Mrs Hahn. She read all the letters he had sent and she told me about his life and career and of his editing the *Literarische Welt*. Bit by bit some private lines entered the business mail. So Mrs Hahn read the letters and she predicted: 'You will marry M. Haas!' I merely replied: 'Are you mad? A man who lives in India and I don't even know him.' 'You will marry him,' she insisted ... One day, and I know exactly where I was standing on the 2nd floor of the shop at the time, the clerk who distributed the mail came up shouting: 'Miss Doktor, Miss Doktor, photographs from Mr Haas!' Everybody scrambled to see the photographs; I was last to see them. The correspondence continued, in English due to the military censorship. All letters still exist, here in my closet. I hope to find someone to pass them on to.

When the war was over and the men were returning. Mr Blackwell, not wanting me to be out on the street, offered me a job at Heffers in Cambridge. 'Well, Mr Blackwell, I must tell you something, I intended to give notice for March the first, because I will get married.' 'What?' 'He is a customer of yours.' 'Who is he, I have not approved him!' But he did approve and accepted my notice for March the first 1947.[23]

A WAR DIVIDEND

While deploring the fact of war, the Blackwells maintained a patriotic stance, as they had in the first war: Christine Blackwell masterminded local food distribution and sheltered refugees; Basil's sister Dorothy returned to nursing duties. Basil donated to the Spitfire Fund and 263,000 books were sent as one-off gifts to POWs, as well as those posted for the Red Cross in Geneva. In 1944 alone, £40,000 of books were sent to prisoners in the Far East and Asia. War was a paradox for the Blackwells: they despised and loathed it but profited by it — although, Basil acidly rejoined, 'most of it was taken in taxes'. Demand for books increased, Basil wrote, from 'ordinary folk' at home and those in the armed forces. Compulsory call-up depleted staff levels to the point where the shop, from time to time, had to close early, but war provided openings in the workplace, brought in women and the physically debarred, though they feared that the jobs were being poached from those away at the Front.

More books than ever were sold in the shop, and sales to America, in Basil's view, helped the war effort.

> There is nothing which gives deeper satisfaction than the knowledge that so many friends in America recognise the tremendous seriousness of the struggle in which we are engaged ... Yet many of you feel that there is nothing that you personally can do to help. But there is one thing that any American citizen can do, at once and easily, and the effect would be enormous if some thousands of you did it – buy a copy of a British book (not published in an American edition), read it, and pass it on to a friend . ... All the ideas we are fighting for are enshrined in our books ... You will know that any money spent on strengthening those ties between us, which are vital to us, will do something at once to fight down the treats of tyranny.

Clifford Collins of Christ Church College in New Zealand, the founding father of New Zealand librarianship, sent food parcels and cakes of soap to Blackwell's in return for their kindnesses.

Blackwell's survived unscathed in the Second World War, and Basil went to the rescue of Benjamin Henry's old bookselling friend and first apprentice, Fred Chaundy, whose shop in London had been bombed.[24] At the first AGM after the war, in December 1945, Basil was his customary optimistic self:

> The war is over, and already five or six of our serving staff have returned [twenty nine had seen active service]. We look forward to the return of the rest ... all but one, Merlin Burborough ... I had a feeling he was the sort of youth the gods loved; and so it was that a very promising career here as an apprentice, and a career of fine achievement in the army, till in Burma he was killed in gallant action, ended with 'darkness and the death hour rounding it'.

Although the August 1947 edition of *Broad Sheet* lamented the continuing economic crises and described Atlee as 'feeble', it applauded Blackwell's contribution to the 'austerity era': 'to try for further exports

Merlin Burborough,
a grammar-school
apprentice: 'I had a
feeling he was the sort of
youth the gods loved.'

to boost national income' and to make sure there are 'no passengers'
on the staff and 'to cut out the cost of the *Oxford Mail* newspaper'
(a privation it undoubtedly recovered from). It was ironic that two
devastating wars, coinciding with the growth of universal education,
had had a civilizing effect; Basil wrote, 'people were more critical,
better informed, and, at all levels of society, more aware of their rights,
as well as their obligations'. He reasoned 'that people had woken up to
the fact that the [Second] war might have taken from them their own
heritage. As a result they developed an entirely new and avid interest
in reading books.'[25]

Kenneth Sisam (head of Clarendon Press/OUP) described publishing
as the luckiest of all trades in wartime. But during the First World War,
both Benjamin Henry and Basil saw it as a form of protest. They could
publish those who were able to write what they couldn't say.

NINE

WAR ON MANY FRONTS

I do not think that very much was said
Of solemn requiem for the good years dead.
                    Dorothy L. Sayers, 'Last Morning in Oxford', 1915

F OR THE BLACKWELLS, there were wars on many fronts, not only
in the trenches but between the classes and the sexes and, in the
workplace, capital versus labour. Most importantly they waged war
against ignorance. And selling and publishing books could remedy this.

It is, of course, Basil Blackwell who is remembered as a publisher,
rather than his father.[1] Beyond Oxford, and only there in rarefied
circles, it is little known that Benjamin Henry had made a name for
himself as publisher as well as bookseller. At first he pinned his hopes
on publishing poetry; he was probably persuaded by his friends Henry
Beeching and Herbert Asquith from nearby Balliol, who remained
favourites at Blackwell's throughout their lives. Dr Johnson, showing
off his college, Pembroke, where he had studied in 1728, had remarked
on the fact that so many of its sons were poets: 'a nest of singing
birds', he had declared. By the time Benjamin Henry was starting out
as a publisher, these singing birds must have flown to Balliol. And
to get into print they turned next door to Benjamin Henry, where
their efforts were rewarded. In 1879, the shop's first year, the imprint
B.H. Blackwell made its debut with a slender volume, *Mensae Secundae:
Verses Written in Balliol College*. The collection, Basil later explained,

'which naturally enough reveals a strong pre-Raphaelite influence', was unsigned, 'but initials appearing beneath the poems manifested the pens of Beeching, Mackail, Rennell Rodd, Bowyer Nichols, Philip Burne-Jones, St Loe Strachey and others of lesser and greater note'.

Following the success of his first experiment, not financially but in the sense that it led writers to seek him out, Benjamin Henry followed it up the next year with *Primavera*, and A.E. Housman, of St John's, was again among the contributors. Blackwell's acquired from a neighbour, Shrimpton, another poetry series, *Waifs and Strays*, and brought out the fifth and subsequent issues, which provided the template for *Oxford Poetry*.[2] When he first published this yearly anthology, wrote his son Basil, 'people laughed, no doubt; that was before the [First] War'. But Benjamin Henry was 'dogged in defence of new writing, ignoring fashion and the critics'. A host of famous writers made their debut in *Oxford Poetry*: J.R.R. Tolkien, Graham Greene, Stephen Spender, the Huxleys, the Sitwells, Dorothy L. Sayers, Harold Acton, Cecil Day-Lewis, W.H. Auden, Louis MacNeice, Laurence Binyon, and many more long since forgotten. Some were lucky enough, courtesy of Benjamin Henry, to have their own slim volumes published. An early Rhodes scholar from America, Christopher Morley, remembered these 'little booklets ... bound in paper and sold (if at all) for a shilling each'. He recalled *Ignes Fatui* and *Metri Gratia* by Philip Guedalla of Balliol and *Play Hours with Pegasus* by A.P. Herbert of New College. Morley risked sending a little sheaf of his own rhymes, and the now elderly Benjamin Henry invited him to Broad Street to discuss his work. 'What I remember best of my bashful interview with him,' Morley wrote, 'besides his pink face and white hair and extreme politeness, was his asking me: "perhaps you don't use commas much in America?"'[3] What Benjamin Henry chose to publish was to be 'confined to such work as would seem to *deserve* publicity'. Morley had no idea if his had merit, but it was published anyway.

Benjamin Henry's reputation of being a demon with the blue pencil, and more painstaking than any tutor, led many young hopefuls to seek him out. They came to look on him as a mentor, and he found succour among the scholars, poets and writers he strove to help in his daily business life.

It was probably Henry Beeching who introduced his scholarly bookseller friend to Arnold Ward, the son of the controversial novelist

Mrs Humphry Ward. Very much an Oxford character, she was living there when religious liberalism supplanted Catholic Tractarianism. In her novels, *Robert Elsmere* for example, she deliberately used fiction to discuss religious problems. As the granddaughter of Dr Thomas Arnold, the famous head of Rugby School, and the niece of the poet Matthew Arnold, she had formidable academic connections. Very much in the family mould, her son Arnold, now in his third year at Balliol, had just won the Chancellor's Prize for his Latin verse. Partial to the lyric verse of Horace, Ward invited seven fellow poets to join him in the formation of the Horace Club, a 'literary club with a difference', devoted to this genre. He had no hesitation in inviting Benjamin Henry to officiate as Keeper of the Club's Records. Benjamin Henry, who doubtless knew that the father of the original Horace was also a tradesman like himself, felt at ease in their company, despite not being a 'varsity man'. And his association with them would have given him some much-deserved recognition. Ward's connection with Matthew Arnold alone would have been enough to compensate Benjamin Henry for giving up his almost non-existent free time. Arnold's loathing of tyranny and advocacy of universal education, Benjamin Henry would probably have thought, put him almost on a par with William Morris.

WARNING FROM POETS

The Horace Club Collection is very much of its time. In his 'War and Arbitration', T. Humphry Ward, Arnold Ward's father, intimated he was aware of future danger:

> When Hark! Across our sheltered life,
> Bourne on a sudden blast of fate
> That rudely rocks the ship of state,
> The rumour and roar of strife ...
> And o'er the seas and round the earth
> Echoes an awful voice of doom,
> From battle guns that harshly boom...

Other club members – Raymond Asquith, Laurence Binyon, Hilaire Belloc and John Buchan – also contributed poems that had this edginess about them. But even if, as they feared, there was to be a more extensive conflict, and there were economic and political portents, they hoped that their poetry would survive. 'Life is short, art only lives and stays', wrote the Reverend A.G. Butler in his poem 'Horace', dedicated to the Club's eponymous hero.[4] He took a similar line in another poem, 'Archaeology':

> Warrior, statesman, sage, a host
> Who have won the heroes' praise ...
> And last but not least in the ghostly throng,
> Will be those who have left behind
> Not warrior's name, or genius' fame,
> But who laboured, and loved their kind.

And John Buchan would perhaps have seen his father on his rounds, comforting battle-scarred families (of the second South African War). But he never risked as overt a criticism as St John Lucas, in 'A Sonnet':

> ... Oh puppets, see
> How the gods mock your ever-shifting states.

Did St John Lucas imagine the 'puppets' as suffering the fate meted out to the Symbolists of the Central Committee of the Paris Commune?

Henry Beeching, almost a generation older than Buchan when he offered his contributions, had a more immediate message: '[he who] Does service in the field/Themselves to slavery yield'. Was Beeching thinking of Housman's 'steady drummer', written in 1896 and as popular at the time of the second South African War as it would be during the First World War? Did Beeching ever read with hindsight Raymond Asquith's:

> Never so was any face...
> Gladder than the springs of laughter,
> Sadder than the fount of tears.

Raymond, the son of Herbert Asquith, was expected to follow his father into Liberal politics, but his life ended on the lines at Ginchy, at the battle of Flers–Courcelette in 1916.[5] We can imagine his words coming back to the Asquith family when confronted with the news of his death. The casualties of war came to be immortalized in Laurence Binyon's 'For the Fallen'. A contemporary of Raymond Asquith and a Quaker, Binyon was a later arrival at the Club and would have been much to the serious-minded Benjamin Henry's taste.

The Club, despite its writers' promise, was doomed. By 1901 it had dwindled to two members, a victim of the natural, transient cycle of student life. But Benjamin Henry, in his meticulous way, had preserved autographed copies of each poem presented by Horace members, carefully pasted into two Kelmscott folios. Thinking now as a publisher, he published *The Book of the Horace Club* in 1901, under the B.H. Blackwell imprint.[6]

Some seventy years later Sir Arthur Norrington confided to his old friend Basil Blackwell that *The Book of the Horace Club* 'served as a tribute to his self-educated father, who had been welcomed as an equal'. The cooperation between Benjamin Henry and the Horace poets certainly bridged the divide between town and gown. They are all now just one small part of literary history, but looking again at the work of these 'last Victorians', Basil later wrote, helps to link 'that earlier period with the younger writers of today and tomorrow'.[7]

In its time, the club helped several young writers along the road to fame, and some remain popular today. Little did Benjamin Henry know that he was assisting the creator of James Bond's forebear, Richard Hannay. But John Buchan had not yet any thought of his future protagonist's adventures on the thirty-nine steps. Benjamin Henry had, according to his diary, sat up 'half the night correcting the proofs of Buchan's Stanhope and Newdigate Prize essays'; he would have been especially glad to help Buchan, who was the son of a Free Church Minister in Scotland, existing on a scholarship.

It was Beeching's friend, William Mackail, a future professor of poetry and biographer of William Morris, who suggested that Benjamin Henry might take on the publication of Oxford's prize essays and poems. They too proved a labour of love and added little to the kitty, but they were simply and elegantly produced, sewn into Oxford blue paper covers and costing 1s 6d. On 17 May 1881 he published C.R. Fletcher's Chancellor's Essay, arranging to pay him £2 for thirty copies, but retaining the manuscript and rights. Three days later he published the Newdigate Essay and the Newdigate Verse (that year it was Mackail's *Thermopylae*). The following June he produced William Hutton's Stanhope and, generous to a fault, Benjamin Henry insisted that Hutton was to have ten copies free and fifteen more at 1s 6d. In his diary (12 June 1882) Benjamin Henry wrote: 'Harry Shaw's Stanhope printed at Clarendon Press – got out of bed twice 12.30 and 1.30 to do proofs'; then, two days later: 'published [the] Stanhope Essay ... the same day as Encaenia'. This tradition continued well after Benjamin Henry's death. The subject matter says much about the priority he gave to the classics.

More than poetry came out under the B.H. Blackwell imprint in those early days. In his diary (July 1882), Benjamin Henry wrote of 'being days correcting the proofs of Dudley Medley's *English Constitutional History*'; it became a standard text, despite becoming affectionately known as 'Deadly Muddly'.[8] When Henry Beeching became rector of Yattendon in 1885, he collaborated with Robert Bridges and H.E. Wooldridge to produce the *Yattendon Hymnal* (words and music). Arguably it is the most notable work to bear the B.H. Blackwell imprint; its influence went way beyond the rural parish for which it had been prepared, and Ralph Vaughan William's *English Hymnal* owed much to it. Henry Beeching also edited an elegant reprint of George Herbert's *The Country Parson* for Benjamin Henry in 1898.

A PRINCE GALEHAUT OF BOOKS

For the Blackwells, father and son, publishing was motivated by idealism. Robert Bridges had advised Benjamin Henry against 'entering the perilous seas of publishing' and he was proved right: he made little or no money from it in his lifetime.[9] Even when a book made a small profit, he didn't keep his takings: for example, he sent the proceeds to help 'relieve the sufferings of our sick and wounded in South Africa'.[10] But few knew anything of his efforts, and those in the know, such as delegates to the University Press, were at first suspicious of the unlettered upstart on Broad Street. But they came to admire and accept him; Charles Cannan, Aristotelian scholar, Dean of Trinity and head of the Oxford University Press until his death, became a personal friend. At the time of his death in 1924, Benjamin Henry rather belatedly received a more public approbation. The *Daily Mail* pronounced: 'Blackwell did a very great service to Oxford in providing encouragement and a chance of publicity to young writers.'[11]

Benjamin Henry had established the Blackwell list by helping writers 'unknown to fame', and Basil, as Edith Sitwell and John Betjeman acknowledged, maintained this tradition.[12] 'Writing is a divine *gift*,' Basil wrote, 'an ability to express and interpret truth clearly and in language that delights ... is not the prerogative of the learned and highly educated: whether from the profound scholar Housman or the peasant Robert Burns, the Harrovian Lord Byron or cabin boy Herman Melville.' Those he helped were from all walks of life. Alf Williams' story, which was of an education against all odds, has been told in 'Scholar Apprentices', but there were other, less learned writers too. Edith Barfoot, for example, over sixty, bed-ridden and in constant pain with rheumatoid arthritis since her teens, told Basil how she had triumphed over her pain under the spiritual guidance of the Cowley Fathers. Encouraged by one of them, she produced a short paper entitled *The Discovery of Joy in the Vocation of Suffering*. Basil, much moved and impressed, published it at his own expense.

Having had a more solid grounding in the publishing establishment than his father, Basil could perhaps take more risks. As soon as he'd finished at university, he had been invited by his father's old friend Sir Henry Frowde to spend at year at Oxford University Press's London office. He seized the opportunity and in September 1911 made his way to OUP at Amen Corner, in the lea of St Paul's, 'there to spend one of the most delightful years of my life'. He revelled in the freedom to 'dawdle in the London Library and the British Museum Reading Room'. Here he had 'all English literature to choose from, and drank insatiably of that pure fount so refreshing after the close and anxious studies of the Oxford School of Literae Humaniores'.[13]

Basil's first task was to complete the selection for *A Book of English Essays* to be included in the OUP World's Classics, and to see it through the press; it had already been three parts done by Stanley Makower before his death. Basil viewed the series as the 'pathfinder for the Everyman Library, launched by that shrewd idealist J.M. Dent', who had reprinted 'the best fiction at the cheapest possible price'; his books were as 'great a boon to poor students as the Home University Library'.[14] Adjoining his narrow office was that of Vere H. Collins, nicknamed Vera Historic, who edited texts to cater for sixth formers and undergraduates, 'a growing market that he understood ahead of his time'. Collins allowed Basil to choose samples to peddle around schools and universities, and it gave Basil an idea which he stored up for the future. He had little to do with 'the great Frowde, except when his father came to visit', but from a distance Basil learned 'to consider the book as a whole', and thanks to the 'kindly Frederick Hall, trained as a printer and later to succeed Horace Hart as Printer to OUP', he was introduced to 'the rudiments [and] the mysteries of book production'. He had little contact 'with the great and the legendary Chapman, back in Oxford', but 'his initials were occasionally employed in green pencil as a sign of disapproval'. Seeing them, Basil admitted: 'we believed and trembled'.

Basil had found his niche, and he made life-long friends, including Gerald Hopkins and Charles Williams. Basil's lasting impression of Amen Corner was 'one of reverence for scholarship and education: for any books which might advance their cause'. Imbued with this, he returned to Oxford, where his publishing efforts, on behalf of his father, assumed an almost religious fervour, stirred up even more by the onset of war.

THE PEN – MIGHTIER THAN THE SWORD?

Shortly before the war, Gilbert Murray had faced down the critics in his preface to *Oxford Poetry*: 'tell me not what I ought to admire or not … in poetry the important thing is to understand and feel something, anything, as intensely as possible'.[15] It was this spirit that inspired Basil and his father to publish so many volumes of poetry, and despite their marked preference for the Victorian and Edwardian vein in verse, they willingly committed to publishing modernist work produced in the 'fog of our despairing gloom', as Iris Tree wrote in 1918.

In the gloom of wartime, Basil reflected on the paradox that war was about love of one's country. Wilfred Owen viewed this as a lie, and Basil agreed. One of his favourite books at the time was Charles Kingsley's *Two Years Ago*: its hero, Tom Thurnall, had seen imprisonment during the Crimean War as the spiritual turning point of his life. Could poetry serve this role too? 'Could weapons of war be replaced by the lyre?' Basil wondered, alluding to Horace's *Nunc arma defunctumque bello, Barbiton hic paries habebit* (But now my arms I quit, And hang them up to rust or rest).

Through the years of war and its aftermath, Basil's authors poured out their feelings into *Oxford Poetry*, *Outlook*, *Adventurers All* and *Initiates*, which included (Captain) Geoffrey Faber's *In the Valley of Vision*, Eleanor Farjeon's *Sonnets and Poems*, Aldous Huxley's *The Defeat of Youth* and Edith Sitwell's *The Mother and Other Poems*, followed by her

Clowns' Houses and (with brother Osbert) *Harlequinade*. Maurice Baring, who survived the Royal Flying Corps, offered up *In Memoriam*, and A.P. Herbert, who served at Gallipoli, produced *Half-Hours at Helles*. Blackwell's also published *Goblin Feet*, whose author, J.R.R. Tolkien, invented a mythological clash of good and evil.[16]

Basil also published war poetry to raise funds: the *Belgium Poems* on behalf of *The Daily Telegraph*'s Christmas Shilling Fund. There were also volumes by names hardly known now: Willoughby Weaving, Bernard Gilbert, Wilfred Blair, Reginald Fanshawe's elegy for a young officer, *By Yser Banks,* and the poems of Francis St Vincent Morris (died of wounds 1917). An Australian poet, Henry B. Higgins, described Gallipoli as the 'Mausoleum of our nation's dead'; his son Mervyn had been at Balliol and survived Gallipoli only to be killed in Egypt in 1916.[17] Publishing war poetry was a way of ensuring that the voices of those who did not come back from the war could be heard. Charles J.B. Masefield (MC) died a prisoner after being wounded, but left his *Poems*; before he died, H.R. Freston wrote prophetically: 'Now the daylight droops and dies ... Like the last notes of a song'.[18]

The Blackwell poets would have agreed wholeheartedly with Carl Stead's much later analysis:

> Britain's late Imperium looked for a war in which to assert itself and stumbled instead into the mud and mayhem ... Rupert Brooke's sonnet, *The Soldier*, was what it was supposed to be like – heroic. Wilfred Owen's *Dulce et decorum est* was what it was like in reality – sordid.[19]

But during the so-called Great War, who would dare to criticize Kipling's 'My Boy Jack ... [who] did not shame his kind'?

Sitting not altogether comfortably behind the Queen Anne façade of their book business, the Blackwells dared; although as tradesman, serving people of all shades of opinion, they had to tread carefully. They did, however, have allies. Basil's efforts were supported by many other old Oxford friends, including the writer Michael Sadleir who became a director of Constable & Robinson; Sadleir was to be a delegate to the Paris Peace Conference in 1919 and a member of the Secretariat of the League of Nations.

By publishing war poetry the Blackwells were able to tell the world, indirectly, about the 'brutality and pointlessness of war'. In this way,

Basil thought, he could provide a counterbalance to the warmongers, bureaucrats and politicians. The Blackwell poets, although they wrote what they truly felt about the war, were not necessarily unpatriotic. The Sitwells, however, were openly in revolt. Even so, Osbert served in the trenches and Sacheverell in the Grenadier Guards; their elder sister, Edith, however, was 'dulcet but radical to the core'.[20]

Edith, her brothers and their associates, blazing a trail of 'irony and scorn', declared war on the war in their poetry cycle *Wheels*. Although it was Edith Sitwell who edited the series, the idea almost certainly came from Nancy Cunard, and her poem 'Wheels' gave the series its title:

So dreams and prayers and feelings born of sleep
As well as all the sun-gilt pageantry
Made out of summer breezes and hot noons,
Are in the great revolving of the spheres
Under the trampling of their chariot wheels.

Nancy Cunard tried to warn, as Owen had: the wheels of war rode over everyone, combatants and non-combatants alike. And 'the enemy was not the German Army', it arose from 'the attitudes of those who created the disaster of modern society' and was made possible by the blind young who responded to the call of the herd: 'a patriotic call to duty'.[21] Sherard Vines, in *Wheels: A Second Cycle* (1917), remonstrated on their behalf:

A soldier's such a common thing,
Besides two years of war have taught
The people it's a soldier's job
To stop a bullet.

In editing *Wheels*, Edith Sitwell displayed her commitment to poets writing outside the University's ambit. She was against 'university poets', including any women, being given preference in any list.[22] Basil, who played a role in opening doors for women poets, wrote that truth, rather than gender, informed his choice of those he published. Even so, he thought, women seemed better able to expose the 'terrible world' that Wilfred Owen had written about.[23] Many of those Basil published are virtually unknown today: those who featured in the *Adventurers*

All series, and individual collections by Elizabeth Bridges, Helen Hamilton, Jane Barlow (whose collection was aptly entitled *Between Doubting and Daring*), as well as Mrs Arthur Scott and the pathos of 'Women's Share':

> Dear, when you said 'Good-bye',
> I smiled , didn't I?
> It was my share...
>
> And should they bring me word,
> Death with his flaming sword,
> Has spoken fair
>
> Then, dear, with head held high,
> I'd count the yers go by;
> It is my share.[24]

Conspicuous on the Blackwell lists were Vera Brittain and, to a lesser extent, May Wedderburn Cannan, who both served in the Voluntary Aid Detachment (VAD), and Dorothy L. Sayers, whose poor eyesight disqualified her. They were moral witnesses who pulled no punches. In 'To a VC', Vera Brittain wrote: 'For on that humble Cross you live to wear/ Your friends were crucified'.[25] Daphne De Waal, wanting to immortalize these victims, wrote: 'Their memories will tell/ Throughout all time ... These died, yet are not dead'.[26] Dorothea Wood thought of civilians: 'Hark to the whistling, shrilly cry/ T'will wake the children soon'.[27] Edith Sitwell imagined 'The Mother': her child, grown to manhood, went 'down to dust': hadn't she loved him enough? Or was it her sin that killed him: had she not opposed war enough?[28]

May Cannan's poems in *In War Time* (1917) were mostly written 'bounded by a desk,/ And the grey streets of a town'. May had been in Rouen alongside 'All the youth and pride of England from the ends of all the earth'; after she returned she helped her father run the impossibly short-staffed OUP. 'Here at your desk I sit and work,/ As once you used to do'. This desk-bound poet struck home when she wrote of 'the hope that's fled' and 'The love we buried deep in fields of France'. Yet at OUP, it was business as usual. She had wanted to put up a sign 'Business NOT as usual', but her kindly father 'just smiled' and said it was a bit much. May wrote, retrospectively, that this attitude had its 'counterpart in the Second World War's "they'll tell you if they want you" and "wait until you're fetched"'.[29] May's poetry was her

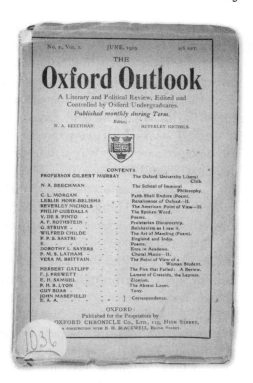

'The Point of View of a Woman
Student', Vera Brittain, *Oxford
Outlook*, vol. 1, no. 2, June 1919.

expiation, and she offered it to others. She ends, 'I have made a Song
for You' where 'Love endures, and memory', and pleads 'Take not from
Them ... If thou hast any need of sacrifice/ Take us! Take us!' And she
captures the poignancy of those who had to carry on at home in 'Any
Woman', written in July 1915:

> I live my life because in France
> You give your life away ...
> I'd give you all my world for thanks –
> And you will never know.

May's own love, Bevil Quiller-Couch, did come back safely, only to
be killed in 1919 by the Spanish flu; her second Blackwell collection,
The Splendid Days, was dedicated to his memory.[30] She offered Basil
a third, *The House of Hope*, but he declined it, explaining that 'times
were changing and he did not, for the moment, think to publish more
poetry'.[31]

It was an unexpected blow for May. Her father admired Benjamin Henry Blackwell, and she and Basil would have been acquainted since childhood; their fathers, not only both publishers, had both served on the city council. Basil liked her work, and Arthur Quiller-Couch had encouraged her to continue 'her practice of poetry'. But, she acknowledged, 'it was on the edge of time ... The new criticism had arrived.' It worked, as Swinnerton wrote in his *Figures in the Foreground*, 'for the destruction of pre-War standards ... nothing was good that was not new'.[32] Basil had seen this: May, an Edwardian, was 'one of the last authentic voices of the traditional modes'.[33] May's third volume was published by Humphrey Milford, but after this little else. She is remembered as a war poet; although she would never herself have had any such 'extravagant' hopes.[34]

Dorothy L. Sayers, the same age as May, was also trying out her feelings about war through poetry. And although she would be better known for her detective stories, poetry was helping her to 'search around' for her place in the literary community.[35] The theme of war crept into Dorothy's work as early as 1908, in her complex poems *Lyrics of War* and *The Prisoner of War* – had she, like May and Basil, seen the Oxford Light Infantry entraining for Cape Town? When war came, although Dorothy never went 'over there', a sense of loss permeated her first collection, *Op. 1*.[36] It included the lament 'Hymn in Contemplation of Sudden Death' and 'Rondels', in which she writes of songs that 'break my heart'. 'Alma Mater' harks back to other wars, to the fate of Troy and the agony of Helen, while in 'The Last Song', Dorothy is gripped by terror: 'And bloody hands of men o'erborne/ Will clutch us by the feet'. Two years later, in her second collection, this distress intensified, though she tried to find solace in 'Carol for Oxford': 'So let us drink at Christmas time to all that dwell by Great Tom chime'.[37] But Oxford gave cold comfort.

Dorothy's horror of war and love of Oxford resonated with Basil, and would have recommended her work to him. Her poem 'Lay', which first appeared in *Oxford Poetry* in 1915, had shown off her scholarly credentials and probably convinced him to publish *Op. 1*. (Their subsequent clashes, when she went to work at Blackwell's, are told in 'Women Warriors'.)

The 'war poets', the women in particular, had said goodbye to their youth in 1914, to emerge into a new and terrible world.[38] They continued to be influenced by, if not preoccupied with, war; there was unfinished business. In *Façade* (1922), Edith Sitwell anticipated another war: 'the drums of death are mumbling, rumbling, and tumbling'.[39] And when it came: 'Everything went Dark as the World of man, black as our loss', as she wrote during the Blitz in her famous poem, 'Still Falls the Rain'. Dorothy wrote her radio play, *The Man Born to be King* (1941–3), and went back to Dante to rediscover her poetic voice: 'Now from the grave wake poetry again,/ O sacred Muses I have served so long'.[40]

First World War women writers in Oxford – Brittain, Sitwell, Cannan, Sayers and their contemporaries – helped to break through the isolation and the fear, and to raise awareness of the social and economic hardship that followed in the wake of war.[41] They understood what Heathcote William Garrod had taught their publisher, Basil Blackwell: that it was a 'scholar's task to relate a new order to the one dying'. Sayers, in particular, helped to bring in a cohort of women from the cold, to join the University's male poets. They were now to provide a route-map to the war writing of successive generations of women. And they never gave up hope. Maurice Bowra wrote that Edith Sitwell, 'by an act of imagination, understood the pain of the soldier ... her poetry ... was healing ... it had a kind of redemption'.[42] Dorothy too saw a counterbalance, in the healing power of faith (in God) combined with the beauty and richness of nature.

May Cannan's hopeful 'Girl's Song', written in October 1916, still resonated: 'Lift up your hearts ... Grant a small hope to light our travailing ... In heaven there be many stars'. Poetry was May Cannan's 'salute to a generation'.[43] After that, she more or less gave up poetry, although her publisher continued to publish it until after the Second World War, when the accountants got the better of him, and of OUP too – Blackwell's could not go back to the days when volumes like Edith Sitwell's *The Mother* had sold so few copies it had had to be pulped.[44]

Osbert Sitwell in his poem 'Therefore is the name of it called Babel' anticipated the desperation that Yeats was famously to describe in his 'Second Coming':

Things fall apart; the centre cannot hold;
Mere anarchy is loosed upon the world.

Although Osbert's work is less well known, it sums up the desperation he felt about the post-war world:

> When all we came to know as good
> Gave ways to Evil's fiery flood,
> And monstrous myths of iron and blood
> Seem to obscure God's clarity ...
> Deep sunk in sin ... Sinks deeper still, and wages war
> Against itself; strewn all the seas
> With victims of a world disease.[45]

Even in peacetime, the awful stench of the trenches would not go away: 'But he grew blacker every day/ And would not brush the flies away', Edgell Rickword wrote.[46] Basil published further cycles of *Wheels*; in the 1919 edition 'the voice of the social reformer' was audible.[47] What attitude of mind had produced the inequalities the troops had returned home to: the 'smut-filled streets and factory lanes'? Importantly, this fourth volume included writers who had been debarred from publication during wartime. Sitwell dedicated it to Wilfred Owen, including his previously unpublished work.[48] In 'A Terre', Owen wrote that war was about ... 'Shooting, war, hunting, all the arts of hurting ... Well, that's what I learnt, – that, and making money ... things best left at home with friends'. Sherard Vines kept a double seal on his lips: 'I shall not see. I shall not know,/ Impotent, stripped of strength or pain', but in 'Elan Vital', he gave notice to quit: 'I will be sport no longer'. Publishing *Wheels* had made Basil a serious player: it had given expression to his own deeply felt, but often necessarily repressed, repulsion as he, everyone, 'supped full' the horrors of the war.[49] As Asa Briggs later wrote, 'he had proved that the pen is mightier than the sword'.[50]

In publishing both poetry and prose, Basil aimed to warn 'the next generation and protect it from tyranny'. Basil's old tutor, H.W. Garrod, had worked for the Ministry of Munitions during the war, but in 1919 was back in Oxford writing about Parson's Pleasure, a reach of the River Cherwell in Oxford:

> Somewhere West, there's a garden
> Laid out with paths of peace,
> That hath no other warden
> Save, at the Gate of Pardon,
> The Angel of Release.

You'd never dream how deep is
the hush of souls around,
Nor how untroubled sleep is,
nor how the peace they keep is
Fenced from human sound.
There's no noise of hearts breaking,
Only, sometimes, the sigh
Drifts in of tired souls shaking
Life's dust off softly...[51]

He had his memories; there was peace now, but the scars left behind
by the war had barely started to heal. He still heard, perhaps, the sighs
of 'tired souls' drifting by, of all those he had known or taught, who
had died. Those that survived, he hoped, would help 'build the world
again'. Studying the classics would help to civilize them, and forewarn
them.

Frank Gray's *Confessions of a Private* was a pointed reminder of the
unfairness that persisted: 'the only equality is that recorded by the
rude, rough graves'; this was echoed in Blackwell publications by the
historian G.K. Rose's *Story of the Oxfordshire and Buckinghamshire Light
Infantry*, and *The Sword of Justice* by the Vicar of Whalley. In his book
for Basil, John Wallis considered the role of the League of Nations,
and W.H. Reade the *Revolt of Labour Against Civilisation*. A Blackwell
pamphlet, *Reconstructors and Reconstruction: A Plea for Common Sense*,
aimed to reconcile competing claims of capital and labour, and an SHP
pamphlet, *Christ and the Modern State,* pursued the idea that 'the rights of
conscience are supreme'.[52] Education wasn't forgotten, as Basil published
W. Warde Fowler's *Essays in Brief for Wartime*, J.H. Badley's *School Talks
in Peace and War* and *Education after the War* (Badley was a headmaster
of the 'alternative' Bedales School), Trevor Berry's *A Forgotten View
of War* and *The Hope of the World*, and Professor J.A. Stewart's *Oxford
after the War and a Liberal Education*. Graham Greene was already sure
there would be another war 'fought out on the Rhine'; he lamented
the (post-war) repression of the Germans by the French particularly.[53]

Rattled by his writers' prophesies – not that he needed any prompt-
ing – Basil published *The War Resisters* by I.M. and Hilda Hubbard,
who envisaged the 'Humid earth hummocks heaped on the hastily
buried dead'.[54] Editing a collection of essays for Basil in 1938, Keith
Briant and Lyall Wilkes asked: *Would I Fight?* It was perhaps easier than

in the First World War for Basil to raise his publisher's head above the parapet. The public, in general, were suffering the privations of the Depression, even if they were lucky enough to have work, and 'were readier than ever before to question the whole basis of society', as John Middleton Murray observed in *Oxford Outlook*.[55] Murray's was a radical voice, reminiscent of, but even more strident than, the Sitwells and their coterie. Yet again, Basil's authors served his purpose: to protest, to educate, to civilize, at a time when they were most needed. And they gave him a voice. Their words may not have delivered their readers from hell but, like the readers of Dante, Basil wrote, turning the leaves (of their books) would have helped to heal the rifts of war: *In quella parte ove surge ad aprire Zefiro dolce le nouvelle fronde di che si vede Europa rivestire* (In that region where the soft Zephyr wind unfurls the new leaves with which Europe is seen to clothe herself anew).[56]

Basil's attitude to appeasement was distinctly illiberal: he despised it. When the Second World War came, he demonstrated his patriotism by joining the Home Guard and waged his own war on local bureaucrats, as chairman of the parish council, churchwarden, school manager and member of the village hall committee. As in the last war, he sent books for POWs through the Red Cross, to the troops in hospitals and to 'the furthest limits of the Postal Union'. 'In an angry and distracted world,' Basil explained, 'when the nations, sundered by political and economic forces, are in danger of forgetting their common heritage of learning ... [this was] the happy lot of Blackwell's.'

As an act of defiance, Basil expanded his business, both its buildings and the scope of its publishing activities, making continued use of his publishing house 'to air controversial issues'. He tried to ensure that all ranks were heard. In 1939 he published *Casting Off and Other Poems*, the work of Private Enoch Powell of the Royal Warwickshire Regiment. Powell was a kitchen hand in the Army, but also a classical scholar – an early encounter perhaps with 'rivers of blood'?[57] In 1943 Basil published *For This Alone*, written by Sergeant R.P.L. Mogg while a POW, his plane having been shot down over Germany. In the preface Basil wrote: 'the world of letters is the gainer for in captivity he [Mogg] has discovered in himself a poetic gift of very high quality ... A fellow prisoner, Sgt J.W. Lambert, has transcribed and beautifully illustrated these poems.' By publishing this volume, Basil hoped yet again to 'extend the healing power' of poetry. And as war broke out he also published a lighter volume, *Balliol Rhymes*, by his father's friend Henry Beeching,[58] which took him straight back to an earlier, happier age.

FANFARE FOR THE COMMON MAN

Basil regarded his publishing efforts as a way of rebuilding Britain. It was as though the public were giving 'Churchill an answer to his question broadcast to our enemies "What kind of people do they think we are?"' Basil's answer can be easily guessed at: they were the kind of people who liked to read, who liked to question; who were no longer prepared to be downtrodden, uneducated. In the process, both Blackwell's reputation and profitability were enhanced. As in the last war, Basil's profit from bookselling rose, but even more so than before: 'demand exceeded supply ... and publishing had to be encouraged'.[59] Despite paper shortages, Basil was able to produce twenty new titles and thirty-one reprints, including *The Problem of Security and the Indivisibility of Peace*, with a preface by Clement Attlee, which came out in 1939 under the SHP imprint. In 1945 he summed up his publishing philosophy:

> there was a very large market for the many good writers, England poets, novelists, scholars, historians, scholars, essayists, humorists ... it was good, serious stuff they read ... These publications served as comfort food during the long years of austerity during and following the war. Similar to the first editions, they were offered at a comparatively affordable price. Their very names conjure up this feeling of security: such series as *World's Classics* of OUP, Collins *Pocket Classics*, the Nelson *Classics*, Dent's *Everyman's Library* and closely followed by the *Novel Library*, the *Zodiac Press* and the *Cresset Library*. Trevelyan argues that it was here, in this Victorian genre, that our English love of liberty, justice and humanity, for which we fought two world wars, is brought into perspective.[60]

Perhaps the best literary products of this period, Basil suggested, were in the realm of satire, being, in Swift's words, 'a sort of glass wherein beholders do generally discover everybody's face but their own'. Basil and his father had held up an allusive glass of poetry; reflected in it were poets of the war generation. For Basil, or more accurately his down-to-earth fellow directors, poetry publishing was sacrificed to profitability.[61] The prices of all Blackwell publications were raised: the reprint of the SHP one-volume Shakespeare, priced at 6s in 1934, was to cost 15s in 1946, despite successfully cutting production costs.[62] Basil seemed to have accepted that 'ideals in publishing, unless tempered by shrewdness, commonly led to disaster'.[63]

Yet, he protested, he was 'not in business to make money, first and foremost'.[64] He was on a personal campaign to 'enlarge the bounds of human empire'.[65] Sending books to developing countries not able to afford them without help was an extension of his education mission.[66] Selling books, either via the British Council or the university libraries of the Commonwealth, for which Blackwell's was a major supplier, took over as the British Raj departed. But it was also, of course, a boost to Basil's plans to expand educational publishing.

'ONLY THE BEST IS GOOD ENOUGH FOR THESE CHILDREN'

Inspired and encouraged by the Fisher Education Act of 1918, Basil had campaigned 'to bring out more children's books and textbooks'. His efforts proved to be 'a curious case of idealism that paid off'. 'In the false dawn of hope and idealism which followed immediately on the First World War, when men looked for a world safe for democracy and the League of Nations deemed to inaugurate a new and nobler age, there can have been few publishers who were not moved to encourage the generous enthusiasms of visionaries.'[67] The Fisher Act had added a year to the school leaving age, and this, Basil suggested:

> called for something new in elementary school books. What were the current books like? I was wholly ignorant. I visited a local Educational Supplier and spent £1 on an armful of them for examination. It was a shocking experience. The dominant consideration was cheapness: of hack-work shoddily produced, and to this were sacrificed the contents, physical and intellectual. My reaction was to thump my desk and cry 'only the best is good enough for these children!'

Basil attributed his subsequent mastery of the art of elementary schoolbook publishing to Ernest Wilfred Parker. Parker, who had been a teacher and the educational manager of Collins, joined Blackwell & Mott on the recommendation of E.H. Carter, who, together with

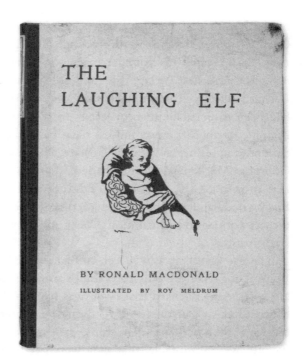

Blackwell's children's books, such as this one, published in 1922, were always upbeat, and fairyland featured regularly; in adult poetry too – Tolkien's 'Goblin Feet', in *Oxford Poetry*, 1915.

C.H.K. Marten, was responsible for the *Histories* series.[68] The *Histories*, appearing first in 1925, were stars in the Blackwell firmament: 'by 1927 they were selling at the rate of 1,000 volumes a week'. Basil was keen to give children the opportunity of studying Greek or Latin: 'to deny them was an act of barbarism'; the *Histories* were written with these sentiments in mind. Eleanor Farjeon's series *Mighty Men*, with illustrations by Hugh Chesterman, starting with 'Achilles', 'made a virtue of the quality of the story telling'. 'Even young children could appreciate stories from the classics'; Basil had read 'Horatius' to his son Richard when he was five: 'he didn't understand but was spellbound by the sense of history and heroism'. Other important school titles included: *A Short Bible* (1930); Edward Mandrake and J. Huxley's *Introduction to Science* (1932–5); and Carter and Brentnall's *Man the World Over* series (from 1941).

Blackwell & Mott had catered for the very young since the end of the war, when they brought out the beautifully illustrated *Babes Book of Verse*, *Farmyard Ditties*, *Ring a Ring o' Fairies* and *Nursery Lays*. *Noddy goes a-ploughing* (1930) by Margaret Baker was a forerunner of

Enid Blyton's work, and no one, then, turned a hair when they saw Cecil G. Trew's pictures illustrating 'Ten Little Nigger Boys'. In 1923, Basil treated his younger readers to a trip down *Joy Street*. The invention of Ernest Parker, this children's annual ran for thirteen years. Richard Blackwell maintained that 'one of Blackwell's achievements had been to persuade men of letters to write for children'. *Joy Street's* list of contributors must indeed have been the envy of every other children's publisher: Walter de la Mare, Hugh Walpole, Hilaire Belloc, Compton Mackenzie, Eleanor Farjeon (famous for the hymn 'Morning Has Broken'), G.K. Chesterton, Edith Sitwell, A.A. Milne, Algernon Blackwood, and so on. 'Added to the distinction of the names was the artwork: good illustrations and good writing go hand in hand,' Basil insisted.

There were misses as well as hits. Blackwell's had first published Enid Blyton, but received 'only the crumbs from her table' when she hit the big time. And Richard Blackwell was to turn down *Asterix*! Richard had read classics at university – didn't he appreciate the humour? Or did he think, perhaps, that comic strips, even ones with a classical flavour, were unsuitable, that they weren't educational?

Basil divided children's books into two classes: under and over twelve. The latter needed little attention, Basil thought. Fluent readers 'could indulge in the great literature available already, the best work by the best authors': Kipling and *Alice in Wonderland*, he suggested. But Basil was so devilishly inconsistent. At other times he decided what was suitable according to whether children had passed the 11-Plus or not; he should have known better. But he advised his customers to buy books as presents for children, not because he was a bookseller, but because of their 'quality of permanence': 'More Books in the Home' was his by-line. It 'made their selection a serious business', but not serious in the sense of 'being instructive; the Victorians had used books in this way'. Just what Basil deemed to be serious could be deduced from his catalogues and advertising, particularly at Christmas time. An insert in the *Daily Mirror*, 13 December 1934, provided:

> An Xmas Book index that solves the children's Gift problem: cut along the dotted lines and let this list make you a model present-giver. The 'girls section' included *Fairies in Plenty* – poems and poetry, 2/6d; *Widdy Widdy Winkey* translated by Rose Fyleman, 3/6; and *New Edition Clear Type Works of Shakespeare*, 6s 4d.

The 'boys section' was instructional: *Simple Science* by Andrade and Julian Huxley; or adventurous: *Tales of Action for Boys* by L.A.G. Strong. There were humorous books, and silhouette books (such as *A Matter of Time* by Margaret and Mary Baker). Had it been intentional, or was it a slip, that *Jobs for Jane,* with illustrations by Thomas Derrick, 4s 6d, was merely classified under 'general'?[69]

The production of school texts flourished and led Blackwell's down the path of academic publishing: science, arts and humanities. Even poetry crept in under the science umbrella in the 1930s with Julian Huxley's *The Captive Shrew and Other Poems*. Foreign languages, too, were given greater weight, especially after the fall of France in 1940, when it became impossible to import French or German texts for school or university use. Blackwell & Mott, with two Oxford professors as editors, initiated a new series, which gave the publishing house its entrée into producing set books, formerly the preserve of the university presses. The 1944 Education Act provided a further incentive to publish school texts, and John Cutforth, formerly a teacher, launched Blackwell's ground-breaking series, *The Learning Library*. Publications such as M.N. Duffy's *The Twentieth Century*, Cole and Benson's *New Ways in Geography*, and Walker and Wilson's *Location and Links* were much lauded, overseas as well as in the UK.

To accompany his educational publications, Basil devised guidelines for teachers and support material.[70] *Reading with Joy*, for example, an innovatory system of reading, included a guide for teachers as well as a workbook for writing in. Teachers across the range of schools, from top grammars to secondary moderns, and later comprehensives, were consulted about subject and content, and regular visits were made to schools and NUT conferences.

In the 1960s, Basil worried that the firm was still 'not coming to grips with either school or university expansion'. John Cutforth, detailed to look into this, advised improving the calibre of authors. He wanted to enlist A.P. Rollett, an HM inspector for schools, for mathematics, and he saw that science also needed books that 'bridged the gap between school and university'. English 'needed extension notes for O and A Levels'; Cutforth suggested approaching Professor Bullough of King's (London) for notes on *Hamlet*.

Basil, back on a favourite hobbyhorse, stressed the need to extend bright state-school pupils.[71] He was furious with the government's comprehensive education programme, the death knell of many grammar schools. This resulted in the publication of 'an anthology for sixth formers on "argument": science and religion going right back to Copernicus; discussing women's role in society for example'. Routh's *They Saw it Happen* was taken up by the history inspectorate as a good introduction to the idea of using primary resources. Books for schools overseas were also considered for publication: 'N Rhodesia wanted a book on native dialect: no problem about costs, just fulfil orders as they come – no advertising or admin.' *Time Remembered* was aimed at secondary modern schools but, Cutforth advised, 'we need to move forward to more modern days'.[72] School titles were displayed in the shop 'so that parents could be involved in their children's education', and there arose a new market 'commensurate with the rise in consumer purchasing power'. Educational publishing was yielding dividends previously undreamt of: sales of textbooks leapt in the 1960s, and by the 1970s Blackwell's was considered a serious academic publisher, but with titles to interest the general reader as well. Fred Hoyle's *The Nature of the Universe* (1950), which sold more than a 100,000 copies, had set a precedent, and Blackwell's had begun to understand the importance of producing paperback as well as hardback editions.[73]

Basil also understood the importance of catering for changes to the school and university curricula. In 1939 Basil and Adrian Mott each gave £500 as initial capital to Blackwell Scientific Publications Ltd (BSP), and Basil was on the board, along with Henry Schollick, Charles Field and Henry Critchley. The managing director was John Grant, who was the inspiration behind BSP's first publication: R. Macintosh and Freda Bannister's *The Essentials of Anesthesia* (1941). Grant had trained at Blackwell's, although his family owned Oliver and Boyd in Edinburgh, publishers of, among other things, medical books and the *Edinburgh Medical Journal*. The moment was auspicious, especially as Lord Nuffield had given £2 million to Oxford University for the establishment of the Post-graduate Medical School.

BSP was to publish medical and scientific research books, to set up a medical lending library and, if possible, to publish a Nuffield Journal.[74] In their design and production, the science books were to perpetuate Blackwell's high standards: John Robson 'set technical standards which were the envy of many a publisher'.[75] The company progressed 'from being the newest and smallest medical publishing firm in Britain to flourishing maturity as one of the biggest with a list of 1,400 titles and a turnover of £5m a year and an international reputation' fifty years later.[76] Blackwell's scientific authors, indeed all educational authors, received the same careful attention as their poets once had, which Hugh Jolly, distinguished pediatrician and head of Charing Cross Medical School, saw as comparable 'to that between patient and doctor'; he always urged his colleagues to try Blackwell's first. But the same could not be said of the poets, who had mostly fled to London publishers.

Basil had grown 'sick of the poetry scene', although he was 'very reluctant to say goodbye to his poets: the Sitwells, Huxleys, Sayers etc'.[77] Unable to cut the cord himself, he told Cutforth: 'rid yourself of Nessus's shirt'; and his son Richard had a very difficult letter to write to the Oxford Poetry Society. Why did Basil allow Richard and the board to put an end to something of which he and his father were manifestly so proud? The excuse was high cost and low demand. But perhaps the truth was that Basil wasn't prepared to stick up for modernist, realist poetry, with its 'lack of rhyme and the broken rhythms'. It may have reminded him too graphically of what he called 'the shaken spirit of the age'? His rejection, he explained, started with what he perceived as 'the lull in poetry and belles lettres [at the] end of the Edwardian period. Meredith had finished his work and Hardy had written his last novel; Swinburne had sung his last.' The first note of revolt against literary conventions of the day was to be heard in *Blast* by Wyndham Lewis, 'an ugly quarto in a harsh magenta cover which shocked, irritated or amused its readers according to their age and outlook ... and the startling notes sounded by Masefield in *The Widow in the Bye Street* and *The Everlasting Mercy*, which multiplied sales of the "English Review"'.

When the world woke up from the 'four-year nightmare' after 1918, Basil found that 'life and letters had changed indeed'. Contributors to *Wheels*, for example, issued a 'counterblast to Edward Marsh's Georgian Poetry', and Basil professed to not understanding their, or anyone else's, modernist writing. But he tried to puzzle it out. Was there 'perchance any relation between the allusive obscurities of their followers, making poetry a matter of "code words among coteries" [the phrase is Godfrey Elton's] and the contemporary diversion of crossword puzzles?', Basil asked. 'Was it the immense celebrity that Lytton Strachey won, debunking Victorian saints and heroes, which prompted Ezra Pound and

Eliot to seek to establish their own poetic reputation by denouncing
that of John Milton?' Basil's view was summed up succinctly by four
lines from his old poetry professor, H.W. Garrod:

> Thou should'st be living at this hour,
> Milton, and enjoying power,
> England hath need of thee, and not
> Of Leavis and of Eliot.[78]

Maurice Bowra added his pennyworth:

> neither magic nor vision are much in favour today nor likely to be.
> Even Mr Eliot's Anglo-Catholicism, with its white leopards and
> jewelled unicorns, can at best appeal only to a limited public, and not
> necessarily a public devoted to poetry.[80]

Garrod had attributed this poverty in poetry to the First World War.[80]
Yet, to Basil's mind, there were no signs of any revival. 'How many
poems, verses, or lines written in the years between [the wars] have
sung themselves into our memory and passed into common use, like
those of "A Shropshire Lad" and Rupert Brooke?' The 'absence of the
mnemonic effect' meant that he didn't remember lines of poetry any
more.

During and just after the First World War, it had been important
for Basil to publicize his authors' anti-war message; that the Modernist
Wheels' 'light brigade charge against [poetic] convention' offended his
personal taste was overlooked. He perhaps sympathized with their view
that 'too long has poetry been confined to one side of life', and he may
also have observed that they were not averse to leaning on the past.

Alternatively, had poetry lessened its appeal because Basil had out-
grown his need to protest? Perhaps there was no longer anything to
protest about, in the peace that followed the Second World War when
Britain 'had never had it so good'? Yet clearly Basil felt that there *was*
still much to protest about: nuclear weapons, the tax man, the Post
Office, the antiquarian Ring, the destruction of ancient buildings, the
condition of the prisons, the decline of the grammar school and the
teaching of classics, the stupidity of British opposition to the Common
Market ... the list was endless. If his poets had still been hammering
on his door, instead of decamping to London, Basil may well have

faced down the board. But he kept his hand in, publishing poetry for children. He could justify this: it was educational in the broadest sense; 'it stretched children creatively'. Back in 1922 his publication of *Fifty New Poems for Children* had met with success; now he could expand into a new market for secondary schools. If he still needed to persuade the board, he had no better advocates than the in-house ex-teacher John Cutforth and the poet Cecil Day-Lewis.

Basil published Day-Lewis's *Poetry for You: A Book for Boys and Girls* (1944): 'on the enjoyment of Poetry'. A schoolteacher and a former editor of *Oxford Poetry* (1927), he had gone elsewhere to be published after university, but in the 1930s he came back to Basil to compile an anthology of verse for children. Had Basil invited him because he detected a lyrical, traditional element in Day-Lewis's own work?[81] Day-Lewis's *The Echoing Green*, taking its title from Blake's poem of children joyfully playing outdoors, ran to three editions. The popularity of the first edition, Day-Lewis suggested in *Poetry for You*, proved that 'poetry wasn't daft ... soft and unmanly ... in the present war, many of our young poets are fighting, and some have been killed'. But was it 'any use ... did it help you to get on in life?' Poetry, Day-Lewis explained, was 'something to be enjoyed', and it 'tells you about inside as well as outside'.[82] Poetry, he added, would also develop children's critical faculty: 'What was a good poem; if it did not run sweetly, then why?'[83] As much a romantic as his publisher, Day-Lewis had held out *A Hope for Poetry* (1934), that it would help the healing process.

The third edition of *The Echoing Green* (1957) moved away from narrative verse, and included the work of Yeats and Eliot. After this Basil thought to ring the changes, calling on John Betjeman to make *his* choices. The new Blackwell anthology was to be aimed specifically at schools, and Basil hoped that 'television's top boy in poetry' would persuade the authorities to include it on the examination syllabuses. Betjeman agreed to 'review' Day-Lewis's selection, which he judged 'good', but he, echoing Basil, didn't like 'the younger poets who often have faulty ears and are careless of rhyme and meaning'. Instead, to Basil's hearty agreement, Betjeman suggested that narrative verse should be reinstated: Tennyson, Campbell, Southey.[84] He also wanted to include Kipling's 'Way through the Woods' and 'Danny Deever', Newbolt's Drake and, possibly, Lear's 'Said the Table to the Chair', but 'wasn't "ducky" just a little juvenile?'[85] Betjeman wouldn't be the editor of the proposed new anthology, he said, but he would collaborate.[86]

The exchange of views about what was to be included makes uncomfortable reading. Basil wanted it to contain poetry that would appeal to grammar and secondary modern children, and to 'thinking teachers' as well as '"B" teachers', who just want 'to be led to a good anthology by a famous name'.[87] 'Narrative and light verse Lear in the latter category', Basil writes to Betjeman, would especially appeal to 'Sec Mod children'. His elitism was not, he claimed, to do with class, but with 'suitability' for this or that type of education, but it did boil down to class. Yet at the same time he was a fierce defender of the grammar school system, which benefitted financially poor children.

Despite the empathy Basil showed, which must have derived from his own background and his belief in self-education, he succumbed to the habit of categorizing people by social class and education. Children, Basil wrote, were judged by their level of, or rather lack of, education. Yet, he admitted, it was 'marvellous how often children will "read up"'; he would have discovered this by observing the apprentices his father had employed. It was this that led him to hit on the idea of asking children, and their teachers, to make their own selections for what became a popular poetry series: *Poems Chosen by Boys and Girls* (1923–5). Taking this democratic approach, Basil redeemed himself. 'Ten thousand is, indeed, too low an estimate' of the numbers of children and teachers involved.[88] The choices the children made – Tennyson, Longfellow, Gray, Wordsworth, Browning, Newbolt, Herrick – affirmed his taste and his faith in juvenile readers, and he would have been gratified that Walter de la Mare's 'Trees' was included: it suggested that the children and/or their teachers understood the suffering endured during the war: 'The Yew alone burns lamps of peace/ For them that lie forlorn'.

A COUNTER-REVOLUTION

Speaking at the celebrations for Basil's seventieth birthday, John Betjeman, who was first published by Blackwell's, reminded his audience of 'those *Oxford Poetry*, beautifully printed, slim volumes, decadent some of them, folksy and some of them obscure, passionate all of them, put forward at the one time in our lives when we really felt we must be published'.[89] It was a reminder of the importance the Blackwells placed, not only on the content of a book, but its presentation and physical quality.

Basil, like his father, had wanted to follow the craftsman's creed preached by William Morris: 'to restore the dignity of work'. Benjamin Henry had more limited resources than Morris, who had the means to employ craftsmen in his textile, furniture and furnishing workshops, but his first volumes were nonetheless carefully produced in hand-printed style by the Vincent Press and bound in brown paper or stiff cards or with wallpaper covers (the cost borne by the increasingly profitable bookselling side). And Basil had stated publicly his opposition to the commercialization of 'the most individual products of the human spirit: as the Victorian giants fell, they were succeeded by mercenary gnomes'.[90] If, as Rex King wrote in his diary, 'the great mass of education is the branding of man with the stamp of the herd, the forcing upon him of convention',[91] then, as a corrective, Basil would publish the best books, beautifully produced but affordable. This would liberate, not only his readers, but the craftsmen who produced them. He wanted 'by word and deed ... to show the difference between crass commercialism and the ideals and satisfaction of the handcrafts ... [which] in the field of book production, the hand-brake of the Private Press Movement halted for a time'.

Basil, in his maverick way, saw the chance to trigger a counter-revolution, aided by his publishing partner, Adrian Mott. 'No changing of place at a hundred miles an hour, nor making of stuffs at a thousand yards a minute will make us one whit stronger, happier, wiser,' Basil wrote. 'There was always more in the world than men could see, walked they ever so slow; they will not see it for going fast.' Basil shared Ruskin's 'bitter bias against his own materialistic and mechanical age', and looked as ever to William Morris, 'the ideals of the arts and crafts movement'. He wanted to experience 'joy in handling and making' (books), while at the same time making them affordable for the 'common man'. He proved to be quite up to the challenge, with the help of some formidable hands.

TEN

PROFLIGATE PRINTERS &
A SPELLBOUND PRINCESS

Mackail's *Life of William Morris* turned my head to fine printing, and so brought me friends who have enriched my life and bequeathed gracious memories. Among them I treasure most highly May Morris and Bernard Newdigate, the typographer inspired by Morris, whose friendship I wove into the pattern of my life until I stood at their graves.

Basil Blackwell

'ONE NIGHT, not quite 30 years ago,' wrote a reviewer in *The Times*, 'the late A.H. Bullen, by divine providence scholar and poet and divine inadvertence publisher ... had a dream.'[1] Bullen, who was living in London at the time, dreamt of walking in Stratford-upon-Avon. He heard a voice say to him: 'You're not going away without seeing the book?' 'What book?' he asked. 'Why, haven't you heard of the noble edition of Shakespeare that is being printed here – the first complete edition ever printed and published in Shakespeare's own town?' The dream cried out to Bullen, 'and he determined to set up a press of Stratford men'.[2]

Bullen and his business partner, Frank Sidgwick, accordingly set up the Shakespeare Head Press's printing works, with four compositors, on 6 June 1904. The Stratford Corporation granted Bullen and Sidgwick the lease of an old Tudor house which Julius Shaw, wool-striker and close friend of Shakespeare, had leased in 1579, the same year that Shakespeare had purchased New Place, two doors to the south. Bullen would hardly have believed his luck at having a scholar printer, like himself, as a partner. Frank Sidgwick, the son of a Greek scholar, had grown up in Oxford, but had been sent off to Rugby and then to Trinity College Cambridge. As a contributor to the undergraduate magazine *Granta*, under the name Sigma Minor, he was known as a bit of a wag, parodying Kipling and Artemus Ward (alias Charles Farrar Browne).[3] But he had a serious side, and he too became an authority on early English lyrics.[4]

From 25 May 1904 to 23 March 1905, Frank Sidgwick kept a diary of the setting up and day-to-day running of the press.[5] He could, Basil Blackwell wrote, 'turn his hand to anything and had to turn his hand to everything at SHP [Shakespeare Head Press]'. Sidgwick's diary of Thursday 28 September 1904 tells of 'a day of troubles'. 'Faulty rollers, broken letters and spoilt paper' all demanded 'the utmost patience'. In addition:

> there were financial problems, complaints of the noise of the machines from neighbours, awkward employees and structural difficulties ... (discovered bones in a wall cavity when piercing the foundations of the machine-room for shafting) ... gardens and gardeners to cope with, the accounts to be kept, the selecting of a cask of beer and, if the Press was to be kept active, public subscriptions to be canvassed.

Bullen, modest, kindly and otherworldly, scholarly rather than entre-preneurial, was oblivious to practical matters. After three years Sidg-wick had had enough.[6] In 1907 he founded his own publishing firm, Sidgwick & Jackson; Jackson was killed in 1917 but Frank, who served in the Army, returned safely.

But at first the partnership had augured well. Sidgwick's daughter wrote about how a townswoman brought her father an old book, with some pages torn out and others drawn on by her children. It was, Sidgwick discovered, a Second Folio Shakespeare, which 'showed how Shakespeare had survived in his home town'.[7] And here, in a house where Shakespeare must have been a frequent guest, Bullen and Sidg-wick printed the *Stratford Town Shakespeare*. In ten volumes, completed in 1907, it had the original Old Face type, as cut by William Caslon. It was printed on 'a little platen press, one side of the sheet at a time' on English hand-made paper specially manufactured with Shakespeare's crest and coat of arms as a watermark.

Bullen and Sidgwick were on a high, and thought of dedicating the *Town Shakespeare* to their new king. Edward VII thought otherwise and Sidgwick received the royal response: 'his Majesty only accepts dedication of works by authors with whom he is personally acquainted'. Sidgwick ruefully comments: 'I suppose his knowledge of Shakespeare is all second-hand.' The King wasn't interested in the Shakespeare, but surely the literate proletariat would be? Yet the reaction of the vicar of Stratford, G. Arbuthnot, Sidgwick wrote, 'was more bizarrely daunting: "H'm, you won't sell any Shakespeare here: we don't want him."' Then, on the day of the pressing of the bound copies of the Shakespeare, Bullen 'was fined £1 4s, with costs, for letting his chimney go on fire'. In spite of the King, the local vicar and the fire, the *Town Shakespeare* made its mark. 'It was a beautiful piece of work and there were one or two very pretty editions of Shakespeare's Sonnets: Bullen and Sidgwick were certainly among the first to revive the use of the fleuron ornaments and "dainty booklets".'[8]

There is no record of what Bullen thought of his dream's fulfilment. He mostly hid away in the cosy, untidy bookshop, which was his front room, with the little printing offices at the back. On sunny days, this impressive-looking man, tall with a mass of curly hair, could be seen pacing the garden and muttering to himself. Perhaps it was on one of these perambulations that he had another dream. Could a 'collected Defoe, in two hundred volumes at a Guinea a volume, if taken up, make £200,000 profit?' This really was wishful thinking, coming from someone trying to raise a public subscription to keep his firm from going bust.[9] But as *The Times* reviewer remembered forty years later:

> Bullen produced some solid scholarly books like W.J. Lawrence's *The Elizabethan Playhouse*, Dr Moore Smith's edition of Gabriel Harvey's marginal notes, Charles Crawford's *Collectanes* and Dugdale Sykes's *Sidelights on Shakespeare* ... Mrs Aphra Behn in six volumes ... W.B. Yeats very incomplete in eight collected and three new volumes ... titbits for lovers of good poetry and good print.

Although Bullen reached out to the modern canon, his lifelong passion was for Elizabethan song and story. Encouraged by a scholarly father, a librarian at the British Museum, he had studied literature at Worcester College, Oxford. Before he took to printing, Bullen had published two volumes of *Lyrics from the Song Books of the Elizabethan*

Age (in 1886 and 1888): 'the first of a long line of similar collections of Elizabethan and Caroline writers'.[10]

In partnership, first with the Elizabethanist W.J. Lawrence (1891–1900) and then with Frank Sidgwick (until 1907), Bullen issued a large number of books, including poetry for the Muses Library series. His 1886 *Lyrics* were reprinted as part of the series with, as Bullen explained, 'a few textural corrections ... the editor [ie himself] has succeeded in discovering the authorship of some songs that he had previously failed to identify'; it is alleged that he was influenced by F.T. Palgrave and Arthur Quiller-Couch. In his preface, Bullen laments (truly, lament is the right word) the separation of song and poetry and issues a challenge:

> Our poets no longer make 'music and sweet poetry agree' ... contrast the poor thin wretched stuff that one hears in the drawing rooms of today with the rich full-throated songs of Campion and Dowland. O what a fall is there my countrymen! In Elizabethan times music was 'married to immortal verse'. Let us hope that the present separation will not always continue.[11]

Basil, still a schoolboy, would, if he had known, have shouted Amen to that!

As a scholar, Bullen made waves, but as a printer he made mostly debts. Despite the quality of his work, especially at his SHP, he had no head for commerce, and sadly at his death, in 1919 at the age of sixty-three, the Press was left derelict, as symbolically his grave would become. The weather-beaten board which marked his resting place in Luddington, three miles outside Stratford, was hidden by a tangle of coarse grass until, forty years later, the poet laureate John Masefield set out to restore it. Masefield and others wrote of Bullen's achievements to a local newspaper:

> One of the distinguished classical scholars of his day ... an outstanding authority on English Literature of the Sixteenth and Seventeenth centuries whose editions of John Day, Marlowe, Peele, Middleton, Marston and others are today a valued possession. He re-discovered Campion, and identified and published for the first time an immense number of fine lyrics from long-forgotten manuscripts [lying] in the Bodleian and elsewhere. A small committee has been formed to raise a fund to enable a bust or plaque to be suitably placed

in Stratford upon Avon to commemorate A.H. Bullen's 16 years' residence in the town, and to provide for the erection of a permanent memorial in the churchyard where Shakespeare's Avon *purls beside him sleeping*.[12]

SHAKESPEARE HEAD REPRIEVED

Bullen's Press, however, was to win the accolades that he himself had so craved in his lifetime. It was revived by Basil Blackwell, 'and furnished with all that [Bullen] had been unable to give it. Furnished, inter alia, with two very potent sources of energy, H.F.B. Brett-Smith, scholar, and Bernard Newdigate, bookman and printer.'[13] It was Basil's dream to 'jump from authors beginning their careers to those who had finished theirs'. And through the medium of the Shakespeare Head Press, his dream was to come true.

At the time Bullen died, Basil was managing the publishing side of Blackwell's for his ageing father and dreamed of producing books of the standard William Morris had set. But it was Morris's friend and adviser at the Kelmscott Press, Emery Walker (1855–1933), who suggested Basil's name to Bullen's executor. Walker was 'the grand old man of English printing'. 'It is scarcely too much to say that his [Walker's] influence, direct or indirect, can be discerned in nearly every page of type that now appears; Bernard Newdigate detected his influence internationally, in German book production,' wrote Morris's executor, Sir Sydney Cockerell.[14]

Walker had started out as a printer in 1873, when he joined the old Typographical Etching Company. In 1886 he founded a partnership with Walter Boutall, process engraver, which became, successively, Walker and Cockerell, then Emery Walker Ltd. Reputedly, it was his lantern lecture to the Arts and Crafts Society in 1888 (had Benjamin Henry perhaps attended?), 'Letterpress Printing and Illustration', that had moved Morris to set up the Kelmscott Press.[15] May Morris often told Basil 'of the assistance she received from Walker in the preparation of the mammoth edition of her father's works'. In her introduction she suggests that the Kelmscott Press could not have existed at all without Walker's active cooperation.

In 1900, after Morris's death, Walker, with Cobden-Sanderson, formed the Doves Press at Hammersmith, naming it after the local pub. His work, notably using the Doves type, showed 'even more convincingly than Morris had done, that sheer excellence of typography is the essential thing in fine book production, quite apart from any decoration or ornament, or novelty in types or composition, or doctored papers, such as are sometimes used to give an added, and spurious, attractiveness to printed books', Bernard Newdigate later wrote. Sadly, the types ended up in the Thames. Walker, having departed from Doves, was devoting himself to photo-engraving, but his interest in letterpress printing never waned. In the year before his death, Walker produced an edition of the *Odyssey*, translated by T.E. Lawrence (Lawrence of Arabia). Assisted by Wilfred Merton and Bruce Rogers, 'it was printed in Centaur type, designed by Rogers, and cut by the Monotype Corporation for use with their composing and casting machines; it had fine illustrations in black on gold background'.[16]

Walker was knighted in 1930 for services to the printing trade, although Basil liked to say that *he* had been the first 'tradesman' to be so honoured (in 1956). But the work of Walker and his associates, just as much as Morris's, had inspired Basil as he learnt the 'gentle art of publishing' at OUP. It may have been Benjamin Henry who introduced him to Walker during one of his London trips to visit Basil while working at the Press. Basil remembered the occasion fondly:

> I spent a magic hour in his office in Clement's Inn, while he
> discoursed on the subject which was dear to him, punctuating his
> words of counsel with 'D'you see? D'you see?' I remember that as I
> listened I thought of the princess in the fairy tale who never spoke
> without dropping a jewel from her lips. It was an unforgettable
> encounter, and I think it was remembered by him, for when
> Bullen died, it was at the prompting of this lovable man that his
> executor invited me to acquire the Press and carry on its tradition of
> scholarship in fine printing.

To start with, Basil's acquisition of the SHP did not go smoothly. In a letter to M.A. Spielmann, a scholar who had contributed an essay to the *Town Shakespeare*, Bullen's niece and former secretary, Edith Lister, asks if he 'might know someone who will buy the Press'.[17] Mr Bullen had 'died in great poverty', and the Press would have to be wound up 'unless a publisher can be found'. Lister writes of 'selling Bullen's books volume by volume ... to pay wages: the printer-compositor's wages are

£7.5.7d, and the ordinary compositor's £3.17.6d'. Bullen's brother, E.L. Bullen, had put a price on its head: 'he wants £2,500 for the Press and all the effects in the houses, antiques etc'.[18]

At probate Bullen's estate was valued at £2,660 including books; could this 'asset be used to set up a school: Bullen had always intended to take on pupils?' A letter from Charles Whitby, probably an executor, suggested that he was happy about the idea of 'an Indian prince' purchasing SHP. There would be political and economic advantages if this 'rich prince could give as a gift to the world the [SHP's] valuable re-prints of Elizabethan literature'.[19] In the New Year, 1921, Lister writes again to Spielmann offering to cut the price of this 'scholar's press' to 2,000, informing him that 'an American syndicate is thinking of taking it over'.[20] Meanwhile, Basil appears to procrastinate. Lister tells Spielmann: 'Basil, who wants the press, has not yet paid – maybe he will yield it up to the Syndicate?'[21]

Three days later Lister announced: 'Basil now owns the press', but 'the Maharaja' was still hanging in.[22] A series of telegrams crossed the world, but in the end the prince lost out to a little-known publisher, in comparison almost a pauper, in Oxford. Basil's father was still chairman, and much in favour of continuing Bullen's work. Could Benjamin Henry have remembered him giving a series of lectures in Oxford on Elizabethan writers, breaking new ground when English was only admitted as a subject for a pass degree?[23] With no more equivocation Blackwell's board agreed to purchase the Press for £1,500, to be run from Stratford for nine years after its incorporation on 21 February 1921.

Bullen's former partner, W.J. Lawrence, wrote to Basil praising him for taking over the SHP.[24] Lawrence's motive for getting in touch with Basil may not have been entirely selfless, however. He had written an article on Shakespeare 'from a new angle for a lecture delivered at Harvard, printed in *Studies*, Dublin, Sept 1919, and this was to be part of a book to be published by Bullen'.[25] Did he reckon that Basil would fulfil Bullen's promise?[26] In an undated letter, T.S. Eliot also praised Basil's efforts. He took 'the liberty' of suggesting:

> texts ... not of great length ... [but] practically unobtainable: Marlowe's and Golding's translations of Ovid, Philemon Holland's selections from Livy, Suetonius or Pliny, selections from Donne,

The Martin Marprelate Tracts, Campion's and Daniel's *Treatises on Versification*, Gawain Douglas's Vergil, Underdowne's *Heliodorus* and Nashe's *Terrors of the Night* and *The Unfortunate Traveller*.

Basil expressed his own hopes and intentions in 'Fine Printing at Lower Cost'.[27] Morris had 'set the book printer a standard he could not hope to reach: widening rather than diminishing the gap between the ideal book and the book of every day'. But surely, Basil added, 'this was not the point; the important thing was the statement of aims and practical solutions in one man's eyes ... Modifications in line with modern production needs would have to be made.' But Morris's message had been seen and understood: 'books from Pelican and Nonesuch, Symon's First Edition Club, the University presses, hard-backed pocket editions offered by many of the regular publishers, the ubiquitous Penguin [from 1939]'.[28] Among these accessible classics were, of course, the library editions of the SHP. Its standard editions were finely printed and, although more affordable than was usual, none was in the same price bracket as the Penguins; they were however more durable.

For twenty years, until the outbreak of the Second World War, Basil and Adrian Mott 'engaged in a series of books, some glorious, all dignified, the work of authors ranging from the Venerable Bede and Chaucer to the Brontës and Anthony Trollope'. Reasonably priced, they gave the less well off an opportunity to build their own 'library' of fine books – more often than not just a shelf. And those involved in the production of the books benefitted too. Basil, as his father had, tried to create a working environment where 'individuals thrived, where they learned and improved their skills, where creative, and artistic considerations were as important as commercial realities'. In the SHP workshop, fine design, printing and binding promoted closer union between art workers, scholars and craftsmen, and gave young artists an opening.

John Frederick William Charles Farleigh (1900–65) was a classic Blackwell case. Leaving school at fourteen, he was apprenticed to the Artists' Illustrators Agency, London, where he learnt lettering, wax engravings and how to make black and white drawings for advertising. He attended evening classes at the Bolt Court School until the war intervened; he served for the last few months until the armistice. A government grant enabled him to study full time at the London County

Wood engraving by John Farleigh for the Shakespeare Head Press
edition of Pindar's *Odes of Victory*.

Council Central School of Arts and Crafts (later the Central School of
Art and Design).[29] Amongst his teachers were Bernard Meninsky and
Noel Rooke, who introduced him to wood engraving. Farleigh was to
make a name for himself as a wood engraver, but his first important
commission came when Bernard Newdigate 'asked him to do the head
pieces for Pindar's *Odes of Victory*, 1928', which perhaps led Constable
to choose him as the designer for Bernard Shaw's *The Adventures of
the Black Girl in Her Search for God*. He also produced 'some marginal
drawings for a [Blackwell] school geography ... beautifully engraved
on pear wood blocks'.[30]

John Mason, a former printer and binder at SHP, who taught at
Leicester College of Arts and Crafts from 1930, wrote in *Bookcrafts and
Bookbinding* that 'the revival of bookcrafts was a lifeline for the art's
preservation – in schools and colleges'. Mason's definition of 'bookcrafts' included everything 'from stationery and blotters to boxes using
card, paper and linen: even very young children thus grow the seeds
of interest in the next generation', which 'may revive interest in and
appreciation of English hand binding'.[31]

In his own fervour to resurrect fine printing, Basil set off on his
knightly charger to save William Morris's Kelmscott House in Hammersmith and his flatbed Albion press.[32] After Morris's death, in 1896,
the Kelmscott Press had been dismantled and the Albion went to C.B.

Ashbee of the Chipping Campden Guild. When the Guild was dissolved in 1903–4, the Albion had passed on to Arthur Bullen and then, with the SHP, to Basil.

Basil intended to carry on SHP's traditions with Bullen's scholar printer Bernard Newdigate, and H.F.B. Brett-Smith, who wanted to cover art and architecture as well as literature. Still in Benjamin Henry's lifetime, the publishing side was regarded as 'a naughty baby brother and an infernal nuisance', Adrian Mott wrote. One of Blackwell's printers had hitherto been Bertie Ashcroft. 'Besides being one of the finest in Oxford, he was a bit of a villain,' Adrian Mott remembered. 'If ever the black market returns, Bertie would be the man to know. I believe there is still a bit of a racket in nylons; I can only say that I have no proof he had anything to do with it.' What did the rigorous and austere Newdigate make of Blackwell's motley publishing crew?

THE 'FIDGET' PRINTER

Basil had been overjoyed to inherit Newdigate from Bullen, yet his reputation as a 'fidget printer ... [was] fit to break your heart', Kendrick (the composing room foreman) warned. Or did he, perhaps, mean break the bank? Walker, who was himself not easily satisfied, recounted that Newdigate had once over-run a page, and adjusted throughout six times before he was satisfied. Nevertheless, Basil counted himself lucky. As 'aesthetic and technical adviser' to Bullen, who was 'an amateur albeit an inspired one', Newdigate had proved himself to be a professional.

Emery Walker had already suggested that Basil 'make some modest experiments with a new fount of type based upon the model of Jensen and produced by the firm of Shanks'. But actually making 'money from fine printing' remained 'a Herculean task ... one seldom accomplished', recorded Basil. At his first meeting with Basil, Newdigate 'calmly informed him of this fact'. Basil, under pressure from the board to rein in his support for struggling living writers, hoped to subsidize them by resurrecting dead poets with a selection of finely printed belles-lettres. Added to which he hoped, by using modern machinery 'side by side with the highly prized Kelmscott hand-press', to 'prove that a fine style in printing need cost no more than the uninspired routine work of the commercial printer'. Other presses, such as 'Gregynog, Raven,

Curwen, Alcuin, Golden Cockerel, Nonesuch, Cresset, Chiswick and many more amongst modern printers, in this country at any rate', were making 'a serious effort to achieve the happy union of design with industrial art'.[33]

Newdigate described the Kelmscott, Doves and Ashendene presses as the 'trinity standing high above any lesser followers'. But they were no more immortal than the Shakespeare Head. The Ashendene Press, founded by St John Hornby, had come under Walker's guiding hand in 1904. It produced in 1933 a fine edition of Amyot's French translation of *Daphnis and Chloe*, printed in black, blue and red, and graced by skilled hand-working calligraphers under Graily Hewitt's supervision. Newdigate applauded Gwen Raverat's wood engravings, especially 'her sense of needing to be subordinate to the printed page – a rare quality'.[34] But the press closed the following year. The Golden Cockerel Press endured until the 1960s, but closed when the necessary resources and skills became too expensive. It had been founded in 1920 as a co-operative venture in Berkshire, where Eric Gill contributed fine wood engravings to its edition of *Troilus and Cryseide*, *The Canterbury Tales* and *The Four Gospels*.[35]

As for the Shakespeare Head, while 'Bullen may have had the dream, the scholarship and the vision, it was Blackwell and Mott who had the faith and the courage – and the money'. But it was 'because of [Newdigate's] superb organisation of the words, shapes and patterns that the Press is best remembered … With his arrival, the concept of the *new* Shakespeare Head began to appear and his typography flowered.' Basil recorded his first impression of the man he came to admire so much.

> He called to my mind first and always a descriptive passage in Dickens … As I contemplated the great brow, and the bald dome fringed with hair, the circular spectacles … and the beaming eyes twinkling behind those glasses, I was perforce reminded of the man who had traced to their source the mighty ponds of Hampstead. And indeed there was something Pickwickian in his innocence … his enthusiasm for antiquity … But *his* was the spiritual dignity and remoteness of the later, post-Fleet Pickwick.

Newdigate's scholarly pedigree appealed as much to Basil as it had to Bullen, and his family connection would have had an added appeal for the Blackwells.

The Blackwells' early publishing work had put them within the ambit of what Virginia Woolf called the 'status group'. Could Newdigate widen this circle? He was the kin of Sir Roger Newdigate, who had founded the Oxford Prize for English Verse – published, of course, by Blackwell's. Newdigate's father, son of the third Earl of Dartmouth, had trained and worked as an Anglican priest. He converted to Catholicism and succumbed to the enthusiasms of a Benedictine monk, Fr. Strutter. This modest monk, who had founded St Gregory's Press of Stratford-upon-Avon, where he ran 'a halting enterprise printing devotional books', was more renowned for his faith than his business acumen. Bernard's father threw caution to the wind and sank his capital into the venture, opening his little press in 1888. His wife, the daughter of Sir Henry Boynton, looked askance at the family's finances, and feared for her ten children's futures. Somehow funds were found in 1878 to send Bernard to Stonyhurst, the Jesuit public school whose curriculum, coming from the late sixteenth century, emphasized figures, rudiments, grammar, syntax, poetry and rhetoric.

Stonyhurst possessed 'a splendid collection of early printed and manuscript books', and years later Basil took a party of printing students on a visit there. 'I could well imagine the conditions under which the very young Newdigate started out on his academic career.' Basil likened his situation to that of Stephen Dedalus in James Joyce's *Portrait of the Artist as a Young Man*. Joseph Thorp, in his survey of Newdigate published for the Double Crown Club, 'affirmed that in all probability, Newdigate's character and attitudes were moulded by his two main Jesuit tutors; one a most solid figure of learning and the other a more quick-silver exponent of the Catholic Philosophy'. The breadth of his reading and scholarship was remarkable, and his impatience was tempered by 'the idealism of Morris and the practices of Emery Walker'. Sensitive to the family's financial difficulties, Newdigate took an external London BA degree and set about preparing himself for the Civil Service examinations. But he was not destined to be a Trollope-like clerk. His father's enterprise, the Art and Book Company, had moved to Leamington but was showing symptoms of collapse. Bernard tried to come to the rescue.

It was in his father's print shop that Newdigate was introduced to Emery Walker. He always told Basil that 'he learnt more about the conditions of fine printing from Walker than from any other source

... that red ink alone did not make for an impressive title page, that the unit of a book is not one page, but a pair of pages, and ... it was preferable to use bigger type solid than smaller type leaded'. Newdigate set about following his advice. From his father's small establishment he created the Arden Press. Newdigate's most famous work at Arden, between 1911 and 1914, was the printing of the twenty-four volumes of Longman Green's monumental *Collected Works of William Morris*.[36] But Newdigate's fine work had buttered no parsnips: by 1905 the Press was already sold to W.H. Smith's. It had not made Bullen solvent. How was Basil's SHP to avoid the same fate? Try as he might, Basil could not restrain his friend's perfectionism. 'So,' Basil recorded, 'we had to ask for an estimate, formally accept it, and leave Newdigate to dedicate the profit to getting it right!'

Under Newdigate's direction, and the scholarly eye of H.F.B. Brett-Smith, literary editor 1921–8, many fine books came out under the SHP imprint. First off the press was Michael Drayton's *Nymphidia*. In quick succession, *Twenty-Five Sonnets of Shakespeare* appeared (1922), and in 1924 the book was transformed from a mere pamphlet into a limited edition on Kelmscott hand-made paper, with hand-printed boards, covered in buckram with silk ties.[37] *The Loves of Clitophon and Leucippe* (1923) was also printed on Kelmscott paper, with a few special vellum copies. 'This,' Basil gleefully recounted, 'was a fine beginning to the new order ... and the style of Newdigate is already apparent: close word spacing, judicious leading, strong title page opening, and a crisp letterpress on firm white paper.' Next came Greene's *Newes both from Heaven and Hell* and *Funeralls* from the 1590s, which made use of the original sheets of Bullen's 1911 edition. Less ambitiously, but just as fastidiously, came a raft of poetry and some inspired books for children, such as Madeleine Nightingale's *Ring a Ring o' Fairies*, with woodcuts by Charles T. Nightingale.

In the beginning Newdigate favoured the Caslon type and, Basil wrote, 'he was, in all probability, its greatest exponent, but he took other typefaces, particularly the new Monotype revivals, in his stride'. Other printers, like Cobden-Sanderson, imposed their 'will on the book'; the Doves Press, 'coldly formal', shaped 'with the chisel', while Morris, more human, carved at it. Newdigate, Basil expounded, was subtler, 'with more delicate clothing for the words ... and quite impeccable tailoring of the subject to be printed'. To make ends meet, the Press also took on jobbing printing and some vanity publishing, especially verse, but the work still had to pass muster with Newdigate. Some editions were printed for Cresset Press: Bacon's *Essays or Councels Civill and Morall* and Bunyan's *Pilgrim's Progress* in 1928, with wood engravings by Blair Hughes-Stanton and Gertrude Hermes; Milton's *Paradise Lost and Regained* in 1931, using the Cloister typeface (unusual for Newdigate). In 1930 Newdigate was commissioned by the Limited Editions Club of New York to produce Thomas De Quincey's *Confessions of an English Opium Eater*.

The hand-coloured Froissart's *Chronycles,* published in 1927–8, distilled in Basil's view 'the essence of Newdigate's style'. His *Chaucer* (collected works), (1928/9), was a more flamboyant exercise, livelier and with more calligraphic flourishes between the stories. The Lynton Lamb illustrations, based on the Ellesmere manuscript, added a touch of lightness and gaiety to the pages.[38] Colin Franklin, comparing the SHP version with two editions from the *real* private presses, Kelmscott and the Golden Cockerel, plumped for Newdigate's simplicity and careful planning. Two volumes of the Venerable Bede's *History of the Churche of England* (1929) displayed the skills Newdigate deployed in his Cresset Press *Pilgrim's Progress*, as did Chapman's *Homer*, produced in 1930/1 with over fifty wood engravings by John Farleigh. Newdigate used the newly available 16-pt Centaur, demonstrating 'that the Caslon was not always inevitable or necessary for a superb design', Basil declared. Malory's *Morte Darthur* followed in 1933. Basil judged it 'perhaps a little less fine, but knowing the subtle interpretations of Newdigate for tenor and time, it is probably deliberately coarser and a more rugged feel prevails ... Newdigate's wizardry has made the page easy – pleasant – charming to read.' His scholarly credentials were also evident in *The Ben Jonson Poems* (1936), which he edited. The make-up of poetry, he believed, required the exercise of care and certain nicety of judgement. Newdigate's Book Production Notes, which appeared in the *London Mercury* from 1920 to 1937, 'formed one of the most valuable critical analyses of printing and book production during this time'.[39]

To publish a complete works of Michael Drayton had been one of Bullen's unfinished ambitions, which Newdigate saw to fruition in *Michael Drayton and His Circle*, which appeared in 1941. 'It was produced in the grand scholarly tradition of a long line of scholar-printers –

Aldus, Caxton, Plantin – and will surely have granted Newdigate a place in the printer's Valhalla', Basil enthused.[40] Four volumes were edited by the American scholar John William Hebel (1931), the fifth by Kathleen Tillotson and the sixth by Newdigate himself.

If Newdigate could make works of antiquity 'easy – pleasant – charming to read', perhaps his skills could be used to produce texts already in great demand by the general public'? Could he, Basil Blackwell wondered, endow a one-volume Shakespeare with merit? Newdigate seized on the suggestion. The *Shakespeare* was commissioned in 1934: a complete edition of 1,260 pages in a production run of 50,000 copies, to be sold at 6s each. This was no limited edition! It was printed by Billings of Guildford, and the speed of production did not allow any of Newdigate's 'fidgeting'; its success ensured a reprint in 1937. 'In 1940,' Basil recalled, 'our dear enemy destroyed the moulds, and the book was re-set leisurely.' Newdigate, now an invalid 'kept at home', read the proofs, 'improved the setting, and wrote a short life of Shakespeare to introduce the plays. He lived to see the new edition, and saw that it was good.'[41] The venture's success was 'staggering', Basil wrote, 'since it coincided with the terrible economic depression of the Thirties'. Despite the lack of profit and the slump, SHP continued to produce fine editions, while Blackwell's bookselling and educational publishing provided ballast. Newdigate's reputation for helping printers and artists during hard times also helped to keep the good ship afloat. As well as John Farleigh, the Press used other notable illustrators, including Lynton Lamb, Paul Woodroffe and Thomas Lowinsky.

It is ironic that hard times *made* many artists: writers, painters, musicians, as had the First World War. But the Second World War did for the SHP. When the US Army requisitioned the premises of SHP, 'we had to clear everything', and Basil 'found a good home for the Albion press at Oxford's Technical College'.[42] (When Kelmscott House was bequeathed to the William Morris Society, Basil tried to return the Albion.[43] But it wouldn't fit through the door. 'I will house it, if Kelmscott cannot,' Basil insisted; two years later, after some restoration, it was successfully re-installed.[44]) And with the death of Bernard Newdigate in 1944, the SHP chapter closed – almost for ever. Henry Schollick, a Blackwell's director since 1931, didn't want to look back: 'The time, the place and the man are gone.'

Basil deeply mourned Newdigate's passing and, when he had more time on his hands, he hoped to provide 'a more permanent memorial to the man who made the SHP'.[45] In his lifetime, Newdigate was always 'quite indifferent to praise, and discouraged attempts of other writers to give publicity to his own work'. In self-justification, he would quote George Wither: 'if he be a Printer he makes conscience to exemplify his Coppie: to compose his book fayrely, and truly'.[46] After a lifetime 'of effort to inspire tread printing and publishing with the ideals of the Arts and Craft movement, Newdigate remained the most under-rated of typographers'. The books designed by Newdigate are 'a monument to his ability as a designer showing a recognizable technique using very simple means', Basil explained. He had 'a steady eye for the minutest detail, a disciplined use of a good and fitting typeface, a complete understanding of the unity in the book page(s) ... and a feeling for a period. And he married typeface, illustrations and page format to fit the spirit of the job.'[47]

Although not so learned a man as Bullen, in Basil's view (and this is debatable), 'Newdigate matched him in familiarity with Elizabethan literature and even surpassed him with his knowledge of that era ... Among all the good things he produced for the Shakespeare Head Press, perhaps the most characteristic are the sturdy, unpretentious editions of Defoe, Richardson and Fielding ... Out of all his work there shines an almost child-like integrity.' Writing ten years after his death, Adrian Mott wrote that 'of all the men I have ever met I think perhaps he was the one I most admired. The quite exceptional uprightness of his character, his charm and his genius were unique.'[48] But for Basil, Newdigate's genius lay in his ability to preserve what had been so valuable in the craft of Emery Walker and William Morris. His admiration for these men's work and ideals led him to Morris's daughter, May, and resolved him to realize her publishing dream.

THE SPELLBOUND PRINCESS

Basil first set eyes on May in the early 1920s, when she came to Oxford to give a lecture on pattern for an Arts and Crafts exhibition. He had invited her to speak, knowing she was anxious to promote the memory of her father and was hoping to attract subscriptions towards a memorial in his honour. He fell instantaneously under her spell: 'what a knowledge of loveliness she showed, and how modest she was in presenting it'. But she had to be handled with kid gloves. 'How like a whip were her words when a foolish woman came up to her afterwards and suggested she might give that lecture before some body in which she was interested: "My fee is ten guineas." She had given us the lecture freely.' But he also saw her softer, more vulnerable side: he 'remembered comforting and encouraging her when she came to Oxford to address Sir Michael Sadler's Town and Gown Luncheon Club, remote and timorous among two hundred men. I remember the lovely substance of her dresses, beautified by rare but unprecious jewellery.' Her face 'of noble and austere beauty' was, however, 'somewhat haggard, with her eyebrows set at an angle reminiscent of a Greek tragic mask'. But Basil thought there must have been a time when, in the gloriously exciting company at Kelmscott Manor, like Hardy's Phena, 'Her dreams were upbrimming with light, and with laughter in her eyes.' And he wanted to see Kelmscott for himself.

William Morris had imagined an earthly paradise where women and men were free, healthy and equal, and that they would live in countryside reclaimed from industrial squalor. At Kelmscott his daughter did indeed live 'where roses were rolling over one another with that delicious super-abundance of small, well-tended gardens which at first sight takes away all thought from the beholder save that of beauty', as her father had written in *News from Nowhere*. But her life was far from paradisiacal. As Basil Blackwell came to know her, 'she would remind me of a spellbound princess, such as may be found in those poems, half story and half dream, which enchanted me in reading that earliest collection, *The Defence of Guenevere and Other Poems*'. She was, he wrote, 'the captive of her father's memory, who had, as it were, to complete the tapestry of it before the spell could be broken'. For all he admired William Morris, he wished that May would come out of the 'desolate land of ghosts' and follow her own star. Her 'aesthetic and mental equipment and her excellent prose style', Basil reflected, 'fitted her for creative work in her own right'. May's *Decorative Needlework*, written in 1893, was, as an old friend later reminded him, 'quite wonderful – plainly written ... [about] both the techniques and the utility of embroidery'.[49] May was closely associated with the Arts and Crafts movement and became the virtual leader of craftswomen in England, founding the Women's Guild of Art in

1907.[50] That Basil's grandmother had taught embroidery would also have recommended her to him.

Basil's first excursion to Kelmscott was made by river, sculling from his home in Appleton. He counted himself lucky to be considered a 'pilgrim: mere sightseers and any who betrayed a trace of patronage were frozen by May's hauteur, and dismissed with a cutting phrase'. Making his way up the path, he came across May in the garden where he was treated to a rare glimpse of her happier persona. Finding her 'in knickerbockers, pruning the vine: something of this happier face was captured in Rossetti's chalk drawing of May in girlhood'. Basil was reminded of her 'lovely mother Jane Morris; one of the most painted of the Pre-Raphaelite women'. But when, Basil wondered, had the eyebrows of Jane's beautiful daughter begun to assume their tragic slant? Were hers the 'lips and eyes of the loved and the lover' that Morris had written of in 'Love is Enough', or had she not been loved enough? Could he sense that May had not been her father's favourite? He would perhaps have known of her failed marriage, but did he also know of her 'mystic betrothal' to George Bernard Shaw?

As a comrade-communist, Shaw had come to frequent the Morris household.[51] 'Among the many beautiful things in Morris's two beautiful houses was a beautiful daughter then in the flower of her youth. You can see her in Burne-Jones' picture coming down the *Golden Stairs*.' Shaw thought himself too poor to marry and, in deference to her father, didn't dare to try to win May's hand (he omitted to mention that he was already engaged in a sexual liaison elsewhere). Instead, 'I light-heartedly indulged my sense of her beauty.' One Sunday evening, Shaw recounted, he 'had looked at her rejoicing in her lovely dress and lovely self and she looked at me very carefully, and quite deliberately made a gesture of assent with her eyes. I was immediately conscious that a Mystic betrothal was registered in heaven to be fulfilled when all the material obstacles should melt away ... and I did not think it necessary to say anything ... Suddenly, to my utter stupefaction, and I suspect that of Morris also, the beautiful daughter married one of the comrades.'

For a time Shaw shared the house with the young couple, but 'finding the situation too exacting, and lest he should be the cause of breaking the marriage, he vanished'. But 'the ménage that had prospered so pleasantly as a ménage à trois proved intolerable as a

ménage à deux ... and the husband vanished too'. Presently there
was a divorce. 'The beautiful one,' Shaw wrote, 'abolished him root
and branch and resumed her famous maiden name.' Thereafter, Basil
surmised, 'May buried her unhappiness in her tireless efforts to prom-
ulgate her father's ideas, and to preserve his work ... to keeping her
father's memory not only green but dynamic. In an age that regarded
the Pre-Raphaelite movement as a Victorian episode, his faith was to
be preached entire, his crusade to be pressed home.' May's task was
'heroic', Basil wrote, 'for all the current of present-day life ran away
from or counter to so much for which William Morris had lived and
worked'. This 'championship of an artistic creed outworn' perhaps
added to her sadness, Basil thought. She lived on at Kelmscott as
chatelaine ('the word is almost inevitable', wrote Basil), but not quite
alone. Basil recorded his first sight of her companion, Miss Mary
Lobb, and a less Pre-Raphaelite character could hardly be imagined:
'large, hearty, crop-headed, and always dressed in a Norfolk jacket
and knickerbockers'.

In reality May was not the fey wraith of Basil's imaginings. She
took an active role in village life, and on one occasion wrote to the
principal of Somerville to see if she had a likely candidate to fill the
post of village schoolmistress. Margaret Horton, née Thomson, takes
up the story of her encounter with May Morris in June/July 1925, much
the same time as Basil's own first visit.

> Somerville College, Oxford: end of Midsummer Term after Finals.
> Going-down interview with Miss Emily Penrose, Principal. As is her
> way, she puts me face to the light of the big window while she is at
> her desk in a dimmer corner: shrewd eyes, white hair, questioning
> and scrutinising, terrifying but tolerant. 'And what reading have
> you most enjoyed?' 'Chaucer and William Morris.' 'William Morris?
> How extraordinary!' It seems that Miss May Morris has written from
> Kelmscott wanting a village schoolmistress. Would I be interested?
> Like to think about it? Go for an interview? (Visions of a many gabled
> old house; visions of happy children doing poetry and craftsman's
> work in the Land of Nowhere!) I would. She will arrange it. Smiles,
> delight, farewells. Spanner then neatly thrown into the works by
> my tutor C.R. Young, a shrewd, realistic and downright Scot. (I
> have to thank her for punishing me for, and I hope curing of, purple
> passages and dim meanderings.) 'You will *not* take such a job. Inferior
> status and salary. Elementary school or worse. If you want to be a

teacher you must take a training year instead. You are a specialist. All the same, you *will* go for the interview as it has been arranged. Interesting!'

Somewhat crushed and down-to-earth, I'm still going. I receive a telegram from May Morris addressed to 'Somerville Cottage, Oxford'. Train times to Lechlade Station, where I shall be met. July 9th, my birthday. Having carefully ironed my green linen jerkin (stencilled round the hem, save the mark, with yellow crocuses!), brown skirt of Irish homespun, shoes worn out but tremendously polished (all this in honour of the Arts and Crafts Movement, to which I had been introduced at school by my English mistress), I set off mid-morning for Oxford railway station with my friend Betty Freeth (who intends to remain invisible at Lechlade but will wait for me at Fairford till afternoon). On the way she buys me at Blackwell's a red-covered book, 'The Wood Beyond the World'. It is before me now; on the flyleaf: 'Margaret Thomson, on the day that Mary Lobb rattled her off to Kelmscott in a dog-cart.' An almost empty local train, pottering through enchanted country: Yarmon, Eynsham, South Leigh, Lechlade; my friend vanishes off to Fairford. Outside the station the dog-cart indeed: brown-painted, polished and smart, brown pony small and plump (Icelandic in style at least) and Mary Lobb herself. I don't think there were the famous plus fours but there indeed was the burly figure, the mannish brown tweeds, the Tyrolean hat, the red cheeks and loud voice of legend. 'Jump up! I'm Mary Lobb.' We rattle off westwards, into the breeze.

The noon sun shines on us from the wide blue sky. There are wide fields covered with corn, scattered with red poppies (l remember or imagine a scent of bean fields). Mary Lobb points out landmarks with her whip, discoursing amiably. She came from the West Country as a landgirl during the War and never wanted to leave. She loves ponies, the land: the life. I catch aslant her shining eyes, red cheeks, enthusiasm. Nevertheless, guilt troubles me. False pretences! Teacher training! We have arrived. I 'recognise' over the hedge and under the elms, those often read of, even dreamt of, golden-grey gables, the roof tiles 'in their orderly beauty as a fishes scales or a bird's feathers'. 'Out you get!' Mary Lobb has disappeared. I don't remember seeing her again. I am through the latched door in the stone wall and walking up a flagged path. There is a scent of roses from standard trees on either hand, a scent surely of box and lavender; I recognise it all from descriptions and illustrations in Mackail [William Morris's biographer]. The front door is open. May Morris. I knew, I suppose, that William had been dead twenty-nine years, Janey eleven; I don't think I knew much about Jenny Morris. May was at that time sixty-three. I had thought she was some sort of spinster living alone on her inheritance and certainly she looked remote and withdrawn enough. I expected flowing draperies but she was dressed conventionally for the occasion in a dark 'costume' with a frill of white. She was tall, slim, upright, pale face strikingly oval, greying hair smooth, eyes calm and kind. There was a feeling of very gentle hospitality long practised. She led me along a flagged passage to a washroom, where, she said, 'You will find powder and everything you need.' (Powder seemed to me at that time the height of sophistication.) In the washroom I looked at my undistinguished features framed for the first time in what seemed a silver mirror of Florentine work. My guilt returned. Perhaps I should not be there.

In the dining room I am presented to the Vicar, a stout middle aged gentleman, clerical black and a dog-collar, gold watch chain displayed over a good deal of front. We eat at a long refectory table. The vicar is rubicund and happy, loves to talk, loves food. We eat fish nicely cooked in a white sauce (was it a Friday?). Whether it was gudgeon from the river or fish from the fishmonger I know not. I am exceedingly taken up with the loveliness of the surroundings and find it difficult not to stare and remain silent. Hand-spun embroidered linen, engraved glass, painted plates, wrought silver spoons heavy with ornament – surely some of the 'best things' brought out for a visitor, however humble. Furniture and hangings, 'but little, and of the simplest forms'. Do I remember or may I have imagined head-height light-coloured tapestry with a pattern of stags and trees? The talk is between the Vicar and Miss Morris – of parish matters, and then of me. He says, 'Well young lady, have you got your certificate?' I think this the height of ignorance in relation to my BA Honours Oxon, and I reply rather stiffly that I hope to, then it occurs to me that I am here on false pretences, but I am unable to explain just then. Back in the drawing room of the Manor (the Vicar having vanished) *I'm* sitting opposite Miss Morris. Confession seems inevitable. 'Miss Morris, I'm really here on false pretences …' She is listening most attentively, even smiling. Out it comes, the specialisation, the teacher-training. Still smiling; she understands completely. 'So the whole thing has been a rather happy mistake.' Now would I like to see over the house?

I now feel quite at home as, pleasantly talking, she leads me upstairs, downstairs, through the simple, carefully tended rooms. There is a sense of space and peace, few but choice furnishings, a carved chest, a rush-seated chair from Morris and Co., a Persian carpet. There are strange, evocative objects, bringing one up sharply, heard of but hardly believed, like things from Tutankhamen's tomb: Morris's Elizabethan four-poster, with its embroidered legend (forty weeks to embroider) 'The wind's on the wold – And the night is a-cold – And Thames runs chill …' (and cold it must have been in that passage room, covers and hangings much needed). In the Tapestry Room so much associated with Rossetti, the tall Samson figures, 'the indigo blues, the greys and warm yellow browns', more faded and ancient than ever; in the garden room, a round table of English oak, typical Morris and Co., simple, solid, almost immovable. In this room there is a handloom with a tapestry just begun. May Morris gets up early to work, as her father did. The hand-dyed, hand-spun wools are bright reds, blues, greens, yellows; flowers are growing in ever-fresh invention out of the grass, into the air, a beginning as vital as spring.[52] This I like best of all. The house with its treasures and memories is being lovingly preserved but better still the work and tradition is seen in action. In this room, Miss Morris takes down from the wall two pastel drawings of herself and her sister. 'These are by Rossetti.' I feel her pride. In spite of everything that happened it is clear that as a child she loved Rossetti. As I'm going I'm offered the shillings for my fare to Lechlade. Though poor I'm happy to be able to refuse, and to return thanks for a memorable day as to a kind friend. She puts a big bunch of roses in my hand. 'From my father's garden.' As I go on to Fairford through dusty lanes feathered with July flowers, herbs, stitchwort, cow parsley and campion, I think something like this: 'There goes a kind and quiet woman, simple and intelligent, who has known trouble and turning points and is not too busy or important to talk and listen to a very young student and to set her worried mind at rest.' A few days afterwards Miss Penrose received and passed on to me a note saying among other kind things that Miss Morris would have liked Miss T. for the teaching post, but that Miss T. had decided for further training on the advice of her tutor. This indeed I did. I treasured this note for many years until the mice ate it.[53]

Basil's accounts of both May and Kelmscott are similar in many details. Some of his ideas, like Margaret's, are borrowed from Mackail, but his perspective is that of a middle-aged man who wanted to help *her*, rather than of a young student who had mistakenly thought *she* might be helped. His first sightings of the upper part of the house were as fanciful as Margaret's.

Upstairs one passed into a shrine dedicated to the memory of 'My Father'. There, in the frozen stillness of a museum, the pilgrim stood, surrounded by lovely evidence of that versatile genius, most memorable among them his painting, *La Belle Iseult*, showing at once rare achievement and promise of mastery, had he persisted, in the supreme art of 'silent poetry'; and on the bed (four-poster and surprisingly short) his noblest memorial, a copy of the Kelmscott Chaucer – that masterpiece of typography whose artistic glories are so strangely alien from the robust spirit of the author. Thence you passed to the chill of the tapestried chamber, where, perished with cold, while a wooden fire sent its modest warmth straight up from a huge open hearth, the hieratic May would turn for you with an ivory knife the pages of some manuscript of her father, or sit at her loom, surrounded by grim titanic figures portraying the blinding of Samson

– which again reminded him of May's 'tragic eyebrows'.

Basil always had what he termed a 'dual relationship' with May: private friendship and public support for her work. 'There were times when, with Miss Lobb and my wife, she would talk happily of trifling matters, of their camping holidays, of their visits to Ireland, or of the Kelmscott snowdrops of rare pedigree whose descendants each Spring carpet the bank beneath the beech hedge in our orchard.' And there were times when they talked of the progress of Memorial Hall, which May 'had set her heart on building and endowing. It was to perpetuate her father's memory and in craftsmanship be worthy of his ideals. Many contributed to the cost, but the inspiration and the burden were mainly hers: the reward of many years of sacrifice and work in lecturing and writing.'

When the Hall finally opened in 1934, the centenary of Morris's birth, her friends 'came but could not get in; for they found the Hall thronged to the limit by an unexpected multitude of unknown disciples. With difficulty, and by way of the coal cellar, an entry was contrived for Ramsay MacDonald; the rest of us,' Basil recounted, 'stood outside listening to Bernard Shaw's allocution relayed by an intermittent microphone.' Despite a gap of almost forty years, Shaw had been back in touch with May. Motoring through Gloucestershire, the spell of Kelmscott came upon him and he turned aside to visit the grave of William and Jane Morris, which he had not seen before, and was moved to knock at the door of the manor, and 'presently the beautiful daughter and I, now harmless old folks, met again as if nothing had happened'.[54]

By 1934 William Morris's ideals and scholarship had been eclipsed in the public mind by his political persuasion, his iconoclasm and his 'creed outworn'. Basil had an idea of how to resurrect his reputation. He wrote to May, suggesting 'that if any scrap of her father's writing should still be unpublished, we might help to commemorate his centenary by printing it handsomely at the Shakespeare Head Press on the very same hand-press which once had been part of the equipment of the Kelmscott Press'. Keen that May too should be given an opportunity to show her talents as a writer, Basil had in mind that she should be the editor. She responded almost immediately. Some days later, a huge parcel arrived from Kelmscott House. It included a mass of typescripts, pamphlets, periodicals and off prints; upwards of half a million words. Basil recorded this memorable day: 'My first thoughts were of Alf Button [and his] overwhelmingly obliging genie whose ministrations proved to be, in the author's words, "too bloomin 'olesale" for him.'[55]

Thrown by May Morris's wholesale response, Basil looked to his publishing colleagues for help. His first port of call was Longman's, who had already published twenty-four volumes of Morris's work. They, however, regretted that this was 'quite enough for them'. May had herself asked Longman's in 1932, and been bitterly disappointed by their refusal. Basil then tried Allen & Unwin, having in mind their Ruskin, which, according to Basil, 'had made the firm'; his dear friend Stanley Unwin 'had a unique ability in finding markets for difficult books'. 'But', Basil wrote, 'Sir Stanley's generous heart was controlled by a strong and clear head', and his answer was no. For over a year, Basil was haunted by the 'silent reproaches' of May's 'thumping parcel'. Unlike his other publishing friends, Basil's heart was more susceptible. As it had for his father, sentiment, rather than commercial reality, often prevailed. But could he publish everything May had sent? He thought not. Basil set off for Kelmscott Manor, hoping to persuade May to make a selection; he would sweeten his offer with an invitation to her 'to add a written account of the chosen pieces in her own admirable words'. 'Once more we sat in that grim and chilling room, and in the end May, dismayed and hesitant, agreed to see what she could do.' But 'the look on May's face spoke legions' and Basil could only think of making a speedy escape before she changed her mind.

Basil got as far as the car but no further. He found his progress blocked by Miss Lobb. As strong as any farm labourer, she used her own special charms to strong-arm Basil into the Memorial Hall, on the pretext that he hadn't been able to get inside at the opening. Penning Basil in a corner, 'her legs a-straddle and her arms akimbo', she said her piece: 'Now look here Mr Blackwell, you are worrying May, and I won't have her worried. You've got to publish all that stuff. Don't think I care a snap for the writings,' she bellowed. 'I hate old William Morris – dreadful old bore – but I'll not have May worried. You go home and write tonight telling her you will publish everything.' She then proceeded to offer her life savings as an inducement to the bemused Basil. 'I've no money,' she told him, 'I've only £50 in the world, but you shall have that and welcome if you do as I tell you.'

Basil was no match for May Morris's minder: all 500,000 words were saved. Miss Lobb was never called upon to relinquish her life's savings and May Morris saw two volumes of her father's remaining unpublished works roll off Basil's Shakespeare Head Press in 1936. The work was entitled *William Morris: Artist, Writer, Socialist*, and its production was 'appropriately under the direction of Bernard Newdigate, who had designed and printed the twenty-four volumes of *The Collected Works* during his time at the Arden Press at Letchworth'.[56] George Bernard Shaw, forgetting a wrangle he and Basil had had over his own collected works, agreed to write an introduction to the second volume. It gave an account of Shaw's relations with Morris in the early days of the socialist movement and of his youthful love for May. Was their love rekindled? As an old lady, May did 'a lot of knitting of socks to keep her hands supple and whenever she saw Shaw she gave him some'.[57]

After the book was published, May had only two more years to live. 'The last time I saw May Morris was in fulfilment of a vow that I would bring my family to visit her by river,' Basil recorded. From the Blackwell home in Appleton:

> it was but sixteen miles up river and so it was that on August Bank Holiday 1938 we shipped our sculls at Kelmscott and made our way up to the house. I saw her at a distance in the paddock: she turned and gazed at us stonily as we advanced, looking very like dishevelled trippers, and I had a moment's anxiety lest she might not recognise us and speak words of rebuke which she might regret. I called out to her,

May Morris and her companion Mary Lobb around 1937. The Blackwells, like May and her father William Morris, tried to reconcile socialism and capitalism.

and her manner changed: she admitted that she was about to chase us away deeming us to be a party of idle curious who had come by cabin-cruiser.

After a feast of home-made wine and cake, May walked the Blackwell family back to the riverbank where their boat was moored. She told Basil that 'she no longer cared to go out either to the front or the back of the Manor House; for the long peace of Kelmscott had been invaded by an aerodrome behind the village, and on the river the old wooden weirs and bridges had been replaced by concrete work, and rollers had given way to lochs for the benefit of motorboats'. 'How much they miss,' Basil commented.

Unknown to them the subtle music at the water-level, from swaying rushes, from the kiss of sculls precisely dipped, and the quiet mirth of little eddies as the blades are pressed home; unknown the deep

content in healthy weariness and the sense of achievement at the day's
end. Such joys were known to May Morris in the hey-day of life at
Kelmscott, but are now almost forgotten on the upper reaches of the
Thames. It is all part of the passing of an age. The noise and vulgarity
of the world were pressing hard upon her, and I was aware of a
weariness of spirit that day.

Basil's sense of May's world-weariness was not ill-founded. 'Before
the year was out I stood at her grave. It was 1938. The chapter was
finished and the book closed; William Morris had passed into legend.'
And Miss Lobb? 'She for a little tried to live without her, liked it not
and died.'

Looking back, Basil tried to get his feelings about May in perspective. She was not after all, he now thought, her father's captive.

> I see the daughter as the complement of her father. High priestess of
> his cult, hers was the Pauline function of ordering and interpreting
> the manifestations of his volcanic genius. In the devotee I see also
> the partner … It is the measure of May Morris's achievement that
> Morris has remained an inspiration and a household word to this
> day; and I am glad that I was able to contribute a little towards that
> achievement.

If Basil's *Morris* served to show off May's talent as a writer, it also
accorded with his aim to make book production an art form. He had
fought valiantly to halt the dead hand of mass production, but after
the Second World War his enthusiasm 'declined until it fell away'. He
excused himself; he was a 'fading Cheshire Cat'. Was he sentimental? No, he didn't think so, he wrote. The cessation of hostilities in
1945 'marked the end of an epoch in many spheres of human life and
thought, and not least conspicuously in the tradition of English Letters'.
Hence, like Virgil, Basil took solemn leave of those who had accompanied him: 'So, away with the conventional and the sentimental! Away
the tenderness and veneration! Away with reticence … So good-bye
to all that.'[58]

CONCLUSION

A man's work in literature, like water, eventually finds it own level ... its survival depends on the instincts of ordinary people, not 'Professors of Literature, writers of Literary handbooks, or expert librarians' ... We are our own jury.

Basil Blackwell

THE STORIES told and retold here point to many conclusions, depending on how the reader chooses to see the material. But the underlying message must be that books are of paramount importance for self-betterment. Some, like Lord Nuffield, saw no need of them, but where would Rex King, Alf Williams and their contemporaries have been without them? Rex King and, at the other end of the social scale, Hugh Walpole, like countless others of all classes, started their literary lives with 'penny dreadfuls'. But a character like Sexton Blake was as iconic to that generation as Harry Potter is to today's. Like the Hogwarts adventures, Blake and the other 'penny dreadfuls' were disparaged by some highbrow critics, even though they played an important part in encouraging children, especially boys, to read.

Basil Blackwell always argued that reading should neither be censured nor steered. He read his own son ancient myths and legends, but he himself had started out with Andrew Lang's *Fairy Books*, and then, as an adolescent, was 'suckled in the rhythms of Swinburne and the novels of Stevenson'. In adulthood he kept an open mind. He 'didn't (just) read the classics': by 'classics' he meant 'books that survived';

that were 'the best'.[1] But this troubled him. What if a book that was held up as an example of the best was as false as the emperor's new clothes? A supreme example, he felt, was the reception by the critics of *Finnegans Wake* (1939). 'I longed to see some critic of standing state that this was an exercise in gibberish,' said Basil, 'but Joyce and his claque had been so convincing that only fools could fail to recognise its beauty.' Reasoning in this way, Basil advocated some censorship. It was, for example, his 'duty to censor any book that he judged to be pornographic'. But this 'offered a choice between two evils: censorship insults the spirit of man by depriving us, though not for gain, of the right of private judgment. Pornography, for gain, degrades the spirit of man by seducing us to contemplate ignoble things.'

His father, Benjamin Henry, had been caught up in this conundrum. The *Yellow Books* associated with the 'naughty Nineties' were prominent on the shelves of his workroom.[2] Yet in 1893 he refused to publish Lord Alfred Douglas's *The Spirit Lamp*, after he detected 'something tainted' in the opening contribution: 'a letter written in prose poetry by Mr Oscar Wilde to a friend, and translated into rhymed poetry by a poet of no importance ... "*Hyacinth, o mon coeur! Jeune dieu doux et blond*"'.

Basil kept his father's *Yellow Books*, and supported writers who were by no means 'good boys and girls'– many of the contributors to *Wheels* anthologies, for example.[3] 'But why couldn't modern writers make vice a virtue?' Basil asked. The genius of writers such as Goldsmith and Fielding was that they could 'make vice interesting and made it a virtue ... [but] virtue is fast becoming old-fashioned ... Could any writer today create a Dr Primrose or an Amelia?' Obviously not Joyce, whose *Ulysses* Basil deemed 'obscene'. He was deeply troubled by what he called this 'frank writing'. 'As legal sanctions in sexual matters are relaxed we find writers exploiting the techniques and vocabulary of fornication.' He would not have seen himself as homophobic, but the 'homosexual's charter [1967] opened a new chapter' and Basil did not want to read of 'acts of foul sexual perversion [that] offend good taste and good morals'. As a child of his time, Basil's stance could be understood. As he explained, it had 'been formed in the years when Wilde had gone to prison and his father had refused Alfred Douglas's *Spirit Lamp*'.

The publication of Hubert Selby Jr's *Last Exit to Brooklyn* went too far. At Basil's son Richard's instigation, a Tory MP undertook a private prosecution of the novel in 1967 on the grounds of 'unrelieved barbarity'. Basil, called as a witness for the prosecution, was asked if it had corrupted him. 'There was silence in the court when he replied: "my memory has been defiled by it"'; the publishers (Calder & Boyars) were found guilty, but won on appeal.[4] Basil's objections were probably aesthetic as much as anything: he disliked its style – the lack of grammar and the seditious use of the Bible.

Seven years later he faced Calder again, at the Oxford Union. The motion for debate was: 'This house would rather have pornography than censorship'. Calder was to propose the motion and Basil to oppose it. The derisive laughter can be easily imagined as Basil told his student audience: 'booksellers from time to time have been accused of officious censorship'. They would have known he had form, and not only over censoring *Last Exit to Brooklyn*.

In 1959, when Weidenfeld & Nicolson had published *Lolita,* Basil withdrew it from Blackwell's shelves: he said he wasn't 'worried about the young, but old men'. The student magazine *Isis* undertook a libellous campaign against the shop.[5] The 'adolescent scribblers', including Dennis Potter (who was reading PPE at New College), 'were banned forthwith from mentioning Blackwell's'. A don made an apology in the *Oxford Magazine* on their behalf:

Who are they that they should question
Orders of that learned knight,
Or hesitate the least suggestion
That he has not judged aright.
Let the Isis roll in silence;
Cherwell's waters have the right
To sing with tumbling genuflections
'Blackwells are a source of light.'

When, the following year, the unexpurgated version of *Lady Chatterley's Lover* hit the bookshops, Basil was up in arms. 'Here was a gutter-born Lawrence exacting social vengeance ... a manifestation of genius in decay ... the work of a sick man at the end of his life.' *The Times* judged Basil's explanation 'sour grapes', but he may in part have been defending the reputation of his old friend Ottoline Morrell, who, Lawrence knew, had trysted with a young stonemason.

Facing a 1970s audience, suckled on Larkin and the sexual revolution, Basil argued that *he* always obeyed the sixth commandment in Clough's 'Latest Decalogue':

> Thou shalt not kill, but needst not strive
> Officiously to keep alive.

Intellectually, Basil aligned himself with Milton, who had championed the 'Liberty to know, to utter, to argue freely'. Yet in Roman times, Basil continued, 'the censor was an inspector of public morals'. But today's censors 'could condemn on just reading a selected passage ... as was the case of Havelock Ellis's magnum opus and of *Ulysses*'.[6] They were all too often as 'reactionary, ineffective and absurd' as the Vatican, which had forbidden, for example, '*Pamela, Virtue Rewarded, A Sentimental Journey* and *The Laws of Organic Life* by Erasmus Darwin'. Really absurd, said Basil, had been the expunging in Bowdler's *Family Shakespeare* 'anything likely to offend or bring blush to the cheek'. He cited 'Leonatus's letter in Cymbeline where the omission of a single letter saves the cheek of modest innocence with the reading: "Pisanio, my wife hath played the trumpet in my bed"'. When Basil read something that repulsed him, he said he overcame it by thinking of Shelley's description of Naples: 'Such statues! There is the Venus, an ideal shape of the most winning loveliness, a Bacchus more sublime than any living being, a satyr making love to a youth in which the expressed life of a sculpture and the inconceivable beauty of the form of the youth overcomes one's repugnance to the subject.'[7]

To further inform his 'thinking on the issue of censorship', he turned to '*The Decameron*, because Boccaccio was the first refiner of Italian prose ... *Lolita*: brilliantly written, but has no worthy or noble sentiment'. Basil recounted how he shocked A.E. Housman by failing to discern fully the excellence of *Gentlemen Prefer Blondes*; yet *Moll Flanders* he found acceptable as 'only a picture of the times'. All good books, Basil concluded, had their imperfections: 'for authors are men with passions like ourselves ... The poet Martial, in the dedication of his book of Epigrams, fairly admits this frailty,' which Basil rendered as: 'good things, some not so good more frankly bad, this book contains, that's how all books are made'. Even Shakespeare had his faults:

> we should remember what Ben Jonson, who 'loved the man and did honour his memory' said: 'I remember the players have often mentioned it as an honour to Shakespeare that in his writing (whatsoever he penned) he never blotted out a line. My answer hath been "would he had blotted a thousand ... but he redeemed his vices with his virtues, there was ever more in him to be praised than to be pardoned".' And that perhaps is as much as we can say of the work of most authors. Ben Jonson by refusing to 'go with the crowd' of uncritical admirers did Shakespeare a notable service.

Such authors, Basil argued, survived because their work contained an 'immortal spark', which he defined, borrowing from Housman, as 'a moment of truth' that goes 'to the core of the human mind and the unalterable element in its constitution'.

Such a moment of truth, in Basil's view, was sublimely captured in *Middlemarch* when Mrs Bulstrode, on learning that 'her husband's reputation is blasted by the discovery of some villainy in his early life ... seeks him out as he sits abjectly "feeling himself perishing in unpitied misery". Putting one hand on his, which rested on the arm of a chair, and the other on his shoulder, she says, "Look up Nicholas!" So she espouses her husband's shame and sorrow; no more is spoken, they weep together.' Against this, he suggested, the twenty-two stanzas of Browning's 'Any Wife to Any Husband' appeared 'ponderous and inadequate'. *Middlemarch* became a classic. A book that has 'an immortal quality, stirs the mind', whether it was Mrs Bulstrode's silent absolution or 'the cruellest line in English drama: Lightborn's "And get me a spit, and let it be red-hot"; Chaucer's "Allas, Allas, that ever love was synne!" or William Wordsworth's "To me the meanest flower that blows can give, Thoughts that do often lie too deep for tear"'. Did Basil think this sentimental? 'Absolutely not!

Towards the end of his life, he spent most of his time 'searching through books to see if they contained this immortal quality'. Was it this preoccupation that hampered Basil in his efforts to write his own book? He said that he 'ran out of time'. In truth, he was by his own admission averse to being 'eminent in one small field' or 'holed up in academic institutions'. Like his father, he venerated the intellectual

Basil Blackwell in his Broad Street office, on the first floor in the bookshop, circa 1970. He is reading his much-loved copy of Morris's Kelmscott Chaucer.

life of the cloister, but he upheld the freedom of the 'scholar gypsy': someone travelling through life and 'acquiring an education, through books, and not necessarily in formal surroundings'. According to this maxim, almost everyone could have an Oxford education.

VERTEX

Greek and Latin are the alphabet of the humanities even as
mathematics is the alphabet of the sciences.

Basil Blackwell

T HIS COLLECTION of Oxford stories, although largely literary in
tone, appeals to the mathematician in me. Its narrative describes
a vertex – a point at which two lines meet – where high Victorian
elitism met a new era of outreach and inclusion, and where scientific
subjects were placed on an equal footing with other disciplines. Yet
this had been the situation when Merton was founded, 750 years ago.
Back then it was poor scholars, without a benefice, who were admitted
as full members. By the fifteenth century, Merton was to become as
famous for its mathematicians as for its classicists, and there was no
clear distinction between them. The term 'mathematics', coming from
the Ancient Greek, means simply a subject of instruction. Perhaps what
the Greeks (Pythagoras and his followers, for example) had in mind
was a system – a methodology, a language – which would help them
to think and learn so that they might discover the 'truth'.

Many of the real-life characters that appear in this book were intent
on finding the truth. The autodidact Rex King, whose diary is an
important addition to the Merton Blackwell Collection, wrote about
his search. But whereas literature was a help, science 'was all too often
an impediment', he wrote.

Literature is the criticism and portrayal in seemly and ordered words, of human thought and experience. Science is but a larger parable of the ways of God – the effort of the finite to comprehend the infinite ... [It] has solved none of the great ultimate problems of life – it has only wrapped them up a little differently. They are not laws. [Yet] the results of scientific enquiry went all too often unquestioned ... By the simple conjuring trick of putting into the hat all that they wished to get out of it they [scientists] succeeded for a time in deceiving a superficial and over-credulous public. Hypnotized by a glib phraseology, by the light coinage of superficial knowledge, people accepted mere generalizations of observed phenomena as adequate and satisfying explanations.

Rex King's preoccupation with the shortcomings of the scientific method reflected the concerns of many in Oxford at the time. In the Quaker circles he frequented, there were many successful scientists ready to question any scientific theory, doctrine, creed or belief. King went further. 'Scientists cannot tell us how such strange beings as ourselves came to inhabit such a strange world.' The Bishop of Stepney, addressing the boys of Magdalen College School in 1902, when Basil Blackwell had just started as a pupil, warned them that 'those always urging so-called scientific training were making the greatest possible mistake'. Reared among the classics in his father's shop, Basil needed no persuading. His conviction hardened when he went on to read classics at Merton. Their study, he thought, more than 'historical facts' or the 'proven conclusions of logic or mathematics', would help him 'to get at the truth'. Aeschylus, for example, in the *Agamemnon*, wrote that 'the sinful deed begets more in the likeness of his own kind in an unending and unbreakable chain'. This was 'a *terrible* truth', one that came home to Basil when the 'nations of Europe' were caught up 'in this ineluctable coil of mischief-breeding mischief' after the First World War.

While poets tried in vain to warn, scientists looked for solutions. More of them had to be trained, and for this books were needed. Basil Blackwell made a start in the early 1930s, with the publication of a series for school children: Edward Mandrake and Julian Huxley's *Introduction to Science* (1932–5). In 1939 he formally established a separate scientific publishing house and was on the lookout for authors, experienced teachers especially, to extend the range of his books for schools. He found mathematics books sadly inadequate, either for children staying on longer at school or to 'bridge the gap between school and university'. Serendipitously, one of the Blackwell mathematics books that resulted was entitled *Vertex*. Like medieval scholars, the characters in this book, imaginatively reconstructed by Rita Ricketts, lived at a high point where science, social science and the arts came closer together. They were no more successful in uncovering any ultimate truth, but they may have encouraged us to try out a few solutions of our own, or at least to write about them.

Sir Martin Taylor, Warden of Merton College

NOTES

PRIMARY SOURCES

Although reference is made to Arthur Norrington, *Blackwell's 1879–1979: The History of a Family Firm* (Blackwell, Oxford, 1985), and Rita Ricketts, *Adventurers All* (Blackwell, Oxford, 2002) the original drafts in the Merton Blackwell Collection were used and should be relied on rather than the printed books. Where sources are not given in the text, they are taken from the Merton Blackwell Collection (MBC).

BH   Benjamin Harris Blackwell
BHB   Benjamin Henry Blackwell
BB   Basil Blackwell
MBC   Merton Blackwell Collection
MCS   Magdalen College School
RK   Rex King
SHP   Shakespeare Head Press

THE ARCHIVIST'S VIEW

1. When Blackwell's took over Parker's its records were kept. Also in the archive is information on other illustrious practitioners of their day, such as Parsons' of Oxford, George's of Bristol, Thin's of Edinburgh and, more recently, Heffers of Cambridge.
2. Bordering Mercia and Wessex, Oxford had been a meeting place for parliaments, synods and parlays, between the English and the Danes, for example. Edward the Elder's great mound, built in the tenth century, had guarded the valley against the marauding Danes. After the Norman Conquest, Baron Robert d'Oili erected a formidable castle, subsequently a prison and now a hotel. And trade followed the flag. Merchants had easy access to the Midlands, a ford to the south over the Thames, and the negotiable River Isis provided an effective means of transport for goods and people.
3. R.W. Southern, *The History of Oxford University*, vol. 1: *The Early Oxford Schools*, Clarendon Press, Oxford, 1984, p. 33.
4. Catestreet had lost all trace of the early book trade by 1712–13, when all old dwellings were cleared for the Clarendon Building. David Vasey, 'Anthony Stephens: The Rise and Fall of an Oxford Bookseller', in *Studies in the Book Trade*, Oxford Bibliographical Society, 1975, p. 93.
5. See, for example, H.C. Maxwell Lyte's *A History of the University of Oxford*, Macmillan, London, 1886, pp. 2–15; of note is the list of texts studied (p. 9). See also H.L.

Thompson, *St Mary the Virgin, Oxford*, Constable, London, 1903, p. 9: The Trivium and Quadrivium: 'Ligua, tropus, ratio, tonus, angulus, astra'.

6. See R. Gameson and A. Coates, *The Old Library, Trinity College*, Trinity College, Oxford, 1988.

7. The Stationers' Company was given a royal charter in 1557.

8. David Vasey in *Studies in the Book Trade*, pp. 91–8.

9. Until the sixteenth century there were few colleges outside the city's walls; most were in the network of streets bordering the High Street east of Carfax.

10. The Benedictine Durham College, to the east of Balliol College, became Trinity College; the former Cistercian College of St Bernard on St Giles became St John's; the conventual buildings of the Austin Friars in Parks Road became Wadham. Worcester College was later to incorporate the surviving buildings of the former Benedictine Gloucester College, and Exeter College gradually extended into Broad Street in the nineteenth century.

11. Until the passing of the Municipal Corporations Act (1835), a bookseller within the walls of the city had to be either a Freeman or a matriculated member of the University, and many chose the latter, enjoying the protection and privileges that it brought. These avenues were not open to BH when he wanted to set up shop in Oxford.

12. The principal provincial booksellers for whom records survive from the second half of the eighteenth century are the Clay family of Daventry, Rugby and Warwick, and Timothy Stevens of Cirencester. For an important examination of the eighteenth-century provincial book trade and its customers, see Jan Fergus, *Provincial Readers in Eighteenth-Century England*, Oxford University Press, 2006.

13. Richard Altick, *The English Common Reader: A Social History of the Mass Reading Public, 1800–1900*, University of Chicago Press, Chicago, 1957.

14. Joseph Parker was born the third son of the Rev. Richard Parker of Duntesbourne, Gloucestershire in 1774.

15. Sackville Parker worked in the business of James Robson of New Bond Street. Robson himself was a native of Cumberland who, at the age of sixteen, had also seen London as a means of 'getting on', entering the business of his bookselling relation John Brindley.

16. Fletcher had previously traded with his father, also James Fletcher, until the latter's death in 1795, whose father was probably Stephen Fletcher, a native of Salisbury who migrated to Oxford at the turn of the seventeenth century. Fletcher's business clearly flourished; as the antiquarian Thomas Hearne recorded, he also kept a shop at Westminster, 'having in all a great stock of books the best of which he removed to London'. Fletcher appears to have spent much of his time in London, going up to Oxford occasionally on business, where his wife and five children resided. The arrangement must have suited Mary Fletcher if Hearne's account of her husband's character is to be believed: 'He was a very proud, confident, ill-natured, impudent, ignorant fellow, peevish and forward to his wife (whom he used to beat) … and of no credit.' James Fletcher senior took over the leases of the former Ransford family properties in Turl Street and Broad Street from 1731 onwards, and by 1788 they had built a new shop looking onto the newly widened and extended Turl Street, after which the Broad Street site served as a warehouse.

17. FHP were used to giving long credit, but had to be prepared to play the long game. For example, in April 1798 the account of Mr Marshall of Corpus Christi College stood at £10.19s.3d. By April 1801 it had been reduced to £7.5s.9d, when Joseph Parker determined that the remaining debt should be paid off by half-yearly instalments, and the bill was finally paid off in May 1806. But it was not just the large sums that mattered; FHP were prepared to wait for even the smallest debts to be settled. In May 1798 James Holloway, undergraduate of Exeter College, bought a copy of *Juvenal* at 3s. It must have been with satisfaction that Joseph Parker eventually struck through the entry as paid in February 1813, when Holloway resigned his fellowship! At times, though, the company had to treat its customers with a degree of latitude as when, in

May 1795, it accepted a hamper and a dozen bottles of wine against £10 off the bill of Joseph Fern of Brasenose.

18. In principle, all students were bound by the same rules, but as the higher-ranking paid higher fees and enjoyed various privileges, a certain laxity often crept into their observance of their college obligations, be it attendance at chapel or their academic studies. They might start out with the best of intentions, but many were readily led astray by fellow students, as many colleges provided superior accommodation for their sole enjoyment, such as Corpus Christi's Gentlemen Commoners Building or, the acme of desirable apartments, Christ Church's Peckwater Quad.

19. The Servitors were not always the sons of the desperately poor. They either came up to university at an age older than other students, probably having worked beforehand to put some money together, or they were the sons of tradesmen of limited means. John Ireland, the last Servitor admitted at Oriel in 1779, was the son of a Devonshire butcher – see Jeremy Catto (ed.), *Oriel College, a History*, Oxford University Press, 2013, p. 227. By the late eighteenth century, Servitors had all but disappeared, their offices replaced by college servants, but the FHP daybooks show that they clung on at Christ Church and Jesus, at least.

20. I am grateful to Judith Curthoys, archivist of Christ Church, for identifying the 'Mr Grinley' of the FHP daybook from the Christ Church admission register DP iv.a.1, where he is recorded as a cathedral lay clerk.

21. Eligibility had previously been restricted by geographical location (members of Queen's College, for example, were historically drawn from Cumberland and Westmorland; Wadham College from the West Country).

INTRODUCTION

1. RK, diary entry, Saturday 13 July 1918.

2. Some of it was published, such as the articles and speeches of BB and poems and review articles of RK, but the circulation was very small. The MBC also includes the publishing ledgers, annotated catalogues and business records of B.H. Blackwell's. The latter was drawn on by Norrington and Ricketts; drafts of both books are available in the MBC.

3. RK, diary entry, Saturday 8 November 1918.

4. The Bodleian Blackwell Collection (BBC) publishing papers, post-Second World War, contain some exceptional material: preparation of children's books – contentious at times – with important contributions from C. Day-Lewis, John Betjeman and Enid Blyton; *Oxford Poetry* during its last days in Blackwell's hands; monographs showing Blackwell's passage to academic publishing, from the classics and poetry to science and social science, with famous names from academia creeping in – Plamenatz's *English Utilitarians* (1957–8); Ludwig Wittgenstein's *Notebooks* (1957+); reissues of belles-lettres in the SHP style.

5. The 1919 volume of *Wheels* introduced the work of Wilfred Owen (MC), and was dedicated to his memory.

ONE

1. In her book *My East End* (Penguin, London, 1999, pp. 20-31), Gilda O'Neill gives a graphic description of London at the time.

2. BB cites his grandfather as the founder and his father as the 're-founder'. See *British Books To Come*, no. 45, 1948, pp. 13–15.

3. Spiers' bookshop was demolished in 1909 to make way for the Rhodes Building of Oriel College.

4. Ruth Fasnacht, *A History of the City of Oxford*, Basil Blackwell, 1952, p. 140.

5. Richard Altick, *The English Common Reader: A Social History of the Mass Reading Public, 1800–1900*, University of Chicago Press, Chicago, 1957, p. 39; taken from Lackington's memoirs.

6. ibid., pp. 99, 128, 350.
7. Isaac came to be much respected in Oxford. His nephew, BHB, writes of his funeral in his diary: 'to Uncle's funeral 2.15. Long procession to Osney, coffin borne by the old teetotallers'.
8. Milton's phrase was used by BHB at the beginning of his catalogue, no. 39, October 1893.
9. 'That the [Blackwell] shop was situated outside the city limits was significant, for unless he were a freeman of the City, or the son or apprentice of a freeman, no one might set up a new business in Oxford without the payment of a fine.' Reflecting on his grandfather's life, BB took pride from the stand BH had made as 'one of a number of young adventurers in trade who refused on principle to submit to this tyranny, and opened shops just beyond the City's eastern boundary across Magdalen Bridge'.
10. The city council became increasingly aware of the need to relax the 'Freeman' regulations: allowing more people to open up in trade created employment opportunities, even if this meant sacrificing the preservation of Oxford's beauty; see also Fasnacht, *A History of the City of Oxford*, p. 203.
11. *The Oxford Directory*, 1846.
12. BB's thoughts on early beginnings.
13. Fasnacht, *A History of the City of Oxford*, p. 193.
14. BB, notes on the 'Functions of a Good Bookshop', 30 September 1952.
15. Scrapbook, Oxford City Library, 1855–1954, p. 5.
16. Ibid., p. 4.
17. Dutton, Allen and Co.'s Directory and Gazetteer for 1863.
18. To Chas Richards from George Routledge, of 2 Farrington Street, London, 20 June 1851.
19. Norman Franklin, Routledge, Kegan & Paul, to BB, 28 February 1975.
20. The site is mentioned in the Domesday Book. In medieval times it had been part of a small village of fullers and weavers, with a manor house, a green, a church and the 'holy wells', which gave the site its name.
21. The social historian David Kynaston speaks of a period in the mid-twentieth century when 'Sunday was still Sunday'.
22. The new parish church in North Oxford, SS Philip and James, which had been consecrated in 1862, was designed by George Edmund Street, famous not only for his churches, but also the Law Courts in the Strand.
23. BHB diary entry, 1 March 1880.
24. Notes on work contained in a notebook dated 1868.
25. John Gideon Wilson was chairman of the Educational Board of the Booksellers' Association, writing the syllabus for young booksellers. His manual, *The Business of Bookselling* (1930), BB wrote, 'remains a treasury of good counsel'.
26. BB's typed notes for *The Bookseller*, 14 September 1963; also for the *Dictionary of National Biography*, Supp. 1961–70, Oxford University Press.
27. ibid.
28. Included among the run-of-the-mill were a few very fine editions: two Aldines, 5s and 5s.6d, and a Baskerville, 5s, for example. Over two-thirds of the items in his first catalogue were less than 5s, only forty-five cost over £1, and these were often in two volumes.
29. Norrington, p. 22.
30. ibid.
31. ibid., p. 41.
32. Orlo Williams, 'Browsing in Bookshops', *World*, 18 October 1910.
33. Norrington, p. 40.
34. *The Oxford Magazine*, 1939.
35. Interview with BB, John Owen, *Oxford Times*, 25 May 1979.

36. Opened in 1875, it was already preparing girls for the University; the first Oxford women's college was to open in 1878.

37. BB's notes.

38. For further details, see A. Crossley, C.R. Elrington (eds), *A History of the County of Oxford*, vol. 4, Victoria County History, 1979.

39. David Starkey, *Henry*, Harper Perennial, London, 2009, pp. 174, 364.

40. R.S. Stainer, *A History of Magdalen College School*, Basil Blackwell, 1958, p. 82.

41. A contemporary group of year 9 boys, using the school's archives, helped to build up a picture of Basil's school life. Among the boys who were enrolled alongside Basil were Maltby, a chorister and a Thespian, who played Leontes in the school's production of *A Winter's Tale* and spent his spare time rowing. R.F. Cooper, too, was a rowing man. Woodhead had a social conscience. Like Basil, he was concerned about poverty, beggars and the industrialization of Oxford. Obsessed with keeping fit, cricket was his bag and Wisden took precedence over Sweeney Todd and Sherlock Holmes.

42. See volumes of *The Lily* (1901–6), MCS archive.

43. Come, oh my muse; and with majestic broom
    Sweep thou the chords of my responding lyre,
    And tell me why, without a blazing pyre
    And eke unhallowed by a hollow tomb
    There lies this object by the lily's bloom
    Half in the water, half upon the mire,
    That skirts the stagnant stream. Say who its sire?
    And why it lies neglected? Direful doom!
    Oh! cat, for thou wert as once of yore,
    And singing this I scarce suppress a tear,
    In Memphis' fane was reverenced with awe
    Yet of thy power rests there somewhat here,
    (Wrapt in thy sack-cloth shroud), not in thy claw,
    Though lost in sight, to smell alas; too dear.

44. BB to Sir Arthur Norrington, 3 December 1975.

TWO

1. The long and controversial trials of an Australian who claimed to be heir to the fortune of the Tichborne family enflamed Victorian society in the 1870s. The claimant became a *cause célèbre*, with support and outrage split along the social divide.

2. 'To the Electors of the North Ward', Oxford City Council Elections 1911, Liberal Candidates G.E. Underhill, 10 Northmore Road, and B.H. Blackwell, 1 Linton Road, Election Material, Oxfordshire County Records Office, P324.23.

3. Clive Waters, 'William Morris and the Socialism of Robert Blatchford', *Journal of the William Morris Society*, vol. V, no. 2, Winter 1982, pp. 20–31.

4. RK, review of A.W. Humphrey's book *International Socialism and the War*, P.S. King and Son Ltd. Dudley Ward, writing in the *Manchester Guardian*, 15 August 1914, argues that for the Socialist party, as for the rest of Germany, the war was a war of aggression from the side of Russia – they condemned the bungling diplomacy of their own (German) government and the actions of Austria but argued that their own government wanted peace. During the war they fought for fair play for the enemy. Rex comments that the book gives 'a glimpse of the workings of a movement that is destined to play a great part in the future of Europe'.

5. Even Lord Darling's Act of 1927, outlawing bidding agreements, had 'proved to be inoperative'. By the mid-1950s, collusive bidding at auctions began to attract uncomfortable publicity, especially after a major trade journal went to the wall. But castigating the Ring brought the revenge of less upright members of the trade, who refused to renew their subscriptions to the Association.

6. *The Times*, 1 August 1956.

7. *The Times*, 24 May 1969.
8. *Daily News*, 20 November 1885. See also Robert Blake, 'Oxford Divided', *Spectator*, 21 October 1955: 'Not since the heyday of the disputes provoked by the Tractarian Movement 120 yrs ago have passions raged more furiously in Oxford.' There was a proposal to make roads through the University parks and meadows. The city council was in favour of the Vice Chancellor's idea of blocking Magdalen Bridge, BB was not in favour and the University divided. The Warden of Merton accused the VC of riding his hobby-horse round the re-medievalized Oxford of his dreams.
9. *Oxford Times*, 1 June 1951.
10. BB, 'The Urban Mind', *The Countryman*, vol. 57, no. 4, Winter 1960, pp. 620–25.
11. BHB wrote in the 1915 city guide on behalf of the Visitors and Entertainments Committee and printed it on hand-made paper with an Oxford blue paper cover.
12. The president of Rochdale's Layhelpers' Association wrote that 'in all their holiday experiences no place had ever given them such a welcome as had been had in Oxford.'
13. *Book World*, vol. 3, no. 1, February 1984, p. 4.
14. Arnold J. Toynbee's actual words were: 'The spirit of Nationality is a sour ferment of the new wine of Democracy in the old bottles of Tribalism.'
15. From Lord Lloyd of Kilgerran (CBE, QC, JP), Joint Treasurer of the Liberal party, to BB, 28 July 1981.
16. Letter from BB to Lord Lloyd of Kilgerran (CBE, QC, JP), 4 August 1981.
17. Richard Blackwell presented as evidence in court an analysis of a complete day's orders in Blackwell's: see 'The Day's Bag in a Bookshop', *Journal of Industrial Economics*, 1960, which lists the functions that Blackwell's has to perform: special orders, searches for books out of print, provision of endless information to the public, i.e. bookshops have a 'community role'. The bookseller's problem is one of being open to demand for over 300,000 titles from thousands of publishers, to Marks & Spencer's which sold, at the time, only 5,000 items. His article concluded: 'books are not the result of processing a stable and calculable raw material: they are the product of creative minds, which makes them wayward and unpredictable to handle as articles of trade', ranging from 'Mrs Tittlemouse, to Teretullian's Treatise Against Praxeas from Town and Planning circular No. 92, HMSO, to the First Interim Report of the Conservative Sub-Committee of Education produced by the Conservative Party. The judge admitted books were different in that no two were alike, unlike many commodities (eggs and oranges, he cited) and that their production and marketing is different from other commodities' but still he lost the case.
18. This is a matter of debate within the family and there are letters which voice his concern. In general, BB's attitude to religious differences was rather ahead of his times: he was one of the first to design, print and sell Eid cards in his shop. While reticent on religious discrimination, Basil was more vocal on racialism. He had come out strongly against the colour bar after visiting Kingston, Jamaica. Meeting the Governor General at dinner, he writes to his secretary that there are: 'many guests, blacks of many shades … This is an up and coming part of the world and I am convinced that the colour bar is an evidence of barbarism. We will have none of it!'
19. See 'Portrait of Penelope Jessel', *Oxford Times*, Friday 3 June 1988.
20. *Oxford Mail*, 13 January 1970.
21. Interview Corinna Blackwell, September 2013, just before her ninetieth birthday.

THREE

1. Harold Macmillan, at Balliol, had also commented on the absence of women, *The Times Saturday Review*, 18 October 1975, p. 7.
2. This account of his life at Merton was written by BB for *Postmaster* (Merton) in 1971 and reprinted in *Broad Sheet* in 1984.
3. BB's notes, 30 September 1952.
4. She continued to ply her trade, despite going up in the world. In the *Oxford Directory*

of 1880, Nancy is described as a dressmaker, even though she was now living with her son over the Broad Street shop.

5. Jews Mount was subsequently renamed Bulwarks Lane: letter, BB to M. Maclagan (Oxford Library), 7 January 1954, including some of the notes and material he used for his Christ Church speech.

6. BB's notes.

7. The 1871 census records Anne Blackwell living at 1 Bulwarks Alley, formerly Jews Walk, with her three children, an apprentice and a servant. The 1874 *Oxford Directory* records the dressmaker living at 46 Holywell.

8. BB, Christ Church speech.

9. Letter to BB, 25 November 1951.

10. Dorothy Blackwell's notes.

11. Lilla must have told him of Jack's departure when she was visiting her sister in Oxford, before they married.

12. See, for example, Flora Thompson's memoirs in Margaret Lane (ed.), *A Country Calendar and Other Writing,* Oxford University Press, 1979, pp. 188–9.

13. Lady Margaret Hall led the way in 1878, followed by Somerville (1879), St Hugh's (1886) and St Hilda's (1893).

14. Sumner Austin (1888–1981), MCS and St John's, was a founder member of Oxford University Operatic Society: the first production was *The Bartered Bride* in 1929. He did German and Italian translations for Basil's publishing ventures, and had his own work published there. A distinguished baritone and technical director of Sadler's Wells, he sang in Greek in Sir Hubert Parry's production of *The Frogs*. He started in the Indian Civil Service but abandoned it to study music in Dresden. In 1919 he was snapped up by the Carl Rosa Co. and then went to the Old Vic; he was a frequent broadcaster.

15. BB used these memories of his sister for Dorothy's funeral address.

16. Interview Julian Blackwell, 20 April 2001.

17. Christine Soans was the daughter of the headmaster of a girls' boarding school, where she herself was almost certainly educated. It must have been academic enough for pupils to gain places at university, as Christine had done.

18. Interview BB and Ved Mehta.

19. See, for example, a letter to BB on his eightieth birthday from Nigel Hugh (? name illegible – possibly a German refugee?), from 2 Pikes End, Pinner, Middx, 25 May 1969: 'I was ill one day and you asked in the shop who was looking after me. They said: nobody, you told them to let me know that you would fetch me at 6.00 and take me to Appleton.'

20. BB's notes for his life of May Morris.

21. Interview Roger Highfield, 19 July 2001.

22. Scraps of drafts, mostly in pencil, are in BB's archives.

23. Interview Roger Highfield, 19 July 2001.

24. Interview BB and Ved Mehta.

25. Letters, Christine Blackwell to BB, September 1919, Ramsgate.

26. The Archives of Milham Ford School are in the Oxfordshire County Records office, S126/5, but no personal details of individual girls have as yet been released.

27. Milham Ford School County Archives, S126/5; S126/5/2/A1/2.

28. Subsequently the school was acquired by the city of Oxford, and in 1947 it became a state grammar school.

29. *The Bookseller,* 27 July 1968.

30. MCS, *The Lily,* 12 November, Xmas 1906.

31. The Representation of the People's Act (1918) enfranchised women over thirty who met minimum property qualifications, even though it was rather deprecatingly known as the 'flapper vote'.

32. RK diary entry, 15 December 1918.

33. Vera Brittain, 'To My Brother, In Memory of July 1st, 1916'.

34. Vera Brittain, 'The Lament of the Demobilised'.
35. *Oxford Outlook*, March 1919.
36. Mark Bostridge and Paul Berry, *Vera Brittain, A Life*, Virago, London, 2001, p. 153.
37. Vera Brittain, 'To a VC', *Oxford Poetry 1917–19*, Basil Blackwell, 1920, p. 126.
38. Bostridge and Berry, *Vera Brittain, A Life*, p. 156.
39. ibid.
40. Virginia Shull, *Lysistrata*, vol. 1, no. 2, May 1934, p. 58.
41. Virginia Woolf, 'Why?', *Lysistrata*, vol. 1, no. 2, May 1934, pp. 5–12.
42. Review article, based on an interview with Eric Whelpton, in *The Sunday Times*, 23 February 1975, of Janet Hitchman's *Such a Strange Lady*, New English Library, London, 1975. It suggests that DLS's first full-length Wimsey story resulted later on.
43. 'To members of the Bach choir on Active Service' was published in the *Oxford Magazine*. See also James Brabazon, *Dorothy L. Sayers: A Biography* (Preface by Anthony Fleming and Foreword by P.D. James), Charles Scribner's Sons, New York, 1981, p. 60.
44. James Brabazon, *Dorothy L. Sayers: A Biography*, pp. 60–1.
45. She had playfully submitted it under her stage name, H.P. Rallentando, and it was published in *Saturday Westminster Review*. See James Brabazon, *Dorothy L. Sayers: A Biography*, p. 61.
46. DLS, *Op. 1*, 1916.
47. DLS to Muriel Jaeger, 8 March 1917, DLS papers, Bodleian Library (MS ENG MISC C. C. 698 folio 1).
48. DLS, *Op. 1*, Fifth Song in 'Rondels'.
49. *The Times*, 7 May 1981; James Brabazon, *Dorothy L. Sayers, The Life of a Courageous Woman*, Gollancz, London, 1981. DLS and Brabazon were fellow churchwardens at St Anne's, Soho; they also had a shared interest in the theatre. His book was said to be sanctioned by DLS's son, who gave him her papers.
50. Janet Hitchman, *Such a Strange Lady*.
51. Basil to Professor Thorpe, 7 March 1977. See also Lewis Thorpe in *As Her Whimsey Took Her*, Margaret Hannay (ed.), Kent State University Press, Ohio, 1978; and A.S. Dale to BB, 28 February 1928 – she, like Basil, finds Hitchman's book inaccurate, misleading; she does not like the 'tone and treatment' of DLS.
52. Ralph E. Hone to BB, 16 February 1976. Hone's book, *A Literary Biography*, Kent State University Press, Ohio, 1979, was generally seen as more reasonable than Hitchman's, but it was not that favourable to DLS.
53. 'Homage to the Gaffer', *Oxford Times*, 4 February 1983.
54. The Bodleian has the oldest surviving copy of the manuscript of *Chanson de Roland*, which DLS may have been able to view. She produced her own translation for the Penguin Classics series in 1957, just before she died. In 1929 she had translated *Tristan in Brittany*.
55. Although her work as an editorial assistant may have been erratic, she was brilliant at writing creative copy for the London advertising agency S.H. Benson: the Guinness toucan advertisement was her doing (*The Times*, 7 May 1981). This work tided her over until she began to earn enough money from her writing to maintain herself and a son. The experience also provided material for her novel *Murder Must Advertise*.
56. 'My wife and I occasionally entertained her': letter from BB to Mrs A.S. Dale, 7 March 1978; see also Dale's biography of DLS, *Maker and Craftsman*, 1978.
57. Letter from Mrs Graham Greene to the *Oxford Times*, 18 February 1983. Donna MacPherson also makes a similar suggestion in her PhD thesis ('The Modern Scriptor', in progress, University of Sussex). MacPherson argues that Sayers had not just wanted to make money by writing popular fiction. Is she suggesting, perhaps, that she wanted to expiate her sexual desires? Harriet's marriage to Wimsey is DLS's dream, and Lord Peter Whimsy is BB. Doubtless DLS was captivated by BB; she says so in her letters, writing of him with his 'sweet baby' after meeting him at his home.
58. DLS's most prolific period was in Oxford between 1915 and 1921, even though during

this period she taught in Hull, and another year in Normandy with Eric Whelpton. She continued with her translation of the Anglo-Norman poem 'Tristan', and in 1937 she was invited to write a verse drama for Canterbury Cathedral (The Dorothy L. Sayers Society, 1996, p xii). See also *The English War,* published by *The Times Literary Supplement,* 1940, anthologized by C. Day-Lewis, Stephen Spender, Laurie Lee: 'Ariel Reconnaissance' and 'Target Area'.

FOUR
1. 'The Tragic Life Story of Alfred Williams', *North Wilts Herald,* 8 June 1945.
2. See *North Wilts Herald,* 8 June 1945, and AW's autobiographical poems *In a Wiltshire Village,* 1912. In collaboration with George's of Bristol, Basil published Leonard Clark's *Alfred Williams: His Life and Work,* 1945. See also *The Listener,* 16 April 1981, p. 509, reviewing a radio talk by John Wells (the right-wing satirist and principal author of *Mrs Wilson's Diary* and *Anyone for Dennis?*) on Radio 3, 31 March 1981; Basil was the chief source for this programme, as acknowledged by BBC letter to BB, 24 February 1981. See also Basil's account in A.M. Hardie and K.C. Douglas (eds), *Augury: An Oxford Miscellany of Verse and Prose,* Basil Blackwell, 1940, pp. 57–61. In the MBC, BLK/3/7, is Basil's hand-corrected typed version: *The Tragic Story of Alf Williams,* 1940. Basil wrote about him for *The Sunday Statesman,* 16 April 1950. See also BB's *Retreat from Grammar,* Presidential Address delivered to the Classical Association, University of Manchester, 1 April 1965, John Murray, London, 1965.
3. *North Wilts Herald,* 8 June 1945.
4. Oral account, Lou Robins to BB.
5. 'Liddington Hill', published in *Songs in Wiltshire,* 1909.
6. *North Wilts Herald,* 8 June 1945.
7. *GWR Magazine,* 1915.
8. *North Wilts Herald,* 8 June 1945.
9. ibid.
10. A Berlin reviewer of his first book, *Songs in Wiltshire,* went so far as to describe Williams as the greatest living poet; see Leonard Clark, *Alfred Williams: His Life and Work.*
11. Basil started to write his article on AW in March 1940; he wrote various versions of the story and contributed to others.
12. The blind friend was Lou Robins, who undertook to see AW's work published; see *Alfred Williams: His Life and Work.*
13. Originally composed in India in the second century BC, they are believed to have been written by the scholar Vishnu Sharma and others.
14. The letter writer had been an undergraduate in Oxford and had always loved Blackwell's, where he was treated as a friend rather than a customer: letter from St Xavier's College, Calcutta, 2 June 1950.
15. Brian Aldiss, *The Brightfount Diaries,* Faber & Faber, London, 1955.
16. Bernard Quaritch's famous shop at No. 15 Piccadilly, in the old gaslight days, drew the great and the good well into the night; William Morris was a regular.
17. Richard Blackwell; all references come from MBC unless otherwise stated.
18. BHB lectured at the WEA and Quaker evening classes, and collaborated with one of the leading educationalists of the day, Sir Michael Sadler. Sadler had been one of the young hopefuls BHB had helped while an undergraduate at Trinity in 1880, the year after Blackwell's opened its doors. He became a renowned educational pioneer, Vice-Chancellor of Leeds University (1911–23) and Master of University College, Oxford (1923–34). They worked together to establish the Oxford Extension Movement, the pioneering outreach programme which has today metamorphosed into the University's Department for Continuing Education. Ruskin called these extension courses 'bridges between the worker and the university educated'. See also Jonathan Rose, *The Intellectual Life of the British Working Classes,* Yale University Press, New Haven and London, 2001, p. 277.

19. John Betjeman to BB, 43 Cloth Fair, London, EC1 (undated).
20. National insurance was introduced in 1912: men 4d, employers 5d, women 3d and young persons, boys and girls 1d per week.
21. Coincidentally, Chaundy's bookshop at 104 High Street was succeeded by Sanders, where Brian Aldiss worked his apprenticeship on which he based his fictional *Brightfount*.
22. A compendious German grammar.
23. Interview Corinna Blackwell, 2 October 2013.
24. Conversation with Henry Chadwick in Christ Church, August 1998.
25. Crutch was a major player in the drafting of the Norrington history of Blackwell's.
26. Sent on 25 March 1947 from Adisadel College, Cape Coast, Ghana.
27. See article on Christopher Francis, *Oxford Times*, 18 December 1987.

FIVE

1. George Eliot, *Middlemarch, A Study of Provincial Life*, 1874.
2. RK's diary contains inserts on the common-place, on his philosophy of life, an extract from Samuel Daniel's poem 'To the Lady Margaret', a one-liner from Daniel's poem 'Delia': 'here I unclasp the book of my changed soul', and some pencil notes about James Hinton's *Philosophy*.
3. For a discussion on common-place books, and an exemplar, see Elizabeth Smither, *The Common-Place Book*, Auckland University Press, Auckland, New Zealand, 2011.
4. Robert Darnton, *The Kiss of Lamourette*, Norton, New York, 1990, p. 212. See also Jonathan Rose, *The Intellectual Life of the British Working Classes*, Yale University Press, New Haven and London, 2001, p. 1.
5. Flora Thompson, *A Country Calendar and Other Writings*, ed. Margaret Lane, Oxford University Press, 1979, pp. 3–4.
6. David Kynaston, *Austerity Britain 1945–51*, Bloomsbury, London, 2007, p. vii. See also Kynaston's *Family Britain 1951–57* (2009) and his earlier work, *King Labour* (1976).
7. Thomas Hardy, preface to *Poems of the Past and the Present*, 1901, quoted in Kynaston, *Austerity Britain 1945–51*, p. viii.
8. Richard Altick, *The English Common Reader: A Social History of the Mass Reading Public, 1800–1900*, University of Chicago Press, Chicago, 1957.
9. Jonathan Rose, *The Intellectual Life of the British Working Classes*. Rose is indebted to the work of John Burnett, David Vincent, David Mayall et al., *The Autobiography of the Working Class*, 3 volumes, New York University Press, New York, 1984–89. See also John Carey's *The Intellectuals and the Masses: Pride and Prejudice among the Literary Intelligentsia, 1880–1939*, Faber & Faber, London, 1992.
10. *London Review of Books*, vol. 23, no. 24, 13 December 2001, pp. 33–5.
11. Hugo Dyson to BB, 27 December 1965.
12. Hugo Dyson to BB, 7 March 1972.
13. Hugo Dyson to BB, 27 December 1965.
14. A stretch of the Cherwell in Oxford, long enjoyed for male-only bathing.
15. Thompson, *A Country Calendar and Other Writings*, Introduction, p. 11.
16. Delafield wrote for Blackwell's, contributing a story to BB's *New Decameron*. See Nicola Beauman's Introduction to E.M. Delafield, *The Diary of a Provincial Lady*, Virago, London, 1984, p. vii.
17. See Quentin Bell's Introduction to Anne Bell (ed.), *Virginia Woolf, Selected Diaries*, Vintage, London, 2008, p. x.
18. RK, other material, MBC.
19. VW diary entry, (Easter) Sunday 20 April 1919.
20. Thompson, *A Country Calendar and Other Writings*, p. 31.
21. J.-P. Sartre, *War Diaries* (3 December 1939), 1983, p. 90.
22. Hardy's *Jude the Obscure* was first serialized in 1895, when King was almost ten.
23. Thompson, *A Country Calendar and Other Writings*, p. 10.
24. ibid.

25. Hermione Lee, *Virginia Woolf*, Vintage, London, 1997, p. 13.
26. Virginia Woolf, *Granite and Rainbow: Essays by Virginia Woolf*, Harcourt, Brace, New York, 1958, p. 25.
27. Michael Holroyd, *Works on Paper*, Little, Brown, London, 2002, pp. 4–5.
28. RK's's own notes on his childhood, written in the 1930s and 1940s. King called these jottings 'The Day Book of Mr Folio Kynge-Penguin'; dated 15 January, there is no year.
29. See MBC, BLK/3/97.
30. BB, October 1950, in *The Broad Sheet*, Blackwell's.
31. *Times Literary Supplement*, 29 September 1950.
32. John Sparrow to BB, 15 September 1950.
33. Bodleian Library Record, 1950.
34. RK's diary contains lengthy passages exhorting the 'ordinary' man to find good right under his nose.

SIX

1. BHB's catalogue, No. 39, October 1993.
2. Oxford's prominence in church history is well known, particularly the phases of the English Reformation, the Oxford Movement and the rise of Nonconformism after the repeal of the Test Acts. Mansfield College, founded in 1886 as a theological college, soon became a powerhouse of Congregationalism.
3. During an Ascension Day procession in 1268, Jewish merchants attacked the cross and the crucifer. To make amends they were ordered to provide two replacements, bejewelled and made of precious metals. Feeling hard done by, they gave away all their belongings and pleaded poverty. They were expelled by Edward I's Edict of Expulsion (1290), after which there was no openly acknowledged Jewish community for almost 500 years. By Victorian times Jews were allowed to sit in Parliament, and Jewish-born Disraeli became prime minister.
4. Campion was later beatified by Pope Leo XIII.
5. In writing *Eikonoklastes*, Milton was responding to pressure. He defends regicide and republicanism.
6. Under the Quaker Act of 1662, they were made to swear allegiance to the Crown, although it was against their conscience to put earthly rule above God's. Their meetings, deemed secret, came under attack in the Conventicle Act of 1664. But under the 1689 Toleration Act, it became illegal to disturb the Christian worship of any group.
7. The Test Acts were put in place during the reign of Charles II, and it was not until 1871 that Fellowships were open to everyone, whatever their beliefs.
8. Oxford's Museum of Natural History, 1860.
9. The New Road Chapel was one of the bastions of Congregationalism. See also Michael Hopkins, 'Congregationalism in Oxford: The Growth and Development of Congregational Churches in and around the City of Oxford since 1653', MPhil thesis submitted to University of Birmingham, January 2010.
10. RK, diary entry, 23 April 1919: 'Hinton's thoughts have been quite an inspiration throughout the day'.
11. RK, diary entry, Sunday 16 June 1918.
12. Review of Percy Gardner, *The Ephesian Gospel*, Williams & Norgate, London, 1915.
13. RK, diary entry, Sunday 29 September 1918.
14. RK, diary entry, Sunday 5 September 1920.
15. Other reviews: *Bible Essays for the Times*; Mutual influence; Recent theology: W.R. Thompson, *Studies in Isaiah* etc., The Books of the Apocrypha, Faith and progress; The thought of Canon Scott Holland; Ezekiel, The Division of Christendom, the Life Hereafter, the Hidden romances of the New Testament; the foundations of belief, nature's sermons; Dr Gore's Christology; *A Preacher's Essays*; the Rev. R.J. Campbell's *Life of Christ*: the Christ of Faith and the Jesus of History.

16. Jonathan Rose, *The Intellectual Life of the British Working Classes*, Yale University Press, New Haven and London, 2001, p. 29.
17. H.J. Bridges, *The Religion of Experience*: *A Book for Laymen and the Unchurched*, Macmillan, New York, 1916.
18. D.W. Forrest, *The Christ of History and of Experience*, Charles Scribner's Sons, New York and Edinburgh, 1901.
19. T.R. Glover, *The Jesus of History*, George Duran, New York, 1917.
20. N. Schmidt, *The Prophet of Nazareth*, Macmillan, New York, 1905.
21. RK, diary entry, Saturday 23 Sept 1922.
22. J. Nicolson, *The Great Silence*, John Murray, London, 2009, p. 17.
23. Fox's *Journal* was published in 1694, but written while he was in prison in Derby.
24. Henry David Thoreau, *Civil Disobedience*, 1849.
25. RK, diary entry, Monday 27 May 1918.
26. RK, diary entry, Sunday 9 June 1918.
27. RK, diary entry, Monday 22 July 1918.
28. BB, October 1950, in *The Broad Sheet*, Blackwell's.

SEVEN

1. S.R. Fischer, *A History of Reading*, Reaktion Books, London 2003, pp. 287–9
2. Rose puts the antipathy towards penny dreadfuls down to prejudice against education of the poor, but his research into their reading habits suggests that they easily saw the difference between bad and good, and they read both interchangeably as children: Stead's Penny Poets alongside the Penny Dreadfuls. Jonathan Rose, *The Intellectual Life of the British Working Classes*, Yale University Press, New Haven and London, 2001, pp. 36–71.
3. Fischer, *A History of Reading*, p. 272. For girls, who were expected to help with the housework and the younger children, the opportunity to read was even more limited.
4. Stefan Collini, in his *TLS* review of Rose's book.
5. Rose, *The Intellectual Life of the British Working Classes*.
6. Of particular note is Lydia Wevers' account of autodidact reading: *Reading on the Farms: Victorian Fiction and the Colonial World*, Victoria University Press, Wellington, 2010.
7. S.R. Fischer, *A History of Reading*, pp. 287–9.
8. RK, MBC.
9. RK, MBC.
10. RK, MBC.
11. RK, MBC.
12. RK, MBC.
13. RK, MBC.
14. RK, MBC.
15. RK, MBC.
16. RK, diary entry, Sunday 27 April 1919.
17. RK, diary entry, Wednesday 21 July 1920.
18. RK, diary entry, Thursday 24 April 1919.
19. RK, diary entry, Sunday 27 April 1919.
20. RK, MBC.
21. RK, diary entries, 31 July–1 August 1918.
22. RK, diary entry, Sunday 27 April 1919.
23. RK, diary entry, Thursday 12 June 1919.
24. RK, diary entry, Saturday 23 August 1919.
25. RK, diary entry, Sunday 20 October 1918.
26. In reviewing J.W. Frings' *The Immanent Deity*, Rex tried in vain to identify the unifying cosmic elements underlying the great mystery of life.
27. RK, diary entry, Sunday 19 September 1920.
28. RK, diary entry, Wednesday 7 August 1918.
29. RK, diary entry, Friday 9 July 1920.

30. RK, diary entry, Tuesday 27 May 1919.
31. ibid.
32. RK, diary entries, 18–20 June 1918.
33. RK, diary entry, Wednesday 10 July 1918.
34. RK, MBC.
35. RK, diary entries, 14–15 June 1918. It was some twenty years since Wilde had been imprisoned and still homosexuality was abominated. Rex does not subscribe to this heresy. It could be, given his unhappy marriage, that Rex had some inclination in this direction. But this is mere supposition on my part, albeit one suggesting itself by reading his life.
36. RK, diary entry, Wednesday 1 May 1918.
37. RK, diary entry, Tuesday 9 July 1918.
38. Thomas Carlyle's major work, *Sartor Resartus*, meaning 'The tailor re-tailored', was first published as a serial in 1833–4.
39. RK, MBC.
40. RK, diary entry, Sunday 18 August 1918.
41. RK, MBC.
42. RK, diary entry, Wednesday 22 May 1918.
43. RK, diary entry, Thursday 23 May 1918.
44. RK, diary entry, Saturday 25 May 1918.
45. RK, diary entry, Monday 27 May 1918.
46. RK, diary entry, Friday 16 August 1918.
47. RK, diary entry, Wednesday 7 August 1918.
48. RK, diary entry, Saturday 17 August 1918.
49. RK, diary entry, Wednesday 21 August 1918.
50. RK, diary entries, 10–12 September 1918.
51. RK, diary entry, Saturday 9 November 1918.
52. RK, diary entry, Sunday 18 May 1919.
53. RK, diary entry, Monday 28 July 1919.
54. RK, diary entry, Thursday 11 December 1919.
55. RK, diary entry, Sunday 29 February 1920.
56. RK, diary entry, Thursday 1 April 1920.
57. RK, diary entry, Thursday 8 April 1920.
58. RK, diary entry, Friday 16 April 1920.
59. RK, diary entries, 13–17 May 1920.
60. RK, diary entry, Sunday 6 June 1920.
61. RK, diary entry, Thursday 17 June 1920.
62. RK, diary entry, Sunday 4 July 1920.
63. RK, diary entry, Wednesday 7 July 1920.
64. RK, diary entry, Sunday 29 August 1920.
65. ibid.
66. RK, diary entry, Monday 30 August 1920.
67. RK, diary entry, Thursday 14 October 1920.
68. RK, diary entry, Thursday 14 April 1921.
69. RK, diary entry, Saturday 29 July 1922.
70. RK, diary entry, Friday 4 August 1922.
71. RK, diary entry, Sunday 6 August 1922.
72. RK, diary entry, Thursday 5 October 1922.
73. RK, diary entry, Sunday 15 October 1922.
74. Jottings dated Thursday 6 September 1923 'while vegetating in the Cotswolds'.
75. RK, MBC.
76. RK, MBC.
77. RK, MBC.
78. RK, MBC.

EIGHT

1. Jon Stallworthy (ed.), *The Oxford Book of War Poetry*, Oxford University Press, 2008, p. xxvii.
2. T.E. Lawrence (of Arabia) was a neighbour of BB's. He attended school in Oxford (Oxford High School for Boys) and was at university at the same time as BB. Two of his brothers, William and Frank, were killed in the trenches in 1915. BB published a volume of their letters in 1954.
3. Notes for *Postmaster* (not the final version).
4. Interview BB and Ved Mehta.
5. Geoffrey Barfoot, Memories and Thoughts 1912–1968, MBC.
6. J.-P. Sartre, *War Diaries* (3 December 1939), 1983, p. 90.
7. RK, diary entry, Sunday 14 July 1918.
8. RK, diary entry Saturday 27 July 1918.
9. RK, diary entry, Thursday 30 May 1918.
10. DLS papers, Bodleian Library.
11. RK, diary entry, Saturday 1 June 1918.
12. RK, diary entry, Wednesday 3 July 1918.
13. RK, diary entry, Sunday 15 December 1918.
14. RK, diary entry, Monday 2 September 1918.
15. RK, diary entry, Saturday 7 September 1918.
16. RK, diary entry, Sunday 15 December 1918.
17. This poem was published, probably in *The Daily Citizen*, a short-lived labour journal. It was also used by BB in 1977.
18. Lloyd George shared his concern. Speaking on the ineffectiveness of the League of Nations in the 1920s, he said: 'it provided elaborate devices for preventing wars between small nations, but between big and small – it was only quick march. The big nations are sharpening their swords upon the very temples of peace.' Speech at the Oxford Luncheon Club, remembered in an article by Fay Young, *Oxford Times*, 21 February 1975.
19. RK, diary entry, Sunday 5 October 1924.
20. RK, diary entry, Sunday 27 March 1921.
21. BB, Minute Book, Blackwell's Ltd, p. 402, and valedictory address as President of Booksellers' Association, 1935.
22. Herta Haas, née Doktor, was born in 1907. She eventually went back to live in Hamburg. This is a shortened version of her memories, recorded when she was in her nineties by Dr Marion Hulverscheidt, 27 December 2004.
23. Another German refugee, probably desperate for work, walked into Blackwell's off the street, and after being told to learn to type was employed. 'After 2 weeks he ran out of money: to survive he sold the gold coin which his mother had given him when he left Germany. After 4 weeks he received an envelope "so thin that I did not think it could contain more than £2". Much to his surprise, he found a generous cheque. "I felt very rich!"' Nigel Hugh (? name illegible) to BB, 25 May 1969.
24. When Fred Chaundy moved from Oxford he took over the antiquarian booksellers Dulau & Co. in London. After the shop was bombed, killing Chaundy's son, BB invited Chaundy back to Oxford, bringing Dulau into the Blackwell's fold.
25. *St Louis Despatch*, July 25 1956. See also BB, 'The Bookshop – Yesterday, Today and Tomorrow', *The Author*, vol. LIII, no. 1, 1942, pp. 1–3.

NINE

1. With the acquisition of the firm by Wiley's, even the memory of his imprint is fading fast: Wiley's vast company history concedes only one page to Blackwell's.
2. *Books To Come*, April 1948.
3. An extract sent by Jack Wolsdorf from an essay 'Concerning the First Edition of "The

Eight Sin" by Christopher Morley', published by Colophon, 1934; see Blackwell's *Broad Sheet*, March 1985.

4. *The Spectator*, 29 June 1901, p. 25: 'Out of many excellent pieces of English verse we may especially select for commendation Mr. A.G. Butler's charming address to the eponymous hero of the Club.'

5. Basil wrote to Miss Dorothy M. Ward (sister of Humphry Ward), 29 May 1952; she replies saying she has retrieved for him the Horace White copy, which had belonged to Raymond Asquith. It is now in the MBC.

6. Of the original ninety-five, sixty-three poems were included in *The Book of the Horace Club*: six in Latin, two in Greek, one in French and the remainder in English. The volume was made to last, on hand-made paper and bound in vellum. Hilaire Belloc made a rebus design for the book, with the motto *Sumite castalios nigris da fontibus haustus* (From the Black Wells make ye the Muses draughts). Only 500 copies of the book were published, and it became a highly prized collector's item, commanding a good price on the second-hand book market. *The Times* judged it 'almost invidious to select where almost everything of its kind is good'. Other reviewers rather predictably gave pride of place to the already famous 'names', but found space to praise Asquith, Buchan and Medd. Popular acclaim went to Belloc's 'Sussex Drinking Song' and 'The South Country'. Henry Beeching's 'Fatherhood' was judged by *The Spectator*, and later by BB, to be among the best. And its contents deserve a rereading. Its contributors are now mostly forgotten, but the collection still has strong resonance for the present generation of student poets from all walks of life, whether they are writing for *Oxford Poetry*, the *Big Issue*, or to raise money for the local homeless sanctuary, the Gatehouse.

7. *Books To Come*, April 1948.

8. BB's speech to celebrate 100 years of Blackwell's publishing, 6 September 1979.

9. All the way through the early accounts books there is evidence of the costs of production for *Mensae Secondae*: £2.8s.10d in January 1880, for example, but nowhere a sign of any profit!

10. W. Warde Fowler, preface to *Memories of Some Oxford Poets*, 1900.

11. *Daily Mail*, 12 November 1924.

12. John Betjeman saw BB's publishing as a 'metaphor for everything he loved and respected ... And it reveals the dark side of life: poverty, the lack of recognition that Basil strove to correct when he published the work of the practical man cum scholar manqué [Alfred Williams] who took on the battle of life.'

13. BB's notes, May 1956.

14. BB commemorated the work of Dent in the first Dent Memorial Lecture. Dent's Everyman's Library was one of the series, between 1830 and 1906, charted by Richard Altick; others included Charles Knight Library of Classics; Bentley's Standard Novels; Bohn's Standard Library and British Classics; W. and R. Chambers' People's Editions; Chapman and Hall's Standard Editions of Popular Authors; Murray's British Classics; Routledge's British Classics; British Poets and Standard Novels, which were not so cheap but led to Dick's Waverley novels at 3d, his Shakespeare at 1d, W.T. Stead's Penny Poets (1885) and the Penny Novels (1896), which anticipated *Readers Digest*. See Jonathan Rose, *The Intellectual Life of the British Working Classes*, Yale University Press, New Haven and London, 2001, p. 131.

15. Gilbert Murray, Introduction to *Oxford Poetry*, B.H. Blackwell, 1910–13, pp. xviii–xx.

16. Tolkien wrote to Basil that his first published poem 'Goblin Feet' (*Oxford Poetry*, 1915) made 'you (Blackwell's) ... my first publisher, as I remember with gratitude'. MBC.

17. Henry B. Higgins, 'An Epitaph', *Oxford Poetry*, B.H. Blackwell, Oxford, 1919.

18. H. Freston, *Oxford Poetry*, 1914.

19. C.K. Stead, *Risk*, Maclehose Press, London, 2012, p. 195.

20. John Pearson, *Facades: Edith, Osbert and Sacheverell Sitwell*, Macmillan, 1978, p. 104.

21. Ledbetter, 'Battles for Modernism and Wheels', *Journal of Modern Literature*, vol. 19, no. 2, Fall 1995, pp. 322–7.

22. Letter, E. Sitwell to *The Spectator*, 29 June 1954, p. 123.
23. *Poems of Wilfred Owen*, BL, Add. MSS 43720–43721.
24. Mrs Arthur Scott, *Scattered Leaves*, B.H. Blackwell, 1916, pp. 18–20.
25. Vera Brittain, 'To a VC', *Oxford Poetry, 1917–19*, Basil Blackwell, 1920, p. 126.
26. Daphne De Waal, *Soldiers Immortal*, B.H. Blackwell, 1918; poem of the same name.
27. Dorothea Mary Wood, 'A Mad-Song', *Parson's Pleasure*, 1928, p. 45.
28. Edith Sitwell, *The Mother*, Benjamin Henry Blackwell, 1915, pp. 15–18.
29. May Wedderburn Cannan, *Grey Ghosts and Voices*, Roundwood Press, Kineton, 1976, p. 88.
30. May Wedderburn Cannan, *The Splendid Days,* Basil Blackwell, 1919.
31. Cannan, *Grey Ghosts and Voices*, pp. 182–3.
32. ibid., p. 184.
33. ibid., BB's Foreword.
34. ibid.
35. Barbara Reynolds writes that DLS 'began as a poet … [and] she always remained one, even in her prose works'. See Barbara Reynolds' Introduction to Ralph E. Hone (ed.), *Extracts from the Poetry of Dorothy L. Sayers*, Dorothy L. Sayers Society, 1996, p. xiii. Reynolds argues that this 'poetry of search' became the 'poetry of statement' in DLS's more mature years; see, for example, *The House of Zeal* (1937) and *The Devil to Pay* (1939).
36. Published in the *Adventurers All* series, no. 9, B.H. Blackwell, Oxford, 1916.
37. *Catholic Tales and Christian Songs,* B.H. Blackwell, Oxford, 1918.
38. BB's Foreword to Cannan, *Grey Ghosts and Voices*.
39. From 'The Last Gallop', *Façade II*, 1922.
40. 'Il Purgatorio', *Divine Comedy*, trans. DLS, 1955–, i, vii–viii.
41. See Juliet Nicolson's Introduction to her book *The Great Silence*, John Murray, London, 2009.
42. Leslie Mitchell, *Maurice Bowra, A Life*, Oxford University Press, p. 46.
43. Cannan, *Grey Ghosts and Voices*, p. 152.
44. Jon Stallworthy, for example, bitterly regretted that OUP and Blackwell's turned their back on poetry.
45. Osbert Sitwell, in Edith and Osbert Sitwell, *Twentieth Century Harlequinade*, Benjamin Henry Blackwell, 1916, p. 23.
46. Edgell Rickword, 'Trench Poets', *Oxford Poetry*, 1921.
47. C.H.B. Kitchin, 'Wheels: A Tricycle', *Oxford Outlook*, 1919, p. 182.
48. Only five of Wilfred Owen's poems had reached print before his death: a childhood competition winner in an evangelical magazine, 'Song of Songs' in *The Hydra* and 'Miners', 'Futility' and 'Hospital Barge at Cerisy' in *The Nation*. See BB letter to Arthur Norrington from Ithaca, NY, 4 September 1977.
49. Letter, Alan Thomas to BB, 20 October 1979.
50. Asa Briggs took over from BB as chairman of the William Morris Society, and she wrote of Basil for the *Journal of the William Morris Society*, vol. vi, no. 1, Summer 1984.
51. H.W. Garrod, *Worms and Epitaphs*, B.H. Blackwell, 1919, p. 29.
52. *Western Morning News*, 14 January 1935.
53. Graham Greene, 'The French Peace', *Oxford Outlook*, vol. vi, no. 28, June 1924, p. 212.
54. I. and H. Hubbard, *The War Resisters*, SHP, 1934, p. 2.
55. John Middleton Murray, *Oxford Outlook*, vol. xii, no. 58, May 1932, p. 88.
56. Dante's *Divine Comedy* was a favourite of BB and BHB.
57. This anti-immigration speech, on 20 April 1968, made Enoch Powell infamous.
58. W.G. Hiscock (ed.), *The Balliol Rhymes* from rare original *Broad Sheet* with the notes of J.W. Mackail, Lord Sumner and F. Madan, with manuscript from Christ Church (Oxford), Basil Blackwell, 1939.
59. Basil, 'The bookshop – Yesterday, Today and Tomorrow', *The Author*, vol. liii, no. 1, 1942, pp. 1–3. Blackwell & Mott's profits soared, too, from under £500 a year before

the war to nearly £9,000 by the end. The nation's book bill in 1939 was £10,000,000; by the end of the war it was £25,000,000.

60. BB, *Books to Come*, no. 45, April 1945, pp. 10–11.

61. BB to Arthur Norrington, 29 September 1976: he wanted 'to have written up the difficulties that fine printing went through'; this led to a 'turning away from poetry and fine printing' to make money (especially after Richard Blackwell, H.L. Schollick and Per Saugman came on the scene). See also publishing Minute Books in MBC.

62. See exchange of letters between Oldham's Press and BB, 1943–6.

63. Basil cited J.M. Dent as a notable example of the successful combination of the qualities of idealism and shrewdness.

64. Clare Squires has the same idea as BB: that the book trades are caught between 'capitalism and culture'; see her essay in Alexis Weedon (ed.), *The History of the Book in the West: 1914–2000*, Ashgate, Farnham, 2010, pp. 191–2.

65. BB, 'Letters in the New Age', The First (William Francis) Jackson Knight Memorial Lecture (8 March 1968), Abbey Press, 1969, p. 3.

66. See series of letters to and from Blackwell's, often BB, to the Brit Council; for example BC to H.L. Schollick, 26 May 1955, publishing papers in BBC.

67. *The Sunday Times*, 7 June 1959.

68. Carter was a former school inspector; Marten was Under Master at Eton. The latter was to teach constitutional history to the young Princess Elizabeth.

69. Special mention was made of this children's list in the *Sunday Times*, 3 November 1935.

70. 'The Teacher's World', 16 January 1924, also given as a talk on the BBC Home Service at the same time.

71. This included BB's own school. 'The future of Magdalen College School was in doubt in the 1920s and 30s, and there was no large body of Old Boys on whom to call for support ... Had it not been for the help given by John Johnson, the University Printer,' wrote BB, 'the school may well have ceased to exist.' BB played his part. From 1944 he helped with the governing of the school, serving on the School Committee for the next twenty years. During his time as a governor he pushed the introduction of scholarships and bursaries, and after the war, as the school grew and prospered, 'it was able to provide places for boys from all different kinds of backgrounds'.

72. John Cutforth notes for Richard Blackwell, 19 April 1963 and 22 April 1964.

73. Plea for academic books in paperback from Alan England to Henry Schollick, 31 January 1969.

74. BH had first sent catalogues to America in 1946; how surprised he would have been if he had known that his embryonic firm was to cross the Atlantic over 130 years later, as Blackwell Scientific Book Distributors, based in St Louis, Missouri.

75. John Robson became a director; his very fine collection of books on printing and typography is housed in the Robson Collection in Merton College Library, Oxford. He was modesty personified ('he would never let his colleagues treat him to lunch') and little known of since his death, despite many prizes.

76. See *From the First Fifty Years: An Informal History of Blackwell Scientific Publications 1939–89*, Blackwell Scientific, 1989.

77. BB's notes to John Cutforth, 1 September 1978.

78. Dr H.W. Garrod, late Professor of Poetry at Oxford (and a young Fellow when BB was at Merton College). BB published his *Epigrams*: for example, four stinging lines 'On the late detractors of Milton'; see *The Observer*, 4 January 1948.

79. *Oxford Outlook*, 1932.

80. H.W. Garrod, *Worms and Epitaphs*, B.H. Blackwell, 1919, p. 54.

81. C. Day-Lewis, 'Sonnet', *Oxford Poetry*.

82. C. Day-Lewis, *Poetry for You*, Basil Blackwell, 1944, pp. 1–11.

83. ibid., p. 5; he would also ask 'his publisher', BB, for another volume to answer children's questions about poetry, p. 112.

84. Exchange of letters, BB and John Betjeman, July 1957 and 22 June 1959. Also Cutforth to W. Mason of Manchester Grammar School, 3 July 1959.
85. John Betjeman to BB, 15 March 1962.
86. The anthology, entitled *A Wealth of Poetry*, edited by W. Hindley, a grammar school teacher, appeared in 1963.
87. See exchanges of letters; for example, John Cutforth to HMI N. Walley, 3 July 1959.
88. Preface to Book 3, p iii; the series were arranged by Fowler Wright and Crompton Rhodes.
89. Betjeman was not an *Oxford Poetry* contributor, but joint editor with John Sparrow of a volume of *Oxford Outlook*. Blackwell's was his first publisher; see *Daily Telegraph*, 14 March 1959.
90. BB, printed pamphlet, *A New Order in the Book Trade*; an address given to the Society of Bookmen, 29 January 1943.
91. RK, diary entry, Monday 27 May 1918.

TEN

 1. Review, *The Times*, 17 March 1930. *From Avon to Isis*, p. 15, Exhibition of Shakespeare Head Press books at Bumpus, 350 Oxford St.
 2. Frank Sidgwick's diaries and other material relating to the Shakespeare Head Press are in BB's notes and his 1975 essay on Bullen and Newdigate.
 3. See Frank Sidgwick's obituary, *The Times*, 15 August 1939.
 4. F. Sidgwick, *Early English Lyrics: Amorous, Divine, Moral and Trivial*, chosen with E.K. Chambers, was announced in SHP booklets 1–2, 5, 1906.
 5. Discovered later by his daughter, Mrs Ann Boer, and published as *Frank Sidgwick's Diary and other Material Relating to A.H. Bullen and the SHP*, Blackwell's, SHP, Oxford, 1975.
 6. A.E. Bullen letter to confirm dissolution of partnership with Sidgwick, 31 March 1907; Bullen to continue at Stratford-upon-Avon and Sidgwick in London.
 7. Ann Boer in *Frank Sidgwick's Diary*, p. vii.
 8. *The Times*, 1930.
 9. What is little known is that Bullen's nieces, Alys and Edith Lister (Edith under the name E.M. Martin), wrote copy and edited for Bullen. They helped with the appeal to keep his Press going, launched on 18 April 1911.
10. *The Cambridge History of the Book.*
11. See Editor's Note and Preface in A.H. Bullen, *Lyrics from the Song-Books of the Elizabethan Age*, Lawrence & Bullen, London 1891, pp. i–xxv.
12. John Masefield letter to *Western Daily Press*, 24 March 1960, also signed by T.S. Eliot, J.C. Masterman, John Betjeman, Basil Blackwell, F.P. Wilson (Merton), the Provost of Worcester College, et al.
13. Review, *The Times*, 17 March 1930. *From Avon to Isis*, p. 15, Exhibition of SHP books at Bumpus, 350 Oxford St. The Press was removed to 5 Alfred St, Oxford.
14. BB's account, MBC.
15. Further notes on E. Walker, W. Morris and the Kelmscott Press in BB, *A Note on Kelmscott Press*, proofs, 6 January 1983 – BB read and approved – the note written by BB in 1982. Further note on W. Morris and the Albion press by Ray Watkinson, many from W. Morris's 'A Note by William Morris on his aims in Founding the Kelmscott Press, together with a short description of the Press by S.C. Cockerell and an annotated list of books printed thereat', which was finished in 1898 after his death. His involvement in fine printing came after he intervened in the production at Chiswick Press of his *House of the Wolfings* and *Roots of the Mountains*. He spent much time developing the Golden type modelled on Jensen's, used in his *Pliny* (1476): 'it is roman not gothic, made as near as possible to that of the 15c'. He bought the second-hand Albion press at the end of 1890. William Bowden, who had recently printed *News From Nowhere* for Reeves Turner set his press going, intending to print William Morris's *The Golden Legend*, but with over 12,000 pages more hands were needed. On a sample of new paper,

on Saturday 31 January 1891, Bowden pulled the first trial page watched by William Morris and Emery Walker; Bowden's daughter (Mrs Pine) helped, and his son too. The paper was too small and Morris, hurriedly revising, printed his recently serialized *The Glittering Plain* instead, on 8 May 1891. This was the only book printed at 16 Chiswick Mall. More space was needed and another press, and the company moved to no. 14, taking half of this Georgian mansion; Emery the other half as a photo-engraving workshop. Bowden's son took over and used new compositors, including Thomas Binning, one of the printers of *Commonweal* and a member of the London Society of Compositors. Binning was elected Father of the Chapel, and took on other Kelmscott staff, including Mrs Pine, who became the first woman member of the Society. Morris began work on his Troy type for his Chaucer: 'more Gothic than Golden … modifying pen forms but by no means a conventional black letter'. Morris, despite his illness, finished in the autumn.

The second Troy type press was delivered in January 92, and a trial page of Chaucer printed on larger paper. Troy was clearly too big, and it was reduced from 18 to 12 pt, to be called Chaucer after the book. The Chaucer type was delivered in July 1892 and it was a very long process given the size of the book; actual printing began in August 1894. In 1895, no. 14 Chiswick Mall was given up for no. 21 on the river side of the mall: 'reflection from the water enhanced the light here'. The new Albion, built for the Kelmscott Press, was set up and William Morris, by this time very ill, was determined to get the book finished with Burne-Jones. In the winter of 1895–6 Morris worked on the binding and title page and on 8 May 1896 the last sheet was pulled. He had the first two copies on the 2 June, just four months before he died. The Chaucer was still in production, and ten more planned. It was taken on by F.S. Ellis and Cockerell, Morris's executors, who also printed William Morris's little volume *Aims in Founding the Kelmscott Press*. C.R. Ashbee, 'one of the hands' (and a scholar printer too) who had set up his own Essex House Press, bought most of the Kelmscott Press plant, acquiring William Morris's compositors Binning and Tippett in the process. They printed Ashbee's own translation of Benvenuto Cellini's *Treatise on Goldsmithing* to 'keep alive the traditions of good printing refounded by William Morris'. The plant was all moved to Chipping Campden when the Guild of Craftsmen transferred there in 1902: printing by hand was still in place in 1906, producing *Socialism and Politics*. Ashbee had to abandon it the following year, and the older press bought by Bullen, whence it went to BB.

16. BB's account, MBC.
17. Lister to Spielmann, 1 November 1920.
18. Lister to Spielmann 8 November 1920.
19. Whitby to Spielmann, 27 November 1920.
20. Lister to Spielmann, 14 January 1921.
21. Lister to Spielmann, 21 January 1921.
22. Lister to Spielmann, 24 January 1921.
23. English could be studied for a pass degree from 1873; Merton was in the vanguard, with a first Professor of English in 1885.
24. W.J. Lawrence to BB, 12 February 1921.
25. Among Bullen's unfinished works (see the publishing ledgers in MBC and the Paul Morgan handlist) were:
    Thomas D'Urfey, *Songs Compleat*, pleasant and diverting – one sheet with pp. 1–16 and two settings on each sheet
    Ralph Edwards, *Tredington and its History*
    Sir Philip Sidney, *Arcadia*, typeset 8 March 1905 as a projected first volume of Shakespeare's Books – this was referred to in Sidgwick's diary
    A.H. Bullen, *Readings in the Cambridge Platonists*, announced in List of Books, 1915
    Holland's edition of Pliny's *Natural History*, C. Whibley (ed.), announced in the *Daily Mail* appeal for finds – by Bullen and his friends, 18 April 1911

Early English Lyrics: *Amorous, Divine, Moral and Trivial*. Chosen by E.K. Chambers and
  F. Sidgwick – announced in SHP booklets 1–2, 5, 1906

Accounts of Chamberlains of S upon A, announced in 1905, eventually incorporated into
  Dugdale Society Publications, vols 1, 3, 5 (1921–6)

Thomas Shadwell, *Works*, Montague Summers (ed.), 1915, but Bullen wanted orders in
  hand before he printed it in a set of 5 vols to be sold at £2 12s 6d

Sir Charles Sedley, *Works*, Montague Summers (ed.), fifty copies on hand-made paper
  and 750 ordinary paper in 2 vols, announced by Bullen in his book SHP, 1915

Cornelius Agrippa, *The Vanity of Arts and Science*, Englished by James Sandford, R.B.
  McKerrow (ed.), also mentioned in the appeal in *Daily Mail*, 18 April 1911 and 1912
  list

Thomas Heywood, *Works*, ed. 'by a young American scholar, a Harvard man', mentioned in the Bullen appeal

Sir Francis Fane (d.1680), Stuart anecdotes; passages from the manuscript commonplace
  book – announced 1914 – galleys were produced and corrected by Bullen – see
  also article on Fane by Bullen's niece Edith Lister (E.M. Martin), 'Shakespeare in a
  Seventeenth Century Manuscript', *English Review*, vol. 51, 1930, pp. 484–9

Thomas Dekker, *Works*, R.B. McKerrow (ed.), mentioned by Bullen in his SHP list,
  1912

The following were taken over from Bullen:

The Beacon, E.R. Appleton (ed.), vol. 1, no. 1, and then eleven more until 1922, printed
  at Kemp Hall but SHP in the adverts; after Oct 1922 by Allen and Unwin, finished
  in 1924

1215 – 6 July 1921, *Shakespeare's Sonnets*, cr 8vo designed cover 10/6 SHP –

This had been started by Bullen – has a foreword on Bullen by H.F.B. Brett-Smith
  reprinted in *Sidgwick's Diary*, SHP, 1975, 'sheets of the text printed by late A.H.B.'

1268 – 1 February 1922, *Greenes Newes both from Heaven and Hell* (1593) and *Greenes
  Funeralls* (1594), reprinted from the originals with notes by R.B. McKerrow – 8vo
  Crown paper boards canvas back 7/6 SHP

26. W.J. Lawrence to BB, 26 February 1921.

27. BB, *The Bookman's Journal*, vol. v, no. 3, 1921, pp. 98–9.

28. Allen Lane took 'Morris's ideals to the nth degree: his Penguins were produced and
    printed in such a way that classics, new and old, were more affordable than ever before'.
    The Penguin resulted from a tea party in BB's garden, when he was president of the
    Booksellers' Association. BB explained: 'four dailies, in competition for increased
    circulation, were offering sets of Shaw, Dickens, etc. at bargain rates. Here was a
    portent not to be ignored. I suggested to Stanley Unwin that we arrange an informal
    conference of publishers and booksellers at Ripon Hall, Oxford, and Allen Lane went
    away with the idea of Penguins, which came to him in my garden while others played
    tennis, swam, or indulged in intellectual chat.'

29. From 1922 to 1925, Farleigh taught art at Rugby School before returning to London
    to take up a part-time post at the Central School of Arts and Crafts. While teaching,
    Farleigh worked as a designer, notably for London Transport (1933–63), and as a book
    illustrator, employing his great talents as a wood engraver. He exhibited at Royal
    Academy summer exhibitions and had a number of solo exhibitions at the Leicester
    Galleries and Lefèvre Gallery, London. In 1940 he was appointed chairman of the Arts
    and Crafts Exhibition Society (now the Society of Designer Craftsmen) and from 1950
    to 1964 was chairman of the Crafts Centre of Great Britain, which he had helped to
    form; his CBE (1949) was for his work in its founding.

30. He was elected as a member of the Society of Wood Engravers in 1925 and a fellow of
    the Royal Society of Painter–Etchers and Engravers in 1948.

31. See the role of SHP in rekindling interest in the printing trades: *Leicester Mercury*, 6
    September 1936; *The Builder*, 4 October 1935; and H.J.L.J. Masse, *The Art Workers Guild
    1884–1934*, SHP, Oxford, 1935.

32. *Daily Telegraph*, 28 December 1981.
33. Review in *The Bookman*, February 1935, of the Royal Academy Exhibition, where SHP's productions were much praised.
34. Newdigate writes that the Amyot was quarto in Ptolemy type, copied by Hornby from the fount used for Ptolemy, printed in 1482 and, as far as he knew, not used elsewhere.
35. The Golden Cockerel Press's fount was 'a clear and rather heavy roam', Newdigate judged; later, it used Perpetua designed by Gill for the Monotype Corporation.
36. This edition of *The Collected Works of William Morris* was in medium 8vo, 12-pt Caslon, 'with hanging headings and a very agreeable title page', BB wrote.
37. Newdigate was as fastidious about paper as print: when he was appointed to the Board of Education, to assist in the inspection of printing classes, he jibbed at the use of poor-quality paper.
38. This edition was the subject of a finely produced booklet and exhibition at the Bodleian Library: R. Ricketts, *A Moment in Time*, Bodleian, Oxford University, 2004.
39. See Bernard Newdigate, *London Mercury Book Notes*, October 1933. See also Newdigate's essay, 'Fine Printing in Great Britain 1925–34', in 1935 Year Book of the Gutenberg Society of Mainz, Germany, tenth in the series, quarto, 370 pages; see also G. Betteridge, *Scholastic Studies in Printing*, Advisory Council for Further Education, Manchester, June 1969.
40. The *Drayton* was reprinted by SHP in 1961.
41. Double Crown Club address.
42. Now Oxford Brookes University. BB's old friend John Brookes, principal of the Technical College, had been associated with the Campden Guild.
43. Kelmscott House on the Upper Mall was where William Morris lived for eighteen years.
44. The deed, struck between BB and the Stevensons, is in the MBC.
45. Newdigate's life and work is commemorated in Joseph Thorp, *B.H. Newdigate, Scholar-Printer 1869–1944*, Blackwell's, 1950; and in an article by BB in *Signature*, 1, July 1947, pp. 19–36. See also J. Thorp, 'The Work of B.H. Newdigate', *Printing Review*, Winter 1938–9, pp. 803–9; BB's notes in MBC; and Bernard Newdigate's *The Art of the Book*, The Studio, London, 1938.
46. George Wither, the seventeenth-century poet and pamphleteer, to George P. Brett, 1625: 'An honest Stationer (or Publisher) is he, that exercizeth his Mystery (whether it be in printing, bynding or selling of Bookes) with more respect to the glory of God & the publike aduantage than to his owne Commodity & is both an ornament & a profitable member in a ciuill Commonwealth … If he be a Printer he makes conscience to exemplify his Coppy fayrely & truly. If he be a Booke-bynder, he is no meere Bookeseller [that is] one who selleth meerely ynck & paper bundled up together for his owne aduantage only: but he is a Chapman of Arts, of wisdome, & of much experience for a little money …'
47. Bernard Newdigate's books and papers are at Heriot Watt University, Edinburgh, as part of the Edward Clarke Collection (Basil originally sent them to the printing department of Napier College of Commerce and Technology). His family were last known to be living in Canada.
48. Adrian Mott's notes, 1954.
49. Basil was not the only one who wanted to promote May's work. *Decorative Needlework*, originally published by Joseph Hughes, London, 1893, was later reissued by Elizabeth Masterton. She too wanted to bring May out from her father's shadow. When working for Bernard Quaritch, Masterton had executed an embroidered binding for Norman Stone, who gave her some photos of May's embroidered binding on William Morris's *Love is Enough*. In her letter to Basil of 14 March 1979, Masterton writes of how she came across May: 'some ten years ago when I joined the Embroiders' Guild I borrowed *Decorative Needlework* from their library. It was quite wonderful: plainly written there

was all that I had been vaguely thinking about both the techniques and the utility of embroidery.'

50. Fiona MacCarthy, *William Morris: A Life for Our Time*, Faber & Faber, London, 1994, p. 677.

51. May Morris (ed.), *William Morris, Artist, Writer, Socialist*, Blackwell's, 1934 (2 vols). The account of May is in Shaw's Introduction to vol. 2, pp. xxvi–xxvii. See also Michael Holroyd, *Bernard Shaw, The Search for Love*, Chatto & Windus, London, 1988, pp. 223–30.

52. May Morris never did get very far with her tapestry work; see Joan Edwards to BB, 7 February 1979. Joan Edwards first wrote to BB after he had sent his article on May Morris, the one Betjeman so admired. In a letter to BB of 18 July 1979, Edwards explained that she had lectured at the V&A on twentieth-century embroiderers and was collecting material for a book, *Seven Notable Embroiderers 1840–1960*; she wanted to included May Morris and wanted BB's help.

53. Margaret Horton, 'A Visit to May Morris', *Journal of the William Morris Society*, vol. v, no. 2, Winter 1982; in the MBC, among BB's papers.

54. George Bernard Shaw, Introduction to *William Morris as a Socialist*, Blackwell's, 1936.

55. *Alf's Button* (1920), a popular novel by W.A. Darlington, told of a soldier in the First World War who discovered a button made from a fragment of Aladdin's lamp. When he polished it, the genie who appeared granted Alf's wishes, but never in quite the way Alf hoped.

56. BB, *The Bookseller*, 27 October 1962, p. 109.

57. Joan Edwards to BB, 30 January 1979.

58. BB, *Literature Today*, 23 July 1948.

CONCLUSION

1. BB's own notes, 'Origins of the Classics', for his speech and paper for the Classical Association.

2. Hugh Speaight, *Period,* Basil Blackwell, 1929, p. 31.

3. A review of *Wheels 1918, Third Cycle*, described it as 'as notable a phenomenon as the Yellow Book'.

4. *Guardian*, 29 May, 1969.

5. *Isis* is an Oxford University undergraduate magazine, founded in 1892.

6. Moore Crosthwaite, *Oxford Outlook*, vol. X, no. 47, November 1928, pp. 120–24.

7. P.B. Shelley (ed. Mary Shelley), *Letters From Italy*, vol. 11, 1840 edition, letter XV, PBS to TLP, Naples, 22 Dec, 1818.

SELECT BIBLIOGRAPHY

MAIN SOURCES

Bodleian Blackwell Collection (BBC): publishing papers and back copies are housed in the Bodleian Library, University of Oxford. It contains some exceptional material: preparation of children's books – contentious at times, with important contributions from C. Day Lewis, Betjeman and Enid Blyton; Oxford Poetry during its last days in Blackwell's hands, monographs showing Blackwell's passage to academic publishing: from the classics and poetry to science and social science (with famous names from academia creeping in: Plamenatatz's *English Utilitarians* 1957–8), translations and hand-drawn illustrations, Ludwig Wittgenstein's *Notebooks* 1957– for example; reissues of belle letters in the SHP style etc.

Merton Blackwell Collection (MBC), memoirs, diaries, letters, family, associates, authors and business records, publishing and bookselling etc. are housed in the Library, Merton College, University of Oxford. Of particular note are the Robson Collection, which includes a very comprehensive set of books on printing and typography, publishing ledgers, early records of the bookseller Parker's, Rex King Diaries, Basil Blackwell's stories and articles.

Sir Basil Blackwell Library: an eclectic collection housed in the Bodleian's Weston Library.

Poetry and prose anthologies published by B.H. Blackwell and Basil Blackwell, especially *Oxford Outlook, Oxford Poetry, Adventurers All, Initiates, Wheels, Lysistrata*.

Reid, J., R. Ricketts and J. Walworth, *A Guide to the Merton Blackwell Collection*, Merton College, University of Oxford, 2004.

McKitterick, David, ed., *The Cambridge History of the Book in Britain 1830–1914*, Cambridge University Press, Cambridge, 2009.

Altick, Richard A., *The English Common Reader: A History of the Mass Reading Public, 1800–1900*, University of Chicago Press, Chicago, 1957.

Fischer, R.S., *A History of Reading*, Reaktion Books, London, 2003.

Rose, Jonathan, *The Intellectual Life of the British Working Classes*, Yale University Press, New Haven CT, 2001.

COLLECTIONS

Bodleian Library: papers of Dorothy L. Sayers.

City of Oxford Directories, including Dutton, Allen & Co's Directory and Gazetteer.

Dorothy L. Sayers Society: records and publications.

Oxfordshire County Records: City Council and school records.
Society of Antiquarians: papers concerning William and May Morris.
William Morris Society: records and publications.
Times Literary Supplement and *London Review of Books*.
University of Heriot Watt, Edinburgh: Bernard Newdigate, *London Mercury Book Notes*.
Magdalen College School, archive of *The Lily*.
Paul Morgan's papers, 'Bibliography of the SHP'.
John Robson Collection, publishing, typography and printing.
Gutenberg Society of Mainz, Germany, Year Books, e.g. *Fine Printing in Great Britain 1925–34*.

BOOKS AND ARTICLES

Aldiss, Brian, *The Brightfount Diaries*, Faber & Faber, London, 1955.
Andrews, P.W.S., *The Life of Lord Nuffield*, Basil Blackwell, 1955.
Barker, Nicolas, *The Oxford University Press and the Spread of Learning, 1478–1979: An Illustrated History*, Clarendon Press, 1978.
Bell, A.O., ed., intro. Quentin Bell, *The Diary of Virginia Woolf*, Vol. 1, Hogarth Press, London, 1977.
Bell, A.O., ed., *Virginia Woolf, Selected Diaries*, Vintage, London, 2008.
Bell, Quentin, *Virginia Woolf: A Biography*, Pimlico, London, 1996.
Blackwell Scientific, *From the First Fifty Years: An Informal History of Blackwell Scientific Publications 1939–89*, Blackwell Science, 1989.
Blumenthal, Joseph, *The Art of the Printed Book*, Pierpont Morgan Library, New York, 1973.
Bone, Gertrude, and Muirhead Bone, *Came to Oxford*, Basil Blackwell, 1953.
Bostridge, Paul, *Vera Brittain: A Life*, Virago, London, 2001.
Brabazon, James, *Dorothy L. Sayers: A Biography*, Charles Scribner's Sons, New York, 1981.
Brabazon, James, *Dorothy L. Sayers: The Life of a Courageous Woman*, Gollancz, London, 1981.
Bridges, H.J., *The Religion of Experience: A Book for Laymen and the Unchurched*, Macmillan, New York, 1916.
Buchan, William, *John Buchan: A Memoir*, Harrap, London, 1982.
Byatt, A.S., *The Biographer's Tale*, Vintage, London, 2001.
Cannan, M.W., *Grey Ghosts and Voices*, Roundwood Press, London, 1976.
Catto, Jeremy, ed., *Oriel College: A History*, Oxford University Press, 2013.
Clark, Leonard, *Alfred Williams: His Life and Work*, Basil Blackwell, 1945.
Crossley, A., *A History of the County of Oxford*, Vol. 4, Institute of Historical Research, Oxford University Press, 1979.
Delafield, E.M., *The Diary of a Provincial Lady*, Virago, London, 1984.
Sartre, J.-P., *War Diaries: Notes from a Phoney War, 1939–1940*, Verso, London, 1983.
Darnton, Robert, *The Kiss of Lamourette*, Norton, New York, 1990.
Davidson, Maurice, *Medicine in Oxford: A Historical Romance*, Basil Blackwell, 1953.
Davidson, Maurice, *Memoirs of a Golden Age*, Basil Blackwell, 1958.
Eliot, Simon, and Jonathan Rose, *A Companion to the History of the Book*, Blackwell, 2007.
Fabes, Gilbert H., *The Romance of a Bookshop*, privately printed, 1929.
Fasnacht, Ruth, *A History of the City of Oxford*, Basil Blackwell, 1954.
Fergus, Jan, *Provincial Readers in Eighteenth-Century England*, Oxford University Press, 2006.
Fields, J.T., *A Shelf of Old Books*, Osgood, McIlvane, 1894.
Foster, Margaret, *Rich Desserts and Captain's Thin*, Vintage, London, 1998.
Gameson, R., and A. Coates *The Old Library, Trinity College*, Trinity College, 1988.
Geering, Charles, *Notes on Printers and Booksellers*, Thoroton Society and Nottingham Sette of Odde Volumes, 1900.
Green, V.H.H., *A History of Oxford University*, Batsford, London, 1984.
Hey, Colin, *Magdalen School Days*, Senecio Press, London, 1977.
Hitchman, Janet, *Such a Strange Lady*, New English Library, London, 1975.
Hobhouse, Christopher, *Oxford*, Batsford, London, 1952.

Holroyd, Michael, *Bernard Shaw*: Vol. 1, *The Search for Love, 1856–1898*; Vol. 2, *Pursuit of Power, 1898–1918*; Vol. 3, *Lure of Fantasy, 1918–1950*, Chatto & Windus, London, 1988, 1989, 1991.

Holroyd, Michael, *Works on Paper*, Little, Brown, London, 2002.

Hone, Ralph, *A Literary Life*, Kent State University Press, Kent OH, 1979.

Hone, Ralph E., ed. *Extracts from the Poetry of Dorothy L. Sayers*, Dorothy L. Sayers Society, 1996.

Horton, Margaret, 'A Visit to May Morris', *Journal of the William Morris Society*, vol. v, no. 2, Winter 1982.

Humphrey, A.W., *International Socialism and the War*, P.S. King, London, 1915.

Jackson, Holbrook, *The Printing of Books*, Cassell, London, 1938.

Kemp, S., et al., *The Oxford Companion to Edwardian Fiction*, Oxford University Press, 1997.

Kynaston, David, *King Labour*, George Allen & Unwin, London, 1976.

Kynaston, David, *Austerity Britain*; *Family Britain*; *Modernity Britain*; Bloomsbury, London, 2007, 2009, 2013.

Ledger, Sally, and Roger Lockhurst, *The Fin de Siècle: A Reader in Cultural History*, Oxford University Press, 2000.

Lee, Hermione, *Virginia Woolf*, Vintage, London, 1997.

Lee, Hermione, *Penelope Fitzgerald*, Chatto & Windus, London, 2013.

MacCarthy, Fiona, *William Morris: A Life for Our Time*, Faber & Faber, London, 1994.

McKenzie, D.F., *Making Meaning*, ed. Peter McDonald and Michael Suarez, University of Massachusetts Press, 2002.

Masefield, John, *Shopping in Oxford*, Heinemann, London, 1941.

Maxwell Lyte, H.C., *A History of the University of Oxford*, Macmillan, London, 1886.

Mitchell, Leslie, *Maurice Bowra: A Life*, Oxford University Press, 2009.

Morgan C., and R. Ricketts, *Initiate: An Anthology of New Writing*, Blackwell and Kellogg College, 2010.

Morris, Jan, *Oxford*, Faber & Faber, London, 1965.

Morris, May, *Decorative Needlework*, Joseph Hughes, London, 1893; reissued by Dodo Press, 2010.

Morris, May, ed., *William Morris: Artist, Writer, Socialist*, 2 vols, Blackwell, 1934.

Murray, John G., *A Gentleman Publisher's Commonplace Book*, 1996.

Murray, Nicholas, *The Sweet Red Wine of Youth*, Little, Brown, London, 2010.

O'Neill, Gilda, *My East End*, Penguin, London, 1999.

National Portrait Gallery, *The Sitwells*, exhibition catalogue, 1994.

Nicolson, Juliet, *The Perfect Summer*, John Murray, London, 2007.

Nicolson, Juliet, *The Great Silence*, John Murray, London, 2009.

Newdigate, Bernard, *The Art of the Book*, The Studio, London, 1938.

Newdigate, B.H., et al., *Modern Book Production*, The Studio, London, 1928.

Norrington, A., *A History of the Firm*, original drafts, from various contributors, for 1879–1979, MBC.

Pearson, John, *Facades: Edith, Osbert and Sacherverell Sitwell*, Macmillan, London, 1978.

Ray, Gordon N., *The Illustrator and the Book in England, from 1790 to 1914*, Pierpont Morgan Library and Oxford University Press, 1976.

Raymond, Harold, *Publishing and Bookselling*, J.M. Dent Memorial Lectures 8, Stationers' Hall, London, 1938.

Read, Herbert, *Paul Nash*, Penguin Books, London, 1944.

Reilly, Catherine W., and G.K. Hall, *English Poetry of the Second World War: A Biobibliography*, G.K. Hall, Boston, 1986.

Ricketts, Harry, *Strange Meetings: The Poets of the Great War*, Chatto & Windus, London, 2010.

Ricketts, Rita, *Adventurers All*, Blackwell's, 2002; see also original drafts in MBC.

Ricketts, Rita, *A Moment in Time: Blackwell's at the Bodleian*, catalogue and commentary on an exhibition of selected editions of Chaucer's *Canterbury Tales*, 2004.

Rickword, Edgell, *Trench Poets*, Oxford Poetry, 1921.

Sackville-West, Vita, *The Edwardians*, Virago, London, 2011.

Shaw, George Bernard, introduction to *William Morris as a Socialist*, Blackwell's, 1936.

Smither, Elizabeth, *The Common-place Book*, Auckland University Press, Auckland, 2011.

Southern, R.W., *The History of Oxford University*, Vol. 1: *The Early Oxford Schools*, Clarendon Press, 1984.

Stainer, R.S., *A History of Magdalen College School*, Basil Blackwell, 1940, 1958.

Stallworthy, Jon, *Wilfred Owen: Poems Selected by Jon Stallworthy*, Faber & Faber, London, 2004.

Stallworthy, Jon, ed., *The Oxford Book of War Poetry*, Oxford University Press, 2008.

Starkey, David, *Henry*, Harper Perennial, London, 2009.

Stead, C.K., *Risk*, Maclehose Press, London, 2012.

Sutcliffe, Peter, *The Oxford University Press: An Informal History*, Oxford University Press, 1978.

Sutherland, John, *Stephen Spender: A Literary Life*, Oxford University Press, 2005.

Thompson, Flora, *A Country Calendar*, ed. Margaret Lane, Oxford University Press, 1979.

Thompson, H.L., *The Currch of St. Mary the Virgin, Oxford in Its Relations to Some Famous Events of English History*, Constable, London, 1903.

Thorp, Joseph, *B.H. Newdigate: Scholar-Printer, 1869–1944*, Basil Blackwell, 1950.

Vasey, David, *Anthony Stephens: The Rise and Fall of an Oxford Bookseller* in *Studies in the Book Trade*, Oxford Bibliographical Society, 1975.

Waters, Clive, 'William Morris and the Socialism of Robert Blatchford', *Journal of the William Morris Society*, vol. v, no. 2, Winter 1982.

Webb, Barry, *Edmund Blunden: A Biography*, Yale University Press, New Haven CT, 1990.

Wevers, Lydia, *Reading on the Farm: Victorian Fiction and the Colonial World,* Victoria University Press, Wellington, 2010.

Wiley, Margaret, *Three Women Diarists*, British Council, London, 1964.

Williams, Orlo, 'Browsing in Bookshops', *World*, 18 October 1910.

Wilson, Charles, *First with the News*, Jonathan Cape, London, 1985.

Wilson, J.G., *The Business of Bookselling*, Three lectures at the London Day College, Booksellers Association, 1930.

Woolf, Leonard, ed., *A Writer's Diary*, Hogarth Press, London, 1953.

Woolf, Virginia, *Granite and Rainbow: Essays*, Harcourt, Brace, New York, 1958.

ACKNOWLEDGEMENTS

I AM INDEBTED to Julian Blackwell, youngest son of Sir Basil, for his munificent support of the Blackwell History Project over a decade and a half. This has spawned two books, a stream of articles, the renovation of Benjamin Henry's and Sir Basil's workroom in Broad Street and the establishment of the Merton Blackwell Collection. Without Julian's prescience, much of the Blackwell archive could have ended its life in a skip and stories of surprising lives would have been lost for ever; such had been the fate of most of the records from the early days of Blackwell publishing. The idea of preserving the archive germinated when Julian Blackwell dropped a vanload of cardboard boxes on my doorstep. Examining the contents, I called on the help of Sir Basil Blackwell's old college. It more than turned up trumps. I would like to thank the then Warden of Merton, Professor Dame Jessica Rawson; the then acting librarian, Steven Gunn (Fellow in History); and the former archivist Michael Stansfield. I have had the continued support of the present Warden and his wife, Sir Martin and Lady Sharron Taylor, the Fellow Librarian Julia Walworth, current archivist Julian Reid, and previous Common Room steward, the Rev. Dr Simon Jones. I must thank other fellows and staff of the college who have helped me during my research, and for the invitation to enjoy the privilege and fellowship of the Common Room.

I am also beholden to Corinna Wiltshire (Blackwell), Sir Basil's youngest daughter, who as Blackwell's unofficial archivist was unpaid and unsung for many years. Her guidance, friendship and encouragement have been bountiful throughout years of research. Just as her namesake Korrina reputedly nurtured the young Pindarus, she had the energy and foresight to husband the tales of 'writers known and unknown to fame' and countless other Blackwell associates; in turn, Corinna relied on the generous help of Joan Baskerville and Joyce Ferguson. Thanks to the efforts of other family members some long-lost materials came to light. Will King's Diary, for example, came to hand courtesy of Miles Blackwell's estate, adding considerable weight to the Merton Collection. I would like to thank other Blackwell family members, particularly David Jessel, Sir Basil's grandson, who talked about his parents and family; Adam Butcher, Helen Blackwell's son-in-law, who always took an interest in the history project, as did Julian Blackwell's loyal and long-serving staff members Derrick Cook and Sandy Hales.

From afar, but no less enthusiastically, I would like to thank Martin Hanks and the family of Fred Hanks, and the granddaughter of Dr Herta Doktor who told me her grandmother's remarkable story. Sadly, I have not been able to contact descendants of Bernard Newdigate, William Rex King and Margaret Horton, née Thompson. Staff, past and present, who worked at the Broad Street shop were ever-helpful: manager Rebecca MacAlister, irreplaceable classicist Peter Saxal, theology guru Richard Kingston, Phil Brown, who trod in Will King's shoes, and his contemporaries Len Fry, Ken New, David Retter and Keith Cleck. Bards Heather Slater and Kaye Heelas helped me with literary sources and frequently gave up their own free time to help with readings. Basil Blackwell and his sister Dorothy held Saturday evening readings in the shop for fledgling writers. In its new form, World Writers at Blackwell's, the sessions were open to anyone who happened to be writing in Oxford, wherever in the world they originated. I am grateful for the guidance of Michael Haslet and fellow members of the John Buchan Society, and members of the Dorothy L. Sayers Society. I am particularly grateful to a succession of *Oxford Poetry* editors and contributors, especially Carmen Bugan. I am grateful to Blackwell's and the president and fellows of Kellogg College, particularly Clare Morgan, who undertook to publish *Initiate: An Anthology of New Writing* (ed. Jon Stallworthy, Clare Morgan and Rita Ricketts).

In beginning my research on the publishing side, I was given a great deal of help by the late John Robson, director of Blackwell Publishing, who subsequently donated his library of books about printing and typography to the Merton College Library. My research was given an extra fillip in 2007 when, thanks to the generosity of Wiley Blackwell, Philip Carpenter in particular, aided and abetted by Sarah Thomas and Richard Ovenden, a parallel Bodleian Blackwell Collection was made possible. It consists of back copies of Blackwell's early publications – under the imprints B.H. Blackwell, Basil Blackwell, Basil Blackwell & Mott and Shakespeare Head Press – and such publishing papers as escaped the ravages of time and two world wars. I am grateful for the hands-on support of Ronald Milne, Clive Hurst, Chris Fletcher, Sarah Wheale and Michael Hughes in establishing and husbanding this collection. Of particular note were the exertions of Julian Reid, as we trawled through an army of dusty old boxes. Avidly pawing the contents, hoping for treasure, our labours were amply rewarded as more jigsaw pieces fell into pace. Lodging two collections, Merton Blackwell (MBC) and Bodleian Blackwell (BBC) permanently has been one of the many rewards of working on this project. Just as Alexander the Great spared the house of Pindarus, I am grateful to Oxford University's Bodleian and Merton College libraries for safeguarding collections that will provide rich fodder for future literary enthusiasts, book historians and cultural historians to plunder and enjoy.

With two collections at my elbow the book threatened to assume epic proportions, until Caroline Bell was charged with the thankless task of cutting my thrice-overlong text. Deepest thanks to her, Samuel Fanous, Dot Little, Janet Phillips, Deborah Susman and Su Wheeler at Bodleian Library Publishing as well as Lucy Morton of illuminati. Other members of the curia in the Librarian's office in Broad Street also merit thanks, especially Janet Walwyn. Various other groups and individuals have also influenced the content of the book. Richard Blackwell, as recorded in the MBC, asked for the stories of writers and readers associated with the family firm, particularly the first-hand accounts of Blackwell's early apprentices, to be set within the political-economic matrix of time and place: the growth of universal education, the years of war and depression, the emergence of women in the workplace, the tension between socialism and capitalism, and the march of modernism in art and science. Added to this implicitly political economic underlay, stemming from years teaching the subjects, two other areas of scholarship shaped my approach. First the History of the Book Project (Merton and the Bodleian), especially scholars Richard Ovenden, Julia Walworth and Giles Bergel, and secondly, the Oxford Centre for Life Writing (OCLW) at Wolfson, Hermione Lee, Elleke Boehmer and Rachel Hewett. Their work has been a vital source of information and an example that I have humbly tried to learn from. Paul Nash merits high praise for the way he generously gave up his time to initiate me in the art of fine printing.

Staff of other institutions also helped me to gather material. Master of Magdalen College School Tim Hands, and his predecessor Andrew Halls, took a keen interest in my research, as did Linda Beaumont. MCS archivist Rebecca Roseff and members of the Department of History lent me a team of young historians, during Artweek 2012. Alex Marsh, Charles Bond, Greg Garnett, Guy Bailey-Williams, Tom Elder and William Klemperer researched the lives of teachers and boys at the turn of the twentieth century; I was able to build up a similar picture of girls' education with the help of staff at the Oxfordshire County Records Office. The Society of Antiquarians generously gave me access to their Morris Collection, adding depth to my understanding of May Morris's life, and the librarian at Heriot-Watt University gave me access to Bernard Newdigate's papers. Further afield, Blackwell's American connection, dating back to the 1840s, survives today much to the credit of Katina and Bruce Staunch, who allowed me try out my ideas in a series of articles for their journal *Against the Grain* and at one of their famous Charleston conferences. Similarly, my stories of Blackwell's women war poets infiltrated the University of Tbilisi in 2008, thanks to Professor Manana Gelashvili, just as people sheltered within its portals during the clash with Russia.

Closer to home, the Ricketts ménage, Willy de Leeuw and my very biddable grandchildren, especially Pippy and cRicket who provided light relief during long concentrated hours of research, more than deserve a mention. Tommy and Jamie Ricketts, Maddy Crowe and Charlotte Swing constituted a tribe of young transcribers, while Charlotte Paszkiewicz acted as my artistic and graphics advisor. Friends too played a part in keeping my feet under that table. Chief among these must be New Zealand historian Malcolm McKinnon, who painstakingly reviewed and corrected drafts. Other old friends guided me in my earlier writing career: Tom and Sarah Larkin in particular. Rose Beauchamp and Felicity Day revelled in the stories but tactfully applied the handbrake. Chiara Agnello, who gave me a refuge at her farm in Sicily where I could draft undisturbed, must also be thanked. And I cannot forget my dear friends Jackie Williams, Christine Castle and Peta Georgeades, who, before they succumbed to cancer, provided a captive audience for early versions of these stories. Their verdict on the characters sums things up: most were 'modest, hard-working people who loved books and valued the pursuit of knowledge for its own sake'.

I have lived with these characters in the imagination, and seen them daily in my mind's eye. Many of them would never have dreamed that their diaries, memoirs, letters, poetry and prose, written despite long hard days in relatively low paid work, would lay alongside those of eminent writers to be valued by subsequent generations. This book acknowledges them.

INDEX